It wasn't *meant to be like this*

LISA WILKINSON

It wasn't *meant to be like this*

HarperCollins*Publishers*

In several instances names have been changed to protect privacy. Refer to the Acknowledgments at the end of this book.

Extract from 'I Am Woman' by Helen Reddy on page 43: Words and music by Ray Burton and Helen Reddy. © Buggerlugs Music Co./Irving Music, Inc./Rondor Music Australia Pty. Ltd. All rights reserved. International copyright secured. Reprinted with permission.

We gratefully acknowledge the permission granted by copyright holders to reproduce the copyright material in this book. All reasonable attempts have been made to contact the copyright holders; the publisher would be interested to hear from anyone not acknowledged here, or acknowledged incorrectly.

HarperCollins*Publishers*
Australia • Brazil • Canada • France • Germany • Holland • Hungary
India • Italy • Japan • Mexico • New Zealand • Poland • Spain • Sweden
Switzerland • United Kingdom • United States of America

First published in Australia in 2021
by HarperCollins*Publishers* Australia Pty Limited
Level 13, 201 Elizabeth Street, Sydney NSW 2000
ABN 36 009 913 517
harpercollins.com.au

A catalogue record for this book is available from the National Library of Australia

ISBN 978 1 4607 5017 9 (hardback)
ISBN 978 1 4607 0445 5 (ebook)
ISBN 978 1 4607 8952 0 (audiobook)

Cover design by HarperCollins Design Studio
Front cover image by Steven Chee/Newspix
Back cover images: Lisa at her desk at *Dolly* in 1984, going through transparencies of potential covers for the magazine; and Lisa with her school friend Michelle, at Campbelltown High, 1974, both supplied by the author
Unless otherwise credited, all photos are from the collection of Lisa Wilkinson
Typeset in Bembo Std by Kirby Jones
Printed and bound in Australia by McPherson's Printing Group

MIX
Paper from
responsible sources
FSC
www.fsc.org
FSC® C001695

To my father, Ray Wilkinson, whose gentle,
loving star I still steer by.

CONTENTS

Foreword

MY BEAUTIFUL LATE DAD once told me that a person needs just three things to be truly happy in life: someone to love, something to do, and something to hope for.

I have been wonderfully fortunate to have experienced all three.

But none of it was guaranteed. None of it just happened. There were, in fact, many times when all three seemed unattainable, because so much of my life wasn't actually meant to be like this.

Growing up in Sydney's south-west, there were very few expectations placed upon me. Like every little girl in 1960s Australia, my life looked decidedly predestined: probably married by 23, with a bunch of kids before 30. And if I were to have a job, it was more than likely going to be limited to that small window before the arrival of kids because, from then on, 'a woman's place is in the home'. In most workplaces, pregnancy was grounds for dismissal, and in many others, so too was marriage; reliable childcare was almost non-existent; and women's wages were considered almost 'pin money' because, really, the plan was … to get a man to support you.

If I wanted to venture down a professional or corporate path, the glass ceiling – still decades away from even being recognised as 'a thing' – ensured that opportunities for women were rare. Meanwhile, the gender pay gap was just accepted as normal; reliable contraception was difficult to access; abortion was illegal; domestic

1

violence was rarely spoken of; women were banned from drinking in public bars; getting any sort of bank loan or even a passport to travel was impossible without the approval of a male guarantor; and there was no such thing as a no-fault divorce.

And, oh yeah, bachelors were desirable, but 'spinsters' were not.

If I were to marry, I would have had to promise henceforth to 'obey' my husband for the rest of my life. As for the name I was born with, with its achievements, history and sense of self-identity? That would all immediately disappear. Just as my mother went from a 22-year-old Beryl Eastall to Mrs Ray Wilkinson, all trace of that young woman's origins was wiped out, at least on paper.

None of it appeared right through my young eyes, and though the vision I had for my path forward was far from clear, I always felt that what was ahead for me was going to be a little different, more circuitous, less predestined.

By the early 70s, thanks to the efforts of generations of women before me, I could feel the ground shifting, as Helen Reddy's rallying anthem for the ages, 'I Am Woman', filled the airwaves. That song demanded that we women raise our voices and finally be heard. It encouraged us to tell the truth of our stories and to listen to the stories of others, because staying quiet wasn't getting any of us very far.

But while I could sing along at the top of my voice to Helen's unifying cry like every other young girl, it would take me decades to have the courage to finally find my own voice, and fully realise that I, too, knew too much to go back and pretend. Because when it comes to women speaking out against injustice, the societal pressure – however subtle or unspoken – is to say nothing, for fear of a possible backlash, or worse: being accused of trying to stand out. When, in fact, all you're doing is standing up. For yourself. And ultimately, all women.

As women, the rules we are taught from a very young age are conflicting: excel, but not too much; value your inner worth, but here, buy all this makeup; love your body, but why not buy these torture garments to smooth out all that unsightly cellulite while you're at it?

And when the prizes for women are so few, what does that do to our psyche? What does that mean for our desire to see other women succeed? How does it affect the camaraderie we feel with other women when we are all essentially set up to be in competition for the few tiny slices of the pie that we're told exist?

It means that our choices become limited. And in a man's world, that's a win. For men. So as a woman, it can often feel like you can't win. And when you can't win, the temptation is to give up.

And there were times when I almost did. Times when the career moves I made felt too big, too high profile, too high pressure for me to believe I could succeed, and I lived with the daily knowledge that, with every challenge I took on, I was probably headed for a very public fall.

I've often wondered why I keep doing that to myself. Why, just when I have felt comfortable in a job, proud of the work I was doing, and pretty sure of what each new day was going to hold, I've decided to shake things up and move on. Why do I keep testing myself like that? Why the need to keep proving myself?

Perhaps because I've never felt completely comfortable with the opportunities that have come my way over the years. As a kid from Sydney's western suburbs with no private schooling, a pretty ordinary pass in Sixth Form, no uni degree, no presumptions of entitlement, and a more than healthy dose of convict blood deep in my DNA, I've always wondered: why me?

But when those opportunities did come along, I made damn sure I never wasted them. I also didn't want to disappoint those who were brave enough to take a chance on me. To keep moving forward, though, I had to learn to love myself along the way – with all my flaws and foibles, contradictions and inconsistencies.

Not all of us are dealt the easy cards in life, but that doesn't mean you can't reshuffle the deck once you've seen the light and the possibilities of a better outcome.

My mother was dealt terrible cards, but she was a hero and a survivor. As a kid she was forgotten, ignored, and made to feel like she was an inconvenience. And yet, after everything she had been through, she was able to show up and keep going.

I've been truly blessed by the good people I have had in my life who, over the years, have so unconditionally believed in, loved, and supported me. But I've also seen people I didn't want to be like and situations I'd never want to be in. I now know that those people have been my teachers, too.

So, in some ways, this is a book about both thanks and forgiveness, showing gratitude for the good angels and making peace with the bleak ones, because all of them have taught me valuable lessons.

To be human is an ongoing process, and part of that is making mistakes. I've made plenty, as you're about to find out. The important thing is to always look for what we can learn from them to keep growing, keep choosing, keep evolving, keep challenging, and to welcome change when it comes.

And live with kindness. I hope I have.

TV is an unforgiving business where the stakes are often all or nothing, where worth is judged on daily ratings, shows and people are axed without warning, and egos can be made or broken by unrelenting scrutiny. It demands a strong backbone to cope with it all. And when you spend a significant chunk of a lifetime sitting in the public gaze, people can have a lot of ideas about who you are, and how you can be most easily defined. The good and bad impressions and suppositions others apply to you can make your head spin if you allow them to.

So, I don't know if my story will confirm what you already think you knew about me, or if maybe it will change your mind. All I know is, for me, it's never really changed.

I always was, and always will be, Lisa Wilkinson from Campbelltown. A magazine junkie kid from the suburbs who lucked out big time.

And this, with all its mistakes and missteps, flaws, and fabulously unexpected joys, is my story …

Lisa Wilkinson
October 2021

CHAPTER ONE

Little girl lost

'The moment you doubt whether you can fly, you cease
forever to be able to do it.' – J. M. Barrie, *Peter Pan*

The trip along the dusty driveway out of Dalwood Children's Home was not a long one, but it was enough for six-year-old Beryl to look back through the taxi's rear window and take in the enormity of the old sandstone building.

Once more she bore witness to its grand columns, sweeping arched verandahs and monstrous black front door. To some, that magnificent exterior would have conjured thoughts of romantic fairy tales and magical castles where beautiful princesses would live out their happily-ever-afters.

But to young Beryl, this was no fairy tale. There was no happiness. This was instead a place of endless anguish and deep distress.

Inside the home were scores of disadvantaged children left in the hands of staff whose job it was to raise them. Dalwood was ruled with an iron fist, and punishment was as swift as it was harsh if ever the children stepped out of line.

Abandoned, unloved, malnourished and scared, some of these children just didn't know any better – and at least the slaps broke up the numbing monotony of their daily existence.

Beryl looked once again at that huge front door receding in the distance – the same one where, just three months before, her mother, Marie, had unexpectedly left her standing, before herself disappearing into the night without so much as a backward glance in the direction of her little girl.

It was one of a number of orphanages and foster homes Beryl had so far experienced in her young life, as Marie tried to sort out her own complicated, ever-changing living and dating arrangements – arrangements that rarely included Beryl.

But here was this tiny girl, obediently sitting in the back of a taxi – a hotbox on this stifling December day – with her little legs already sticking uncomfortably to the vinyl seat, her mother now right by her side, and the two of them going who knows where.

It had all happened so quickly. Just ten minutes earlier, she had filed into the lunchroom with dozens of other scruffily dressed kids, surprised to find it decked out in brightly coloured handmade decorations, ahead of tomorrow's Christmas Day lunch. The saying of Grace had only just finished … *Bless us, O Lord, and bless the food we are about to eat …* when the word came.

'Your *mother* is here,' the woman hissed, in a tone almost as if Beryl had been caught stealing a Milk Arrowroot biscuit – a rare treat the children would only ever be afforded on special occasions.

And it was true. On one of those whims that sometimes possessed her, Marie had decided that she wanted her daughter back, and had no sooner arrived unannounced at the entrance than she had demanded that it happen immediately – *Do you hear me?*

There had been no warm embrace when they met, for Marie just wasn't like that. Nor was there a 'thank you' to the woman manning the reception desk, who handed her the little girl's small, already-packed bag on the way out the door. Marie wasn't like that either.

Beryl was simply told they were 'going home', and that was it. Exactly where that home would be was not yet clear.

In her six short years, Beryl had moved to more places than she could count up to. Paddington, Glebe, Annandale, Parramatta, Brighton-Le-Sands, Chippendale, Marrickville and Fairfield were just some of the down-at-heel, raggedy-pants workers' suburbs they'd moved through, living mostly in housing commission tenements, sometimes on acquaintances' couches – all temporary stays and make-do.

Until the next one – *So don't get comfortable, OK?* And young Beryl never did.

She had so many questions she wanted to ask her mother, but as she sat there studying anew this woman sitting silently beside her – all dressed up in one of her finest sundresses and probably on her way to somewhere else – Beryl figured she had better keep her mouth shut if she knew what was good for her.

Besides, Marie was already concentrating on the powder compact she'd retrieved from her purse, trying to minimise the beads of sweat forming along her top lip, while simultaneously rearranging her recently done hair after the havoc this afternoon's heat had wrought upon it.

Beryl knew all too well her mother's moods, and how volatile she could be. In moments like these, Beryl would always reach for the one thing that comforted her: her much-loved Shirley Temple doll. It had been a Christmas present three years before from her grandmother Clara, who looked after Beryl when Marie could not, which was ... mostly.

Wait. Shirley! Where was she?

Inside Beryl's small bag of belongings, there was no sign of her dearest possession, the beautiful rag doll she'd held on to so tightly during all those long, lonely nights in the orphanage.

With scrabbling hands, she reached over to her almost empty bag and rummaged through the few items of clothing she had, but there was no sign of it. Looking to see if it was at her feet, then spinning around to check behind her, Beryl realised ... the doll just wasn't here.

'Oh no. Shirley! Where is she? Did they give you Shirley, Mummy?'

Marie snorted in reply. *Oh, god, is this kid going to start already?* She'd never quite got the whole Shirley Temple thing in the first place. While Marie herself had always been something of a tearaway, by contrast, that little American girl – who had so captivated Hollywood with her perfectly ringleted hair and cute tap-dancing routines in sweet movies with a moral – was just a bit too cute for Marie. That her daughter had now invested so much love in this pathetic doll was a little too much for Marie to bear.

'No, they didn't give me Shirley, but I'll give you something to really cry about if you keep carrying on.'

The ache Beryl felt for Shirley in that moment was almost unbearable. She knew that tears would get her nowhere with her mother, and she tried – she really, really tried – not to cry. But knowing she shouldn't cry and stopping herself were two different things.

She felt the hot stinging behind her eyes, blinked, and before she knew it her face was wet with tears.

'Mummy, *please*, I can't leave without her,' she said, softly pleading. 'I *need* Shirley. *Pleeeease*, Mummy.'

But Marie was unmoved. She was dropping Beryl back to her mother Clara's for Christmas and then Marie had a date. Softening a little, perhaps – with Marie, you could never tell which way she would go in any given moment – she said they would return some other time to get it. 'Maybe next time I drop you at the orphanage? Promise.'

But as much as Beryl, kneeling by her bed each night in the weeks and months that followed, prayed that her mother would keep her promise, Marie never did.

And with that, Shirley, the only doll Beryl had ever owned and loved, was gone forever.

*

It could have been so different for Marie.

Despite her descent from generations of the hardscrabble of 19th-century convict and colonial Sydney, at 16 she had been given a real shot at escaping it all when she fell in love with young Gordon Power, a 20-year-old budding journalist at the *Labour Times,* the son of a one-time Federal Labor Senator, with ambitions to follow in his father's footsteps. Suffice to say, Marie was thrilled when she and Gordon started dating, but terrified when she discovered she was pregnant with his child. Gordon had been reared a strict

Roman Catholic, so this bastard child was going to be cause for deep shame, and Gordon had no intention of marrying someone of Marie's station. In other families, there might have been talk of 'getting rid of it', but Marie was also from a strict Irish-Catholic family and that idea was never on the table.

In any case, by the time Beryl arrived on 12 December 1928, all of Marie's hopes that actually meeting his sweet little daughter might change Gordon's mind about marriage and fatherhood had evaporated, as Gordon had fallen gravely ill.

In the months before he died from the ravages of tuberculosis, Marie would take her daughter to the darkened rooms of Randwick Hospice to visit. But as Gordon's health continued to decline, so did any dreams Marie had of a secure future with the father of her child.

Neither Marie nor Beryl was mentioned in the death notice placed in the *Sydney Morning Herald* by the family. Nor were they invited to Gordon's funeral, with dignitaries from far and wide turning up in huge numbers for the son of the distinguished former Mayor of Paddington and NSW State and then Federal Senator.

For Gordon's family, Marie and wee baby Beryl might as well have not existed, and it was clear they wished that continued to be the case as there was never any further contact. With the Great Depression now in full swing, Marie just had to get on with it and do the best she could.

As the years passed, and various 'fathers' moved in and out, Marie always insisted that Beryl change her surname – if not legally, then at least publicly – to fit whichever man was present in her mother's life at that time. Marie assured her that things were 'less complicated that way'.

*

For Ray Wilkinson, life couldn't have been further from the experience of young Beryl's.

As the son of Elsie and William Wilkinson, Ray was the apple of his parents' eye – a much-cherished only child, who had grown up in a stable home filled with love and laughter.

Particularly talented at drawing, he would sketch for hours on the back verandah of the home William had built at 33 Osborne Street, Wollongong, on the NSW south coast.

Music and rugby were Ray's other two great loves, with the latter curtailed in his late teens when a mild heart murmur was diagnosed, and all strenuous exercise discouraged on his doctor's orders. It was that same diagnosis that put an end to any talk of Ray signing up to the war effort in Europe as he reached conscription age – something Elsie was not displeased about, as disappointed and frustrated as Ray was.

While understanding Ray's feelings on the matter – the lad craved a physically robust life – William, too, could not have been more pleased that his son was going to be spared firsthand experience of war. Himself a veteran of the blood-soaked French battlefields of the First World War, including the appalling loss of Australian lives at Villers-Bretonneux, he knew more than most the abject horror of young men dying all around him. Catching the Spanish flu in 1918 in the final months of the war and then spending six months in an English hospital as a result had possibly spared him from dying in a hail of bullets, as so many promising young men of his Company had.

William returned to Australia and settled back in Campbelltown, 35 miles south-west of Sydney. It was a place where the roots of the Wilkinson family tree went deep, dating back to the 1870s. The buildings on its main street – Queen Street – were still much the same as they had been on the day they opened, and certainly the way they had been when William left for war. It was a comforting relief for a man who had spent so long in European towns that had been reduced to rubble.

Decades later, William would regard even the *idea* of his son – his only child – going off to war as anathema.

So, with his heart murmur keeping him firmly on Australian soil, Ray had thrown himself into his music studies instead, mastering the double bass and guitar, while courting a local lass by the name of Skippy.

CHAPTER TWO

A love story

'I want to know about your dreams and listen to you talk
about your day. I want to hear your childhood stories and
what makes your heart race. I want you to tell me your
fears and trust me with your secrets. I want to listen to your
favourite music while we lie in the middle of your bedroom
floor and kiss until we can't think anymore.'
– Courtney Peppernell, *Pillow Thoughts IV: Stitching the Soul*.

I T WAS A COOL December night in 1949 that just-turned-21 Beryl
would remember until her final days.

Sydney was only just beginning to recover from the ravages
of the Second World War. She and her best friend, Daphne,
were thrilled to be heading to Sydney's magnificent Town Hall
to see one of the hottest jazz bands around: Jack Allen & The
Katzenjammers.

From the moment the house lights went down, the joyous
swinging harmonies of the eight musicians on stage, with the
charismatic Jack out the front, had totally captivated the packed-out
crowd, intoxicated not just by the beer but by simply being young
and in one of the grandest places in Sydney.

There was one particular member of the band, however, that
Beryl just couldn't take her eyes off, despite the haze of cigarette
smoke and being seated so far down the back of the hall.

'See, Daphne? That one, in the second tier.'

She was pointing at the handsome double-bass player on the crowded stage, suited up, as they all were, in a white tuxedo and black tie, and wearing a look of pure joy on his face. She couldn't help feeling she knew that face, and then she realised why. He was, make no mistake, a dead ringer for Frank Sinatra.

Beryl was smitten. No matter that for the past year she had been going out with a lovely young man by the name of Keith Morris; this just felt so completely different that, just before the band launched into the next tune, she leaned over and whispered to Daphne, 'That's the guy I want to marry.'

Daphne giggled – until she saw the look on Beryl's face. She was serious.

'That's ridiculous. You don't even know him. Besides, what about Keith? You guys are almost engaged!'

'I know,' Beryl replied. 'But look at him – I'm sure he just smiled in my direction. He looks so lovely. There's just something about him …'

A few days later, when the two met up after work as they regularly did, Daphne had almost forgotten about her friend's passing crush. But Beryl certainly hadn't – and for very good reason, but we'll get to that.

After leaving school at 15 to help Marie pay the bills, Beryl was now working the reception desk and switchboard at Clyde Engineering, in the inner-west of the city.

Beryl loved feeling needed and appreciated, and she was, with every brightly answered incoming call to that switchboard. 'Good morning, Clyde Engineering! How can I help you? Mr Evans? Let me try that number for you now, sir …'

So, when Beryl sat down in the booth opposite her friend at the local milk bar just across the road from Beryl's work, Daphne wasn't at all surprised to see Beryl's always beautiful smile. But today, that smile was brighter than usual.

'You'll never guess who came into work today applying for a job in the sales department!' Beryl gushed. Then, before even waiting for a reply, 'He asked me out … and of course I said yes.'

'Sorry?' Daphne replied. 'You're going on a date with someone you don't even know?'

'No! Well, yes. Well ... sort of. It's the double-bass player from the Town Hall on Saturday night. Remember him? His name is Ray Wilkinson. And he got the job! We're going to be working together. Well, sort of together. He is *so* lovely. And Daph, he's even more handsome up close!'

And so began an all-consuming romance between the 28-year-old budding salesman from Surry Hills, now knuckling down for the first time to something a little more secure than life as a travelling musician, and the sweet 21-year-old switchboard operator from Chippendale, who was happy to have a job at all and, now, even happier to have Ray.

Sadly, Keith was heartbroken, as was Skippy, whom Ray had been engaged to for many months.

Also nonplussed about the whole affair was Marie.

'I don't trust him. He's too perfect,' she would tell Beryl, time and again. 'He never gets upset about anything. I'm telling you, Beryl, you can't trust any man that nice.'

But Beryl did, and on 19 January 1951, at St Oliver Plunkett Catholic Church at Harris Park, Ray and Beryl – or 'Beb', as he called her – were married in a simple service, with Daphne as chief bridesmaid. Also in attendance were a proud William and Elsie, along with a disapproving Marie, now with three young sons, Ronnie, Neville and Alan – all half-brothers to Beryl – watching on.

Once again, Beryl was changing her name, this time to Wilkinson. But for the first time, she wasn't changing it to suit Marie, and it wasn't out of embarrassment or coercion. She was doing it because *she* wanted to. It would be the last time Beryl would ever change her name, and on that January day, as the two emerged from the church into the warm sunshine of a promising new life, there was nothing she'd ever been more sure of.

To this point, the men Marie had brought into Beryl's life had been a disappointing collection of reprobates who had only just tolerated her or, worse, simply denied her existence.

Now she was Beryl *Wilkinson*, bearing the name of a good man, a kind man, a man she knew she could finally trust.

The marriage began with a short honeymoon in the Blue Mountains, not far from venues like the mighty Carrington Hotel and Hydro Majestic, where once Ray had taken to the stage with his beloved double bass.

But just as Beryl had been told by her boss that, as a married woman, she now had to leave her job at Clyde Engineering, Ray had packed his double bass and guitar back in their cases and stowed them away for no more than the sweet memories they brought.

Together, the couple found a tiny two-bedroom rental in the small village of Narellan, just outside Campbelltown, and started saving for a home and planning a family.

CHAPTER THREE

And so it begins

'We didn't realise we were making memories,
we just knew we were having fun.'
– Winnie the Pooh, Disney's *Winnie the Pooh*, 2011

I DIDN'T WANT TO go. I told Mummy that. But she insisted. Tears were rolling down my cheeks as I peered out the window of the brown Morris Minor that had come to collect me from our little terracotta-coloured weatherboard home at 17 Sturt Street, Campbelltown. My cries only got louder as Mum, waving goodbye to me from the front verandah, receded in the dusty distance.

I was just three years old and on my way to my first day of community day care at a neighbour's house four blocks away. It was also my *last* day, as it turned out. The only thing I remember about the whole dreadful experience was crying such a river of tears halfway through fingerpainting that they had to call Mum to come and get me. She decided to never put me, or herself, through it again.

I loved being at home with Mum, playing with my little baby brother, Brett, and our big, beautiful boxer dog, Sparky. And the best thing was that big school was two whole years away! There were still cubbies to be built out of sheets and pegs on our Hills Hoist, sprinklers to play under in Campbelltown's unforgiving summertime heat, tall trees to climb and conquer, and Miss Pat and Mr Squiggle to watch on TV. School could definitely wait.

While our street was not exactly on the outskirts of Campbelltown, it was new enough that most of it was still dirt track and devoid of streetlights. It wound its way back up the hill towards the bush and other small pockets of new 'baby boom' developments, where other young families were similarly making a go of it here on the south-western fringes of Sydney.

The block Dad had bought and built upon had, until recently, been part of a much larger farm. From our sloping block and the big, sliding kitchen windows high above our backyard, we had a clear view of the original old timber farmhouse, still with a smattering of grazing sheep, veggie gardens, huge mulberry trees and a neat row of willows by the creek that always overflowed when the rains came, to our great delight.

Because that meant frogs. Lots of frogs. And there was nothing that my big brother, Kyle, and I liked better, than catching some of those frogs – apart from silkworms, that is, and those mulberry leaves were their food of choice.

The life expectancy of both said frogs and silkworms, once they were placed inside the shoeboxes Mum would helpfully keep for just such occasions, was a bit of a moot point. Despite a constant food supply of earthworms for the frogs and fresh leaves for the 'silkies', and the holes we would punch in the lids to help both breathe, sometimes our little friends wouldn't make it – just like the many goldfish we had to flush down the toilet every six months almost always because of overfeeding.

Which is why there were few greater joys in my young life than seeing my juicy silkworms, their tummies fat with mulberry leaves, slowly spin their silky cocoons and then disappear inside their new, cosy, little white houses.

While I waited for them to re-emerge, I loved playing the role of 'mummy' – caring, feeding and nurturing my little babies until they were ready to leave home and be out in the world on their own. Every day I would gently lift the lid and look inside the darkened cardboard space for signs of a moth about to break free from its chrysalis.

And yet, when they did, I was always sad. I couldn't understand why they didn't come back and visit. Ever patient, Mum would then have to comfort me through that process. 'You just have to be happy for them, darling. Remember, it's the cycle of life.'

Along with our big backyard, our pretty little front yard – bordered by, yes, a white picket fence – held its own joys; most particularly, three evenly spaced brick garden beds Dad had thoughtfully built right next to the verandah, in which each of us kids could plant seeds and grow flowers of our very own.

The verandah itself was the perfect size for riding my blue-and-red Cyclops tricycle round and round and round. For hours. My specialty was reverse parking, and many was the time when Dad would arrive home from work and I would beg him to stand there and watch my latest tricks.

'Watch this, Dad. I can do a three-point turn!'

Dad was patience personified, and he always did stop and watch, as if witnessing all this precision driving for the very first time.

'Well done, sweetheart,' he would say encouragingly. 'You're getting really good. Keep going.'

But if Dad was home and now heading inside, that was where I wanted to be as well. My tricycle could wait until tomorrow.

That was everyone's reaction to my dad. An exceedingly wise and gentle man, Ray Wilkinson was a highly respected member of the Campbelltown community. As the much-loved president of the local Lions Club, there were few in the town who didn't have a story about Dad's kindness. And now, as the well-regarded area sales manager at Cyclone Fencing in Granville, his popularity and standing only grew.

Granville was 25 miles away, so his role demanded a long commute every day in his fawn-coloured EH Holden along the Hume Highway (although at the time, 'highway' was a bit of a stretch). I remember once my whole family going to the annual Cyclone kids' Christmas party at his office. On the way, we counted how many traffic lights and STOP signs Dad had to pass through before he arrived at work every day. Forty-three. That made a total of 86 every day, as he took his place in that slow-moving, never-ending, stop-start river of red lights back and forth from home.

In the evening, usually around 7.30, when he did get home (if I wasn't out driving my own set of wheels on the front verandah), I would thrill to the sound of his key going in the front door. *Daddy!* I would then run down the hall and straight into his arms, and he would pick me up and swing me around.

Sometimes, if Dad was home particularly late – damn those traffic lights – I would stay up and wait for him. When I saw through the venetians the flash of his headlights coming down the driveway, I would jump on the lounge, close my eyes and pretend that I was asleep. Then, just as he sat down, he would quietly whisper to Mum, 'Is our little girl asleep?' at which point my eyes would spring open and I would yell, 'Surprise!'

Dad would always laugh heartily and give me a huge hug. And even though we had played this game so very many times before, neither one of us ever tired of it. It was *our* game. And it would always make me feel special.

Ray was someone everyone loved spending time with. Despite being an only child, he had become the centre of his own wider Wilkinson family, including the slightly eccentric Harry Wilkinson, Dad's uncle, who was in his eighties by the time I arrived on the scene.

Uncle Harry lived in a humble turn-of-the-century cottage directly opposite the town's Central Infants' School, which I would soon be attending. He was rich beyond his wildest dreams, after buying up much of the town's cheap farmland in his early years as a plumber in his father's business, and more recently selling off those lands as the area grew in popularity. Not that you could tell, because there were only three things that Harry loved in life: his wife, Rita; his vast array of prize-winning potted orchids, which spilled well beyond the giant greenhouse in his back garden; and, with no kids of his own, playing ventriloquist at just about every children's party in the town. Including my own fifth birthday party just before I headed off to big school.

It was my first-ever birthday party, and my over-excitement must have been obvious to everyone, especially when I accidentally peed my pants just as proceedings were about to begin. All the neighbourhood kids were there – the three Sullivan kids from number 16 across the road, my friend Sharon from three doors up at number 23, and Susan from next door at number 15.

Mum had knocked herself out blowing up balloons and providing every possible party-food treat: fairy bread thickly coated in hundreds and thousands, homemade toffees, jellybeans, GI cordial in big glass pitchers and – joy of joys – little cups of red Aeroplane Jelly, my favourite.

The plan was set: once Uncle Harry had made his appearance and thrilled us all with his amazing talking doll, we would play Pin the Tail on the Donkey and Pass the Parcel, and then it was birthday-cake time! At the end of the party, each child would be able to take home with them a cute little lolly basket Mum had stayed up all night to make, filled with a rich assortment of snakes and cobbers, Fantales and Jaffas, Freckles and chocolate bullets.

Except none of it ever happened. Just ten minutes after everyone arrived and we settled into the garage around the makeshift party table holding all that delicious food, I somehow lost my balance. That saw-horse of Dad's I was sitting on to get a good ringside seat on the whole food situation had somehow toppled over, taking me with it, and I cracked my head wide open on the garage's unforgiving concrete floor.

Mum had to tell everyone to go home so I could be rushed to the doctor. With blood dribbling down my forehead and all over my pretty pink party dress, I was carried out into Dad's car. The crestfallen looks on the faces of all the kids who had just been robbed of an afternoon's worth of sugar and games – not to mention Uncle Harry and his talking doll – would never leave me.

As Mum and I disappeared up the driveway, Jamie Sullivan from across the road called out, 'Can I take my lolly bag, Mrs Wilkinson?'

In the distance, I could hear Jamie's mum who had come to collect him.

'Jamie, Lisa's bleeding – don't ask that! And say "please"!'

Before a wan, 'Please, Mrs Wilkinson?'

Fortunately, my head wound healed quickly; sadly, my humiliation didn't. Nor did my disdain for birthday parties. And it would be many decades before I would ever gather the courage to have one again.

*

If Dad was a pillar of the community, with a wide circle of friends and colleagues outside the home, Mum more easily found her purpose within it, and took comfort in sticking close to home.

She was proud that in this life she was working hard at building with Ray – after a childhood filled with so much transience, trauma and uncertainty – her own three children knew the stability of living in just one house, with two loving parents and the same bed with the same pillow upon which to lay their heads every night.

Like every stay-at-home mum I knew – which was pretty much every mum I knew – Beryl did everything around the house: the lawns, the meals, the washing, the ironing and the cleaning. While I'm sure Mum would have liked a bit more domestic help from Dad, he was the 'breadwinner' in charge of everything financial, and that was just the way things seemed to naturally divide up between them.

Mum always said that all those chores helped keep her weight down, too. Not for her were those Ford Diet Pills to 'keep you slim and regular', advertised during her favourite daytime show, *Beauty & the Beast.*

Nor did she like those Bex Powders her own mother seemed to rely upon so much. The recommendation to housewives across the country at the time, at least according to those ads, was, when life gets too much, just 'have a cup of tea, a Bex and a good lie down'. And Marie would have one of those 'good lie downs' most afternoons, as she struggled on a small pension to raise her three sons, largely on her own.

But Bex was in fact a highly addictive compound analgesic, and the powdery contents in those little blue-and-yellow envelopes I so often saw in Nanny's handbag, combined with her growing love of alcohol, were not a good mix.

Mum didn't want any of it. She wanted to keep her slim, 34-24-34 figure naturally. Even if that meant missing the occasional meal.

Or two. Or sometimes three. And walking everywhere. Mum said that one day, when she could gather the confidence, she would learn to drive and get her licence, like lots of other mums in our street were doing. But for now, walking was fine, and that included trips to the small supermarket four blocks away in Queen Street, to do the week's shopping.

Mum always let me help with putting all the groceries in the basket for the lady at the checkout, and then into our portable vinyl shopper trolley for the slightly harder and heavier trip back home.

Always my reward for being such a good little helper was to stop by Andrews Milk Bar just across Queen Street for an icy-cold chocolate milkshake served in a big stainless-steel milkshake cup, the frothy brown top punctuated by two red-and-white striped paper straws. One for me and one for Brett. I loved sitting there with Mum, sipping our milkshakes, and watching my sunny Campbelltown world outside go by. I felt lucky, and so grown up.

*

I was right. Two years was exactly the amount of time I needed to be ready for big school. And from the very first day I arrived in Mrs Yabsley's kindergarten class, I absolutely lapped it up.

I couldn't get enough of learning the alphabet, numbers, reading, painting and drawing pictures to take home to Mum and Dad, and playing with my new friends, Lisa and Michelle.

Every day Mum would walk me to school, me often clutching a big pink camellia flower from the bush in our front yard for the kindly Mrs Yabsley.

I loved doing well at school and became quite addicted to the whole gold-star reward system given out for excellent schoolwork. Everything I did was in the hope of having one of those much sought-after shiny stars licked and pasted by Mrs Yabsley right next to my latest writing practice – Bb, Bb, Bb, Bb, Bb, Bb – knowing that Mum and Dad would get to see it at the end of the week when my exercise books came home for signing.

The only thing better than the gold star was one of Mrs Yabsley's animal stamps – the red ink applied either on the back of the hand or, better still, right in the middle of your forehead, so the *whole world* could see what a very good girl you had been to be so publicly decorated.

If I got one of those stamps on a Friday, and was really careful and worked around it when I washed my face that night, I would get to display that stamp on my head all weekend. Even better if the animal stamping fell just before a weekend when we were visiting my beloved grandparents Da and Bappy, as they were known, down at their place in Wollongong, right after Sunday School at our local Methodist Church.

While Dad was largely agnostic, Mum was a self-described 'lapsed Catholic', her experiences as a child too harrowing to lead to any greater piety than that. The Methodist Church was simply the happy medium we ended up with.

And Sunday School was just what every kid in Campbelltown did. The deal was, if Kyle, Brett and I sat still and listened during those Sunday-morning teachings, Dad would take us for ice-creams at Con's Milk Bar straight afterwards as a reward, before we headed to Wollongong.

Con himself was a huge local character, one of a wave of post-war European immigrants drawn to the area in recent times. Con had an enormous affection for Dad and would always yell from behind the counter whenever he saw him, 'Ray, where have you been, my *frrrriend*?!'

Con's Milk Bar boasted all the basic essentials of a corner store, but one of its biggest selling points was the shiny glass lolly cabinet right by the front door, and its treasure trove of ice-creams in the shop's big stainless-steel bins. I used to love the distinctive sound of Con slamming those metal lids back to reveal …

'Pine-a Lime-a Splice-a? Paddle Pop-a? Or maybe just a big-a scoop of icy vanilla in a cone-a, Miss-a Lisa?' Con would ask.

'Mr Kyle, young Brett-a? For-a you?'

Con's was also where Dad would always stock up on his favourite brand of cigarettes – Consulate – in their soft, green-

and-white packaging that, to my young nose, never completely hid the sweet, enticing smell of the rich tobacco within. For years I presumed that Con made these 'Con'-sulate cigarettes just for Dad, and that Dad's two-pack-a-day habit was, in turn, just his way of supporting his friend Con.

Then, with Sunday School attendance and ice-creams done, it was time to pile into the family Holden, collect Mum, and head south to Wollongong, playing I-spy and spelling games, led by Dad, all the way.

Da and Bappy had together seen themselves through plenty of hard times. Family was precious to them; and beyond each other, the thing they loved most in life was when their much-loved son and his young family came to visit.

Their home was actually a combination of three cleverly designed flats: two one-bedders at the front – providing Bappy and Da with a small rental income – and their own three-bedder at the back, with its sunny timber verandah and huge meandering back garden featuring the biggest mandarin tree imaginable.

In one corner of the garden was the long-drop dunny 'outhouse', and right next to it, the garden shed, where tumbledown blooms of purple wisteria flourished in springtime. Inside the shed was a dark wonderland full of the tools of Bappy's various trades from his younger days. He was a handyman to beat them all, my grandpa, and could fix anything. You only had to ask.

Beneath the verandah was the big old, cavernous open laundry – always filled with the sweet waft of Sunlight soap – with its long cement washing tubs, a shiny 'copper' for boiling the clothes, and a large rubber-handled wringer for squeeeeeezing out any excess water, before everything was hung out on the line. If Da wasn't cooking in the kitchen or mending clothes in her tiny sewing room, this was where I would always find her.

Beyond the laundry was the garage, permanently housing the beautiful lines of Bappy's perfectly preserved dark-green Ford Cabriolet 'automobile', dating back to the 1930s. I don't remember ever seeing Bappy actually driving that beautiful machine, but every so often I would catch a glimpse of him gently pulling back the large protective cover, giving the wooden dash and leather seats a gentle dusting, while possibly, briefly, remembering all the happy family outings it had once afforded them.

Often Kyle, Brett, Mum and I would spend our school holidays there in Wollongong, while Dad stayed behind doing his daily Campbelltown/Granville/Campbelltown trip, to and from work.

Those holidays were full of long, happy days spent at North Wollongong and Austinmer beaches. We would bake ourselves brown beneath the Aussie sun, build endless sandcastles, and jump in and out of the waves with our bright-orange Zippy boards while Mum watched from the shoreline, before returning to Osborne Street for dinner and nights filled with games of '21' and 'Old Maid'.

In the mornings I would often watch, transfixed, in the washroom just off the back verandah as Bappy – now in his late seventies – would lather up his face, and sharpen the blade of his razor, back and forth, back and forth, on a long piece of leather hanging from the small, silvery mirror above the basin. Then, he would artfully scrape off every last whisker, pat his face dry and give me a kiss on the forehead, before excusing himself to get dressed. Neat cardigans, collared shirts, sharply pleated pants and, sometimes, a tie.

No matter that Bappy's days of actually needing to dress up at all were now few in number – with the important exception of the annual ANZAC Day march down Crown Street. With many of his former infantry mates now gone, though, and the lingering pain of his own war-time mustard gas burns becoming increasingly bothersome, his attendance was no longer guaranteed.

William was raised to be a gentleman in the truest sense of that word. And he was. He also had a keen eye for a bargain. With still-sharp memories of the need for 'rationing' during the wars, tinned corn, tinned ham, tinned pineapple and tinned peaches were repeatedly purchased, cut-price, in their dozens, all of them then placed under the kitchen sink, as insurance against the day government rationing might be implemented again. It never was, but Bappy and his constantly replenished cache of tinned food were always ready, just in case.

I always remember seeing him purposefully walking up the steep hill of Osborne Street, his empty leather port and string shopping bag in each hand, his once-strong legs still managing the climb, but the old soldier slower now. And those trips were starting to take it out of him.

Da adored her husband, and we in turn adored her. Small, cuddly and utterly low-key in all she did, she devoted any spare time she had to her role as president of the Wollongong Legacy Club, such was the gratitude she felt to have got her much-loved William back, safe from the war.

Da delighted in a growing love I had for performing, and would patiently sit and dutifully clap with *every single rendition* of 'Chopsticks' I would play on the big pianola in the corner of their lounge room. Ballet performances were soon added to my night-time show repertoire after we bought a pretty pink, but slightly limp, second-hand 'tutu' during a visit to the local Wollongong Vinnies, with Mum.

Mum and I would often disappear into that Vinnies for hours on end – me helping her sort through the jumble of discarded clothes piled high into the variously priced bins. With items priced at 5 cents, 10 cents and 50 cents apiece, depending on the quality, Mum loved the thrill of finding bargains she declared to be 'good as new'.

Mum never wanted for much, and was a demon with leftovers and a great believer in recycling. I dare say, the haunting spectre of her troubled childhood accepting hand-outs and living in hand-me-downs never left her.

*

I always felt sad when those holidays with Da and Bappy were over and it was time to head back up the Bulli Pass to home. With the lights of Wollongong and the flaming fires of the Port Kembla steelworks falling away behind us, I would rest my head on the windowsill in the back seat of the EH, look up to the sky and watch the moon, transfixed as it raced along beside us, somehow going at *exactly* the same pace as our car.

When I asked Dad how that happened, he said it was because he would adjust the speed of our station-wagon so we would always arrive home at exactly the same time as the moon, so it was there outside our window as we fell asleep that night. How very clever, I thought. How very Dad.

Around this time, I was given my very first pair of ballet shoes. Inspired by my Vinnies tutu, and the excellent response I was getting to my performances in front of Da and Bappy, I joined the Lurnea School of Classical Dance. One of the girls at school, Leanne, was already going, and when I told Mum I would like to try ballet too, she didn't hesitate. And so began my after-school lessons with the supremely elegant Miss Dean at the old Masonic Hall in Allman Street, not far from school.

I was smitten from my very first class. Miss Dean moved in a way that was crisp and precise, and quite unlike anyone I'd ever met. Her jet-black hair was always scraped back into the tightest of buns, while her long, lithe limbs made the act of simply walking across a room a stunning stage performance in itself.

Her own dreams of making it on the world's stage having possibly already receded, it was clear she still took enormous joy in passing on those dreams to young ones like me. She was patient and kind and extraordinarily encouraging, and every afternoon when I would arrive for my lessons, she would beam. And so would I.

Two lessons a week quickly became four, and as my progression whizzed through the various ballet 'grades', Miss Dean told Mum that I was 'good enough to go all the way'. I wasn't sure exactly what 'all the way' meant; I just knew that the more I danced, the more I wanted to dance. Everything was possible when I slipped on my pink ballet shoes and criss-crossed those shiny slim ribbons once, twice, three times around my ankles. To my amazement — and certainly to the amazement of my two brothers — I could will my body to move and lift and leap and hold with complete control, to feel lighter than air, and to dance!

Every December, all the Lurnea dance schools from across Sydney would hold their annual eisteddfod at the Footbridge

Theatre at Sydney University. Classical ballet, jazz, tap, highland – every one of the dance disciplines on offer was enthusiastically represented.

Our class would practise our group performance for months, and somehow, every year, I was asked to do the only solo classical ballet performance on the night's rundown. Every time, I would stand in the wings behind the massive stage curtain, terrified, just before my chosen music would begin. And every time, on Miss Dean's cue, I would take a deep breath, get out there in the footlights and ... *love* every second of it. I never felt more alive than when I got on that stage, and I would *live* for seeing Mum's and Dad's smiles out there in the audience, and then the look on their faces afterwards when they came to collect me backstage.

One performance, though, more than any other, will stay with me forever. It was 17 December 1967 and my neon-white tutu, with its sharply starched tulle skirt sprinkled with tiny diamantes, was glowing as I waited patiently side-of-stage for the girls from the Hurstville chapter of Lurnea to complete their tap-dancing rendition of 'Hello Dolly'.

Standing next to me was Phyllis Wheatley, who was in the performance after mine. Phyllis was one grade ahead of me in ballet, and two years ahead of me in life. She had been forced to grow up more quickly than most in recent times though, as, just two years before, her father, Kevin, had tragically been killed in the war in Vietnam. At the age of 28, Phyllis's dad was protecting a fellow soldier who had been mortally wounded as the Viet Cong closed in. Even though he had been urged by medical personnel that there was no longer anything he could do to save his comrade, the young soldier never left his side. Kevin Wheatley was posthumously awarded the Victoria Cross as a result, and Phyllis and her siblings were growing up without their amazing dad.

Right now, though, as the Hurstville tap-dancers were beginning to take their bows, and just as I was about to take my first steps onto the stage, Phyllis leaned in to whisper something.

'Did you hear what happened?' she asked, clearly very upset.

I hadn't, but I hoped that whatever it was could wait, as by now the last of the girls were off stage and I needed to prepare to go on. I asked if she could tell me later.

'The prime minister,' she continued, unable to wait. 'Harold Holt. He's dead. He drowned at a beach in Victoria today. It's so sad. Our prime minister is dead. And ... he has ... three kids.'

Phyllis had tears rolling down her cheeks. She understood the loss felt by the Holt children, the same pain she and her siblings had experienced just two years before.

With just seconds to spare, I gave my friend Phyllis the biggest hug I could. I'll never know if it helped, because right then I really had to close my eyes and focus.

With that, the spotlights came back up, immediately igniting the diamantes on my tutu. I lifted my arms into first position, pointed my toes and delicately stepped out onto the stage, a huge forced smile on my face. Phyllis never moved throughout my whole performance, and I kept looking over to see if she had someone with her.

As I lay in bed that night back in Campbelltown after the long trip home and thought of Phyllis, I wondered what it would feel like to no longer have your dad around. I tried to imagine it, but I simply couldn't. And I hoped I would never find out.

CHAPTER FOUR

'Bappy' days

'I will never have this version of me again. Let me
slow down and be with her.' – Rupi Kaur

I F GOING TO VISIT Da and Bappy was a dose of pure sunshine, then
going to visit Nanny, as we called Mum's mother, Marie, was a
dark agony.

Years of taking Bex powders and an increasing dependence on
alcohol had proven to be a toxic combination, and after suffering
a series of strokes, Nanny was now living in a semi-vegetative
state in a nursing home in the inner-south-west Sydney suburb of
Lakemba.

These were difficult trips for Mum, and Dad knew it. Mum's
relationship with Nanny had always been fraught; all the more so
now as Mum increasingly found herself dealing with the demons
and disappointments visited upon her by Marie's lifetime of motherly
indifference.

I could always tell when one of these dutiful Sunday-afternoon
visits to the nursing home was coming, because right after Sunday
School Dad would cheerily collect us – the car already packed
with swimming costumes and towels – and take us straight from
ice-creams at Con's to the Woolwash, Campbelltown's favourite
swimming spot out the back of the bush at Kentlyn. With its array
of long rope swings tied to the ancient gums on the Georges River

shoreline, small sandy 'beaches' and gentle freshwater flow when the rains came, this place always gave sweet relief to locals escaping Campbelltown's searing summer heat. For us kids on these 'Nanny visit' Sundays, the Woolwash was an unspoken reward in anticipation of what we were about to endure.

From the moment we would open the aging frosted-glass door at the nursing home's entrance, the smell would hit us: an unmistakable pungent punch in the nose of stale urine, antiseptic and old age, all seemingly in competition against one another – the urine often winning. That is, until the cleaners would start up the whirring discs of the floor-polishing machines, at which point waves of industrial-grade chemicals would have a momentary olfactory win. Then as we would walk down the long sunroom corridor, passing various snoozing elderly residents in wheelchairs as they took in the afternoon rays, the strong aroma of today's lunch – or was that last night's dinner? – would take over.

Arriving at Nanny's shared room, we would gently pull back the grey plastic curtain, trying not to disturb her similarly bedridden roommates. And there would be Nanny, half propped-up by pillows, staring into the middle distance, her mouth slightly agape, unable to speak and, from the moment we entered, entirely unmoved by our presence.

Always, Mum would arrive with freshly washed nightgowns for Nanny – after having gathered the dirty ones during the last visit – and flowers from our garden, hoping against hope that those small gestures would bring a smile or a flicker of recognition to her inanimate face. But … nothing. Undeterred, Mum would busy herself with putting away the clean nightgowns and placing the deep-pink camellia blooms in a small cut-glass vase that sat by the bed in anticipation of these fortnightly visits.

Unlike Da, Nanny had never smothered us in cuddles – that was all a bit too soppy and sentimental for her. In fact, I don't remember ever receiving any kind of affection from Nanny when we were little, so we didn't really miss it now that we were older, and her arms had become almost as useless as every other part of her weak, emaciated body.

I'm sure it took all Mum's strength, and Dad's too, to try and remain upbeat during these visits. But no matter the subject – my ballet, Kyle's judo, Brett's footy, or how we were all going at school – still Nanny remained unresponsive.

Occasionally, she would lift her eyes and stare at one of us, or a small trickle of dribble would roll down to her chin, and Mum, always doing what she could to keep some semblance of Nanny's dignity intact, would dutifully wipe it away. For all the years of hurt, she was still her mum. And yet, the only emotion I ever remember witnessing from my maternal grandmother towards her only daughter – even when she was well – was indifference and detachment.

To help pass the time while Mum and Dad 'chatted' with Nanny, Kyle, Brett and I would sometimes wander out into the long hallway common to all of the shared hospital rooms, and make good use of the super shiny, always freshly polished linoleum floors. Shoes off and socks still on, it was the perfect spot for a game of slip-and-slide and, on a good day – if we didn't squeal too much and get roused on by a passing sister – we could kill a whole half-hour in that corridor.

On the trips back home, Mum would always be a fairly silent presence in the front seat. The very sight of her mother and her slow, sad demise clearly awakened all those grim memories of a childhood that every day she was fighting to leave behind. I am sure she must have dwelt on it all.

How could her mother have so often abandoned her?

How could she have not kept her promise to go back and find her Shirley Temple doll?

How could she have denied her little girl the care and warm embrace of the only parent she knew?

I felt for Mum, as so much of what she had learnt as a child meant that now, in her adult life, taking risks and trusting too much would, in her mind, almost always guarantee hurt. So, living a smaller life and never getting her hopes up on anything was a much less painful path for Mum to take. With no model of caring motherhood to work from, she had to take her cues as to how a family should function from Dad. Dad knew that, and his patience as Mum navigated it all was unending.

As to Nanny, there was certainly something of the fighter in her, as she continued to exist day after day, month after month, year after year in that same darkened corner, silently sharing a room with an array of ever-changing faces she never got to know.

And then finally Nanny, too, slipped away.

It was a small funeral, and Mum said we didn't need to go. It was a school day, she said, and coordinating getting all of us to the church in Parramatta was going to be too difficult. She had to meet up with her half-brothers, and Dad had to come back from work and … *look, just don't come, OK?*

So, we didn't.

It was many years later that I discovered that Mum didn't attend Nanny's funeral either. Those memories, those scars, that hurt, that lifetime of disappointments were all just far too deep for her to pretend to celebrate a life that had so traumatised her own. There had already been far too many farewells when she was a little girl. One more made no difference.

Dad went to the funeral – of course – driven as always by his sense of duty, his desire to do the decent thing, and be there for that little girl not strong enough to face this final moment. The man Nanny never liked, the man she said was 'too perfect', was there – the sole representative of a chapter in Marie's life she had closed long ago.

*

I loved Miss West. And there was no student more thrilled than me when it was announced that our entire class was going to have her for another whole year as we moved from Fourth to Fifth Class.

Miss West was a traditionalist, both in her style of teaching and her, well, style: cable-knit vests, kilt skirts, knee-length socks, sensible court shoes, and a neatly waved hairstyle straight out of the playbook of Her Majesty the Queen (that's her there in the wattle-yellow ballgown in that big picture just up above the blackboard). With no kids of her own, still living at home with her mum, and in her early thirties, Miss West was known to everyone as a 'spinster'.

Not that she seemed to mind, because all that ever really mattered to Miss West was teaching 'her' girls and boys, and teaching them well.

I suppose I was one of the 'good girls' through primary school, always eager to please and keep learning. I took pride in getting my homework done on time. I loved being blackboard monitor and was always the first one to put my hand up to clean the dusters. If the teacher needed a note delivered to the principal's office, up would go my hand again.

My favourite job of all, though, was helping to roll out copies of our homework sheets from the big old gestetner machine, with its fading purple ink and heady – somewhat addictive – solvent fumes that would be released during the printing process.

After school, with homework done and if Kyle and Brett didn't already have a game of cricket going with the other kids in the street, I would often head three doors up and play with my friend Sharon. Along with making mud pies, and playing jacks, elastics, chasings and hide-and-seek, we loved playing with our dolls.

Everyone I knew had Barbies, but somehow I just couldn't bring myself to get on board the Barbie train. Her proportions bothered me, knowing that, were she human, she would have been incapable of staying upright with that ridiculous boobs-to-waist-to-hips figure ratio.

That said, Barbie did have quite the array of careers: school teacher, doctor, nurse, astronaut, flight attendant, fashion designer and ballerina. Still, I just couldn't relate. All those endless job choices seemed much more about fashion and selling more dolls than any suggestion of what the future might hold for young girls with ambitions for a life beyond 'wife' and 'mother'.

My favourite doll was the less popular, much shorter, rounder Skipper, with her flat chest; bob-cut hair; kind, makeup-free eyes; and a sprinkling of adorable freckles. If I'd had a sister – and I always wanted one, for I envied those girls blessed with the closeness of what I imagined as a familial female other half – I wished she would have been Skipper. So that was the doll I always took to Sharon's.

Sharon's family had a huge backyard and it was always the location of the neighbourhood bonfire on Cracker Night, even though it would invariably leave a deep blackened scar in their lawn. Skyrockets, penny bungers, throwdowns, Catherine wheels and sparklers were the once-a-year treat we all saved up for, and the three-dollar bulk-sized bag from Con's was always the best value for money.

Campbelltown's well-known hoons, excited by the bonfires blazing in just about every street, always saw Cracker Night as full permission to put on a show and perform endless screaming burnouts and 'doughnuts' in the otherwise quiet cul-de-sacs right across the town. The small number of local police would be too busy to worry about squealing tyres though, as every year there would be countless other mishaps to attend to. Cracker Night invariably ended in a busy emergency ward over at Camden Hospital – bonfires that got out of control, misfired skyrockets and skylarking with penny bungers often causing the most harm. Burst eardrums; third-degree burns; eyes, fingers, toes forever taken; and sometimes, deaths, always featuring on the 6pm news the following night.

Before school, at least in our house, we watched *Miss Marilyn's Super Flying Fun Show* starting at 7 o'clock every morning on Channel 9, with its games and cartoons; the lovely host, 'Miss Marilyn' Mayo; and the slightly crazy Rod Hull, with his out-of-control life-sized puppet, 'Emu'.

There were lots of kids at school who weren't allowed to watch TV in the morning, but Mum didn't have a problem with us switching on the old black-and-white – as long as we kept getting ready for school, and didn't dare touch the delicately placed antenna ears that extended out the back *juuuust so*. There was a fine art to getting those silver sticks in *exactly* the right position so you could see the picture rather than just an infernal rolling black band across the screen or, worse, a screen full of snow – so woe betide any one of us who ever moved them!

All through primary school I had something of an obsession with *Archie* comics, which featured four wholesome, quintessentially American teenagers in the 1960s. After school, I would regularly head down to the local newsagent to see if the latest weekly instalment in the series had arrived.

Archie Andrews was the slightly hapless, red-headed, freckle-faced 'boy next door' and the quasi 'nice-guy hero' of every story. Then there was his rich football-star mate, Reggie, whose shiny black hair, we suspected, was as dark as his heart. Reggie was always in competition with Archie: from his starring role as the school's touchdown-scoring quarterback to those shared Harvard ambitions; from the cars they both drove to the affections of the two central women in their lives, Betty Cooper and Veronica Lodge. And this is where all of us playing along at home had to make a choice between Betty and Veronica – because both girls were rivals for Archie's love, and every story revolved around Archie trying to decide which of the girls he would choose.

Betty was the 'good' all-American 'girl next door': the always sweet, always available one, hopelessly in love with our hero, and often the loser in this game of romantic roulette for Archie's affections. Veronica on the other hand was the much more exciting, glamorous, brunette vixen whose life epitomised the 'American dream': a vast family mansion to rattle around in; a wardrobe stuffed full of designer clothing; and European summer vacations with her distracted millionaire father who appeared to spend all of his excellent life making money, while Veronica excelled at spending it.

It all came so easily to the beautiful Veronica, including having Archie wrapped around her little finger. We just knew this self-centred villainess was bad for him, and much better suited to the dastardly, equally self-obsessed Reggie; but more than all that, we wanted our favourite, Betty, to win out. If only Archie would wake the hell up.

With every new instalment, I was always willing Betty to stop playing the waiting game: if you want him, go and tell him, for heaven's sake, and stop putting up with all those back-stabbing antics of Veronica's. And why does he get to do all the choosing anyway? What happens if he ends up choosing neither of you? What are you doing about planning for your future – an education, a job, a career – like the boys both are?

Complicating it further was the fact that Betty and Veronica were cast in this ongoing love triangle as BFFs. They were the original, ultimate 'frenemies'.

Archie's world was a clearly drawn example of a theme that permeated much of my childhood (most particularly in the fairy tales that were read to me, as they were to every other little girl and boy I knew, at bedtime): that when it comes to your future happiness, there is only ever one prince, one glass slipper, one magical kiss that will 'save' you, and you'd be best advised to do whatever you can – decency be damned – to get that guy. Oh, and by the way, that guy you want? *He* gets to do all the choosing. So stand in line, sister!

Because we all knew the deal: getting the guy was your meal ticket for life. And we heard it again and again in the tales of Cinderella, Snow White, Rapunzel and Sleeping Beauty (who was actually in bed *fast asleep* when that random passing prince started kissing her!). The stories of these female characters involved a happily-ever-after that only came if you were lucky enough to be chosen – chiefly because you were the most beautiful one, and usually after being in direct competition with a whole bunch of other women.

Stepsisters? They were always 'ugly' and mean. Stepmothers? Let's paint them as seethingly jealous harridans, ready to throw you into the oven, or better, banish you into the darkened forest with nothing but stale bread. And let's not forget to throw in a nasty female witch, just to be extra sure we drive home the women-are-always-in-competition-with-one-another message.

As to each story's ending, I couldn't help noticing that, once these young damsels had bagged their handsome guy, their lives suddenly stopped – at roughly 20, with nigh on six decades of their lives yet to be lived. The conclusion? The most interesting thing that would ever happen to these young women was already in the rear-vision mirror.

While I was reading *Archie* comics, my brothers were devouring *Mad* magazines, where the hero of the piece was a goofy kid of indeterminate age, called Alfred E. Neuman, who stood for mocking all he observed in the world, including those fairy tales.

It was in fact the pages of *Mad* magazine that cured me forever of that whole 'damsel in distress' theme when I saw their complete carve-up of Rapunzel who, locked up for years in a tall, tall tower for crimes unknown, grew a couple of hundred feet's worth of hair before yet another prince (presumably one with hair-climbing abilities) came and rescued her.

Mad magazine – ironically enough put together by an almost exclusively male team of writers and comics – had decided that if that prince was going to be worthy of Rapunzel's forever affections, she had to set him a challenge to prove his love was real. And so, in their version, when that prince appeared at the bottom of Rapunzel's tower and uttered that infamous line, 'Rapunzel, Rapunzel, let down your golden hair', what she threw down was not the silky golden tresses from atop her pretty blonde head, but the slightly darker, somewhat more coarse growth from years of not shaving her underarms.

The moral of this totally updated take on the story was all the more superb for its final comic frames, as this edgy, feminist version of Rapunzel saw her square-jawed prince unable to cop a joke (or her bodily sproutings) and hastily gallop off, at which point she tied that underarm hair to a nearby hook that had been there all along, expertly climbed down it and rescued herself. She didn't end up with that dopey prince because he was too superficial to see past the hair. But Rapunzel was free. And she'd done it on her terms. And I liked that.

As for Betty? She never did wind up with the always undecided Archie, but that was a good thing. Betty – and every woman, I decided – deserves better than ambivalence.

Meanwhile, as I got older, there were plenty of other stories and characters for me and my girlfriends to take our cues from. American sitcoms formed a large part of our daily pop-culture diet, and looking back, they probably had a bigger influence on me than I realised at the time.

Every afternoon after school, there was a smorgasbord of TV shows to choose from, many with sharply drawn female characters who, at first glance, appeared tied to their kitchen and usually kid-bound married lives: *Bewitched*, *Get Smart*, *The Addams Family*, *The Munsters*, *The Beverly Hillbillies*, *I Love Lucy*, *I Dream of Jeannie*, *The Flintstones* and *The Jetsons*.

At closer inspection, however, there were much more subtle messages at play in these sitcoms: firstly, they seldom ended without some sort of moral lesson having been learnt. The good guy or girl always won, kindness mattered, and bad people could be thwarted by heroic collective action. Secondly, if you were a woman with a few wily tricks – often way too sophisticated for the men in their lives to understand – you could navigate your way through a man's world and turn most situations to your advantage.

When it came to the men they were married to, or in the curious case of *I Dream of Jeannie* became 'slaves' to, these men were often clueless bumblers – Fred Flintstone, Darrin Stephens, Major Nelson – repeatedly unable to succeed at anything without the help of the much sharper women guiding them through.

One of the few sitcoms to show a woman in an actual workplace was *Get Smart*, starring the goofy secret agent Max and his groovily dressed female sidekick, Agent 99. Of course, 99 was hopelessly in love with Max and, like a 'good girl', was always waiting for him to make the moves. But when it came to ultimately beating the baddies, it was usually the clever, capable and eagle-eyed 99 who did so. While 99 pretended that Max had done it all himself and always gave him the credit for saving the day, we at home knew better.

And then there was *The Brady Bunch*, with its iconic opening theme song ('*Here's a story, of a lovely lady …*'); cute-as-a-button kids; and teachable lessons delivered by squeaky-clean caring parents, Carol and Mike – as it happens, the first TV couple ever to be seen sharing the same double bed.

Every afternoon at 5.30pm, right before the Channel 10 news, there I was on our lounge-room floor – as the cameras zoomed in on the Bradys' super-cool, split-level ranch-style home – ready to see yet another perfectly resolved episode of gentle sibling rivalry, unrequited crushes or giving the kid that didn't make the team a helping hand.

So addicted did I become to this series, that I used to try to impress Kyle and Brett by guessing in the opening seconds of the first scene which episode was being screened that afternoon. Would it be the one where Cindy and Bobby attempt to beat the teeter-totter record? Or the one where Marcia gets hit in the nose with the football? Or when Davy Jones from the Monkees is her date for the prom? Or that god-forsaken Hawaiian two-parter with the unlucky tiki charm that eventually spelled the end of the show? I always guessed right; yet my brothers, inexplicably, were never impressed.

This was the first 'blended family' depicted on mainstream TV, and with three evenly age-matched boys and girls thrown into the mix, we all had our favourites. While many of my girlfriends had a crush on the oldest, Greg, and we all tried to recreate Marcia's perfectly centre-parted sun-kissed mane of hair, I was always drawn to Jan. Jan was quintessential middle child: not the prettiest, not the showiest, not the most popular, and the least likely to ever rock the boat.

Jan was also the one with the biggest heart, the sharpest spark of adventure and a keen eye for justice. And if the Jan-featured episodes had a theme, it was usually that it's the quiet one who does the work and no-one sees coming who often prevails. As a middle child myself, I liked that.

In one episode, probably my favourite of all 117 that made up the show's five-year run, Jan finds a childhood photograph of her permanently single, adventure-loving, kinda crazy Aunt Jenny who occasionally comes to stay before she jets back off overseas to her next far-flung exotic destination. Aunt Jenny is already in her later years and, boy, has she lived a life. But she is not what you'd call conventionally pretty, and that picture of her as a young girl is the spitting image of Jan as she is now.

Aunt Jenny soon discovers that Jan is worried she is looking into her future – and her future face – when they meet. Jan can't hide her disappointment, but Aunt Jenny, God love her, is not offended, and instead teaches Jan important lessons of cherishing the beauty within, and why living an interesting, adventurous and fulfilling life will always bring far greater joys than any cares Jan may ever have about the superficial. Jan immediately gets it, and vows from that moment forward to live life just like her magnificent, risk-taking, *beautiful* Aunt Jenny.

Every time I watched that episode, I cried.

CHAPTER FIVE

Off to high school

> 'Mockingbirds don't do one thing but make music for
> us to enjoy. They don't eat up people's gardens, don't
> nest in corn ribs, they don't do one thing but sing
> their hearts out for us. That's why it's a sin to kill a
> mockingbird.' – Harper Lee, *To Kill a Mockingbird*

IN THE CAMPBELLTOWN OF the early 70s, you were either a Holden family or a Ford family (we were Holden). You had a TV or you didn't (we did). A caravan or you didn't (unfortunately, we didn't). A home phone or you didn't (we did – 21165!). Your parents smacked you or they didn't (thankfully, ours didn't). Your parents smoked or they didn't (sadly, ours did). And you were either Catholic or 'other' – and we were definitely 'other', due in no small part to Mum's perplexingly un-Christian Catholic upbringing – a confusion she was determined we kids would never have to experience.

That meant, when it was time to choose a high school, there was no choice to be made: I was headed for the come-one-come-all public school, Campbelltown High. There were two other high schools catering for the town's growing baby boom, but both were Catholic and stood high on the two big hills that marked each side of the old town.

On one hill sat St Gregory's for boys; on the other, St Patrick's for girls. And sitting almost exactly between the two, just a couple of blocks from our house, was Campbelltown High.

And while going the non-secular route meant I would never get to experience any of those traditional celebrations some of the girls from my ballet classes would – like taking confirmation and, perhaps eventually, making their 'debut' – I didn't mind. I never quite understood what the purposes of those events were anyway.

Besides, when I saw that St Pat's strict uniform code dictated a heavy woollen blazer at all times (scorching hot summer days included), a handmaiden-style bonnet and immensely sensible brown school shoes, I figured missing out on a couple of chances to wear pretty lace frocks was a small price to pay.

At Campbelltown High the dress rules were somewhat more relaxed. Even though on day one of First Form we were told that our skirts had to be long enough so that when we knelt down our hem would *touch* the ground, that rule never stuck. We worked out pretty quickly that with our belts pulled tight enough around our waists we could always hitch our skirts, and no-one said a thing when we ditched our blazers. The headmaster would occasionally frown when he cast his eye over morning assembly, but none of us ever took his threats of detention seriously. He knew, I suspected, that there were bigger issues at play in a worthwhile education. The most important, of course, was encouraging good teachers, and my greatest hope was that here in high school I would find another 'Miss West'.

As it happened, not everyone had turned out to be a fan of Miss West's gentle teaching style – most particularly Miss Stupples, my much tougher-talking, Kiwi-born teacher in Sixth Class. And she *didn't miss*.

'I'm not going to spoon-feed you kids,' she had warned us in that final year of primary school. 'I know most of you have come from two Miss West years, but let me tell you, this year is going to be different. I'm different. Because high school is different. It's time to toughen you lot up.'

And she was right. Transitioning from being one of the 'big kids' of Sixth Class, to one of the all-too-easily identifiable First

Formers – in our oversized uniforms, brand-new Globite school cases in hand, nervously sitting on the sidelines at lunchtime trying to work out exactly where you fitted in and who you fitted in with – did come as a huge shock.

With students from all the small primary schools in the town landing here together, there were plenty of new kids to meet, too. At least I had my pod of friends from Campbelltown Central with me, including my three besties – Michelle, Lisa and Sharon – who felt as I did: that we needed to stick together until we could work out this place and all these new faces.

The school itself was made up of a random hotchpotch of standard-issue Science, Arts, English, Library, Home Ec (for the girls) and Woodwork (for the boys) blocks, along with a growing number of demountables, surrounded by lots of green playing fields, and big old trees. In the middle of it all, a huge central playground.

Navigating the rules of that playground was a steep learning curve too. Sure, you could draw a hopscotch course on the ground, or set up a genteel game of elastics or jacks like you did back in primary; but in this much more rough-and-tumble space, that line of play demarcation you might have been counting on meant nothing. These older kids were a lot bigger, a lot louder, a lot faster, and a lot less apologetic if one of their frequently out-of-control balls just happened to connect with your game, or your head.

Schoolwork was harder, too, and getting my brain around things like trigonometry, chemistry and *algorithms*, for god's sake (I mean, when in the history of the world would *they* ever have any relevance in most people's lives?), was a bit of a struggle.

Then there was the ever-changing line-up of different teachers that came with our weekly 'timetable'. No longer was there one teacher devoted to nurturing each of us through to the end of the year. High school involved a new teacher for every new subject, every new 40-minute period, every new classroom.

It felt like everywhere I looked, change was happening – and not just at school, but for women, and girls like me, in general. Nowhere was it happening with more speed than in the media, and courtesy of two Australian women who were making a lot of important noise on the world's stage.

The first was Germaine Greer, whose book *The Female Eunuch* was imploring women to challenge the ties binding them to generations of gender inequality and domestic servitude. Greer argued that women didn't have to do what had always been expected of them: that is, be good girls, get married, have kids, be nice and shut up. Detractors blamed the book for breaking up marriages, while generations of dissatisfied women saw simple good sense and real power in its message, and were using it to renegotiate terms across every aspect of their lives on a more equal basis.

Greer begged women to raise their voices and take on the world.

A little less angry, but arguably even more powerful, was singer Helen Reddy, and her number-one hit that quickly became a feminist anthem to women across the generations. From the moment I first heard 'I Am Woman' on More Music 2SM – it spoke to me.

I am woman, here me roar,
In numbers too big to ignore,
And I know too much to go back and pretend.
'Cause I've heard it all before,
And I've been down there on the floor,
No-one's ever going to keep me down again.

Oh yes, I am wise,
But it's wisdom born of pain.
Yes, I've paid the price,
But look how much I've gained.
If I have to, I can do anything.
I am strong,
I am invincible …
I am woman!

Wow. Just … wow!

Suddenly we realised that so many of the songs we all listened to on the radio were about wishing and hoping and waiting for a man. This song wasn't about men at all – it was about *us*. And our unrealised power. Helen Reddy reminded us that we deserved to be taken seriously and celebrated as human beings who could be anything we wanted to be – and without the crushing restrictions faced by our mothers and grandmothers.

Her message was only driven home further in her Grammy acceptance speech six months after the song's release, when she thanked God, 'because *she* makes everything possible'. In that one simple line I felt, like many, as though I had been woken up. Helen Reddy was right. Women were suddenly questioning everything. Why *is* it presumed God is a He? And while we're at it, I wondered, why does Mum get called Mrs Ray Wilkinson? Why do women have to leave their paid employment when they're pregnant? Why are there so many female teachers, but every school principal is always male? Why are all the newsreaders on TV always men? And every DJ on 2SM? And our prime ministers? Why are blokes only ever addressed as 'Mr', but women always defined by their marital status: 'Mrs' or 'Miss'?

Gloria Steinem was another name I kept hearing. Steinem was editor of a US magazine called *Ms* (I loved her and the title already), and sometimes, when I got my teachers to sign my autograph book at the end of each year (in the absence of actual famous people to sign it), they would quote the wise words of others. One that always stuck with me were the words of Gloria Steinem.

'Without leaps of imagination or dreaming, we lose the excitement of possibilities. Dreaming, after all, is a form of planning.'

Dreaming. I liked that.

*

Dolly.

It was a strange name for a magazine, to be sure. But I loved that highly catchy jingle I kept hearing on Graham Kennedy's *In Melbourne Tonight* for a new Australian magazine for teenagers. As the song kept repeating, 'Dolly is a girl like you!'

For years, when I headed to the newsagent looking for my latest beloved *Archie* comic, I'd occasionally see teen magazines from overseas, like *Honey* from the UK and *Seventeen* from the US, but from Australia, there was nothing.

Sure, magazines like *The Australian Women's Weekly*, *Woman's Day* and *New Idea* had always been a mainstay in our house since before I could remember. These were wholesome weekly housewife journals, chock full of recipes, knitting patterns, and cleaning and gardening tips – all the better to 'housewife' with, I figured. There was always plenty of news on the royals, too – any royal would do, really, but mostly it was Queen Elizabeth and her corgis, as well as everyone's favourite former-Hollywood royal, Princess Grace of Monaco.

But *Dolly* was different. And from its very first issue, I was hooked. So, too, were my girlfriends. *Dolly* wasn't exactly a girl like me – but that was the whole point, really. Because now I could dream of the girl I could be.

Dolly quickly became my teen bible. Every month a whole new world of fun, fashion and advice I simply couldn't get anywhere else became mine. Every month I'd open up those pages and dream of which clothes I'd buy if only I had the money, which pop star I'd date if only he knew I was alive, which hair colour I'd use if only Mum would let me, and which of all those Yardley Pot O'Gloss colours for lips, cheeks and eyes I'd save up to buy (for me, Pot O'Gloss Lilac always won).

Dolly was everything. A lifeline. A best friend. A teacher. A trusted confidante. A glimpse into my future.

And then there was 'Dolly Doctor', with its hugely helpful, sometimes lifesaving, intensely personal advice on everything from contraception to pimples, vaginas to periods, tampons to pubes, pregnancy to STDs, and boys … so many questions on boys. Not that that was really an issue for me yet, but 'a girl like me' could always dream …

So much of the pain of our teenage years was lessened when we escaped into that 'other' world of *Dolly*. There was one teenage hurt *Dolly* couldn't take away, though. At the end of Second Form and within just a few weeks of each other, both Lisa and Sharon announced that they with their families were moving away – Sharon to Queensland, and Lisa to Sydney's North Shore.

I was heartbroken, and simply couldn't imagine life without them. So I threw myself even more intensely into my ballet to try to fill that void. I was now at Advanced 1 Level and just about to begin en pointe, so Miss Dean was thrilled when she saw my renewed commitment to the craft and to her.

With Sharon and Lisa now gone, Michelle and I quickly grew closer than ever, with sleepovers becoming a regular thing. And along came new friends like Sue and Christine, Julie and Therese.

But I still missed Lisa and Sharon, and although we all promised to become regular pen pals and visit whenever we could, I just knew life was about to change.

And by Third Form, it certainly did. I just never could have imagined how much.

*

I don't quite remember when I first noticed Raelene Schroeder looking at me menacingly, but she definitely was. I'd known her vaguely since kindergarten, but we were never in the same classes, and now her antipathy towards school, its rules and its teachers was well known.

Raelene was far and away one of the prettiest girls in school, with deep olive skin, stunning almond-shaped green eyes, and a pair of legs that were the envy of all of us. She was one of the first to shave her legs, wear makeup to school, peroxide her hair, pierce her ears, and pluck her eyebrows right down to the thin brown line that was the fashion of the day, and she was regularly on detention for smoking either in or behind the toilets with her gang.

Raelene had already had two 'serious' boyfriends in succession — two of the coolest older guys in town — and it was a common sight to see her being picked up at the school gates by one of them a in their panel van (or shaggin' wagon, as they were much better known). Raelene spent most of those afternoons down at what had now become a quasi-clubhouse for the tougher kids in the town, Andrews Milk Bar.

Yep, Andrews had now become 'Cool Central', with its maroon vinyl booth seats, frosted amber feature glass, plastic hanging ivy, and that new-fangled European-style coffee machine, which all held such lovely memories for me from all those grocery shopping trips with Mum when I was little. There was still a smattering of young mums and their bubs in there, casually catching up over toasted ham-and-cheese sandwiches – just like Mum and I once had – seemingly oblivious to the fact that Andrews had, somewhere along the line, become a hub for many of the town's most intimidating.

If Andrews was now the place where the cool kids hung out, then booth number two, with its perfect view of everyone walking past its big open doors, was its seat of power. And that was *exactly* where Raelene would always be positioned.

If you weren't one of those accepted by the cool gang, just walking past Andrews took huge reserves of courage, knowing there was an audience ready to pass judgment over every one of those ten steps it took to go past that open door. Sometimes, though, I had no choice. Positioned as it was, right in the centre of Queen Street, I needed those streetlights to ensure a safe path as I walked home alone from ballet. So, on these afternoons – particularly in the darker winter months – Andrews became impossible to avoid.

My ballet case, with its various leotards, shoes, tights, leg warmers and hair paraphernalia, was a dead giveaway that I had just come from what was considered the very un-cool pursuit of ballet, so I always tried to pretend I was just casually looking in the other direction when I passed.

But sometimes one of Raelene's gang would call out. Not responding would only up the volume and the humiliation. Glancing over guaranteed a snarl, a dirty look, or worse: 'Wilkinson! Just been off to ya stupid ballet, have ya? Ya dick!' or 'You betta watch yaself, Wilkinson. Raelene's gunna fight ya.'

It was terrifying.

Once, in the lead-up to a big ballet exam, Mum surprised me by turning up to watch my class, and on the way home I mistakenly thought having her by my side would give me a bit of protection. I was wrong.

'Got your fuckin' mum with ya, Wilkinson? That won't save ya. I'd be shit scared if I was you, ya fuckwit.'

I was utterly crushed. I didn't want Mum to see this, to hear this. I knew with her own deep insecurities she would be shattered for me. And in a moment when I needed her strength, I didn't know if she would have it.

It turned out to be the only time in my life I was ever glad of Mum's failing hearing. She had started regularly wearing a hearing aid, courtesy of the not-infrequent slaps across the ear she used to cop as a kid from Nanny. But thankfully, on that day, she didn't have her hearing aid on … so she was shielded from the explicit ugliness of what was happening.

'What did your friends just say, darling? I think they're calling out to you.'

'Nothing, Mum,' I said, before quickening my step and adding, 'Can we go up to Con's on the way home, please? I'm starving.'

At school, it started to become impossible not to notice the signs that trouble was brewing. An 'accidental' push in the canteen line, a not-so-stray basketball to the head while walking to class, a fully packed schoolbag aimed square at my legs in assembly. Never from Raelene. Always from one of her growing number of tough-talking minions.

Then it came: an anonymous note saying that Raelene was going to 'get me'.

*

She was beautiful, but not like those girls in the magazines. She was beautiful, for the way she thought. She was beautiful, for the sparkle in her eyes when she talked about something she loved. She was beautiful, for her ability to make other people smile even if she was sad. No, she wasn't beautiful for something as temporary as her looks. She was beautiful, deep down to her soul.

It was as if F. Scott Fitzgerald had known Miss Jackson when he wrote those stunning words in *The Beautiful and Damned*.

Miss Jackson lived in the most seriously cool, big old double-storey terrace house on the hill overlooking town with a bunch of other young teachers, just out of teachers' college. She wore bell-bottom trousers, had a curtain of shiny black hair, an intellect every bit as imposing as her frame was light, and she was my Third Form English teacher.

A powerhouse of calm and strength in equal measure, Miss Jackson was brilliant and rebellious and nurturing – and gifted me with what became a lifelong love of the written word. F. Scott Fitzgerald, the poetry of T.S. Eliot, J.D. Salinger's *The Catcher in the Rye*, even Shakespeare's previously incomprehensible *ye olde gobbledegook*, all suddenly came alive under Miss Jackson's magnificent teaching spell.

If there was one text we studied, however, that for me stood tall above all others, it was Harper Lee's classic, *To Kill a Mockingbird*.

While the story took place in Depression-era Alabama, the themes were universal, and told through the innocent eyes of six-year-old Scout Finch as she, her brother, Jem, and friend Dill learnt powerful lessons about the impacts of persecution and judgment, poverty, prejudice and racism, and how fear and cruelty only prosper if you stand by and let them. The title refers to an incident in the novel, in which Scout's dad, Atticus, upon giving air rifles to his two young children, tells them they're allowed to shoot at tin cans but never at a mockingbird. Scout, puzzled, learns that there is a proverb, 'It's a sin to kill a mockingbird', because these birds harm no-one and only make beautiful music.

Scout's an astute kid who, by closely observing the actions of her magnificently humble small-town lawyer dad and his ongoing fight for justice, can see the adult world's oft-repeated oscillation from beauty to prejudice.

Everything about that book spoke to me. As the quiet, moral compass of all in his orbit, Atticus was my dad; Scout, still so wide-eyed about learning the sometimes confusing ways of the world, was me. And even though I didn't fully realise it at the time, the tale of the bullied Boo Radley was slowly, inexorably becoming my own … But I'll get to that.

One assignment Miss Jackson set our class that year that I loved more than any other was to examine two of Sydney's afternoon newspapers, *The Sun* and *The Daily Mirror*. The task was to check for the journalistic and marketing-style devices the editors employed to lure readers in. For me, it was more fun than a school project should be allowed to be.

I have no idea why, but something in me just *clicked*. Somehow, I could not only see exactly the formula they were using to attract readers, but I provided commentary on the language used, assessed the layouts, and was even presumptuous enough to offer ideas on how I might be able to do better if ever I was given the chance. Working on that assignment didn't feel like homework; it felt like I had found a home to work in. I even wondered idly if perhaps that might be a career for me?

Come the Monday morning, as Miss Jackson handed back our assignments, my mark in big red writing at the top right-hand corner of the first page was impossible to miss: *10/10!* 'Excellent work, Lisa. You even made ME think about how this is all done. Congratulations!'

I was thrilled, although soon became anxious as Miss Jackson set me a further task of giving an actual speech on the subject in front of the entire class. I agonised about it for days, knowing that two of those who sat on the edge of Raelene Schroeder's main gang, Louise and Jenny, were in my English class and would no doubt report this presentation back to her. Wilkinson, the goody-two-shoes ballerina, sucking up to the teacher *and* drawing attention to herself. Again.

But what could I do? I couldn't let Miss Jackson down, and I didn't want to tell her the real reason I was so scared. I'd become good at hiding the bullying that was going on and not imposing the pain I was feeling on others.

In the end, I gave the speech, proud of myself for getting through it, and loving for just those moments the feeling that this was a topic I just *got*, and that had captivated my imagination and fascination. Miss Jackson had beamed at me throughout my whole presentation, and most of the class seemed to be listening.

And as I stood out the front, with all of those faces staring at me, I tried really hard not to look over at Raelene's two gang-hangers;

but just *once*, I couldn't help glancing over, and of course they were both glaring at me, clearly *aching* to tell Raelene what I had gone and done this time.

Sure enough, two days later at lunchtime, I looked up and saw them coming.

As I so often did in those days, I'd sought refuge in a quiet corner in the sun by the Science block, out of the view of the main playground. My upended Globite schoolbag was performing the role of a makeshift seat, while Leanne, my friend from ballet, and a group of others were enjoying the winter sunshine beside me.

But heading across the sports field straight for me was Raelene Schroeder with six of her henchwomen on either side, including Jenny and Louise.

I don't think I'd ever felt so small or so completely powerless and vulnerable in my life, as my friends, in the path of this approaching cyclone, scattered with the wind. I didn't blame them; what could they possibly do in the face of such a show of impending force? Besides, it was clear this gang wasn't coming for them, now that a gum-chewing Raelene, along with her backup crew, some of whom I didn't even recognise, were just a few feet away from me.

'You're a show-off little bitch,' Raelene spat at me, as her left hand swiped across me, knocking my Vegemite sandwiches into the dirt.

Her right fist? I never saw it coming, but it now crashed into my temple with so much stinging force it sent me flying to the ground, my head only just missing the concrete corner of the building. Even as I went down, the roar of other students went up as a crowd quickly gathered.

'Fight! Fight! Fight!'

I was now on my side, trying to curl up into the tiniest ball possible as Raelene's knee dug into my right hip, making it impossible for me to move, blows now raining down on my head, my nose, my lips, my ears. For the first time, I tasted my own blood.

Still Raelene's fists continued to make contact as the roar of the baying mob grew louder and her mates screamed, 'Get her, Raelene!' Even more kids raced over to witness firsthand the spectacle of two girls – or one at least – going for it, amidst dust flying, on the school grounds.

Were it not for a teacher pulling Raelene off me, I don't know how it would have ended.

This time, however, it ended in the principal's office. Even though I stood there with splatters of blood on my uniform, my left eye beginning to swell and my brain rattled from what had just happened, we were *both* roundly told off for fighting.

I could have told the truth – that it wasn't a fight but a flat-out vicious, unprovoked assault; but in my still-shocked state, with Raelene standing next to me, smirking, and not a single scratch on her, it would have taken more courage than I had.

I could have told Mum and Dad, too, but I just couldn't bring myself to do it. I knew it would have upset them terribly. And I didn't want to dwell on the hurt or the humiliation. I wanted the whole thing to just go away, and for everyone to move on. Raelene had had her kill and, in the eyes of her gang, come out the victor. I hoped that would now be the end of it.

But I had to wonder, was it worth doing well at homework assignments or even ballet, if getting beaten up like this was the result?

And yet, Miss Jackson saw something in me that I was years away from seeing in myself: that I could do this, that I had some kind of intuitive understanding of a small part of the way the media worked, and a feeling for what didn't. My love of words had been ignited, too, and I wanted more. Maybe journalism was for me? Deep inside me a seed had been planted, and I had Miss Jackson to thank for it.

As for my friends, they were sorry for having abandoned me, but they didn't have to apologise – I understood. Raelene was a malevolent force of nature who could not be reasoned with, only fled from. Who would willingly put themselves in the way of that?

What I couldn't understand was, what had I done to deserve all this? I had wronged no-one. Yet I was being attacked in the playground of my own school and was in as much trouble as my attacker? I really couldn't make sense of it; I just knew that to survive, I had to keep my head down and make myself small – while my daily paralysing fear, always lasting deep into the night, was that it would happen again.

*

At least we all soon had a major distraction, and no-one welcomed it more than me.

The pop band Sherbet was coming to town!

For years I'd harboured a crush on the shy, sensitive songwriter in the band, Garth Porter – with his long sandy-coloured curls as he bopped away behind the keyboards – after the group played at our First Form school dance. Shortly afterwards, they won the prestigious Hoadley's Battle of the Sounds competition. I, meanwhile, had bought every record, memorised every lyric, and devoured every magazine with even the tiniest mention of Sherbet. Scrapbooks were made and posters covered my walls. They were now the biggest band in the country, *and* they were coming back to town.

These days I'd also developed more than a passing crush on the lead singer, Daryl Braithwaite – especially the way he always so sweetly cradled that microphone on their hit 'You're All Woman'. So, if the rumours were true that Garth had gone and recently got engaged, at least I knew I had an excellent backup in Daryl.

This time Sherbet was billed to be the headline act at an open-air concert at nearby Leumeah Oval. Michelle, Julie, Sue, Therese and I couldn't believe it, and we spent days planning our outfits, vowing to get there early so we could nab the very best spot near the stage.

We arrived at the oval on that gloriously clear Saturday with a whole six hours to spare before Sherbet was due on stage. Julie had brought a picnic rug (all the better to mark 'our' territory once things got crowded); Michelle, a giant box of Lolly Gobble Bliss Bombs (caramel-covered popcorn heaven); Therese, two family-sized bottles of Passiona; me, 12 piping-hot cinnamon-coated doughnuts fresh from the doughnut-making machine at the nearby bakery; and Sue, a whole bottle of coconut oil – not for eating, but for tanning purposes.

Never ones to squander a tanning opportunity – even holding competitions amongst ourselves to see who could emerge from the weekend with the brownest legs – we pulled up our skirts, opened up our latest issues of *Dolly*, and sat there in the baking sun, laughing, chatting, eating and listening to the line-up of support acts for hours. Life, we all agreed, didn't get much better than this.

As the afternoon wore on, I realised I was the most relaxed I'd been for ages. Raelene and her gang had mostly left me alone – at least, physically. There were still the taunts between ballet and home as I passed by Andrews Milk Bar; and there was one episode where I'd been hit in the leg with a fair-sized rock in the playground, but by the time I realised what it was and looked around, it was impossible to work out who had thrown it.

I was getting through each day as best I could. And right now, on this day, Sherbet was just minutes away!

I was convinced that this was, in fact, going to be the *best* day of our lives after Julie devised a brilliant plan to work our way over and position ourselves right next to those cars over there, which *must* be waiting to take Garth, Daryl, Alan, Tony and Clive back to the city as soon as their set was over. We'd all brought our autograph books with us, and each knew exactly whose signature we wanted to nab before they would suddenly be whisked away. We just had to be quick, and—

Sorry? Did the wind just change?

My girlfriends saw Raelene's gang before I did. 'Lisa, look ...' Michelle said.

Oh no. Not now. *Pleeease*. Don't do this to me now. Not in front of this huge crowd.

It was Raelene, alright. And this time, with what looked like a small army. But strangely, the closer they got, the less Raelene appeared to be at the centre of it. Two steps ahead of everyone else was a girl called Mandy Callan, a girl I'd befriended six months before when she'd arrived at Campbelltown High from England. Dad had always taught me to try to look after the bird with the broken wing. Mandy was one such bird.

With wide, frightened eyes, Mandy seemed utterly lost when she landed midway through Term 3 the year before, so we took her into our group. We bonded over JC sandals, our mutual love of Sherbet, and the fact that actual sex really did sound disgusting.

Mandy had problems at home. Some mornings she would arrive at school, her eyes puffy from all that had happened the night before. I knew life was tough for her, and so I'd really tried to be a good friend. But she was missing a lot of school, and as the months rolled by, on the days she did come, she started to seem quite distant.

And now, she was in Raelene's gang.

The first blow was struck by Mandy herself, the impact to the side of my head knocking me straight down. And with my face now buried in Julie's woollen rug, I didn't see the next savage blow coming. But it was a big one. And suddenly the band on stage that was finishing up its set, with its throbbing guitars and beating drums, may as well have been a million miles away. That last fist had landed just below my right temple, and now I couldn't hear.

Time stood still ... and I wondered in that strange, silent moment, if that was what it had been like for Mum when receiving those blows from her own mum all those years ago.

This time, I decided I was going to run. But as I turned to look to the sky to try and get my bearings, I caught sight of Mandy – white-hot anger in her eyes, and Raelene just behind her, almost mentor-like, that same familiar smirk on her face, proud of the violent work her young disciple was performing for her passing amusement.

The inevitable roar went up. 'Fight! Fight! Fight!'

The crowd, some of them shocked but many excited by this sideshow spectacle, wanted more.

Between blows, I looked over at the faces of my friends, but the gang and the crowd had closed in and I knew if they tried to help me, there were eight or nine others beyond Raelene and Mandy happy to take them on next.

I had to get away.

I leaned over on one elbow, the world spinning like a psychedelic merry-go-round I desperately wanted to get off. If I stood up, I knew there was every chance the biggest punch of all would be waiting for me.

But suddenly the bashing stopped. In the far, far distance I could hear the crowd hushing as an announcement came over the PA. 'Ladies and gentlemen, boys and girls, the boys you have all been waiting for!'

Another roar went up. 'SHERBET! SHERBET! SHERBET!'

'Okaaaaay, everyone, let's give a big Campbelltown welcome to the one … the only … SHEEEEEEERBET!!!!!!'

And with that, Daryl Braithwaite, Garth Porter and the boys burst onto the stage.

Summer love is like no other love,

Oooh yeah-eah-eah,

Summer love is like no other loo-oove …

This was my chance to escape. But the gang wasn't finished. This was their last chance to make their point, and with one final explosion of hate, there was another blow to the back of my head, and from another direction completely a stinging sharp kick to the small of my back.

Was that my kidneys? I wasn't sure, but concentrated on that pain so it took away from the excruciating thumping in my head.

And then, for just a moment, I wanted to die so this whole agony would stop once and for all.

And suddenly, it was all over.

For all their tough-girl exteriors, Raelene and her ever-growing gang of hangers-on were here to see Daryl, Garth, Alan, Clive and Tony, too. One by one, their focus shifted to gaining a spot near the stage. Their work here was done. Once again, they'd taught me a lesson.

Right now, though, I had my moment to escape. So, I rolled over onto all fours, trying to shake the pain and sheer shock. In this bare, treeless space there was nowhere to take shelter or hide. Just a lone red-brick toilet block on the other side of the oval.

As the crowd cleared and my girlfriends moved in to check if I was OK, Sherbet continued to thrill the thousands of screaming fans.

Cloudy skies are blown by with the breeze,
And when that su-un shines, life comes easy,
Bye-bye troubles goodby-ye,
I'm walkin' with my head in the sky-y ...

I was fine, I told them. I just wanted to get out of there. Michelle wanted to come home with me and tell my parents, but I insisted. No!

'I'll just find a phone booth, and Dad will come and get me. Really. I'm fine. Please, go and watch Sherbet.'

And so, with my head still spinning, my right cheek throbbing, blood coming from somewhere above it and now dripping onto the back of my hand as I tried desperately to wipe away the evidence, I grabbed my bag and started gently weaving my way through the crowd, head down, towards those red bricks, and hopefully a cubicle door with a lock I could close on all that had just happened.

What was that shooting pain down my leg? I tried not to limp, knowing there were still scores of eyes following me. For all the pain, every step brought me relief, knowing I was moving further away from the scene, and the people who had witnessed it up close.

I had no idea how badly I was hurt, as all the mirrors in this tiny women's toilet were broken. So, I tried to peer into the reflection of the stainless-steel splashback at the sinks. I couldn't see how bad it was, but as I looked down I could certainly see the blood now dripping into the sink. I closed the cubicle door, staring at the graffiti scribbled on the back of it for what felt like ages. I tried to focus. Blurry at the start, then clearer. 'For a good time call Lynda.'

How long could I sit here before someone banged on the door? What was I going to tell Mum and Dad about what had happened? As I put my hand up to my head, I didn't need a mirror to know that my eye was beginning to swell like a hard-boiled egg.

Somewhere, there was still that cut, too. And for one weird, crazy moment, I laughed. Toilet paper. Toilet paper on cuts on your face made the bleeding stop ... or at least that seemed to be the case with that comedian Norman Gunston on *The Aunty Jack Show* on TV. And after sitting there for ten minutes, holding a big wad of toilet paper to my cheek and temple, I walked ... slowly ... home.

Never calling Dad. And knowing that by the time I got there it would be dark, and Mum would be busy in the kitchen and …

I'll never know how I successfully kept all that happened that day from Mum and Dad. The swollen eye was explained away as me dancing too enthusiastically to Sherbet alongside another girl doing the same thing and, hey, accidents happen. 'I'm a bit sore but fine. And Sherbet were amazing!' I said cheerily, as I grabbed a bag of frozen peas from the fridge before heading to my bedroom, never once looking Mum or Dad in the eye, and then applying this makeshift salve to my own.

I had a lot of homework that weekend too, I'd told them, and that became the perfect excuse to just close my bedroom door, put on some Carly Simon, Carole King and Cat Stevens, and just disappear.

By Monday I had decided to miss ballet that week. The wooziness had hung around, the bruising now too obvious, and I didn't want to have to lie to Miss Dean as well. I needed a break. So often, the taunts I got from Raelene were about me being 'a fucking ballerina'. Time and again, those girls had told me that ballet was for 'stuck-up molls', so maybe if I just stayed away from it for a while, things would change.

But that week's break soon became a fortnight, and then a month, and then …

Mum and Dad were devastated. And Miss Dean even came to our house to try to convince me to come back, telling me she was sure that my future career lay in dance. I hated looking in her eyes and telling her it didn't. Miss Dean had *always* believed in me and given me opportunities I often didn't think I deserved, and here I was, after all she'd done, saying goodbye.

It was a huge wrench, and I missed dancing terribly. So many times in my younger dreams I would imagine I was flying, and the next morning wake up with a smile, knowing that soon I could put on my pink leotard and ballet shoes, and do just that – fly!

But I couldn't do it anymore. The fear I had every night as I closed my eyes, dreading, wondering, hating what the next day could possibly bring, had overtaken everything. Fear of walking down the main street. Fear of being seen as good at anything. Fear of

Mum and Dad finding out and possibly making things worse if they went to the school and demanded Raelene and Mandy be punished.

So, in an attempt to simply get through each day, I decided to do with my life what I had done with my body in those awful, *awful* moments as the blows rained down on me: curl up into as small a ball as possible. The less of me they could see, I figured, the less they could hurt.

If I just disappeared into the cracks, maybe they would finally leave me alone.

CHAPTER SIX

Crushed

'If you and I, every time we pass a mirror ... complain
about our looks ... remember a young girl is watching,
and that's what she's learning.'
– Gloria Steinem in *Miss Representation*, 2011

Boys. WHY WERE THEY so weird? Or maybe it was me who was
weird.

Either way, while most of my girlfriends were 'going' with
someone by Fourth Form ... me, not so much. Perhaps I was too
shy, maybe I'd been too crushed by the bullying, or very possibly I
just wasn't anyone's 'type'. Or perhaps I was dreaming of something
more.

I'd had crushes, sure. Most particularly on Nick Stevens, the
older brother of one of my neighbourhood friends, Anne, who lived
just four doors down – but he was super smart, played competitive
cricket and went to the selective Hurlstone Agricultural High School
near Liverpool, so our paths rarely crossed. When they did, being
his 'little sister's friend' probably didn't add a whole lot to my appeal,
but always, just the merest sighting of Nick was enough for my heart
to skip a whole bunch of beats.

I first spied Nick when I was in First Form; I was with Dad
at a Lions Club barbecue raising funds for a local orphanage. I'd
decided there and then that if Nick was at an event like this, he must

be generous and charity-minded and incredibly kind – just like my dad – and so, thereafter, Nick became the great unrequited love of my early high-school years.

In fact, during those years, the closest I ever came to any boys romantically – if you could call it that – was during the occasional 'kissing party'. These nights were otherwise cleverly disguised as birthday parties – so our parents never suspected a thing. The trick was for the birthday girl to invite all the boys you and your friends were sweet on. Then, at some point late in the proceedings, fuelled by a major sugar hit of Coca-Cola and cake, an evenly divided group of boys and girls would head to a bedroom somewhere in the house. The art was then to try to position yourself right next to the boy you really liked in preparation for what was about to come next.

Ready?

Ready!

Amidst giggles all round, someone would take charge, close the door, turn off the lights and stand guard for ten seconds or so, lest some pesky parent decided to turn up. A sort of Spin the Bottle in the dark ... but with an extra dose of daring, no prying eyes upon you, and a much more targeted approach.

Always, at around the seven-second mark, things would go very quiet. Then, with the lights back on, everyone would jump back up and head straight out, often with heads straight down. Some would emerge with big smiles, others looking embarrassed, and everyone searching for signs that mouths had met. Messy, and awkward, yes. A badge of honour for all those who took part, you betcha. Apart from a few fumbles in the darkness and some smeared lip gloss once, thanks to the lovely Doug Hedge, those kissing parties came to nothing for me.

Over the years, boys would tease me, particularly when I started getting boobs in Fourth Form. 'Jeez, Wilkinson, didn't you grow up over the Christmas holidays!'

Was that a sign that boys were starting to like me? I wasn't sure. I'd had other crushes apart from Nick, but nothing ever in return, so I escaped instead into the romance of the songs and lyrics I loved so much.

Music was always the one thing that never failed to lift me. Cat Stevens, Don McLean, Carly Simon, Neil Young, Carole King, Elton John, America, Slade, Status Quo, Suzi Quatro, Led Zeppelin, Joni Mitchell … I loved them all, and every afternoon, as soon as I walked through the front door, I would put a selection on our three-in-one stereo with its record player, radio and tape player.

We even had one that had an in-built record stacker, so you could pile five albums one on top of another. Once each one had finished playing, the needle arm would automatically pick itself up, return to its cradle, neatly drop the next album down, and immediately place itself in the first groove of the new album – as if by magic. Then, above a light crackle courtesy of years of repeated plays, I would sing …

You're so vain …

The technology just blew us away.

Often on sleepovers, Therese and I would make mixed cassette tapes of all our favourite songs. And with the help of our 'Songster' Top 40 lyric books from the newsagent and all the albums that now had the actual lyrics printed on the fold-out covers, we prided ourselves on knowing every word of every one of those songs off by heart and sang them all at the top of our voices. Especially the romantic ones.

Would I ever have someone who would feel that way about me? Sometimes, on a Sunday night, I would sit at the desk in my bedroom with its clear view across town to the old road that wound its way up the hill to where St Greg's sat, and watch the trail of red taillights as parents drove their teenage boarder sons back to commence another new week of school … and wonder if somewhere out there, there was a boy I didn't yet know. A boy I would end up spending my life with. Was he perhaps in one of those cars? If not in one of those cars, where was he and what was he doing right now? What language was he speaking? was he even *in* Australia? Would I ever even get married anyway?

Choosing just one person to spend the rest of your life with, someone who could meet all your needs, seemed just so huge to me. Was it even possible? So often my friends and I would talk about

'NGBs' – Nice Guy Buts. 'He's a nice guy but, he's not that funny/smart/talkative/supportive/respectful/whatever …'

If I was ever going to be with someone that intensely, I thought, it had to be someone who would add to my life, challenge me, make me think, maybe disagree with me, make me laugh, keep me in line just as I would keep him, but with all the beautiful kindness of Dad.

Would he have nice friends? Nice parents? Would they even like me? What sort of job would he have?

Whatever the future held, I figured the universe would decide. There was one thing that would be a deal-breaker for me when it came to a partner though: he couldn't be a rugby player.

I had nothing against rugby per se, with a lot of my girlfriends now dating footballers from the local Harlequins Rugby Club – of which Dad was now the very committed president, my brother Kyle was playing for; and even Mum was dutifully working for each Saturday sorting the club's sausage sizzles. Sitting with Dad, watching the Wallabies play on TV was enough for me. The players themselves all seemed like lovely enough blokes but … my girlfriends' connection and our family's commitment to the club and the game were already enough. It was just too familiar and safe. Everything there was known. I had a growing craving for the unknown.

And anyway, maybe partnering up wasn't for me. Maybe I would be like Miss West, and simply have a career that I dedicated my life to … or be like Jan Brady's fabulous aunt and travel the world, never sure where my next adventure would take me.

At one point, Mum and Dad had let me travel up to visit my friend Sharon at her new home on the Gold Coast. As I sat on the plane, I wondered if maybe I could be an air hostess? I quite liked those fabulous carnival-coloured Pucci-designed uniforms that the Qantas hosties wore, and they *did* get to travel the world. So as soon as I got back home, I decided to write to Qantas to find out the job's requirements.

There were a lot as it turned out. While the return letter was very polite about the fact I was still many years away from being old enough to formally apply, I was given a few thought-starters for the time when I did.

I had to be single (even being engaged was not acceptable); had to 'present well' (which I figured meant I had to be pretty), with appropriately 'pleasing' measurements provided as a guide (which meant I had to be skinny); had to undertake not to put on weight (which meant *don't get fat*); and was told that mandatory retirement would happen at 35 (which meant *don't get old*).

Well, that was easy. Ah, no thanks.

*

If there was one event that brought all the teenagers of Campbelltown together and alive, it was the dances held once a month at the Old Town Hall, where everyone from Dragon to The Angels, Hush, The Ted Mulry Gang and Farm (soon to be better known as Midnight Oil, with the band's drummer Rob Hirst a local boy from Camden!) had played.

By day, the hall hosted gatherings for the town's historical society, and then became the after-school venue for gymnastics and judo classes. Occasionally, it was used as the meeting spot for the local chapter of Parents Without Partners, a discreet dating site for a small number of mums and dads in the area who were single.

But on the first Saturday of every month, the Old Town Hall would burst into life as the not-so-discreet dating site for hundreds of local teens and early-20-somethings from Camden to Casula, and Liverpool to Leppington.

The pop-coloured posters promised a great time for all, while convoys of panel vans, XP Falcons and EH Holdens, delivering patrons desperate to be a part of the weekend action, prowled up and down the street.

Piled three, sometimes four, abreast onto those front bench seats, these boys had Winnie Blues hanging from their lips and testosterone dripping from their hips.

You could always tell just how strict someone's parents were by the age they started going to the town dances. I was 15 and the very last in my group allowed to attend … and even then, it was on the absolute proviso that Dad dropped me right at the front door on the dot of 7pm, waited until he saw that I was with at least two friends that he knew, and then collected me again at the stroke of 11pm when the dance finished.

I'd been happy to avoid the Old Town Hall dances up to that point, always fearing that somewhere in the crowd would be Raelene Schroeder. But while I was still getting dirty looks in the playground, and her gang members never missed a chance to make nasty comments if they saw me in the corridors, the physical violence, at least for now, had stopped.

So, it was worth the risk. Besides, I loved to dance, and this was now the only chance I got, albeit in very different outfits from my tulle and tutu-filled classical-ballet days.

At the town dances it was all maxi dresses, miniskirts, peasant blouses, boob tubes, Lee jeans (but never ever AMCO, lest you face social death!), JC sandals, 'clunky' wedges, bamboo slaps, and just about anything tie-dyed or made of cheesecloth. Meanwhile, when it came to perfume, there was only one choice to be made: patchouli or musk oil, which always made the air in the hall particularly potent as the night wore on – especially when mixed with the two hottest aftershaves of the day, Old Spice and Brut 33, along with a good-sized dose of sweaty teen-boy hormones.

For those of us without boyfriends, there was always plenty of excitement about who we might see. I always hoped I'd see Nick, but sadly, never did. After years now of wishing and hoping, I'd pretty much given up on him ever noticing me. For those who did have boyfriends, it was a chance to escape into the darkness on a Saturday night, away from the gaze of parents, and make out.

Alcohol was of course strictly forbidden, even though one of the most popular (of the many) pubs in town was right next door. More than once, Dad told me how uneasy he felt seeing all the boys pouring out of the bar clearly looking for girls, or trouble – perhaps both – as soon as the dance finished.

And yet, despite my dad's lovingly protective stance, the real danger awaiting me turned out not to come from any of those wayward drunken boys from the town.

Mine was hiding in plain sight.

*

I always loved sleepovers with my friends.

Chris's place was one of our favourites. Her mum lived in a cool old farmhouse on the road up to St Greg's and, newly divorced, she was the only declared feminist I'd ever met. This was where I caught my first glimpse of *Cleo* magazine, and Michelle, Julie, Sue, Chris and I would often spend hours going through Chris's mum's stash of copies late at night looking for all those sealed sections and giggling over the centrefolds. Chris's mum also used to let us experiment with everyone's favourite hair dye – Magic Silver White. There was a fine art to getting the application right, and success would result in a fetching subtle shade of silvery-lilac; failure gave you an unmistakable shade of premature grey.

When I asked Mum if I could dye my hair like everyone else, the answer was clear and instant. 'If God had meant you to have different-coloured hair, he would have given it to you.' I never wanted to disappoint Mum, so I obeyed her wishes.

When I was much younger, before my friend Lisa moved away, I loved staying at her house where we'd play board games like Twister and Mouse Trap, make cakes, play hide-and-seek with her sister Peta in their big old backyard, and talk for hours to her lovely mum and dad.

Lisa's dad smoked a pipe that left the sweet, smoky scent of wood fires wherever he went, wore tweed jackets and, as the town doctor known for making house calls at any time of the day or night, was loved by everyone. He was the closest man I knew to my own beautiful dad.

Therese's father was not. I always felt strangely uncomfortable around him. He was a fellow member of Dad's much-loved Lions Club, which meant that, in my eyes, he was a sort of 'friend' of Dad's. Whenever Therese invited me for sleepovers at her place, Dad would always drop me off and come in to say hi.

Therese's dad was always a brooding presence when I was at their place, and I knew that theirs was a difficult relationship. I had been brought up to respect my elders, though, so I was always polite to him.

On weekends he was mostly hidden in the house's darkened front bedroom, venetian blinds closed tight on the sunshine of the day. Eventually he would emerge bleary-eyed, his clothes dishevelled, his tobacco-stained fingers burnt yellow and clutching a beer, while the smell of his BO would immediately overwhelm the lounge room where Therese and I would often be. Sometimes, if that bedroom door was left ajar as I walked past on the way to Therese's room and I knew he was in there, I would immediately look the other way. I simply didn't want to see what I didn't want to see.

Therese's dad loved a punt on the horses and the doggies, and once when I was walking home after school, I saw him come out of the local TAB. I desperately didn't want him to see me. There was just something about the way he used to look at me when I was in my school uniform that made me uneasy. Beneath those big bushy eyebrows, he would just *leer*. But it was too late. As soon as he saw me, he called out, telling me to wait up. I didn't want to, but I was in the main street, it was daylight – what could he possibly do?

But here he was, now right in front of me, leaning straight in, picking me up off the ground and hugging me – a 50+-year-old man, pressing his lumpy aging body against my 15-year-old one, his putrid breath and disgusting mouth now just inches away from mine.

I dropped my heavy schoolbag on the pavement hoping it would land on his foot, or at least create enough noise for passers-by to see what was going on. But he wasn't budging. I tried to slide out of his grasp and started pushing down on his arms.

Finally, he started to let go, but as I slid down, my uniform began to rise up, and he immediately grabbed onto my now-exposed bottom and panties. As I continued to squirm and try to wriggle free from his body, I could feel his hard erection against my tummy. It was like a bolt of lightning went through me. I wanted to be sick. My feet at last on ground, I grabbed my bag and, without saying a word, raced across the park towards home, never once looking back.

I never said a word about it to Therese, but I vowed never to go to her place again.

But two weeks later, Therese and I were both part of a group English assignment with two other girls in our class and we were far from finished. It was due on Monday, and our teacher suggested we should all spend Saturday finishing it off at Therese's house. When I told Therese I didn't want to go, her response surprised me.

'Don't worry, Dad won't be there,' she said with a look in her eye that I couldn't quite read. How did she know that was the reason for my reluctance? I still hadn't said a word to her about that disgusting moment in the street. I just couldn't; I loved Therese. What happened wasn't her fault. Was it my fault? What had I done to make him think that he could do that?

'I promise, Dad is going to be up on the Central Coast visiting my aunt and, besides, Missy just had her puppies so you have to come and meet them anyway. Go on. Please!'

Missy was Therese's gorgeous Labrador dog and she'd just had a litter of six puppies. I figured, with Therese's dad out of the house, this would be my only chance to meet them.

And Missy's puppies were a milky, messy tangle of two-week-old gorgeousness. All day, we alternated between a bit of work and a lot of puppy play, and with smiles on our faces we managed to get through our assignment work pretty quickly. So, before Dad came to pick me up at 6pm, I went to have one last play with Missy's brood in the outside laundry where Therese's mum had set them up for the night.

It was getting dark now so I turned on the light at the back door so I could see them. Being so tiny, they weren't doing much more than sleeping, eating and snuggling right by their mum's side. I crouched down and picked up one of the teeniest ones and contemplated whether I should ask Dad when he arrived whether we could think about getting one. We had our boxer dog Heidi at home, but she was almost ten now, and I wondered—

'They're cute, aren't they?'

I looked up. A figure was looming in the laundry doorway, throwing a dark shadow across me as I crouched on the ground.

It was him. Therese's father. But Therese said he wasn't meant to be here. Where was Therese? I knew Dad was just minutes away from picking me up. My head started spinning wondering what was coming next. I was trapped. Do I call out? Do I push past him and race out?

Already that disgusting stale smell of his was filling this small space. I decided to stay calm. So I slowly put the puppy down and said, 'Yes, they are, but I have to go. *Dad* is picking me up any second,' hoping that the mention of Ray Wilkinson – his colleague at Lions – would put an end to any ideas he might have had.

I stood up, thinking I had bought myself some time, which was a mistake. It meant he could now easily reach out to touch me. And he did. Without a single word, his large frame completely blocking the only way in and out, his eyes beneath those wild eyebrows now looking glazed, he put his hand on my breast and started stroking it.

'Would you like one of the puppies? I'd be happy to give you one if you'd like,' he said, as I completely froze. *Was this really happening?*

I wanted to scream, but I didn't. I wanted to slap his hand away, too, but I knew Therese's mother was just inside the door, in the kitchen making dinner. If I cried out, she would know that something had gone on and … would I be blamed? I didn't know. I didn't know or understand anything in that moment. Surely, he would stop now. But he didn't. And I couldn't move. Why couldn't I move?

'Just stay here for a moment, Lisa. Don't worry, trust me. This will feel nice …'

With his other hand, he reached down and started rubbing the crotch of my jeans. Once again, that lightning bolt. Once again, I felt sick. Why was this happening again? This was so wrong. A moment longer and I had no idea where this was going to go. I'd had enough!

So, looking straight into his dark, sleep-encrusted eyes, I clenched my teeth and said, 'I have to go now. My *dad* is here.' All the while thinking, *Please Dad, be here!*

Suddenly, I could move again. I threw my elbow up, knocking both his hands away, and turned, simultaneously shoving him with a force I didn't know I had. The risk to him was now obvious. I had not yet screamed, but if he continued to block me, I would. I pushed hard forward, and he ceded.

Immediately I heard the doorbell. I knew it was Dad, so rushing towards the door I thanked Therese's mum, grabbed my things and called out to Therese that I was going.

I don't think I was ever happier to see Dad in my life and gave him a huge hug right there on the doorstep, knowing now that I was safe. In Dad's arms I was always safe.

'Ray, good to see you! How have you been?'

It was Therese's dad. At the door, to farewell me and greet Dad as if nothing had happened. The sheer fucking *audacity*.

And then, with the very same hand that had just moments before been pawing my breast, he reached out to shake my dad's hand. If only Dad knew. But I just couldn't bring myself to tell him. And I never asked Therese why her dad was there that night when she assured me he wouldn't be.

We never did buy that puppy. And I never visited Therese's house again.

*

These were troubled times for me.

Not only was I shaken by the experience with Therese's dad, but I was missing ballet, and my schoolwork had also started to suffer – which was a problem if I was still going to pursue that idea of journalism as a career. And I wanted to, now more than ever.

Every day I would read the papers and every night I would watch all the news and current affair shows, like *This Day Tonight*, *Four Corners* and *Willesee*, fascinated not just by the news of the day itself, but the art of storytelling too.

And then, of course, there was Mary. Mary Richards. The central character in my absolute favourite TV show of the week, *The Mary Tyler Moore Show*. Mary was a TV news producer in her thirties, living her best life in a fabulously quirky attic apartment in downtown Minneapolis.

Mary was strong and vulnerable, funny and fearless, sassy and sweet. At work she was surrounded by men, and her boss was the tough-talking, hard-drinking Lou Grant.

Every day, she showed up to that newsroom, with all its clichéd battles for acceptance of women in the workplace, her shoulders squared. Actually, she didn't just show up, she showed up in go-go boots and a suede fringed jacket, with a total can-do attitude, and a big old white Mustang convertible car out the front to take her home to that coolest of all cool apartments.

Mary wasn't married and wasn't looking to get married. She talked openly about birth control and had gay friends. In one episode, Mary discovered that the man who had previously held her job earnt a higher salary than her. Mary stood up for herself and eventually, begrudgingly, her boss gave her the raise, and closed that gender pay gap.

That character, her grace, those career choices, even the big 'M' on Mary's apartment wall said to all of us watching at home: this is me, this is my space, and *this* is what's possible if you just go for it.

And it was probably all neatly summed up in the opening credits, with Mary standing in the middle of a busy city street reminding us of the joy that life had to offer as she threw her hat in the air, without apology to anyone. She was, according to the song, a girl 'who can take a nothing day and suddenly make it all seem worthwhile'.

That Minneapolis newsroom may have been half a world and a whole generation away from me, but that hat toss and all that it represented showed me that the sky could be the limit in life, if you just aimed for it.

So every Saturday night as I sat there entranced while those final theme-song lyrics drew to a close, I would sing along as if no-one was listening, 'You're gonna make it after all!'

*

'Leese, Nick Stevens is on the phone for you.'

I thought it was a joke. But why would Mum joke about that? Mum knew that I'd had a crush on Nick for years, and practical jokes weren't exactly Mum's style.

But it *was* Nick, and he was ringing to ask me to be his date for his Sixth Form Farewell. His date! I'd seen him a few times more recently down at Anne's, and one night I ended up having dinner with the whole family. And while he was really nice to me that night, I didn't think I'd had any more impact than usual … which was to say, not much.

I was super excited, but I had one problem: Dad had a strict rule that I couldn't date boys until I was 16, and that birthday of mine was a whole month away. To say I begged would be an understatement. But with a little help from Mum, Dad reluctantly agreed, on the strict condition that I be home on the dot of 11pm.

Yes!! I was finally going on a date with Nick Stevens. What would I wear? What would we talk about? Would his friends like me?

The great thing was one of Nick's mates from Hurlstone had invited one of my classmates, Denise, as his date, so I knew I would have at least one friend there if things didn't go so well.

Nick and Anne's dad was a plumber, so Nick had borrowed his dad's ute for the trip to the event venue in Liverpool. As we farewelled Mum and Dad at the door, Nick reassuringly confirmed Dad's strict instructions.

'Don't worry, Mr Wilkinson, we'll be home by 11pm,' he said as he took my hand and we walked together down the driveway.

'Drive safely,' I heard Dad say in the distance.

With a bench seat in the front, that meant I got to sit up nice and close to Nick for the half-hour trip to Liverpool, our legs touching the entire way. And I felt great wearing a little lilac-coloured halter-neck dress I'd picked out with Mum from Carolyn's Frock Salon.

The night itself was fine enough – if a little disorganised – with plenty of pies and sausage rolls, loud music and dancing; but it soon became obvious that there was a lot of alcohol in the room … and a lot of guests who couldn't handle it in the sorts of quantities it was being consumed. But I was with Nick and, apart from having one Bundy and Coke myself that tasted disgusting, I was having a ball.

Until I saw Denise. I already knew she was nervous about the date, but add a good dose of Blackberry Nip to those nerves and … the poor thing was having a shocker. So, I ended up spending the rest of the night holding back Denise's hair in the toilets.

By 10.15, if we were going to meet Dad's deadline, it was time for Nick and me to head home. Nick was serious about making sure we respected Dad's curfew – I just *knew* he was my sort of guy – and I thanked him for that.

He put his key in the ignition and ... nothing. The ute wouldn't start. He tried again. He looked at the petrol gauge. Empty. It was a half-mile walk to the nearest petrol station and back again. Add to that the half-hour drive back to Campbelltown, and we knew we were cooked.

Of course, we tried to get hold of Dad to let him know what had happened, but the three red public phone booths we stopped at on the walk to the petrol station – with their strange signature smell of cigarettes, BO and stale urine – were all either vandalised or simply swallowed our coins.

Nick was furious with himself that he hadn't checked the petrol gauge before we set out. I knew we were in trouble, but hey, I was on a date with the guy I'd had a crush on for almost four years, and we were holding hands all the way back to the car, so I was in actual heaven.

It was well after midnight by the time we pulled up outside my house, so there was only time for one quick 'pash' before we both took a deep breath, ready to face the music. As we walked up the driveway, I could see both Mum and Dad standing at the lounge-room window, watching us as we arrived.

'Mr Wilkinson, I'm so sorry,' Nick started as soon as Dad opened the door, 'we tried to call ... but none of the phone booths were working, and I ran out of petrol and ...'

'Dad,' I added, 'it's really true. We had to walk for ages to get petrol and ...'

Dad looked us both up and down, assessed the situation and, in typical Ray Wilkinson style, accepted our earnest explanation. All he truly cared about was that I was home safe. He could see how apologetic we both were and said that his main fear had been that we must have been in a car accident. With that, Nick apologised once again, said goodnight and headed home, while I floated off to bed.

Mum, too, was relieved that night, though she didn't say much. In fact, around this time Mum wasn't saying much at all. We'd been arguing a lot over silly things. I'd noticed too that it had become rare for Mum to ever sit down and just relax. Every night Mum would cook dinner for us all, and then either stay in the kitchen listening to her beloved talkback radio or quietly go off to bed, the radio still glued to her ear.

Often in these times I would stay up and do my homework at the dining-room table, while Dad did his work. Dad was a beautiful artist, and I would sometimes ask for his help to do a title page in my schoolbooks. And always we would talk.

Dad knew a lot about Mum's childhood – more, I think, than he ever let on – but in this difficult time that Mum was going through, he wanted me to understand, and asked me to be patient.

'She didn't have anything like the childhood you or I had, sweetheart. You have to allow for that.'

Dad. Always the gentle peacemaker.

*

Fifth Form felt like a huge step for me. These last two years of school were meant to be when things got serious, and yet for the past year I'd really struggled at school. Could I really cope with another two? So much had happened, and even though I knew I could do better, I still felt that if I did well, I would once again become a target.

But maybe my senior years could be a fresh start.

The good news was that Raelene and all of her gang had gone, and I felt a huge relief knowing I would never again have to face the spectre of one of those Raelene-led storms brewing on the edge of the playground and heading straight for me.

Sadly, as we moved further into Fifth Form, one by one, all of my girlfriends – Michelle, Chris, Sue, Julie and Therese – left too. I stayed on and tried really hard to knuckle down in my subjects – and I was loving English, French and Art – but try as I might, there was something about still being in that place, against that same backdrop where so much hurt had happened, that was crushing me.

All the other kids in my year now seemed so smart, so assured, so confident about the directions in which they were heading. Increasingly, I felt like I just wasn't good enough.

Making me even more miserable: I was starting to put on weight. My body, always strong and lithe from a decade of dance, with its hours and hours of strenuous rehearsal every week, was confused once it all suddenly stopped. I had struggled to find something, anything, that gave me the same joy, energy and excitement. Sugar seemed to have now become ballet's replacement, and I was uncomfortable in my expanding skin. It felt like so much of who I once was had been taken from me. I wanted that confident, happy girl back; but I felt like she had been lost forever.

Every day as I walked towards those school gates, all those feelings would be stirred back up again, and I wanted all of it to just go away … by going away myself. I was not sure where to go, or what to do – I just no longer wanted to be at school. Maybe leaving and getting a job might make me happy again.

I had never told Mum or Dad about the bullying, but they could tell things weren't right with me. Every report card told the same story: 'Lisa can do better'. And I knew I could too. Just not here anymore. So one night I begged Mum and Dad to let me leave. I had a couple of rough ideas about what I'd do, too. I'd recently got a part-time job selling shoes at Wrench's Shoe Store in Queen Street, so maybe I could see if they had anything full-time, save hard and then go backpacking for a couple of years in Europe. Maybe then, with some experience under my belt, I could try to get a cadetship in journalism.

We stayed up talking for hours that night, and to my astonishment, Mum and Dad reluctantly agreed to contact the school, and write a letter to the principal giving their full consent for me to finish up at Campbelltown High.

*

Dad, always the sentimental one, insisted on dropping me to school on that final hot December morning of Fifth Form. He was on his way to work, and as we pulled up to the school gates for the last time, I could only meet his gaze for a fleeting moment as I kissed him on the cheek, and he handed me the envelope containing that all-important letter to freedom.

I just couldn't stand to see the disappointment on his face, or for him to see my tears, but in that split second, I wanted to pour everything out to him, explain why I couldn't do this anymore, and apologise for not going all the way to the HSC. But the words just wouldn't come.

So I jumped straight out, clumsily struggling with my heavy schoolbag full of the textbooks I no longer needed … and didn't look back. All I had to do now was walk to the main office, hand over Dad's letter and that would be it. No pomp, no ceremony, no farewell, just 12 years of school, over.

By lunchtime, I was starting to realise the full significance of my decision. The uniform I would never wear again, the classrooms I was seeing for the last time, the final ring of the lunch bell as I headed to the canteen to buy my usual: corned-beef-and-pickle sandwich, Orchy orange juice and cream bun chaser.

As I stood there mindlessly waiting in the canteen line, I felt a tap on my shoulder.

'Lisa?' It was the teacher on playground duty. 'Mr Scott wants to see you in his office,' she said with a look I couldn't quite read.

Oh, god. Mr Scott was the deputy principal and our Fifth Form master. That could only mean trouble. Mr Scott was known as the fastest 'caner' here in the west. I'd had him in Third Form for Geography, and many was the time he would take a student out of class for one misdemeanour or another for 'six of the best'.

I hadn't done anything wrong as far as I knew, but as I threaded my way through the maze of handball games and bouncing basketballs in the beating heat of the school's central playground, I wondered if my last day here might be my worst.

Tough as he was, though, Mr Scott was a brilliant teacher, and I somehow always lifted in his classes. He had this uncanny knack for dictating to us – without ever referring to a single note or textbook – the most exquisite stories about countries and cultures and ancient civilisations around the world that we, in turn, would copy down. I would sometimes look back at that perfectly put-together prose and wonder how on earth he did that. His stories of faraway lands always reminded me of just how massive the world was out there. Beyond this school. Beyond this town. Possibly even beyond my imagination. And I wanted to see it all.

So, as I tapped on Mr Scott's office door and heard a voice invite me in, I steeled myself. It was then that I caught sight of Mr Scott deep in discussion with my Biology teacher. I stepped back, not wanting to interrupt, but there was something about the way they looked up that made it clear I was their topic of conversation.

What was it? That missing Biology textbook from First Form I never did quite pay all the fines on? Were they trying to fine-tune my end-of-school reference – like, how do you put a positive spin on 'reads too many magazines in class'?

Whatever it was, it probably wasn't going to be good. So I steadied myself, moved back into the welcome cool breeze of the admin block hallway, and waited, comforting myself with the knowledge that whatever they had to say wouldn't matter by tomorrow, because tomorrow I would finally be free!

But nothing could have prepared me for what came next, as Mr Scott invited me into his office. After a long lead-up about his surprise at receiving Dad's letter, there was also a whole run-through about what leaving one year early without getting my HSC would mean for my future.

All of which was fine, and most of which I didn't take in – partly because my mind was already made up, but mostly because of the distraction being provided by Mr Scott's mesmerising socks-and-sandals combo that day. It was around 30 degrees, and I swear those thick socks he was wearing were made of, was it … tweed?

And then, in amongst it all I heard two simple words I wasn't expecting.

'You're good,' he said.

I looked up. I'm what?

'You're good, Wilkinson. You're too good to leave school. I've spoken to all your teachers, and we really believe you should think about staying.'

Mr Scott had called me to his office to say he believed in me; that all my teachers believed in me.

Yet I didn't. Miss West, Miss Jackson, and even my ballet teacher Miss Dean when I was just five years old and putting my ballet shoes on for the first time, had all believed in me. So why was I having so much trouble believing in myself?

'Look, I know you haven't had the easiest time at school over the years,' he said.

Oh, god. I had no idea he knew about the bullying. I always thought I'd hidden that stuff so well.

'But those girls have all left,' he added. 'You can still get a great result if you do the work. Anyway, I've rung your dad and told him we think you should stay. He said the decision is yours.'

God love you, Dad. He wanted me to stay, and yet he was prepared to leave the decision up to me.

And strangely, after all that angst, with those two simple words, 'You're good', I made the decision on the spot. Having a teacher like Mr Scott tell me that he believed in me was all it took. I was either a pushover, or I just knew in my heart of hearts that not going all the way with the HSC would be a mistake.

When I told Mum and Dad that night that I'd decided to stay at school, Mum was pleased, while Dad, in his usual understated way, silently beamed.

*

I'd never been to Sydney's notorious Kings Cross before, but here we were, getting off this bus on a school excursion to radio station 2JJ in William Street, to see inside an actual radio station.

Even though I was more of a 2SM girl, Double J was the shiny new cool kid on the radio block, with all the credibility of the ABC behind it. As we filed in one by one in our maroon-and-grey school uniforms, I was totally blown away by what everyone in this place was wearing.

The year before we'd had an excursion to the local paper, *The Campbelltown-Ingleburn News*, where the almost all-male staff – even the juniors – were clean-shaven and kitted out in full suits and ties. Here at Double J, the dress code was pure psychedelic 'Woodstock'. Rock-and-roll posters covered every available inch of the walls, and just about every bloke had a beard or moustache. There were lots of women too, and everyone was in jeans. It was unlike any workplace I'd ever imagined. And certainly unlike any workplace I imagined where journalists worked. Sure, these old ABC studios were tired, the carpet was tattered and there was mess everywhere, but the place itself was *alive*!

I stood there mesmerised: a telex machine was noisily punching out breaking news, people kept darting back and forth in and out of sound booths, Skyhooks records were playing through the speakers, and I even saw Bob Hudson – who'd recently had the biggest hit in the country with 'The Newcastle Song' – doing his DJ shift live. And this was all in the same organisation that gave birth to Aunty Jack, Norman Gunston and *Countdown*. It seriously didn't get much cooler than this.

When I went home that night, I told Mum that I was definitely thinking that journalism was for me. Mum was glad I'd stayed at school, but reminded me that cadetships were hard to come by, so I really shouldn't get my hopes up.

Maybe so, but I was going to try. Mum clearly had other things on her mind, though. As I was drawing closer to my final Sixth Form exams, I was heavier than ever, and Mum couldn't hold her tongue any longer.

'You know, darling,' she said to me, 'I think if you just lost a bit of weight, you'd probably be beating the boys off with a stick. You're so much prettier when you don't have weight on.'

Wow. That stung. Is that the way Mum thinks? Did she worry that I was going to be— What was that saying again? 'Left on the shelf'?

I could hardly blame her. In 1970s Australia, if you were female and over 15, the fat-equals-rejection messages were all-pervasive.

The multi-million-dollar diet industry was booming. Every week, women's magazines were touting the latest fad diets. Weight Watchers' classes were popping up everywhere. Ads for any number of diet pills abounded. Trimolets ('Nothing is fun if you're fat!'), Trim Tabs ('Because when you're less of a weight, you're more of a woman'), and Ford Pills ('Keep you slim and regular') were the most popular.

Yep, those ads certainly didn't miss, particularly when it came to reminding women that, without a man – a man you had to continually keep impressing if you were going to be lucky enough to hold on to him – well, what hope in life would there be for you?

Trouble in your marriage? Perhaps you've let yourself go? According to the Ford Pill ads, if you're fat then it's your fault, and you need to get your act together quick-smart lest that man of yours leaves you for someone prettier, younger and slimmer. As these words from one of their ubiquitous, anxiety-inducing ads at the time warned:

> Ford Pills can help make you as attractive as the girls your husband stares at in the street. Looked at him lately? Not as a husband. But as a man? Looked at yourself? Not as a wife. But as his secretary. Don't run away from what you see. Start fighting. Get a pack of Ford Pills. We'll give you a second chance.

Exactly what was in those pills was unclear. One of the girls from school said her mum had tried them and always acted just a little bit weird when she took them. Turns out, Ford Pills were nothing more than a laxative. They were designed to give women the shits … although not in the way they probably should have.

As a devoted stay-at-home mum with no career skills to speak of, few female friends, and a husband working long hours and adored by everyone he met, Mum was ripe for the picking when it came to these 'you're-nothing-without-a-man' messages. Her already fragile self-worth, courtesy of that childhood so full of rejection, was just what the Ford Pill doctor ordered.

Mum regularly bemoaned to me the fact she no longer had the 'girlish figure' of her twenties, or that 24-inch waist. Three pregnancies, she said, had seen to that. Dad would always tell her she looked great, but she would have none of it.

Over the years I'd seen her trying to peel off the pounds by tuning in to a crazy British fitness guru called Sue Becker on the ABC, who would call upon her legion of lady viewers to 'bottom walk' with the cheeks of their behind – left, right, left, right – back and forth across the lounge-room floor. Mum was a regular viewer over at Channel 10, too, for those morning yoga sessions with Swami Sarasvati.

Strangely, for all Mum's self-doubt, I was always taken by how incredibly fit and flexible she seemed to be. And no wonder: when it came to the drudgery of daily domestics, Mum was an absolute Trojan. As well as keeping an immaculate house, cooking every family meal, and being a regular volunteer for canteen duty at our various schools, Mum was also the one who kept the lawns mowed, the trees trimmed and the garden constantly maintained and blooming, with its impressive show of camellias, azaleas and hydrangeas. I always thought our house, with its terracotta-painted weatherboards and neat row of garden beds out the front, was the prettiest in the street and so much of it was because of Mum.

I don't ever remember her asking any of us to share that load, however. I also don't remember ever seeing Mum sitting back and relaxing, reading a book or a magazine. Everything she did, she did for us. Mum liked being useful and keeping busy. Dad told me once, after gently referring to Mum's various stints in orphanages as a kid, that having something to do probably kept her distracted from the demons of her childhood. For Mum, it seems, the spectre of rejection was never far from her thoughts.

So, always, she kept an eye on those scales. A few added pounds, a skirt too tight or a displeasing glimpse of her reflection in a shop window guaranteed a bad day for Mum, something she often took out on the garden.

More than once I came home from school to discover a large branch had been cut from one of the big liquidambar trees we kids would climb in the backyard. Never a branch that actually needed cutting … just a random branch, mysteriously gone.

Sometimes I would notice that despite dinner being on the table, she wouldn't join us. 'Not hungry,' was always the answer. I wasn't so sure.

When Mum first made that comment to me about my weight, I'd put on maybe a stone, and I really wasn't particularly fussed that there were no boys on the scene. Nick had moved away to college, and while I was a teeny bit heartbroken, I too had moved on. I was simply surviving, using whatever means were available to cope with getting through my exams, until that moment not too far away when I could walk out of those school gates forever.

The canteen at school was no help, with its meat pies, apple turnovers, Paddle Pops and chocolate bars. Then every afternoon on the way home from school, I would pass by the Chamberlain Street shops, load up at the corner milk bar and sneak a stash of treats into my bedroom, hidden away from Mum's disapproving gaze. Wagon Wheels, Chokitos, Polly Waffles … the sweeter, the richer, the creamier, the better. I was eating into my savings from Wrench's Shoe Store in the worst possible way, but it was getting me through.

Once, Mum found the hiding place I had in my wardrobe and confronted me. She was furious. 'I found where you've been hiding your food. What are you doing?!' I stood there, unable to find words. She had been snooping and hit the jackpot, announcing that she'd gone ahead and thrown all of that sugary contraband out.

'Have you been on the scales lately? No wonder boys aren't calling.'

She didn't mean it. I knew she didn't mean it. I tried to remind myself that Mum's own greatest fear in life was being left behind. Now she feared that that might happen to her own daughter. I knew she just wanted more for me. But it hurt.

Suddenly, she started cooking diet meals. Out with the chops, sausages and Rice-a-Riso; in with the boiled eggs, fish, veggies and salad (and as the year went on, in ever-diminishing portions).

Mum couldn't see that those treats were my one bright spot in every pressure-filled day as I headed towards the HSC. I knew she was devastated when I gave up ballet – the pride in her eyes when she used to watch me dance was another one of the many reasons I loved it. But I never told her the reasons why I'd stopped. What those punches in the playground felt like in front of all my friends. Or about Therese's disgusting dad and what he did to me. Why so many times I'd wanted to just disappear between the cracks. Perhaps just like she had when she was a little girl.

I also couldn't tell her that I was trying to fill a bottomless hole inside me, all the while knowing that the more I ate, the more I squirrelled away, the emptier I felt.

But there was no more hiding the effect it was having on me. By the time I sat my HSC, that one stone on the scales in the bathroom had become two. My concentration during stu-vac had become a joke, and every single night my dreams became nightmares of walking into that exam hall in the first week of November in an utter panic, completely unprepared and racked with guilt that I was letting everyone down. Every morning I would wake in a sweat.

At my Sixth Form Farewell, I was miserable and came close to not going at all. I'd struggled to find anything to wear that would fit. In the end, the zipper on the floral Prue Acton gypsy skirt I'd saved so hard over six months to pay off remained half undone all night. I even tried to hide when the official photos were being taken, to no avail.

The after-party was out at Kentlyn, not far from the Woolwash, on a beautiful apple orchard owned by the parents of one of the other students … but I only lasted an hour before quietly slipping away while everyone else partied.

I cried as I drove home that night in the little brown Gemini coupe I'd just managed to put my first down payment on. Every so often I would catch a glimpse of my reflection in the darkened windows, my unmistakably rounded cheeks and tear-stained puffy eyes illuminated by every car I passed.

I realised that something urgently had to change. I was sick of feeling like this. My post-school life *had* to be different. I wanted the old me back – with all her optimism, and openness, and courage. I hated myself for all those times I'd allowed others to make her feel so small. I wanted to give her a hug and tell her it's going to be OK, and that this is when we start afresh. And I didn't want Mum to worry about me anymore.

So, as I walked out of the school assembly hall after the HSC, my final exam paper turned over and handed in, and then out through the gates of Campbelltown High for the very last time, I made a promise to myself: no matter what that HSC result turned out to be, never again would I allow anyone to decide on my behalf who I was, what I was worth, or what I was capable of achieving.

A new life was on its way.

I'd gone ahead and booked myself into business college in the city for the following year, hoping to get those skills that might just get me a foot in the door in the media. And, dammit, I was going to travel as well. I was heading for new places, new people, new experiences, and this was finally my chance to prove to myself that those bullying girls hadn't clipped my wings, that I could still fly away and live a great life. I could *do* this!

That night at home, as I so often did, I closed my bedroom door, turned on my portable record player and sang the Beatles' 'Blackbird' at the top of my lungs, the words reminding me of that I was just waiting for the time I would be free ...

*

It was summer holidays, school was done and, with an HSC result much better than I was expecting (Mr Scott was proud!), I found myself with two whole months to get my act together before college.

So, without a word to Mum, I decided it was time to drop all that weight and started looking around for a quick diet fix. And there were plenty available.

There was the Grapefruit Diet (consisting of grapefruit at every meal), the Cookie Diet (involving pre-packaged cookies with a 'secret hunger-controlling formula'), the Scarsdale Diet (almost pure protein and great for those who enjoy being constipated), the Sleeping Beauty Diet (here, take these sedatives to make you sleep up to 20 hours and therefore limit the time you're awake and able to actually eat), and the Limmits Cracker Diet (involving the sweetest/saltiest/butteriest lemon-filled 'meal replacement' biscuits imaginable – presumably based on the idea that if these things don't turn you off food, nothing will).

Then I discovered something called The Israeli Army Diet. I can't say I'd ever particularly noticed the slim silhouettes of the military in that part of the world, but in the late 70s everyone was doing it – particularly because no less than that most trusted of publications, *The Australian Women's Weekly,* was pushing its strong virtues for instant weight loss. It seemed like a miracle cure. And that was exactly what I needed: a miracle cure.

The eating 'regime' required, appropriately enough, military-grade discipline, consisting as it did of nothing but apples for two days, cheese for two days, chicken for two days and salad for two days. The promise was you were guaranteed to lose ten pounds in eight days.

I lost 12. Sure, I was woozy for most of that time, because, as I discovered, you get so sick of eating each food and nothing but that food, that you end up not eating at all. Bingo!

And with my appetite down to just about nothing, I dropped the entire two stone in five weeks. I was weak, but I was slim again, and everyone noticed. Compliments just kept on coming. Once again, all my clothes fitted. I felt better. Sort of.

Even Mum was happy, if a little concerned. 'Make sure you stop now, darling. That's enough.'

CHAPTER SEVEN

Bondi bound

'Another world is not only possible, she is on her way …
On a quiet day, if I listen very carefully, I can hear her
breathing.' – Arundhati Roy

IF JOURNALISM WAS THE end game, I knew I had a lot of work to do first. My world felt small, and I had a burning urge to remove myself from all that was familiar. I wanted to experience what it was to be out there on my own, fending for myself, with people – and in places – I didn't yet know. And return with stories to tell.

I wanted to watch the sun go down on a beach in Spain; fall asleep in a hammock reading Dickens on a Greek island; touch the cool marble tiles on that 17th-century monument to love, the Taj Mahal; live my life from a backpack in Nepal; eat street food in Phuket; and perhaps even fall ridiculously in love for just a moment with the wrong boy at a chance meeting in a Moroccan cafe.

Problem was, I somehow had to finance that whole ambitious travel plan. While I'd saved hard for years with my job at Wrench's, it was only returning $2.70 an hour. So I figured if I could spend a year at business college getting some basic journalism skills, like shorthand and typing, then get an executive assistant's job and save every single cent, I might be able to scrape together just enough to head overseas and get that travel bug out of my system. Then, according to my plan, I could come back more worldly, hopefully wiser, and look for a cadetship somewhere in the media (maybe even with a smile on my face for not resisting the temptations of that boy in the cafe in Morocco).

For now, though, I had to knuckle down and survive the stuffy surrounds of the 'Metropolitan Business College for Ladies' in York Street in the city – a place highly regarded by my high-school careers counsellor for its advanced course in business and secretarial skills.

To my Campbelltown eyes, the place was populated, at least in part, by a sort of privileged, mildly bored 'society girl' I'd never before encountered – the kind that 'did' ski seasons, summers at 'Palmy', and June Dally-Watkins deportment courses. For some, secretarial school seemed like nothing more than a distraction until a similarly well-connected, rich husband came along.

At lunch their talk was of something called 'B&S balls', family beach houses, and chums called 'Dee' and 'Bin' and 'Boo'. Their cardigans were cashmere, and their nails were always remarkably neat and shiny. And, as I quickly discovered, almost all of them were private-school educated.

And that was what seemed to prompt one rather curious question I was regularly asked: 'So, what school did you go to?' I was confused because so often it was just after they'd asked where I'd grown up.

'I'm from Campbelltown,' I would say. 'So, ummm, I went to Campbelltown High?' All the while wondering if this was some sort of trick question, and if I was giving the right answer.

Always, there was a momentary pause, which told me this was not quite the answer they were looking for. It seemed they could cope with the fact that I came from Campbelltown ('There's a bit of good farming land around there, right?'), but their eyes often said: 'But your parents at least got you out of there for your education, yeah? They didn't? Ooooh, too bad.'

While they didn't exactly roll their eyes, I was clearly dismissed as someone with a sadly limited background and of no networking interest to them. Why the school I went to would even matter to them, I had no idea. To some, though, it obviously did.

And then, thank heavens, there was Tia. Tia lived in a rented second-floor flat a block and a half from Bondi Beach with her fabulously bohemian parents, and she was the closest thing to a citizen of the world I had ever met.

Tia drank strong coffee, smoked even stronger cigarettes, and I was drawn to her on day one, as I looked around trying to identify my new, hopefully kinder, 'tribe'. Tia had the most cultured accent I'd ever heard outside of the 6pm news and had already packed so much into her 18 years.

Tia's mum and dad had been firmly entrenched in the deeply secretive Sea Org arm of the Church of Scientology, and at just 14, Tia and her brother had been removed from school to undertake an open-ended stint as cooks on the Sea Org boat off the coast of New Zealand. No matter that they had no experience as cooks. No matter that both hoped to go all the way to Sixth Form. As Tia told it, the whole episode was a complete disaster, and her parents had realised it too late.

Tia's stories of her family's incredible escape from the church and the years of intimidation that came as a result were frightening and inspiring, all at once. She was fascinating and wise, brave and ballsy, and the best-read person I'd ever met.

Going to college and meeting Tia began to fracture everything I'd ever known. Every day, as I excitedly headed into the city on the 7.03am train to Wynyard and momentarily glanced out the window across at the big oval attached to my old school, that knot that had sat so tightly at the base of my being for years started to loosen ever so slightly.

Slowly, I realised that that life – those bullies, those nights I had lain awake wondering what possible horrors the next day would bring – was finally behind me. Those people no longer mattered. That excruciating time, when my world seemed so grey, was over. Every horizon became a rainbow of possibilities.

My liberation was made complete one morning when I unexpectedly came face to face with Therese's father on my train to the city. He was sitting in carriage three, the one I always seemed to gravitate to each morning. I'd never seen him here before. As soon as I saw him, I froze. That face. Those bushy eyebrows. Those ogling eyes. The broken bloodshot capillaries that now scratched their way across his face.

I stared at him. Right at him. Every hair on the back of my neck was raised. He stared back. Then he started to smile, and I could see that he was about to speak.

'Don't you *dare*,' I shot straight back, before he could even open his mouth. 'Don't. You. Even. Dare!'

He froze. And slumped back in his seat.

I moved to another carriage. And never saw him again.

*

The city had become an oasis for me. During the week, we learnt the QWERTY keyboard on manual and (joy of joys) brand-new electric typewriters, studied Pittman shorthand and office etiquette, and muddled our way through bookkeeping. And I loved it all.

Weekends, though, were party time for Tia and me: nights dancing non-stop at Juliana's Disco in the newly opened Hilton Hotel; watching the sun come up with takeaway pizza on the sands of Bondi Beach; or jumping in my trusty brown Gemini coupe to head up or down the coast for weekends away with an always eclectic mix of new friends Tia had a brilliant knack for gathering.

We wore harem pants and Staggers jeans; did 'The Carwash'; and watched *The Rocky Horror Picture Show* again and again and again, as we sang every word and danced every step in unison. Saturday afternoons were spent plastering our faces with Max Factor's bright-blue paint-on/peel-off masks so we could have 'younger-looking skin', and we vowed to get a share-flat together once we settled down to real jobs.

The year flew by, and by December we were both handed our certificates in Advanced Secretarial Studies. We did it!

Many of the more conscientious amongst our year had secured jobs long before graduation. Every so often, I would scan the papers – and there were plenty of jobs going in solicitors' and real-estate offices – but nothing that really grabbed my eye. And besides, I figured, what's the hurry?

Surely, I could have one last lazy-ish summer, still working at Wrench's, and then once the year got underway, I could start hitting the employment pavement with gusto.

But by one particularly wet Thursday morning in late January, Mum had had enough. 'It's time,' she said (the only time I ever recall a famous Labor Party catchcry coming from her lips, even though inadvertently).

'No more hanging around the house. It's time to go and get the paper and find a job.' The fact that it was a Thursday – not exactly a day known for its pick of the job ads – didn't matter to Mum.

'There'll be nothing in there,' I tried to tell her. 'All the good jobs are on Saturdays.'

Mum would have none of it, so just to keep her happy, I headed off to the newsagent at the Chamberlain Street shops – not to buy the latest copy of *Dolly* as I had every month like clockwork for so many years – but to grab that completely pointless Thursday copy of the *Sydney Morning Herald*.

When I returned, slightly rain-soaked, the *SMH* was just as I predicted, as thin as could be for job ads, and I took no little I-told-you-so delight in pointing it out to Mum as I carefully opened up the few dampened pages for her inspection.

'See, Mum, it has just about nothing,' I announced.

It was true. The Women & Girls employment section of the *SMH* was never extensive at the best of times, especially when compared with the endless pages devoted to finding jobs for the boys. (A phrase and a fact that would only reveal its full irony to me many, many years later.)

So, as Mum left the room with 'OK, but on Saturday, you get serious!', I made my way, just for the hell of it, through each and every one of those ads.

Nup, nothing under 'A' for Assistants.

Nope, don't want to be a Credit Controller.

Anything under 'E' for Executive Assistants?

Before I could get there, though, I stopped at the letter 'D'.

Buried right there was a tiny, unassuming three-line ad. I looked again. Not believing what I was seeing. 'D' for ...

Surely not.

It read: 'Dolly *magazine is looking for a secretary/editorial assistant/ Girl Friday who is prepared to do absolutely anything. Phone Kathy on 699-3622.*'

...

...

Dolly. MY magazine.

And there was a job going there! It couldn't be possible? A job that had my name, my qualifications, my everything written all over it. But why was a big job like that being advertised on a Thursday? And where were all the bright lights and big headings it should have around it? There had to be a mistake.

I looked again.

Inspecting.

Every.

Single.

Word.

'Prepared to do absolutely anything.'

That was ME! A job on a magazine, with real journalists working on it. I simply *had* to get this!

Now even though I'd grown out of reading *Dolly* by that stage, I still had a soft spot for it – not to mention a dusty spot under my bed for the stack of much-loved back issues Mum had been begging me for years to throw out.

Somehow, though, I just never could. Those back issues were the stepping-stones of my teenage years and far too precious to throw away. True, these days they were a little dog-eared from having so often been lovingly passed around and shared at sleepovers and sports carnivals ... evoking in all of us musings about a wardrobe, a boyfriend, a life we could only dream of.

If you could go out with any member of Sherbet, who would you choose? If you could have any hairstyle in the latest issue, which one would it be? If you could have any outfit ... and so it went. Dreams. Simple teenage imaginings of what could be.

I looked at the ad again. So that was the actual phone number for the magazine I had long adored? I couldn't quite believe I was just a phone call away from the people who put it out.

How many other girls 'just like me' had seen this amazing ad? I wondered. Thousands, surely. I had to get in quick. It was just before 9 o'clock. Was that too early? What the heck, if I could be first in the queue, they'd see how eager I was. I hesitated for just a moment before I dialled the number for Kathy on Mum and Dad's khaki-green phone on the hall table.

Here goes. Deep breath. First nervously pulling down the six. Then the nine. Another nine. Three. Six. Two. Two.

From Campbelltown, it was a long distance 'STD' call, so I waited for the pips. Dammit. No pips. It was engaged. No matter. I tried again. Still engaged. And for 45 tense minutes I kept turning that dial, until, bingo, someone answered.

'Hello, Sungravure, can I help you?'

Oh no, I was dialling the wrong number!

'Oh, I'm so sorry, I was looking for *Dolly* magazine ...'

'That's OK,' the voice came back. 'I can put you through.' It was the switchboard operator. 'That line is very busy today,' she said. I knew it: there *were* thousands of other girls applying. And with that, the phone connected through.

'Hello, *Dolly* magazine, this is Kathy.' Yes!

Just how many girls had applied for that job, I'll never know. I didn't want to know. But as Kathy and I chatted about the job and she checked on a bunch of my details, the call ended with an interview booked in for the following Monday with the *actual* editor.

Which gave me exactly four days to panic, fall apart, re-read every one of those seven years' worth of dusty back issues under my bed, buy the latest one (gee, it was a lot brighter than I remembered), and choose an outfit that would hopefully win over Kathy – or her boss, or both.

I had three things in my wardrobe that might work. A shirtdress – yeah, that said sensible secretary, so maybe they'd like that. What about my Jag denim jumpsuit? That whole look was all through the latest issue, so maybe that was a big fashion win? In the end, I settled on the red Merivale sundress I'd had on lay-by for six months, and a pair of chocolate-brown Mr Christian wedges.

For four days I could hardly sleep in anticipation. Mum, on the other hand, was not nearly as excited.

'Darling, do you really want to work there? Won't they all look like models? Won't they all be skinny? How would you cope with that?'

The thought hadn't even entered my head. And while I had kept the weight off since I left school, the boys weren't calling like Mum had predicted. But I also didn't want to get ahead of myself, so perhaps Mum putting a dampener on things was a good thing. This job was just too perfect, and surely life didn't work like that.

That Monday morning passed in a blur of nerves. The train to Central took just over an hour, so to ensure I made my 9am interview, I was taking my seat once again on the 7.03am to the city, this time getting off a few stations short of Wynyard.

Of course, I arrived at my stop far too early – a blessing in more ways than one. As I made my way towards 57 Regent Street, Chippendale, and the Sungravure building, I discovered that my chunky brown Mr Christian wedges with their skinny ankle strap and towering six-inch heels weren't designed for actual walking. What should have been a ten-minute trip ended up taking 30, as I gave birth to four separate bloodied blisters on the way. At least now I had only half an hour to kill before I had to walk through those glass doors and up to the second floor, as Kathy had instructed.

It was a warm morning for sure, and as the sun's rays on this sticky February day started to hit the entrance, I moved a couple of doors further along Regent Street into the shade of some trees, just out of view, and watched, transfixed, as workers – journalists? – entered through those doors, and began their working week.

Sungravure was the magazine arm of the publishing giant Fairfax, which included the *Sydney Morning Herald*, the *Australian Financial Review*, *The Sun* and *The Sun-Herald* newspapers over at nearby Broadway; and these four storeys I was about to enter housed many of Australia's most iconic magazines: *Dolly*, *Woman's Day*, *Cosmopolitan*, *Woman's World*, *Electronics Australia*, *People* ... the list went on. An eclectic mix to be sure, but they were magazines! How utterly glamorous it all felt. And here I was, about to see if I was good enough to at least jump through the first hurdle to join their ranks.

I watched, desperate not to be seen, carefully studying each new woman as she entered through those huge glass doors.

Was that Kathy? What about her? Is that one of the editors? I couldn't tell. Then, at 8.55, there was a sudden rush as employees made their way in for that 9am start.

What struck me as I stood there in the shade was just how normal everyone looked. Not like the models that Mum had envisioned at all. Jeans, blouses, simple dresses … and not a single, impractical chunky wedge shoe on any of them.

Well, blisters or not, I now had to compose myself as I walked back to the entrance and pushed open the big glass doors into the cool blast of the building's air-conditioning, trying for all the world to feel like I belonged here.

I'm not sure exactly what I was expecting when those lift doors opened onto the second floor, but it certainly wasn't this.

The rows of *Dolly* posters pinned to the makeshift felt-board partitions marking the magazine's office space made it clear I was in the right place; but as I made my way to the reception desk, I couldn't help noticing the huge bare patches worn into the grey carpet squares underfoot, perfectly lit up by the neon strip lighting above.

As I looked across to the open office with its jigsaw puzzle of bright-blue and yellow desks, I spied the curling smoke of already-lit cigarettes winding upwards from overflowing ashtrays towards the creamy-grey chipboard ceiling. What appeared to be years of accumulated smoke had done a merry circular dance into the air-conditioning system, only to be sprayed back out again across the ceiling, leaving a blackened tell-tale trail before falling once again into the office below.

The shrill sound of ringing phones, the tap-tap-tap of manual and – glory be! – electric typewriters filled that same hazy air, while huge roughly stacked piles of magazines sat like sentinels on every desk. It was chaos. It was utterly unglamorous. It was everything I wasn't expecting. And I was in heaven. I had arrived!

There, in the middle of it all, was the tiny Kathy, with a huge welcoming smile and a mop of stunning blonde curls.

'Hi, you must be Lisa. I'm Kathy. Welcome! And you're right on time,' she said in an adorable Kiwi accent. 'Mrs Goldie has just arrived.'

Kathy was only a few years older than me and, she told me, it was her job that was available, as she had just been promoted to become the magazine's fashion editor. She'd started as the office receptionist, and now she was becoming a journalist, and that meant …

First, though, I had to nail that job interview. Did I have what it takes? Was my HSC mark going to pass muster? Would I be enough? I was terrified.

The editor, Mrs Goldie, was a strapping, extremely business-like Scottish woman in her mid-fifties, clearly not at all averse to a twinset and pearls, and a good set-and-perm.

So, *this* was the Anne from the Editor's Letter in the magazine I used to devour every month? Again, not at all what I expected: she was incredibly intimidating; but her deputy, Vicki L'Green, who was sitting in on the interview, was warm and encouraging. How many words a minute could I type? What about my shorthand? Then, with just a cursory glance at my carefully collated CV, the interview was over.

It was so brief I was convinced I had blown it. Had they seen my embarrassing bleeding blisters? Was my CV not up to par? After all that angst over my HSC mark, they hadn't even asked about it.

Kathy saw me out and promised to call once a decision was made.

The next few days were an agony. Sure, they had other girls to interview, but I literally couldn't think of anything else. There was no other job on the planet for me. Surely, they could see how keen I was – or was I too keen?

By Friday, after four days of refusing to move from within running distance of the phone, I decided to go and have lunch with Michelle, who was now working at the Commonwealth Bank a few suburbs away and loving it. Michelle was dating one of the guys in the Harlequins Rugby Club, and she told me over lunch that they were even talking marriage and babies. Michelle was one of my oldest and most loyal friends, and I was happy for her. But as I arrived home and wandered into my bedroom, I wondered whether that sort of life would ever be in my future.

And then the phone rang, but before I could get up off my bed it stopped. Dammit! Wrong number. Then …

Mum shouted down the hallway, 'Leese, phone for you!' And as I approached the hall table, Mum, still holding the phone, put her hand over the mouthpiece and whispered, 'I think it's the same lady that called about an hour ago when you were out. I said you'd be back soon.'

What? Why didn't you … But there was no time to worry about that.

'Hello, Lisa speaking.'

And with that, came the words that would change my life forever.

'Lisa, it's Kathy. We'd love to offer you the job, if you're still interested?'

I couldn't believe what I was hearing.

'Yes, I certainly am! That's brilliant news. Thank you. Thank you so much …'

Mine! The job was actually MINE!

I was about to become the Girl Friday at *Dolly*. As I looked once again at that latest copy of the magazine and studied the staff list just inside the front cover, I realised that my name – MY name – would be printed right there.

My whole world had just shifted.

The first thing I did was call Dad at work.

'I was never in any doubt that you'd get it, sweetheart,' he said. 'They would have been crazy not to give it to you. It means you're about to work for some really smart people.'

Dad. There he was again. Always positive. Always encouraging. Always believing in me.

CHAPTER EIGHT

Hello Dolly!

'"What day is it?" said Pooh. "It's today!"
squeaked Piglet. "Ah, my favourite day," said
Pooh.' – A. A. Milne, *Winnie the Pooh*.

KATHY WAS A LITTLE bit embarrassed.
It was my very first day at *Dolly*, and as she helpfully began
to hand over the reins of her old job to me that morning, I was given
one of the tasks Kathy said she least enjoyed doing during her
time at the reception desk: going through the reader submissions for
the Poet's Corner page.

There on my new desk lay pile upon pile of manila folders,
chock-a-block with random bits of paper of every size, shape
and colour imaginable, featuring words penned by the readers
themselves.

'I'm so sorry, but that's about six months' worth,' she said.

I couldn't believe Kathy was apologising. What she saw before
us was a job she had been putting off for months; what I saw were
the hearts, the minds, the tears, the fears and the closely guarded
secrets of a generation of young Australian women. Private teenage
thoughts normally locked away from the judgment of others, and I
had just been handed the precious key.

What, though, was that sickly sweet smell? Kind of musky, kind
of woody, kind of overpoweringly awful, really.

'Oh, that. I know, overwhelming isn't it?' she continued with a wry smile. 'Do you recognise any of them?'

Them?

'Most of the readers like to add some perfume to their letter before they send it. Usually, it's Charlie. But sometimes it's 4711, or Babe, or a bit of Cinnabar, some Yardley Lavender, or a few drops of musk oil or sandalwood or patchouli. So, once they're all in a pile together it's a little, yeah ...' she trailed off. 'Just make sure you don't go through them after lunch when you have a full stomach, otherwise it might be a bit much.'

An excellent tip, for sure.

'Look, honestly, don't spend too much time on them. Most of it is pretty ordinary. Besides, Mrs Goldie is thinking of permanently dropping that page from the magazine,' Kathy said, 'so just choose the top six and chuck the rest out.'

Now, what I hadn't told Kathy at that point is that I had been submitting poems to Poet's Corner for years, with not a single one ever being published. Perhaps now I knew why.

So, to find myself, on my first day, allowed into this teenage world of secret, heartfelt meanderings − with the power to choose which ones actually made their way onto the printed page − was a privilege I wasn't sure I yet deserved, but one I certainly wasn't going to squander. Sure, some of the poems were a little strangled, somewhat oblique, and I never did quite 'get' haiku ... but, oh, the trust those readers clearly had in us. It was a unique window into their private world.

And so began a joyous ritual for me. Every Friday night on the train back to Campbelltown, I would gather together all of the week's submissions, reading through every one of them over the weekend.

Kathy was right, some of them weren't great. But some of them were pure gold. And when they were, and there was a name and address attached, I would write back with the thrilling news that they were about to be published, and encourage them to write more and send them in. And, so often, they did.

One, Pieta Malone, a reader from country Victoria with her own dreams of one day becoming a journalist, was so good and became so popular with the readers that I started publishing her incredible words almost every month.

I grew proud of that page. Where, just a few months before, there were plans to completely drop it, Poet's Corner was becoming a reader favourite.

Another job that became mine was choosing the readers' questions to be answered on the Dolly Doctor page. It was, by any rough measure, the most well-thumbed page in the magazine and, no doubt, often the reason so many teenage boys were never averse to a quick flick through their sister's copies.

Here, for curious young teens keen to try and make sense of their rapidly expanding-lengthening-changing-and-ever-more-hairy bodies, was a safe space where no body part, crack, crevice, topic or bodily fluid was off limits.

Vaginas (*Why does mine look so different from my girlfriend's?*), penises (*Are they meant to have a bend?*), sex (*Why is it so painful?*), breasts (*Why are mine so small/big/veiny/hairy?*), nipples (*Are they meant to go in because mine do and my friend says that's definitely weird?*), periods (*How often am I meant to get them because I haven't had one for four months since I had sex that one time, so what does that mean?*), tampons (*Will I still be a virgin if I use one, and which hole am I meant to put it in anyway?*), discharge (*Normally mine is white but is yellow OK too?*), and pubic hair (more often than not referred to as '*public hair*') were just some of the perennial favourites.

The list went on. The themes were often repetitive, and the letters would almost always begin with '*Dear Dolly Doctor, I can't talk to anyone else about this, but ...*'. Just like the Poet's Corner submissions, questions to Dolly Doctor were almost always anonymous and, judging by the paper used – often torn from school exercise books – written in desperate moments when, with no-one and nowhere else to turn to, *Dolly* was their only confidante.

The trust readers had in us was immeasurable, but also heartbreaking, because our long three-month printing deadlines meant that many of their urgent concerns would never be addressed in time.

Contraception and how not to fall pregnant were common themes (*If we don't have a condom, does plastic kitchen wrap work if things, you know, get desperate?*), as was the age-old issue of consent (*How do I say no and make sure he still likes me?*), and tragically, rape and incest (*My step-father says if we have sex I won't fall pregnant … is that right?*).

The vulnerabilities of our young readers often floored me; and even though I was told not to get involved, so criminal were some of the issues girls desperately needed help with that, if names and addresses were included, I would quietly pass them on to the police.

Was I intruding? Was this a step too far? In the end, I simply couldn't let those cries for help pass by unchecked. More than once I heard of charges being laid.

It was an indication to me that even though it was the late 70s and the world was moving in much less straitened times, teen sex education and the crucial issue of consent were still taboo topics for many parents, and often being left for exploration amongst schoolyard peer groups, where misinformation can prosper … along with unplanned pregnancies.

Each month I would choose six letters and send them off to our 'Dolly Doctor', Dr John Knight, who I was told had been looking after the column since the magazine launched.

Dr Knight was actually better known by his media pseudonym of Dr James Wright, the somewhat whacky doctor from TV's *Mike Walsh Show* on Channel 9. His regular small-screen appearances were usually centred around various bodily fluids and functions and designed to generate embarrassed giggles from the middle-aged, mostly female audience members. All manner of gut issues were particular favourites, and discussions of these would quickly descend into Benny Hill–style fart jokes.

To me, Dr Wright seemed an odd fit with *Dolly*'s young readership. Exactly why he was chosen, when there must have been any number of possibly younger, possibly more appropriate – heck, possibly even female – doctors available to write for *Dolly*, was never really clear.

Kate, the staff writer, whispered to me that he may have been a friend of Mrs Goldie's, which was fine, but to me his advice sometimes seemed judgmental. So when I was typing up his words for the editor's approval, I stuck with his medical advice, but tweaked out his moralising – which I knew would cause unnecessary distress. And no-one was ever the wiser.

One of my favourite jobs, though, was when I was sent to find news clippings and photos at the Sungravure library – a central information-gathering 'brains trust' shared by every magazine in the building, as well as all the newspapers over at Fairfax.

Hidden in the bowels of 57 Regent Street, it was a treasure trove of cultural, political and news-making history. Like any library, it was also dark, stuffy and windowless – making those moments when anyone decided to light up a cigarette a tad challenging – but I loved this place and, left to my own devices, could easily spend hours down there sifting through its decades-upon-decades of archives stored on each and every shelf.

Want to see every story ever written on that up-and-coming new actor John Travolta? Just take one of those step ladders and go to the 'T' section, there on the top row, fourth partition from the back wall – but please, just watch out for those boxes on the floor on the way – and pull out the ever-expanding manila folder with his name on it.

Inside these fading folders – carefully cut and glued onto separate A4 sheets of paper – was every article the librarians could get their hands on whatever or whomsoever your heart desired – sorry, I mean, whomsoever your boss had *asked* you to go and research.

Need more info on the Moon landing? Whitlam's dismissal? When women got the vote? Cyclone Tracy? The history of Federation in Australia? The common cold? The death of JFK? The love life of Prince Charles? It was all there, right at your fingertips. The bigger the name, the story, the event, the interest, the greater the number of dog-eared folders, many stuffed to the point of overflowing.

I simply couldn't believe that we had this incredibly rich source of worldwide information so readily available to us. Want a fact checked, an age verified, a photo sourced, a spelling confirmed, an old article found? You could get it right here in the Sungravure library, sometimes within just ten minutes of looking. Amazing!

For our purposes at *Dolly*, it was often the heartthrobs of the day that got the greatest research attention, so it didn't take me long to head over to the letter 'S' one spare lunchtime and investigate the boys of Sherbet.

Sure enough, there they were, six thrilling folders worth of stories going right back to the band's beginnings, many of which even a super fan like me had never seen before. These were accompanied by hundreds of photos, including what appeared to be three whole unedited rolls of film laid out in clear plastic sheeting from a Sherbet publicity shoot.

The ability to see anything in the poor lighting of the Sungravure library was a challenge at the best of times, so I took the film over to the large photographer's light box in the corner and leaned in with a special magnifying eyeglass, all the better to see this golden find in all its glory.

But as I peered in, I suddenly got far more than I could ever have bargained for. There before me in full living colour all the (*cough*) members of Sherbet wrapped around each other on a studio floor, *naked*, save for some strategically placed soap bubbles. Why on earth did we have three original film rolls of this material here in the Sungravure library? I wondered.

As I studied each frame through the small magnifying glass (for research purposes only), by the third roll it became obvious that those bubbles had started to pop, and ... oopsy, someone forgot to put some extra bubbles on ya there, Daryl.

What a world of unexpected delights this job was proving to be ...

*

Everything about working in magazines excited me. The photo shoots, the stories, the deadlines, the design, the incredible reader feedback, and just the pure joy of the creative process.

There were only eight of us working on the editorial side of the magazine, so I put my hand up for everything and was learning something new every day. Sometimes I even got to do a little bit of writing. Lunch was just a sandwich at my desk, and I often didn't head out the door for the train home until 7pm, but I didn't care – so long as I was part of it.

Sure, I was just the Girl Friday. Sure, I didn't get paid much. Sure, I didn't have the uni degree everyone else had. But what I *did* have was something much more important: I had *passion*. And that passion was obvious to everyone.

Interestingly, once I'd started at *Dolly*, I quickly discovered why the magazine had been losing its appeal for me in recent times. Of course, at 19, I was growing up and no longer within its target market. But from where I sat, the real problem was that it just didn't seem to be in touch with its readers anymore. And whispers I heard around the office confirmed that the circulation was in trouble.

This was, in fact, Mrs Goldie's second stint as *Dolly*'s editor. Her first was for the magazine's launch back in 1970. And while she had nailed *Dolly*'s original, fairly difficult mission statement – to reach an audience of 'hip and happening' women aged 14 to 30, who loved fashion and boys, but had no interest in gardening tips and knitting patterns – time had shown that holding on to such a broad female demographic was nigh on impossible ... as the market would go on to prove.

In '72 and '73, two shiny new Australian women's magazines came along, squeezing *Dolly*'s market hard and sweeping up anyone over the age of 18. First, *Cleo* with its (almost) naked centrefold, cheeky Aussie humour and risqué sex-related sealed sections; and then *Cosmopolitan*, with its sexy, sophisticated single-girl glamour and New York–style sass. That just left the teen market for *Dolly*.

And it was one I knew so well. I had just lived all my teenage years with *Dolly* right by my side, and from personal experience I knew it was a market that wasn't to be underestimated in its complexities, passions, discretion, thirst for information or its deep desire not to be talked down to. I couldn't help wondering if Mrs Goldie, at 55, was still the right 'fit' for this publication.

Since Mrs Goldie's return, everything in the magazine was suddenly brightly coloured and saccharine sweet. The articles on dating were dangerously out of touch – one I saw even suggested not wearing any panties on a date and watching the guy's reaction when you tell him – while others featured pop stars like the Bay City Rollers, who were well past their use-by date, with their spiky hair and kooky tartan-trimmed boiler suits.

Anyway, when I boldly suggested in my first editorial meeting that we should do a huge tear-out poster of Meatloaf, I was told in no uncertain terms by a horrified Mrs Goldie that, delicious as meatloaf was, these were NOT the *Women's Weekly* recipe pages.

For an artist and an album as big as Meatloaf's *Bat Out Of Hell* to have escaped Mrs Goldie's attention for the 18 or so months it had been sitting on the charts took some doing, and there was no point trying to fight it. Or even explain it. Meatloaf would not have been in her K-Tel record rack at home nor, I presumed, would she be watching *Countdown* at 6 o'clock every Sunday night (like me and every other teenager in the country).

No matter; I just kept my head down and kept working, taking on ever more responsibility, and cherishing every precious minute of it. What's more, I got paid for it!

Every Thursday, our white hand-delivered pay packets would arrive from the paymaster. Each week, as I pulled back the gently secured tab on the envelope, there, in typed, soft grey numbers it read: $99.90. And inside, that exact amount in cold hard cash. I could hardly believe that I was getting paid to be a part of all this. Shouldn't I be paying them?

Nothing I did – from taping shoes for photo shoots, to running errands, taking dictation, making coffee, writing up all the regular columns, corresponding with readers, licking stamps, picking up Mrs Goldie's dry cleaning, or even cleaning the office kitchen sink at the end of every day – felt at all like work. I wanted to learn, and the best way I knew how was to volunteer for anything no-one else wanted to do and jump on in at the deep end.

And it seems those at *Dolly* knew an enthusiastic staff member when they saw one. Vicki was aware I was keen to do more and more writing, and six months after I started it was announced that I was getting a cadetship as a trainee writer. But it was on the proviso that I keep up my Girl Friday role; and, if everything worked out, a new receptionist would be appointed. That made me a bit of a hard-working, two-for-the-price-of-one deal but, hey, I'll take it!

As the deputy editor, Vicki had championed me from the start. I could see she was a golden child of the organisation and destined, I was sure, for big things. At 23, she was already married to her childhood sweetheart, wore the most exquisite clothes and exuded private-school sophistication and class. Even though our worlds were very different, together we were a great team.

So, with my shiny new cadetship now official, I was given the job of writing and editing 'What Now?', the news and gossip section of the magazine. The role put me in touch with every movie, record and TV publicist in town. The Australian arts and music scenes were on fire, and groups like Australian Crawl, Midnight Oil, INXS and AC/DC, as well as hotshot actors like Mel Gibson and Judy Davis, were all available for interviews … and I spoke to them all.

I was even given my first feature to write. The brief? How to prepare a romantic dinner at home for two.

Right. The fact I was still living at home with Mum and Dad, rarely cooked and had never prepared a romantic dinner – let alone had someone in my life to prepare that dinner for – was never going to get in my way. And I certainly wasn't going to let on. I was about to get my very first byline – I'd make it up!

The article was called 'Dinner a Deux', in honour of the rather exotic Coq au Vin recipe I'd snaffled from the lovely Margaret Fulton at *Woman's Day*, who I often used to run into in the lift, as she would deliver up yet another tray of Fulton-tried-and-tested deliciousness to the smiles of the editorial team on the third floor.

When your heart is set on becoming a journalist, the only thing that comes close to matching the excitement of seeing your name in print for the first time is seeing someone *reading* your words in print for the first time. So, every day on the train, I would look out for someone, anyone, reading the magazine. I would then wait patiently until they got to my story. Will they stop, or just flick past those two precious pages featuring my publishing debut? Every time, I held my breath. Sadly, when they did stop, it was never for too long. But, hey, I was published. It was a start!

Things were certainly moving quickly for me, and they were about to take on an added pace as, just months later, Mrs Goldie was announced as the new editor of *Woman's Day* – where, fortuitously enough, meatloaf recipes really *were* a big seller!

It was a huge move for Mrs Goldie and it would position her in direct competition with the venerable Ita Buttrose, who for quite a few years had not only edited Australia's biggest-selling magazine, the *Women's Weekly*, but also fronted its TV advertisements.

As public profiles went, you didn't get much bigger than Ita. From launching *Cleo* alongside her boss, media heir Kerry Packer in 1972, by '75 she had taken over the institution that was Australia's most treasured magazine for women, with a readership of four million everyday Australians a week. The rise of the woman with the country's most famous lisp and coolest command of all she took on had been exponential. Mrs Goldie certainly had a big task ahead of her.

As did Vicki, with the announcement that she was the new editor of *Dolly*. And that meant she now needed a deputy of her own. I hardly felt ready for it, but somehow Vicki thought I was.

'The only thing is,' Vicki asked, 'would you mind if we just called you assistant editor for a few months while the rest of the staff get used to it? Your rise is happening pretty quickly, and I just don't want to get any noses out of joint.'

I didn't mind in the slightest.

Now, even with my pretty ordinary pass in Two Unit Maths, I'd already worked out that this new position coincided smack dab with that big trip I had planned to go to Europe.

Not anymore.

But I wasn't at all sorry. Besides, I figured Europe was always going to be there; opportunities like those I was being afforded at work might not.

Very quickly, everything at *Dolly* stepped up a notch and the two and a half hours it took every day catching the train to and from Campbelltown no longer made sense.

So, I broke the news to Mum and Dad that I was making the move to the city, and found a place in Paddington. Dad was happy for me and not surprised at all, while Mum worried about whether I was making the right decision.

'Darling, this is all moving so quickly. Are you really sure you're ready for this?'

Mum was right on both counts; I wasn't sure I was ready either. But there was only one way to find out – throw myself in at the deep end and see if I could swim.

*

So much changed with my new role, and Vicki made it clear she trusted me and my ideas completely. The hours were long and my responsibilities had grown significantly, but I loved it, and continued to put my hand up for everything.

And that included heading to a press conference one Sunday morning, at the famed hotel to the stars, the Sebel Townhouse in Elizabeth Bay, as Kiss, the biggest rock band in the world, kicked off their sold-out 'Unmasked' tour of Australia.

The Sebel was known for its intimacy and discretion, and was the hotel of choice for its long list of celebrity guests, Elton John chief amongst them. It boasted of meeting any guest request at any hour of the night or day, as well as an ability to turn a blind eye to the many excesses of stardom.

Autographed photos of past guests and star-studded Sebel events lined each and every wall of its legendary late-night bar and restaurant, and were constant reminders that this was everyone-who-was-anyone's place to be seen. If big names were in town, throngs of teenagers, often holding signs vowing declarations of love, would line the road opposite, screaming for their idols. And this Sunday morning was no different.

I wasn't a particularly huge fan of Kiss or their music, with the band's defiant, lowest-common-denominator machismo, led by its blood-spitting, fire-breathing, tongue-poking bass player Gene Simmons. These days, though, he was becoming increasingly more famous for his long list of celebrity girlfriends, including Diana Ross and Cher (whom he was seeing at the same time at one point). Kiss's lyrics about rocking and rolling all night long and partying every day outraged parents and delighted their children, while their pyrotechnic-led concerts, multi-platinum records, and an estimated 100,000-member-strong Kiss Army in Australia alone, pushed their popularity into the mainstream headlines, so who was I to judge?

Kabuki-style makeup – and four cleverly created cartoon-like alter egos – hid their faces from the world, and in the rock business that manufactured mystique often means money. In Kiss's case, that had produced a more than $100 million turnover from its mostly adolescent-male audience in just the previous year alone.

Even by its own standards, the Sebel had never seen a media turnout like this one, with every major newspaper, radio and TV outlet represented – from Mike Willesee and *Countdown* to ABC News and *Simon Townsend's Wonderworld* – and there to find out what kept the band's crazed fan base coming back for more.

Despite having a seat saved for me right up the front in the second row by my mate Sam from Warner Brothers Publicity, it was hard to see anything at all. As the four band members entered the room in a flamboyant blaze of skin-tight black leather, flailing silvery capes, in-your-face chest hair, and towering eight-inch-high-heeled boots, every photographer in the place stood up and pressed forward, all vying for the best shots of Gene Simmons' 'Demon', Paul Stanley's 'Starchild', Ace Frehley's 'Spaceman' and Eric Carr's 'The Fox'.

Then, as if by magic, in the middle of the packed-out press conference, just as the boys were taking their seats on stage (and to the delight of everyone watching), rose the biggest star in the room … the 'little Aussie bleeder' himself, Norman Gunston.

Gunston's hilarious celebrity interviews – featuring everyone from Paul and Linda McCartney, to Muhammad Ali, Warren Beatty and Mick Jagger – were now the stuff of TV legend around the world, and his comedic ploy of totally disarming his normally media-savvy prey meant we had all just got ourselves a front-row seat to what was sure to be the best show in town. But I think someone forget to inform the guys from Kiss …

Gunston, in his signature bumbling style began, 'OK, can we just sort this out now … which one of you is the construction worker?'

It brought the house down as the gathered press cheered.

The group looked totally confused, and not a little pissed off. This was meant to be *their* moment to shine, and here was some guy in the audience, in an ill-fitting blue tuxedo jacket, a bad combover and pieces of tissue paper on his face (doing nothing to hide what appeared to be freshly bleeding shaving cuts), taking all the limelight.

What the Kiss boys didn't seem to realise was that, for visiting celebrities, having Norman at your press conference was the ultimate compliment. In terms of fame, you had arrived. All you had to do was relax, just play along, and Australian audiences would love you for it.

But with every Norman zinger that delighted all of us in the room, Gene Simmons was growing ever more annoyed. His trick of silently poking out his seven-inch cherry-red tongue – something that normally got the cameras pointed firmly in his direction – just wasn't working, and now Paul Stanley was trying to get in on the gag by suggesting we all cut with the serious questions, because it was time for some mirth.

No-one laughed. There was complete silence. Until Norman chimed in again …

'Can I ask, Mr Frehley, are you over that cold you had when you were interviewed by Mr Molly Meldrum on *Countdown*?'

All eyes turned to Kiss's confused lead guitarist. 'Come again?'

Not missing a beat, Norman continued. 'You know, when you were interviewed by Mr Meldrum? Because your nose kept running, and you kept sniffing all the time … and your face was as white as *snow*!'

Again, cheers from the packed-out room went up. Norman Gunston, as always, the master of speaking truth to celebrity.

The press was loving it as much as the members of Kiss appeared to be hating it. Gene Simmons was clearly not used to losing control in any room he was in, his attempts at humour simply no match for the mastery of Gunston's brilliant one-liners.

Frehley, however, seemingly immune to Gunston's barbs, was now loving it, and wanted to play along.

'Is it true you use more toilet paper on your face than you do on your bum?'

Finally, a laugh for Kiss coming from the press pack, with the loudest from Frehley himself.

By this stage, though, the score was Gunston, 25; Kiss, 1.

It was time for Gunston to cut and run, triumphant. But before he left, he asked about an autograph. 'Sure, come on over,' Simmons said, welcoming him on stage, before Gunston gathered in with notepad and paper, asking, 'Great, who should I make it out to?'

More laughter, and now one quick photo with the band members, who, as if still bewildered by what had just happened, but knowing enough to take the cues of all those flashing cameras, fell into formation around him – with Gunston of course poking his tongue out – before he was gone.

BOOM!

The show was suddenly over. The band looked relieved, until we all realised we were actually there to work, and had to get our own questions in before the band, too, departed. And with that, I squeezed in my one and only question at the press conference, 'Norman is a national treasure. Did you enjoy that?'

The cheesy grimaces on the band members' faces said it all … and with just a few more questions from the room, the promoter called time from the side of the stage, and it was done.

As the film crews, photographers and journalists headed out the door sated by the gold they now had in their clutches, I spied my friend Sam. I told him he looked a little shell-shocked. His job while Kiss was touring the country was to ensure, as much as possible, good publicity for the boys, and to keep them entertained between shows in every new city.

'I'm OK. Not sure about the band. It's Gunston, though,' he said, 'so it'll probably work for us, but I think the boys are a little confused. In fact, I'm just about to take them out on a cruise on the harbour, so I was wondering if you'd like to join us on the boat.'

'Ummm. Sure. But you mean with the *actual* band members?'

'Yeah, but you have to promise me that everything you see remains confidential. The guys won't be wearing their makeup, so you can't put anything in the magazine about that.'

I'm not sure exactly what I was expecting when I arrived at the nearby Double Bay jetty wharf half an hour later, but once I saw the other guests lined up in the Sunday sunshine, I realised I was entering a world in which I was fairly certain I didn't belong: a dozen or so pretty blonde women in an assortment of brightly coloured bikini tops and teeny, tiny shorts were mixing with a similar number of guys, all with wild black hair, black T-shirts, black jeans, silver-studded black belts and black cowboy boots – evidently, the uniform of choice for the rock-and-roll set.

Telling the band members from anyone else in their entourage, however, was difficult; but amongst the girls, I immediately recognised a recent Miss Universe and a Miss World entrant, a couple of 'Page 3 bikini girls' from the afternoon newspapers, as well as a whole bunch of high-profile models. In my sensible long-sleeved, knee-length shirtdress and neat bob haircut, I looked more like I was ready to take dictation than hang out with the cool kids on the harbour.

But hey, I told myself, I was a journalist now. This drawing back the curtains on celebrity had to be good for my showbiz education, and even though I'd promised Sam I wouldn't write about any of this for *Dolly*, maybe one day down the track I would find the right time to tell the story.

I'd never been on Sydney Harbour before (apart from that ferry ride for a school excursion to the Zoo back in Third Form), let alone boarded a luxury cruiser like this one. As I self-consciously handed in my VIP pass and we set sail, I looked around for the one person I knew – Sam – and found him talking to a large group on the top deck, all taking in the delights of the harbour on this stunning Sydney day.

It was only 1 o'clock in the afternoon, but already the French champagne was flowing, the music was blaring, and many of the girls had already splintered off into groups with some of the guys. As I wandered over to Sam – easy to pick out of this line-up, with his strawberry-blond hair, checked shirt and beard – I straight away heard the big American accents of the guys he was talking to.

Sam turned and smiled. 'Hey, great you could make it. Can I introduce you to Gene and Paul?'

And sure enough, there they were, right next to him: a somewhat unrecognisable Gene Simmons on one side, and a more easily identifiable Paul Stanley opposite, both flanked by female companions.

'Um, hi … nice to meet you,' I said, proud I'd even managed to spit out a full sentence in the presence of these global superstars.

'Lisa is the deputy editor at *Dolly* magazine, which is the biggest teen mag in the country,' Sam added by way of introduction.

'Well done at the press conference,' I said, not meaning a word of it, and wondering why the hell I had just mentioned the war. And yet, that now marked two full sentences spoken in something other than gibberish, so *go me*!

Although maybe I still needed a few lessons in small talk, because at this stage neither superstar had contributed a single word to this one-sided conversation. Gene was likely a little distracted by the girl who was … yes, she really was … blowing in his ear.

'Thanks,' he finally said, perhaps to me, but more likely the woman who was blowing in his ear. It was hard to tell.

'So, what time are we planning to dock, Sam?' I asked.

'Probably around five, I reckon.'

It was going to be a looong afternoon.

*

By 4pm, everyone on board had more than a few on board, except me and this nice guy from the Kiss entourage I'd found myself chatting to downstairs, also called Paul. We'd both retreated to the front of the boat to a little sheltered spot out of the wind and the sun.

He, too, was in the rock-and-roll uniform of choice, all black, and with the tell-tale pasty skin of someone who only comes out at night. He told me about growing up in the Bronx in New York, his family life as the youngest of three, and his love of travel. He in turn was fascinated by Australia, my own childhood, and what it was like for me working on a magazine. He wanted to know the best things he could do while he was here, and knowing he probably had to fit everything around the band's performances, I suggested Pancakes on the Rocks at 3am and a trip to Taronga Zoo as a good start.

'Great idea, I want to see one of those koala bears you guys have. Would you come with me? You could show me around Sydney. We could go tomorrow.' Life on the road, he said, was exhausting, and the band's constant partying was taking its toll. He was trying to take a break from alcohol, he went on, and was keen to see something of the city.

Just as I was explaining that I couldn't just take a day off from work without some sort of notice, Sam appeared and broke in, 'Ah, great. I see you've met Ace.'

I turned and looked again at this guy I'd just spent more than an hour talking to.

How could I have not realised? Why hadn't he told me?

'Look, we're about to dock and the captain said he needs us off quickly,' Sam added. 'You guys ready to go?'

Sure. And as we both headed to join the others at the gangplank, me a deep shade of foolishness red, I said to him, 'I thought you said your name was Paul?'

He explained that was his real name, and he only used it because he wanted to have a real conversation with me. 'I wasn't sure if you were a fan … and it always changes things when people are.'

He laughed and added, 'But I could tell pretty quickly you weren't.'

Then he thanked me for the lovely chat.

One last time he tried to convince me to take the next day off, but I politely declined, and Sam directed him to the waiting black stretch limo and away from the fans that had gathered in anticipation of the boat's arrival at the jetty.

And just like that, as the young girls screamed, they were gone.

*

The next day was the deadline for the February issue to head off to the printers, and those hours every month were always frantic, with Vicki and me doing all the final checks and sign-offs on pages that invariably needed last-minute tweaks.

I hadn't even had time to tell the guys at work about the hilarious goings-on at the previous day's press conference, or the quite bizarre harbour cruise that had followed.

So when my phone rang that afternoon, in the middle of a small drama around a missing photo, I only just had time to answer.

'Hi, it's Paul. I mean Ace ... I mean, hi, is that you, Lisa? Sam gave me your number.'

Oh, lord. This was getting weird.

'I was just wondering ... we're off on tour now, but when we get back to Sydney in a few weeks, I have a spare night, and I was wondering if you'd have dinner with me here at the hotel?'

I don't know if it was the lack of time I had to think in that moment, or the implausibility that my diary would already be full at the end of the month, but I said yes.

Remember, this was purely for research purposes, of course. And besides, he seemed like a nice guy – at least from that one small meeting – and nothing like the hard-drinking, hard-partying public image always being portrayed in the press. In any case, I was sure the dinner would be cancelled.

So, when an envelope arrived at work the day before our proposed dinner, with all the details of who I should ask for when I arrived at the Sebel Townhouse restaurant the next evening, I was surprised. I couldn't back out now.

Surprise was soon overshadowed by suspicion early that next night, though, when the maître de at the restaurant told me that Mr Frehley had called down to say he was unwell, and asked if I could join him in his room.

That old trick.

'Did you speak to him?' I asked.

'Yes,' he answered, clearly knowing exactly what I was thinking. 'He didn't sound well at all.'

The restaurant was busy, and just over the sharply dressed attendant's shoulder, there in the darkened back corner, I could see the unmasked face of Gene Simmons, happily ensconced with a young lady, along with a few of the other faces I recognised from the boat. These Sebel staff had seen everything, and I looked once again at the maître de, then across to the lift and asked, 'Did he really sound sick?'

He nodded, and leaned in. 'It's OK. I've seen them all in here. Mr Frehley seems to be one of the nice ones. I'm sure you'll be fine. And if there's any issue, just call the front desk immediately.'

I can't explain why, but I was pretty sure I would be OK. 'Maybe I'll just check on him and make sure he's alright.'

I was soon knocking on the door of the room number I'd been given, unsure what I would find on the other side. With my car keys splayed between my fingers, just in case and just out of sight, one of the biggest rock stars in the world opened his door.

Oh, dear, he really was sick. And even though the early evening summer light was still beaming through the sheer curtains here in his living room, I could see through the open doorway to his darkened bedroom, where it appeared he had been spending most of the day in bed.

'Are you alright?' I asked.

'Not great,' he said through half-lidded eyes. 'But I'm so glad you still came. I'm sorry about dinner, but you can order in. The food downstairs is really good. Order anything you like.'

'Are you sure you're OK to eat?' I asked.

'Not really, but I've got a whole bunch of movies we can watch. Have you seen *The Godfather* yet?'

I hadn't, and on the table next to the TV and video machine were VHS copies of *The Godfather 1* and *2*, *The Deerhunter* and *Kramer vs. Kramer* sitting right next to an almost empty bottle of vodka.

As I walked in, I looked at him again and shook myself back to reality for just a moment. What was this? What was I doing? I was in the hotel room of a man almost ten years my senior. A man with, let's call it, a reputation.

I decided I'd give it ten minutes. Perhaps less.

But over the course of the next few hours – a Caesar salad for me, Berocca for him, and with *The Godfather* playing in the background – Paul/Ace, this guitarist from the Bronx, the youngest son of a church organist, and I talked. His story was as simple as it was extraordinary, as he revealed himself to be just a lonely – albeit ridiculously talented – guy, caught in the most bizarre of circumstances.

Fame, he said, was a bitch. Constantly away from home as he was, he no longer enjoyed the craziness of life on the road, or what it was doing to him. Or more particularly, what he was now doing to himself. Drugs had become a problem, he was no longer close to the guys in the band, and he was looking for a way out.

I wasn't completely sure why he was telling me all this, but this fascinating portrait of celebrity and what it can do to people forever left a mark on me. He was a lesson in how fame, and its many endless temptations and constant free passes on bad behaviour, can corrupt otherwise good souls … if you allowed it. I didn't know it yet, but I would witness it up close, again and again, in the years to come.

Then, just as the darkness outside fully descended on this late November night and the lights of Sydney were starting to twinkle, I looked over at the screen in time to see Marlon Brando's character Vito Corleone had just died. Hang on, was he shot? A heart attack? Dammit. That was, I think, the fourth time I'd tried to watch this movie and lost concentration while simultaneously having a chat.

'Oh well,' I said as I looked over at Paul. But he appeared to have closed his eyes at much the same time as Marlon Brando. And now he was asleep. Fast asleep.

So, I grabbed some notepaper and a pen from the desk, moved aside the bottles and movies on the side table, and left him a note, before quietly letting myself out. And never saw him again.

CHAPTER NINE

Taking charge

'Don't be afraid to go out on a limb. It's where all
the fruit is.' – Frank Scully

Vicki and I were on our way out to Sydney airport to collect four of the finalists for the *Dolly* Cover Girl competition we'd launched just the year before. Thankfully, the traffic this Friday night was better than anticipated, so with time to kill, we settled into the bar at the Ansett terminal for a drink before the first of the no-doubt nervous and excited state finalists arrived.

For many of them, this would be their first-ever plane ride and trip to Sydney. For one of them, it would result in a starring role on the cover of the December issue of *Dolly*. And who knew what awaited them from there?

'I've got some news,' Vicki said, just as I was returning from the bar with a couple of lemonades, 'and I may as well tell you now before somebody else does.'

She had to be pregnant, so I smiled, indicating I had already guessed.

'No, I'm not having a baby if that's what you're thinking.'

Vicki told me she was, in fact, heading overseas on an extended break through Europe with her husband, Peter, for six months, and she wasn't sure that she would be coming back to *Dolly*.

Great. Just as things were really moving forward, and we'd started to take *Dolly* out of the deep circulation dive it had been in under Mrs Goldie, the band was breaking up.

I was happy for Vicki – she was doing exactly what I had hoped to do not 12 months before and maybe, one day, still would – but a new editor could signal huge change for me. What if this new person and I didn't click, or they didn't appreciate my slightly bolshie ideas on what was right for the magazine and this wonderful audience I really cared about?

'But who's going to be the new editor?' I asked, fearing her response.

And I'll never forget the silence echoing off the dark-green walls and sticky formica tabletops of this tiny booth at Sydney airport as Vicki just looked at me and smiled.

'It's you,' she said.

I was gobsmacked. Me? They'd chosen *me*?

I looked at Vicki, not believing what I was hearing. How could this possibly be? And then we hugged, for the longest time, just as the announcement came over the loudspeaker that the flight from Brisbane we were waiting on had arrived.

So that was it. I was about to become the new editor of *Dolly*, with all of Vicki's wonderful blessings. In the Ansett terminal at Sydney airport. Drinking lemonade. At 21.

I didn't really have a '21st'. I didn't want the fuss. For all the confidence I was starting to gain at work, the memories of that deeply embarrassing fifth birthday party were still strong enough that all I wanted was a quiet family dinner at the local golf club. And I hated golf clubs. They always felt more like boys' clubs, where women were merely tolerated rather than welcomed. But in Campbelltown it was a choice between that or the local RSL. So, the golf club it was. Tia came along, Mum got a birthday cake, and it was a nice enough night, but even I knew there was something a bit sad about it. Fortunately, this big new appointment at work more than made up for it.

Unfortunately, if I was expecting champagne corks and congratulations at Sungravure over my promotion, I soon realised they were probably going to be in short supply. With the company full to overflowing with so many other women's magazines, I just knew there would be fully trained-up journalists all over the building with bucket-loads more experience than me thinking, *Who the hell does this trumped-up little typist think she is?*

Truth is, I was thinking exactly the same thing.

That said, I did get one call of congratulations from a kindly, somewhat elderly Fairfax board member, who rang to wish me a helluva lot more luck with the teenage population of Australia than he was currently having with his 15-year-old daughter ...

But those naysayers couldn't have done me a bigger favour. With their predictions of certain failure ringing in my ears, I was determined that this role, this moment – however long it would last – was mine for the taking. I had one shot, and I was going to *do* this!

So, as Vicki headed off on her big trip to Europe, and I further pushed back my own plans to see the world, I knew that my first and most important mission had to be to gain the trust of the team. My staff. A term I couldn't even believe I was thinking, let alone using.

The tricky thing was, most of them had been in their exact same positions when I'd walked through the door just a couple of years before, hoping to be good enough to make *them* coffee and answer the phones. Now I was their boss. If this was all going to work, I had to bring everyone along with me on this new road we would be travelling – hopefully together. Indeed, I'd landed into this role so quickly that no-one had really got around to teaching me any of the specific rules of *being* a boss. So I wrote a few of my own. And probably broke plenty.

I encouraged regular think-tank sessions, and I was honest with the team about what I didn't know. I also sought advice from other editors in the building. I had strong ideas about the way forward, but I also knew you learn nothing when you're doing all the talking. So, I made sure I also did plenty of listening, particularly to our readers.

As to a new office, I didn't really get one. *Dolly* had recently moved to the fourth floor, next to the ultra-glamorous space occupied by our sister mag, *Cosmopolitan*, with its city views, all-white interior and super chic editor Sylvia Rayner. At the other end of the floor were the hushed, spacious offices occupied by management. *Dolly* got the corridor in between the two, with just some frosted glass separating us from the constant foot traffic to and from management, the incessant noise of the building's clunky old lift and, right outside our door, the industrial-strength telex machine that whirred into life 24 hours a day, delivering up the latest news from our New York and London bureaus.

Hearing yourself think in our open-plan office over that combined chorus, along with our constantly ringing phones, the bash-bash-bash of manual typewriters and general office chat was a challenge. But I had plenty to keep me focused, so I became very good at just tuning out and powering on.

The first thing I was desperate to do was change the whole look of the magazine. I was clear on how to get the words and the tone of the magazine right – and that was to treat our readers as the intelligent, compassionate, curious and fun-loving young women I knew them to be – but if I couldn't get the visuals right, then how could I possibly communicate this new chapter for the magazine to potential *new* readers?

Dolly needed an urgent update, and I had a brilliant art team in Ron and Peter, who were just as keen as I was to give the magazine a more contemporary feel, particularly photographically. Unfortunately, however, that was going to cost money – money, I was told, I didn't have.

The problem was, Sungravure had its own in-house photographic department, and budget constraints meant there was a pool of snappers I was told we had to use. These guys were nothing if not versatile. Need a good close-up shot of the latest transistor-radio connectors for Electronics Australia? Or perhaps an extra little glisten on top of that cheesy macaroni bake for *Woman's Day*, or maybe a shot of Grandma in her rocker to go with that hook-stitch crochet rug pattern for the new issue of *Woman's World*? Then the Sungravure photographic department had a lens-man for you.

But getting those same photographers to understand the new, relaxed yet confident look and attitude that I now wanted for *Dolly*'s pages, and most crucially, our covers, was nigh on impossible. Sure, we'd recently done covers in that very studio featuring two promising young Hollywood actors – Brooke Shields from *Blue Lagoon* and Diane Lane from *A Little Romance* – while they'd both been on flying publicity visits to Sydney, but the final results made both of them look like brightly coloured rabbits caught in headlights.

No matter how often I asked management, the money just wasn't in the budget to use the freelance photographers that every other lifestyle and fashion magazine in the market, including our sister magazine, *Cosmopolitan*, were using. I wanted to start shooting outside, on location, away from static-looking studios, and take advantage of all that beautiful Australian light.

And blow me down if that isn't exactly what that scruffy guy who just walked into the office was hoping, too. Just behind the tiny partition that separated my office from reception, I heard the heavy 'click' of the glass door as it opened and … was that a dog barking? I looked up.

'Hi, my name's Graham Shearer, and I'm wondering if I could see Lisa Wilkinson.'

Oh, my lord. I recognised the name straight away. *This* was a photographer whose work I loved. For months, every time I saw a model's portfolio with particularly stunning shots and I asked who took the pic, the answer was always the same: 'Oh, Graham Shearer took that.'

Graham was a ridiculously handsome former model, who turned up to see me in board shorts straight from a surf at Bondi, along with his equally dishevelled shaggy-haired, bandana-wearing dog, Ralph. Graham was clearly a pretty chilled dude and try as I might to act the same when he appeared before me, it just wasn't possible.

'THAT's ME!' I squealed as I bounced out of my seat and ushered him and the wet, sandy Ralph back into my office. Heck, I would have grabbed Graham by the collar had he been wearing one, so excited was I by his work and the fact he even knew my name.

As he opened up his large portfolio, I couldn't believe the stunning array of work I was seeing, or what I was hearing. I presumed Graham had been working for many years, so extensive was his body of work, but he was in fact just starting out as a fashion photographer, and all those photos I'd been seeing were all just 'tests', as he was learning his craft with similarly inexperienced models. And the real kicker? Graham was really keen to work for … did he really just say, *us*?

He, too, thought we really needed to update our look, and he was, he told me with absolute confidence, just the guy to achieve it. All he needed was for me to give him his editorial start.

The whole conversation was music to my ears, and in the space of an unexpected 15 minutes, all of my wishes seemed to be coming true.

Now, though, came the difficult part. As much as I was desperate to work with Graham, I explained, I simply had no money to pay him. The thing was, we both had something the other wanted: I wanted his work in my magazine, and he wanted my editorial 'tear sheet' pages in his portfolio. Editorial work was where photographers got to exercise some creative freedom and take the photos they loved … but it was also what drove the advertising jobs which was where, for photographers like Graham, the really big bucks were.

So, I had to think smart, and come up with a plan – a bit of creative accounting, for want of a better description. I worked out that I was already paying all the film and processing costs for what we shot in our photographic department with our staff photographers, so I suggested that I just quietly pay all those costs for Graham instead, quickly help build up his editorial tear sheets and, if we started seeing the results in our circulation – as I was positive would happen – I promised I would fight the case with management that we *had* to start paying him.

We had a deal.

And just as I had hoped, from the moment Graham's stunning work started appearing in the magazine, the circulation lifted, and I won the financial argument with management. Graham was finally being paid. I now had a firm foothold on the magazine I'd always imagined *Dolly* could be.

The added bonus was, as well as his faithful companion Ralph who accompanied him on every shoot, Graham also had a brilliant

French stylist wife in Pasha. Together they were a collaborative powerhouse, and with Kathy having moved on, Pasha soon joined the team as my new fashion editor.

The new look lifted everyone. Ron and Pete were over the moon. And word was spreading. *Dolly* was on the move. From the 130,000 or so copies we had been selling every month, we quickly climbed to well over 200,000 within 18 months.

*

My share-accommodation digs in Paddington hadn't exactly worked out. My flatmate, a super confident Canadian stockbroker, turned out to have a bad habit of forgetting his keys after big nights out – usually on days ending in 'y' – and I grew a little tired of waking up to him banging on the door to let him in. At 2am. Again.

It became the perfect excuse for Tia and me to finally get a flat together, this time across the harbour in a tiny little apartment at the back of a big old Federation house in North Sydney.

Tia was working as a production assistant at the ABC and dating, on and off, a lovely guy called Quentin who also worked at Aunty. That was him on the phone right now, inviting us both over to watch the New Year's Eve fireworks down by the harbour as the calendar clicked over into 1982.

Tia had been vowing that this seesaw relationship she'd been in with the irresistible Quentin these last couple of years was over, but all it took was one phone call, and we were on our way to pick him up from his home in nearby Cremorne in my trusty brown Gemini – us bringing pizza, and Quentin bringing his good mate Chris. We headed down to the harbour through the bumper-to-bumper traffic, then battled to find a spot on the crowded foreshore in time for the stroke of 12 o'clock. Somehow, we lost Tia and Quentin early on, but no matter.

Chris, it turned out, also worked at the ABC, as a music and radio producer at Radio National, and as Sydney delivered up its usual magical light show at midnight, we found ourselves talking, there on the grassy verge above the water's edge, well into the early hours.

The attraction was instant. He, a lover of classical music, theatre and books, me the girl from Campbelltown, making it in the somewhat less highbrow world of magazines. Of course, no-one thought we fitted, but we did, and six months later, with the lease on the place with Tia now expired, Chris and I set up house together in nearby Neutral Bay.

*

If there was a single ad that entranced Australian TV audiences beyond all others in the early 80s, it was one for Tab diet cola, a brand-new soft drink squarely aimed at young women. It was also the launchpad for a statuesque young model by the name of Elle Macpherson, as she languidly, mesmerisingly, wandered along a generic Aussie shoreline in the teeniest of red bikinis, hair wet, lifting that hot pink can to her lips, driving young boys crazy, and young girls straight to the drinks aisle at the supermarket – not to mention the beach.

In fact, at the time, beach culture was everywhere. Ken Done's brightly coloured sun-sand-and-surf art was plastered on everything from T-shirts to tea towels and bedsheets, Sun In spray was the hottest selling and fastest way to get those summery 'sun-kissed' hair highlights, and 'tan-thru' bikinis were the easiest way to ensure no 'ugly' tan lines after a day basting at the beach. It was the look every girl was aspiring to, or at least that was the popular belief.

So, putting a totally unknown, fair-skinned, freckle-faced, corkscrew-curled 15-year-old redhead on the cover of *Dolly* at that time would have been, for many, simply unthinkable. But that was exactly what Graham had in mind when he and Ralph bounded through the glass doors of our office on this sunny Saturday afternoon in late March.

Ron, Pete and I were working right through the weekend on the upcoming July issue because the giant tear-out Michael Jackson poster we were running that month had brought all of our deadlines forward.

Jackson's album, *Thriller* – with its thumping hits like 'Beat It' and 'Billie Jean' – was dominating every record player, pop-music station and record chart in the country, and Jackson was the biggest star on the planet, so everything was being rushed through, and there was no time to waste. But so far, we still didn't have a cover.

Graham was always on the lookout for new faces and had rung the day before to say he'd found someone really special. She was still at school, he said, so there was no chance for me to meet with her before the Saturday cover shoot. He was sure I would love her, but wanted me to know that her look was a little different – so he asked me to trust him.

By this stage, I had total trust in Graham and Pasha; together, they were a brilliant team. But they also welcomed my direction, and the results – our circulation just continued to climb – now spoke for themselves. But Graham knew the pressure was on for this edition. He understood that this shoot was the last chance we had to make sure the cover went to press on time. This shoot simply *had* to be a good one.

So, as Ralph leaped through the door that afternoon, followed closely by Graham with a clutch of Polaroids in his hand and a big smile on his face, I figured the results of the shoot were a success. Graham said he'd left Pasha and the model waiting at the studio, just in case I wanted some tweaks to the look before they finished for the day.

Before I could see the Polaroids, though, Graham wanted me to know a few things: the young woman had only just started doing a bit of modelling and was, he said, a big fan of the magazine. She'd already even submitted an entry for the *Dolly* Cover Girl competition. Her dream was to eventually make it in acting, and even though she'd just finished filming her movie debut, which would be coming out at Christmas, getting this *Dolly* cover, she said, could be her big break.

Which was all well and good, but where were the pics, and why was he stalling?

Finally, with Ralph still glued to his heels, Graham excitedly thrust a dozen or so Polaroids on my desk.

And there she was. Red-haired, brooding, beatific and beautiful.

With his ability to perfectly capture that relaxed, fun-loving, sun-kissed Aussie look always assured, Graham had this time delivered instead something quite different: a completely arresting portrait, full of autumnal tones, of an utterly compelling young woman, with a most exquisite face, framed by a stunning halo of untamed Titian hair and kissed with a sweet sprinkling of something you simply never saw on magazine covers: freckles.

'Do you like it? I know it's not what we normally do. And not smiling? Are you OK with her not smiling?' Graham asked.

I LOVED it. I loved it all. I told him not to change a thing. And to let Pasha and the model, still awaiting instructions back at the studio, know that they were done for the day – we had ourselves our July cover.

*

By now, *Dolly*'s numbers – circulation and bottom line – were busting all budget predictions, and as the months and years rolled by it had become no more than an occasional courtesy to show the boss any of our covers before they went to press.

Every one of my general managers – I'd now seen three come and go – seemed so unsure about what it was that was working so well behind that wall of frosted glass down the corridor at *Dolly*, that their policy appeared to be no more strategic than leaving me well enough alone and happily counting the dollars as they poured in. Which suited me just fine.

But this time, I figured I just might do my boss the courtesy. This cover was a dramatically different look, and I wanted to prepare him. Not that I had any intention of changing anything. And to ensure that, I even waited a couple of days until I knew the July issue had safely arrived at our printing presses in Singapore before showing him.

My GM at that point was a guy called Peter Gaunt, a tall bespectacled Brit with a penchant for pin-striped suits and long lunches. He'd come from ad sales over at Fairfax, so it was well known that editorial wasn't exactly his thing. He was a 'dollars' man with confidence to burn when it came to the ladies, and as old-school as it gets.

'I've got something I'd like to show you,' I said as I knocked on his door, hoping a quick unannounced drop-in would keep things low-key. 'It's my latest cover,' I added.

'Sure, come on in, I'd love to see it,' he said as I put the mocked-up cover down on his desk.

He looked at me. Then looked down at the cover. Then back up at me.

...

'She's got red hair,' he said, observantly.

'I know, isn't it fabulous?!' I replied.

'But she ... isn't smiling?'

'Nup, but look how strong and confident she is, Peter,' I added, helpfully.

'And,' he said, as he leaned in and pushed his glasses further up the bridge of his nose, still unsure of what he was seeing, 'are they ... are they, freckles?'

'Yep, beautiful, aren't they?'

He looked at me again, then, squinting, looked down one last time and appeared to be imagining how the cover would look without them.

'So ... you're not getting rid of them?'

'Nope, I love them!' I answered.

This time he looked away and out through his large office windows, to the view of the city skyline in the distance.

'I'm not sure your advertisers will like this,' he offered, proving that once an ad man, always an ad man. 'But ... it's your magazine, so it can be on your head if it doesn't sell,' he said.

'Thanks, Peter, appreciate the feedback, but you know plenty of our readers *have* freckles? And red hair?'

He was unmoved, so I decided to quit while I was ahead.

'Anyway, good to get your thoughts, Peter. I think we're on to a winner, so let's leave it to the readers to decide.'

In the end, that's exactly what our wonderful readers did. The July 1983 issue, with the Michael Jackson poster and a young model by the name of Nicole Kidman on the front cover, was my first-ever sold-out issue.

*

One thing I wasn't anticipating with my new role was just how differently I would be treated. I hadn't changed at all, but some of those around me certainly had.

It was all perfectly summed up by one woman from *Dolly*'s ad sales department. She was one of a tribe of glamorous sales reps who spent their days teetering in high heels as they raced between various ad agencies, building business relationships with the powerful over long, often boozy, lunches where those big-dollar advertising deals were clinched for the magazine.

When we first met, I was the lowest on anyone's pecking order and super keen to please, so I copped her rudeness towards me on the chin. I was clearly just some kid who could do nothing for her, save for when she snapped her fingers on the way past my desk through to another meeting in Mrs Goldie's office, which translated, I worked out, to getting her a coffee, quick-smart.

Now I was the editor? Well, sucking up would be putting it mildly. She was a woman who was only interested in being where the power was. It was awful to be around.

Yet, I will always be grateful for what that woman unwittingly taught me: to never ever *be* her. I vowed to always remember what being on the weak side of a power imbalance felt like. As Dad had always taught me, the mark of a person is how they treat those who can do nothing for them.

It was an excellent lesson to learn early on.

*

From a distance, it was clear to me that TV was a cut-throat, high-pressure arm of the media I had no desire to work in. But when I got a call to be a guest on the pilot for a TV show hosted by Ita Buttrose, it was hard to say no.

Ita had made headlines around the country a few years before after a very public falling-out with Kerry Packer, leaving the *Women's Weekly* to work under Rupert Murdoch as editor-in-chief of the *Daily* and *Sunday Telegraph* newspapers. Now that she was widely known as 'the most admired woman in Australia', Rupert had reportedly also promised Ita her very own in-the-round-style chat show on Channel 10, in the image of the two biggest US daytime talk show hosts of the day: Phil Donahue and Sally Jessy Raphael.

I'd never been lucky enough to meet this legend of Australian magazine publishing, and her iconic status had only hit even greater heights with the release of a Cold Chisel song simply called 'Ita', from their chart-topping album *East*. In anyone's eyes, or ears, it simply didn't *get* much bigger than that, so it was an honour to have even been asked on to her new show, and I hoped that at some point afterwards I might get the chance to have a quick one-on-one chat with her.

I'd been invited on to discuss issues around sex education and why, in the much more enlightened 80s, so many young girls were still falling pregnant, despite contraception now being much more freely available. It was an issue I had strong ideas about, so any nerves I'd previously had as I drove out to the Channel 10 studios at North Ryde about appearing in front of all those studio cameras, and actually talking to the great Ita Buttrose, melted away after her very first question.

For someone so new to TV, her command of the audience and the flow of conversation between all the various guests that day was impressive, as was her beauty. Photos simply didn't do Ita justice.

As a former editor of *Cleo*, and mother to a now-teenage Kate (whose childhood stories were so often the subject of her mum's *Women's Weekly* columns), Ita agreed wholeheartedly that giving every teenager access to proper, informed sex education from an early age was the only answer. Everything I'd studied on the issue consistently showed that, for teen girls, knowledge was power – most particularly the power to say no – and the more knowledge girls had around the whole issue of consent, and what that actively looked like, the longer they delayed their first sexual experience.

Tragically, though, those letters to Dolly Doctor continued to tell the same alarming story: that, too often, both parents and schools found the issue too difficult to tackle, and too many girls as a result were being left vulnerable. It saddened me that the responsibility of addressing the issue of consent then fell to the pages of *Dolly*, but ultimately we had no choice. They simply had nowhere else to go. With well over a million sets of young female eyes on us every month, we *had* to pick up the slack. And I was up for it.

From my own experience I knew that, at its best, *Dolly* was an Aussie teenager's first real understanding of her body. It was a trusted, non-judgmental, reassuring friend, and a reliable source of information on all that confused us. It encouraged us to be independent but also nurtured our broken hearts. It helped us to find and celebrate our very best selves, and to enjoy and take charge of our own bodies.

Convincing some of our readers' more conservative parents that that had become our role, however, sometimes proved a little more difficult. After all, it was often their money that purchased that copy of *Dolly*, and it was their eyes that would also scan its pages each month to ensure the influence we were having on their daughters was a positive one.

Thankfully, for many parents, it helped ease a path to opening up the topic with their daughters at home, so that had to be a good thing. I hoped, too, that by appearing on Ita's show, I could further help to spread that important message.

What no-one tells you about TV, though, is that minutes can pass by in seconds, and before I knew it, the show was over. Just like that. Ita was then swamped by producers and sound people ushering her behind a large black curtain, while here in the studio I, and the various other guests in these tiered audience seats, were led back into the Channel 10 foyer and towards the car park beyond.

I never did get to talk to Ita privately that day, but it didn't matter. A short time later, something much more precious happened. A letter, in the most beautiful handwriting arrived at the *Dolly* office, marked as 'Private & Confidential' and addressed to me.

Dear Lisa,
I just wanted to personally thank you for agreeing to appear on the pilot of my show, *Ita*. You were most eloquent on the

topics we discussed, and I genuinely appreciate you taking the time out of your day. Unfortunately, at this stage it would appear that the show is not going ahead in its current form, but if anything changes I am sure the producers will be in touch. On a more personal note, I just wanted to say congratulations on the excellent job you are doing at *Dolly*. As the mother of a teenage daughter I am so glad that the magazine is in such capable hands.

Warm regards,

Ita.

Just ... wow. I treasured that letter. And I will never forget the way it made me feel. It was a small, generous gesture from Ita, but the impact on me as a young woman still finding her way in the media and the professional world? Enormous.

*

Around this time, I was invited to have another crack at daytime TV, also at Channel 10, but now it was to be on a much more established show, *Beauty & the Beast*. *B&B*, as it was often referred to, was a program that had already spanned almost two decades on Australian TV and one that I vaguely remembered Mum having on at lunchtime back in the days before I'd headed off to big school.

The panel-style format was a simple one: one high-profile bombastic male 'beast' in the middle reading out viewers' letters and thereby initiating discussion – from the heartfelt to the argumentative – amongst four famous female faces who filled the role of 'beauties'.

Legendary names, such as John Laws, Eric Baume, Derryn Hinch and Stuart Wagstaff, had all filled the Beast role to varying degrees of success over the years; while a rotating roster of well-known women – from the ABC's silky smooth Margaret Throsby and Channel 9's Sue Smith (the first woman in Australia to host her own TV current affairs show) to film producer Patricia Lovell (better known by many as Miss Pat on TV's *Mr Squiggle*, and to others as the powerhouse producer behind the multi-award-winning film *Gallipoli* starring Mel Gibson) and arch-conservative Ena Harwood (famous for being … an arch-conservative). All strong, accomplished female voices with serious runs on the board … and every single one of them struck the fear of God into me. And yet, the man who had recently taken over the role of 'Beast', the famously grumpy Clive Robertson, didn't.

Clive's razor-sharp mind, dry wit, exquisite voice and daily banter with the highly respected Caroline Jones on 2BL breakfast had become the stuff of ABC radio legend. Clive needling, Caroline exquisitely warm, assured and unflappable. On that daily exchange alone, he was the perfect choice.

But I was in my early twenties – the youngest on the panel by nearly two decades. What on earth did I know? I think I was there to offer 'the young person's' perspective; but really, what sort of 'advice' and life experience could I possibly bring to the table?

Personally, Clive and I instantly clicked. On camera, though, I struggled, and the other women, while welcoming, could see it. And they were right. TV was just not for me, and so after a half-dozen or so pretty underwhelming guest appearances at the panel desk (where I proved to have a quite bizarre tendency to overshare), I went back to concentrating on my real job – magazines – my much more natural home.

Somehow, I never struggled with the way forward at *Dolly*. Every time a decision needed to be made – from the words on the page to the images we published or the best ways to connect with new readers – I just seemed to instinctively know what to do. I found I had a talent for finding talent too – particularly when it came to young writers keen to get a foothold in the industry and, just as Nicole Kidman's star was now well and truly on the rise, other models like Sarah Nursey had become superstars in their own right with our readers.

And as one year in the editor's chair turned into two, three and four, our tight-knit, highly skilled team were kicking goals we could have only ever dreamt of. By the October 1984 issue, *Dolly*'s circulation had hit 320,000, and the company was over the moon.

The bosses wanted more, and Sandra Yates, a sharp-shouldered raven-haired powerhouse of an executive now running the advertising and marketing departments in the company, came to me with a plan. She wanted to take *Dolly* into the US market. Sandra said she'd done her research and *Dolly* was the perfect formula. She was convinced the existing magazines, like *Seventeen*, *Tiger Beat* and *Glamour*, were looking conservative and tired; but with *Dolly*'s sassy mix of straight-talking editorial and signature spirited look, she said she just knew we had the product to take the US by storm.

There was just one problem: the name. *Dolly*. Ah yes, the name. Over the years, we'd *all* had the discussion about that bizarre name. No-one seemed to quite know the origins of 'Dolly', but word was that it came from a late 60s term – 'Dolly bird', apparently a compliment at the time, though not so much anymore.

Somehow there just never seemed to be the right time – or the significant amount of money needed – to mount the massive marketing campaign it would take for a successful name change. We simply consoled ourselves with the idea that the name had become generic and forged on.

Thrilled by Sandra's proposal, and her desire for me to be at the helm of this US venture – *Dolly*'s first foray into the international market – we started workshopping all kinds of new names. Something stronger. Something that spoke to teens of all ages, not just up to the very limiting age of 'seventeen'. Something … something … something … *sassy*?

How about that for a name?

And so, *Sassy* magazine was born. We were going in.

These were special times. I'd never worked harder, but every day was a joy. Mum and Dad had just gone on their first-ever trip to Europe, and Dad had retired from Cyclone, only to be snapped up just weeks later to become Secretary of Sydney Rugby Union. I had never seen him happier. Meanwhile, Chris and I had just become engaged, and were feeling confident enough that we might just be able to put down a deposit on our first apartment together.

Which got me thinking. I had no idea what the going rate was for a magazine editor – salaries were never discussed amongst the women in the building. Apart from my promotion to A-grade journalist when I became the editor, I hadn't had a single pay rise since.

It was a pretty good wage, particularly for someone who'd come from the reception desk – but that wasn't the point, really. Was my overwhelming gratitude for the opportunities I'd been given now standing in the way of me being paid what I was actually worth? With *Dolly*'s balance sheet now many, many millions in the black since I'd taken over, surely a decent pay rise in recognition of that wouldn't be out of the question?

So, after weeks of trying to pluck up the courage – and figuring I had nothing to lose – I went to see my boss and present what I was sure was a very strong case for a long-overdue pay rise. *Dolly* was now the company's highest-performing magazine on a dollars-return basis and had been for the past three years. And if that wasn't enough to convince him, there was also that small matter of the significant job I had ahead establishing *Dolly* … sorry, *Sassy* … in the US.

By this stage there was yet another new general manager in the building, a sober-suited former accountant called John Hemming, whose uncanny likeness to rising British politician John Major always threw me whenever we met up.

The other thing I found unsettling as I stood there in his office was his desk, with its completely spotless surface, save for four evenly distanced Bic pens of every colour – red, black, blue and green – all with lids securely in place, and lined up on his desk, next to two perfectly sharpened HB pencils, and one always-unopened Spirax notepad.

All up, my meeting with him turned out to be a pretty quick affair. John Hemming said he had been anticipating this day for six months, and now that I had asked, he was very proud to say that he could offer me another $1000.

'One thousand dollars?' I repeated. 'As in a year? As in, less than twenty dollars a week?'

'Yes. I even had it approved by the board six months ago, so I can put it straight through, starting next month,' he added, clearly pleased with himself.

'So, you had this approved six months ago, but never told me? And it's already approved, but you still can't put it through until next month?' Who does that?

The man standing in front of me with a big smile on his face does. And did.

I stopped for a moment to gather my thoughts, trying to get clear what I had just heard.

'I thought you'd be thrilled,' he said, clearly a little crestfallen that his 20-dollar pay rise didn't have me jumping through hoops.

'Um, can you let me think about it?' was all I could say.

Then, as I walked out of his office, I looked back and, always the polite, well-brought-up girl, said, 'Thanks, John.'

'No problem, Lisa,' he said, before adding breezily, 'It'll only take one phone call to put that pay rise through, so just let me know,' as he opened that Spirax notepad and started writing. With, weirdly, that green pen.

CHAPTER TEN

Meeting Kerry

'If you're afraid to dive, then just dive
afraid.' – popularised by Viola Davis

As I MADE MY way back to my office from John Hemming's, I felt like an idiot. Was I kidding myself? Sure, I was a Girl Friday–made-good; sure, they'd given me lots of opportunities; and, sure, I'd never asked for a pay rise before. But surely the job I'd done – and my polite patience when it came to my salary – counted for something? (And who the hell writes with green pens, anyway?)

Like so many women of my generation and every generation before me, I knew the gender pay gap was real, but the magazine industry was almost exclusively dominated by female editors. We were running multi-million-dollar businesses, and the buck literally stopped with us. There were no blokes that could do what we were doing. There were also no blokes, I was sure, who would have copped a 20-dollar pay rise. Or even been offered such a piddling amount.

For more than four years, I'd successfully negotiated my way in and out of sticky financial deals for the magazine, stood in heavyweight boardrooms and convinced huge advertisers to put all their dollars into *Dolly*; I'd swallowed my fear and addressed young girls in packed-out school auditoriums about the evils of bullying and the magic that can come from swallowing your fear, believing in yourself and just going for it. But when it came to negotiating my own worth, I was out of my depth. I had no idea how it worked. No-one was teaching that stuff. Particularly to women.

The company had me over a barrel because, really, what were my options? I was in awe of the team I got to work with every day. I loved the relationship I had with our readers. Management knew I was grateful to even have the job, and for the creative freedom I'd been given to do what I wanted with the magazine without interference – to their advantage, as it happened.

I was invested. I didn't want to do anything else. And my boss knew it. I was my own worst enemy.

For the first time, I was pissed off.

Buying the apartment would now be a serious stretch. And frustrating as the conversation I'd just had might have been, was it actually an important signal? Chris had been telling me I was working far too hard. Maybe I needed to take the pressure off and forget about buying the apartment. With the magazine doing so well, maybe I should just start to relax a little, stop working such incredibly long hours, and go with Chris to Europe and have a decent holiday, starting with the place we had long wanted to go to, France. I decided to give Chris a call as soon as I got back to my office.

Dolly had recently moved down a floor and, as the lift doors opened at Level 3, it was just in time for me to farewell most of my team heading home for the weekend. That afternoon we'd settled on the latest cover, another featuring our favourite, Sarah Nursey, so we knew we had another big seller in the works.

As I walked back to my desk, I noticed that my assistant Lisa McDiarmid was still packing up. Lisa was a one-off. A diehard Boy George fan, she often came to work in outfits inspired by the pop star's audacious style; and when one of the record companies sent me a huge handmade cloth doll of the British superstar – one of only ten in the world – there was just one person I knew should have it.

Every weekday, Lisa had that doll sitting on her desk, an amusing sight for anyone arriving in reception for the first time. On weekends, Lisa took her treasured George home and was about to do just that as I wandered through the office and took my seat back at my desk, still trying to take in my conversation with John Hemming.

There, on the top of the pile of work I had already gathered to take home for the weekend, was a white 'While You Were Out' note torn from Lisa's phone-message pad: 'Trevor Kennedy called. Please ring him back on 282 8000.'

I stared at the note … Surely not.

Trevor Kennedy was the former editor of Kerry Packer's august and powerful weekly business magazine, *The Bulletin*. Now he was in charge of all the Australian Consolidated Press magazines, including the *Women's Weekly*. As a company, ACP was the great magazine rival to Sungravure.

Why on earth would he be calling me? My heart was racing. How did he even know who I was? I called out to Lisa in as calm a voice as I could muster.

'Honey, when did this call come through from Trevor Kennedy?'

'A few minutes ago,' she said, 'you just missed him. 'Night. Have a great weekend.'

'Yeah … you too …' I said, only half listening.

I stared at the note again. Maybe I should just ignore it. Yeah, there had to be a mistake.

Cleo was also part of the portfolio of magazines Kennedy was running, and now probably the closest thing *Dolly* had to a competitor. Indeed, one of my strategies in building the *Dolly* audience over the years had been to do all I could to delay our devoted readers' progression to the more sophisticated *Cleo*.

I always figured if I could capitalise on that enduring soft spot our readers had for *Dolly* during their teenage years, while keeping our content sharp, intelligent and relevant to the widest possible age range, it might just give us another six, maybe even 12, months of loyal readership, and surely that meant our numbers would keep growing – while probably not doing a lot for *Cleo*'s. I was right on both counts.

Word in the industry was that *Cleo*'s numbers had been slipping in recent times, while our December issue was already tracking as a sell-out; and if the early projected numbers I was seeing for January were realised, then that issue would hit a record 350,000. These were figures that were unimaginable when I took over.

But what to do with this darn note. I knew I wouldn't be able to think straight over the weekend. Ah, what the hell ...

I grabbed the handset from the phone on my desk and dangled it in mid-air. Its long plastic cord had, yet again, annoyingly coiled itself into a series of strangled knots through constant use, and as I patiently watched the twirling handset do its merry dance, I was thankful for the opportunity to disentangle my own racing thoughts.

What could this call possibly be about? Was I about to get a talking-to? Those executives and editors over at ACP headquarters in Park Street in the city had pretty full-on reputations, so maybe that was the way they did things? Call and intimidate the opposition.

Whatever he had to say, I could take it. He wasn't my boss. There was nothing to be nervous about, I assured myself, as I pulled the phone to my ear, dialled the number, and asked to be put through to Mr Kennedy's office. I was proud of myself that I was dealing with this right now so I could go home to Chris and finally start planning that long-awaited trip to Europe.

'Hello,' a deep, if slightly distracted male voice answered. What, no secretary? Had I just been put straight through?

'Hello, is that Trevor Kennedy? It's Lisa Wilkinson returning your call,' I said tentatively.

'Lisa!' he said, now warmly. 'Thanks so much for ringing back.'

Far from the threatening demeanour I was fearing, Trevor was not only charming, he was full of compliments. He said he liked what I'd done with *Dolly*, had watched its growth in recent years, and simply wanted to know more about me and how I'd done it.

While I had no intention of telling him any of that – particularly when it came to my strategy of stealing readers away from *Cleo* – somehow, over the course of that one phone call, I agreed to have lunch with him.

Apart from the odd snatched moment at sleepovers at Christine's mum's house, I can't say that I did spend a lot of my teenage years buried between the pages of *Cleo*. I couldn't – my mum wouldn't let me: it did, after all, have that naked male centrefold. Besides, at the time of *Cleo*'s launch, I had just started high school and was way too interested in whether or not I would ever get to meet Greg Brady from *The Brady Bunch* to care.

But no matter. My job now, and before that lunch next week, was to find out all I could about Trevor Kennedy. A former editor of the *National Times*, he'd cut his journalistic teeth at Fairfax, then made the move to work with Kerry Packer. At one stage, he was said to have seriously locked horns with Ita Buttrose in a battle for editorial control at the highest levels of ACP. Now, with Ita gone, he was running the entire magazine division, and had started to preside over other areas of the wider group of Packer business interests. He was now seen as Packer's most trusted right-hand man.

So, when Trevor and I met over lunch at a charming little first-floor French restaurant in King Street in the middle of the city, I was as prepared as I could be; and with what I was sure would be a common love of magazines, I figured we would have plenty to chat about.

And we did, for almost two hours. Enjoyable as it was, however, a two-hour lunch on a workday was a rarity for me, and with no sign of there being any actual point to this lunch, I told Trevor I wanted to get back to work before any of my staff got suspicious.

Trevor called for the bill and then, in the space of 30 power-packed seconds, he told me he was convinced I was the perfect person to take over the editorship of *Cleo*, which had just become vacant, and that Kerry would like to meet me, and would next Friday be OK?

Ya what? It was quite the finish to an otherwise very pleasant lunch.

As kind as Trevor had been and as flattering as that offer was, though, I had no interest in meeting Kerry Packer. And while I knew any number of people who would have given anything just to be in the same room as him, I didn't count myself amongst their number.

Paltry 20-dollar pay rises aside (not that I dropped that little tidbit), I told Trevor I was very happy at *Dolly*. I didn't particularly want the stress of working for a high-powered organisation like ACP, or for someone with the fierce reputation that Mr Packer had cultivated.

Sure, I could see some areas of *Cleo* that could do with fixing up … and my downfall in that moment was telling Trevor exactly that, before adding that I was also sure he wouldn't be brave enough to support what I thought needed to be done.

'Try me,' he dared.

'Well, for starters,' I said, 'that centrefold has to go.'

'Not a problem,' he shot back. 'Done.'

'And it's got to lighten up,' I added, 'stop being so obsessed with the "Big O", and get its cheeky sense of Aussie humour back.'

'Yep. Easy. Anything else?'

I was starting to run out of excuses.

He wanted to hear more, and in a strange split-second decision I still find difficult to fathom, I agreed to another lunch – this time with Kerry Packer himself.

He wanted to meet me, this kid from the west, who only a few years before had been cowering in the corner of the school playground paralysed with fear. I had made a promise to that little girl when I walked out of those gates. And I wasn't going to break it now. I didn't want to die wondering. And I knew it would be the only chance I would ever get, so why the hell not? Besides, it might make a good story for the grandkids.

While I hadn't yet got around to backpacking in Nepal, seen the sun come up on a beach in Spain, or fallen asleep reading Dickens in a big old hammock on a Greek island, as life experiences go, 'having lunch with Kerry Packer' had to be a good – not to mention, pretty unique – experience to put on that list.

And so it was that the following Friday I found myself arriving at the address Trevor had given me, right on the swampy shores of Sydney's Darling Harbour. But there was no restaurant in sight.

Half-completed buildings littered the entire shoreline. In fact, save for one old asphalt-covered vacant lot, the whole area was one enormous construction site, in preparation for the coming Australian Bicentenary celebrations of 1988.

But sure enough, there in the middle of it was Trevor, while right next to him sat the large rubber-based skids beneath the whirring blades of the Channel 9 helicopter, ready and waiting, I soon discovered, to whisk us both up to Mr Packer's summer house at Palm Beach.

Now this was all getting a bit much for a Girl Friday from Campbelltown to take in.

Fortunately, though, when Tia had rung earlier to wish me good luck for the big lunch – she was one of the few, along with Mum and Dad, who knew about it – she offered me probably some of the most sage advice I've ever received.

'You've got nothing to lose,' she told me. 'Remember, you've already got a job. Let him try and impress you. And if that thinking fails you, just do what I do when someone is completely intimidating: just imagine him naked. It just keeps things real.'

Right. Good advice. I think.

So, along with Trevor, I got in the helicopter – me up front, Trevor just behind – and decided to just enjoy the view. As it turned out, the man piloting this chopper was the same one who would go on to give Mr Packer one of his very own kidneys in a life-saving operation for the media proprietor a few years later. (And I am so glad I didn't know that was part of *his* job description at the time.)

The view from the Channel 9 chopper was indeed spectacular – the Opera House, the Harbour Bridge, the glittering harbour itself all spread before us – as we tracked the stunning Sydney coastline right up to its northern-most beaches. The whole trip felt like it passed in mere minutes, and soon the pilot announced over our headphones that we were nearing Pittwater.

At that point, just as I could see that we were beginning to descend, Trevor tapped me on the shoulder and shouted from the back seat that it really wouldn't be a bad idea right now to take off my stiletto heels. His exact reasons were lost in the overwhelming throb-throb-throb of the chopper blades above us, but it didn't matter because I soon found out why.

There had been some fairly torrential summer rains in Sydney the previous week and, as far as the local seagulls were concerned, that big old wooden pontoon sitting in the middle of the calm, crystalline waters just around the headland from Palm Beach was not actually a landing spot for helicopters. It was for them.

And so, when my feet finally made it onto the pontoon decking, it was not long before the most unbelievably liquid seagull poo, five centimetres deep, had squelched its way between each and every one of my perfectly pedicured toes.

Fortunately, the James Bond–style speedboat waiting to whisk us over to the jetty had also copped some of the week's rains and, with a pool of water still lying on the floor of the boat, I worked out that I had just about enough water – and just about enough time – to clean off most of the offending poo.

And then I realised: the boat's bench seat was also wet – as was the entire back side of the carefully chosen apricot linen skirt I had spent all of the previous night deliberating about whether or not to wear. And believe me, when moisture hits linen – particularly the rather delicate shade of apricot I was, right up until that moment, so thrilled to be wearing – there's absolutely no way of hiding it. And with the boat beginning to slow as it neared the jetty, I gingerly half stood up to inspect the extent of my, by now, unmistakable wet patch.

Sadly, the very next thing I remember hearing was Trevor's voice saying, 'Lisa Wilkinson, I'd like you to meet Kerry Packer.' And sure enough, there, at the top of the jetty steps to meet us, was Kerry Packer himself – in, thank god, a T-shirt, a very old straw hat, and possibly the loosest pair of Stubbies shorts I'd ever-so-momentarily found myself looking up.

Good one, Lisa.

As I stood there, with poo still stubbornly caked between my toes, precariously trying to balance as the wash from the boat threatened to topple me, and now holding the back of my dripping wet skirt for everyone to see, I once again looked up at Mr Packer. I had little choice but to embrace this whole farcical moment.

'Hello, Mr Packer,' I burbled as I held aloft the back of my skirt with its tell-tale wet patch, before adding, 'Look, I'm sorry about this ... I knew I was nervous, but I had no idea I was this nervous!'

Thankfully, he laughed, extended his hand to help me up and offered warmly, 'Please, call me Kerry.'

*

As settings for job interviews go, this was probably as good as it gets – the stunning deep verandah of the Packer family holiday house sitting in the filtered shade of a row of magnificent old Norfolk pines. Straight ahead, beyond the home's seemingly endless green lawns, there were 180-degree views to the swooping gulls and Palm Beach surf opposite. The cries of the gulls and crashing of the waves all combined to provide a joyous summery chorus – and an appropriately thumping heartbeat – to the afternoon's soundtrack.

Kerry himself – gee, it was going to be hard to resist the urge to call him Mr Packer – had driven me up from the jetty and through the home's heavy automatic security gates in possibly the sleekest European sports car I'd ever seen, let alone been in.

As for Kerry himself, there was little to prepare me for just how completely charming, physically overwhelming and utterly charismatic he was from the very first. This was a man who immediately owned every space he occupied. Yet he was also quietly spoken, almost to the point of a whisper, and, I suspected, a great believer in an economy of words.

And now, as all three of us were each settling into the deep cushions of some oversized cane lounge chairs, I started to realise that me heading off, after just a quick 'nice-to-meet-you and thanks, I've got the story and the mental picture I wanted for the grandkids', wasn't really an option.

For all I knew, the chopper was gone, and so far, naïve young me had fallen for all the extravagant choreography of this Friday afternoon lunch meeting, just as they had both, no doubt, planned. Whether I liked it or not, I was here for the duration.

What was that advice Tia had given me again?

No, not the advice about picturing Kerry naked – the other advice. I already have a job, she'd said. I just needed to stay quiet and let Trevor and Kerry try to impress me. The problem was, I'd just emerged from my first-ever goddamn helicopter ride, so they already had.

'Hello, you must be Lisa, lovely to meet you, I'm Ros.' It was Kerry's wonderfully gracious wife of more than two decades.

'What time are you thinking for lunch, Kerry?'

His response was part in jest, but also everything I didn't want to hear. 'Well, she hasn't said yes to the job offer I've got for her yet, so no-one gets lunch until that's done.'

Great. Now I was intimidated and more than likely about to go hungry.

'Is that the deal?' I asked half joking.

'It is,' he said a little more seriously than I'd anticipated, 'so let's talk.' And for half an hour, as the distant squeals of excited holidaying children floated up from the beach, we did.

At first, generally – about politics, journalism, my childhood, rugby union (seems he'd done his homework), and the recently appointed and somewhat controversial coach of the Wallabies, Alan Jones. Kerry was a fan. I told him that Dad – now more than a year into his role at Sydney Rugby Union and pretty unimpressed with the way Jones operated – was not. Kerry seemed fascinated as to Dad's reasons why, and I was happy to oblige.

Inevitably, though, the time had come to talk about the reasons we were all gathered there. He wanted to know why I thought my strategy at *Dolly* had worked so well, and why *Cleo*'s numbers were falling. He obviously still had an enormous passion for the magazine he started back in 1972, and against my better judgment and with all resolve I had going into this meeting (perhaps because I was so flattered that he wanted to know), I started talking.

Even though I still didn't want the *Cleo* job, I at least wanted him to know what he was missing out on!

'It's original charter,' I said, 'magnificent! Targeted, focused, feisty, resolute in its fight for Australian women. A total game-changer ...'

From there, though, I tried to tread carefully. After all, I was about to give a pretty raw assessment of something he was perhaps still heavily involved in.

Remember Lisa, you've already got a job …

'… And as brilliant and ground-breaking as it once was,' I told him carefully, 'it needs a major shake-up. There's just a very dry, 70s sameness to *Cleo* now. Some of those original battles have been won, but new ones are emerging. It feels to me like *Cleo* has stopped evolving. And what happened to that great Aussie sense of humour it once had?'

In short, I said, it needed more … sass (now where had I heard that word recently?).

Just at that point, the latch at the top of the verandah stairs opened and two strikingly beautiful young women in bikinis, with towels slung loosely over their shoulders and a light dusting of fine Palm Beach sand still clinging to their feet, made their way across the terracotta tiles towards us.

'Oh sorry, Dad, I didn't realise you had a meeting going on …' It was Kerry's 18-year-old daughter, Gretel, with one of her friends, Adelaide, visiting for the day.

There was an immediate softening in her dad's voice. 'Hello, darling, it's fine. Lunch will be on soon, but can you come over and meet Lisa?'

As I stood up to say hello, he announced, 'Lisa's the editor of *Dolly*, and I know you read it. So why don't you tell us all what you like about it,' before adding, 'and what you don't.'

Oh, lord. Gretel was obviously a very polite young woman, but geez, I thought, don't put her through that. Actually, don't put *me* through that! What if she hates it? I looked over at Trevor, trying to indicate just how uncomfortable I felt for poor Gretel, but he didn't blink. After years of working for Packer, raw, awkward moments like this were probably nothing out of the ordinary for him.

And then the gate clicked open once again. This time it was Gretel's younger brother, Jamie, the very picture of strapping Aussie good health, his board shorts still dripping from his own trip to the beach as he too wandered over to join us and say hello.

'Jamie, this is Lisa. Lisa is the editor of *Dolly*, and I want her to come and work for me,' Kerry offered by way of introduction. I remained standing as I shook hands with this good-looking young man who definitely had his mother's warm smile.

With just over a year separating the siblings, Kerry explained, the two were only now embarking on life after school. Kerry wasn't a believer in university and, at his strong suggestion, Gretel was doing overnight shifts packing sandwiches for the onboard catering division of Ansett Airlines, while Jamie would shortly head off to jackaroo at the Packer family cattle station, Newcastle Waters, in the Northern Territory.

'I've told them I want them to know what real hard work feels like,' he said.

Together, Gretel and James formed the fourth generation in the Packer media dynasty, and Kerry was clearly doing what he could to arm them against that well-known curse that often befalls that particular birthright. As far as Kerry was concerned, unless they knew what it was like to do the hard yards, how could they ever possibly appreciate the enormous good fortune they enjoyed now, or the full extent of what they would one day inherit?

The good thing about our brief chat (apart from Gretel and Adelaide both saying they loved *Dolly*, and Jamie admitting that, like most of his friends, he'd sometimes grabbed his sister's copy just so he could have a look at Dolly Doctor) was the excellent thinking time it was buying me ahead of what was surely coming next.

And with that, Gretel, Adelaide and Jamie excused themselves and headed inside for lunch, no doubt about to be sorely disappointed when they discovered that I was the one thing standing between them and the burgers and lamb cutlets Ros had already told us were on the menu.

I, on the other hand, now had no interest in lunch. I felt sick knowing that after all this palaver – flattering as it was – I was still just here to check out Kerry Packer. I'd done that. I didn't want the job. Couldn't I just leave now?

Sure, there was the small matter of needing a lift back to the city in that big old Channel 9 helicopter over at Pittwater, but no matter ... Do they have taxis here in Palm Beach? I wondered.

And then it came. 'So, what are you on over there at old Granny Fairfax?' Kerry asked.

Jesus, how much more excruciating could this afternoon get? Did he actually just ask me how much I earnt? It was a question I simply, stupidly, naïvely hadn't even prepared for. Why would I? I wasn't here to negotiate anything. Except perhaps now, my exit out of here.

Besides, I'd always been taught you don't ask people how much they earn. Or their age. Or their religion. Or anything that might be the tiniest bit personal. It just wasn't polite.

And yet, this didn't quite feel like the time, nor the place, to give Kerry Packer lessons in etiquette.

Then suddenly it got very warm there on that verandah. With beads of sweat running down my back as I shifted uncomfortably amongst the cushions, I realised something rather awkward was going on beneath me. Again. That sopping wet patch on the back of my skirt I had so embarrassingly transported from the boat to Kerry's car and then all the way here to the verandah had still not had any opportunity to dry, and the beating heat of this mid-summer afternoon, not to mention the self-administered blowtorch of my own nerves, was making it all much worse.

'Sorry?' I asked. Kerry Packer was just feet away, but I tried to pretend I hadn't heard his question. If I told him the truth of my salary, I was sure he would think me pathetic. He was starting to look irritated.

'What are they paying you at Sungravure, or is it called something else these days?'

He turned to Trevor, 'What do they call themselves over there now? It's a promotion company or some fucken thing?'

It was true, Sungravure was changing its name to 'Magazine Promotions', which confused everyone, including it seemed Kerry Packer. Now Trevor was looking at me. He could tell I was stalling.

Kerry was losing patience. 'Trevor! You'd know ... what are they paying their editors over at Fairfax these days?'

Bloody hell. Trevor would know. What do I do now? Should I lie? This guy probably knows everything about everything.

Hang on a sec, was I now in salary negotiations? The second salary negotiation I'd been in, in the space of just a few weeks? The last one hadn't gone well. Was this about to be two out of two?

As a gambler of wide renown, stories of Packer's penchant for playing the money game hard were legendary. According to one oft-repeated story, Packer had once been at the casino tables in Vegas next to a boorish Texan – the quintessential ten-gallon hat on a two-pint head – who was loudly boasting to the visiting Australian of his own $60 million fortune. At which point Packer reached into his pocket, pulled out a coin and said, 'Yeah? Want to toss for it?'

Another story told by one of Channel 9's then-biggest stars, *60 Minutes* reporter George Negus, involved a game of chicken during his contract negotiations over lunch with Packer, after both men wrote down on beer coasters what each believed his new annual salary should be. Negus was at the top of his *60 Minutes* game, so he decided to make it a big one.

When Negus, at Packer's invitation, turned his coaster over to reveal his figure, Packer asked him which number he wanted: his, or Packer's as-yet-undisclosed one. As Negus recalled, 'Packer turned to the head of Nine, Sam Chisholm, also in attendance at the lunch, and said, "This bloke's an idiot, he's asking for less than I was gonna give!" And then I remembered I was dealing with a gambler, so I said I'd take his.'

Packer agreed instantly and proceeded to tear his own coaster up.

On the drive back to Channel 9, Chisholm informed Negus that Packer had told him he'd written down a much higher number on his coaster, and so an extremely generous pay rise was on the way. Negus had called it well.

But had he? Packer was also renowned for his extraordinary generosity when it came to talented, hard-working and, most particularly, loyal employees, so the truth as to whether Packer really had written down a much bigger number on that now-torn-up coaster, only Packer knew. But Negus certainly got that pay rise.

Now it was my turn for a game of 'salary chicken', and as a handful of possible dollar figures rolled around in my head, I realised if – hypothetically – I ever did work for this increasingly terrifying man in front of me, surely there had to be some danger money in it?

So, I just went for it. What did it matter anyway? Be confident, I thought, as I started to sit up in the chair. Be confident, and think of a number, quick!

OK, I had it … but it was unrealistic, so I knew it would need a run-up.

'Well, as you know, *Dolly*'s circulation has gone through the roof over the last few years,' I said, 'so, given that … you know, I am making a lot of money for them … like, you know, millions more, then …'

Now he was definitely out of patience, so I momentarily closed my eyes and blurted out, '$50,000!' I had fibbed wildly.

By the time I opened my eyes again I could see Kerry Packer staring back at me.

He blinked.

I blinked.

He looked down.

Had I gone too far? Was that it? Discussion over?

He shot a glance at Trevor.

'Did you hear that, Trevor? $50,000! Since when did Fairfax open the cash drawer? Did you know about this?'

I had gone too far. I knew it. I had one chance to name a number and I blew it. He knows I'm lying.

No, hang on … wait a minute. Was that … was that a wink I just saw from Trevor to Kerry?

What an idiot I was. Not only did they both think I was telling the truth, but it was now obvious I had no skills in the fine art of bargaining. You're meant to embellish in these moments. And I had, but they thought I hadn't. They thought that was what I was actually on.

My head hurt.

Why didn't I go for something much higher? I probably could have doubled that number and he wouldn't have even blinked! Let alone winked. Dammit.

And then I saw an opening. Some room to negotiate. The extras. I had extras!

Realising I was now slumped deep down into the damp cushions of this cane lounge chair, I pulled myself up, not wanting either of them to think I was done, that I was some sort of Fairfax pushover. An ingenue who couldn't argue her own worth.

I cleared my throat. 'Ahem … oh, and of course, I've got a company car.'

Kerry shot me a glance and then looked straight over to his right-hand man. 'Trevor! They give their editors company cars at Fairfax these days? I bet you didn't have one of those when you were there!'

Trevor smiled. But I had more …

'And a Shell Card for petrol!' I added.

'You get petrol as well? Trevor, she gets petrol AS WELL!'

At that point, I wasn't sure if I was in salary negotiations, or just desperately trying not to look pathetic as I sat there, totally out of my league with the two most powerful men in publishing.

Then, realising I was only going to get one go at this moment, I added meekly, 'Um, and they pay my home phone bill … because I, you know, I work hard, so I use my home phone a lot for work …', as I scrambled around in the small change drawer of my 'salary package' for something, anything that might make it look like at one point in my short professional career, I'd cut a sharp 'deal' in exchange for the millions I was minting for Fairfax.

'Sorry? What was that?' Kerry asked.

Ugh, I couldn't do it again. 'Um. Nothing …' I said.

'Anything else you want to add to that long list?'

Yes, there was. But how could I say it? I had to get to the actual truth of the situation: the reason why I was feeling so uncomfortable, and why I knew I could never accept any offer he might have had to work for him.

I'd come this far, so I just said it.

'Look, I really don't think you'd want me to work for you. One of the big reasons *Dolly* has been so successful is because I have around me the most incredibly talented team. I've hand-picked almost all of them, nurtured them and I just couldn't bring myself to leave them.

'Besides, management don't understand *Dolly*, and so they never interfere. I get to do exactly what I want, and I never have to check anything with them. They've pretty much left me alone ever since I took over. That's the only way I know how to work. I just don't want to give up all that autonomy right now.

'And I'd want to make some significant changes to *Cleo* and I wouldn't want to have to fight in order to get them. And I know that magazine is your baby, so I really think this is probably all a big waste of time, and I'm really sorry ...'

But, before I could finish, it was Kerry's turn to sit up in his chair. He looked agitated and had obviously heard enough. He wanted this deal done, and was no doubt growing impatient for lunch now, too, so it was his turn to launch.

'Are you kidding me? I pay my editors a shitload of money so I *don't* have to interfere. Why the fuck would I do that? And if you've got talented people, bring them with you. Trevor?'

Trevor agreed, saying he could easily shuffle some of the existing *Cleo* staff, who he said were keen to move to other titles anyway.

'But I'm talking like, five, six people,' I said.

'Great,' he replied. 'If they're as talented as you say they are, I want them.'

Fairfax would be furious, I said.

'Well, if you're prepared to come, then they should have valued you more.'

...

Bingo. I looked around. There wasn't a green pen or an unopened Spirax notepad in sight.

With that, the offer was made. And I blinked a lot. It was several times what Fairfax was paying me.

'So, are we done? Are we agreed? You're happy with that and we can get on with lunch? I'm fucking starving.'

Not so fast, Mr Packer. I'm not quite sure where I got the wherewithal to push back in that moment, but I really did need some time to regroup, to think through the enormity and the logistics of this huge move.

If I could just have a few days to think about it, I said, talk to my fiancé, Chris, and Mum and Dad, I promised I would give him a final answer by Tuesday. Dad and I were already planning on having lunch in the city, just near the rugby head offices down by Circular Quay on Monday so without his counsel, I said, I wouldn't be deciding anything.

Surprisingly, almost confusingly, he said he was fine with that, and lunch was served.

*

It was 7 o'clock on Monday morning and far too early for the phone to be ringing, especially after the sleepless couple of nights I'd had trying to make a decision on the Packer offer.

I still loved every day I spent at *Dolly*, and felt an incredible loyalty to our wonderful readers, but the chance to turn this iconic ACP magazine around on my own terms, with a lot of my own talented team beside me, seemed just too good to be true.

When *Cleo* began its life, it was the only women's magazine in the country with no knitting patterns, no recipes and no royals. Instead, readers were encouraged to be independent, take control, study, be politically active, get a home loan, ask for a pay rise, strive for workplace reform, demand the best from relationships, enjoy themselves in bed, and, most crucially, to make decisions about their lives and bodies without reference to a man at all.

Yes, it was an extraordinary opportunity, but I just wanted a little more time to think about it.

Oh. The phone.

'Have you seen the paper yet?' It was Dad calling and he sounded concerned. 'Dorian Wild's gossip column in the *Telegraph* says that you're leaving *Dolly* to edit *Cleo* and you're taking half your staff with you. Didn't you say you were giving them your answer tomorrow?'

I was confused. Dad wasn't.

'Darling, I think Packer's people have leaked it to the papers to force your hand,' he said.

I was in a gossip column? How weird. And once again, how naïve. God, I was so new at this game. They had totally snookered me and there was no going back now.

Telling the team at *Dolly* that morning, while also quietly approaching each of those I wanted to take with me, wasn't easy. It was in fact a very delicate exercise, with furtive meetings in bathrooms throughout the building. There were tears — mostly from me — but I was thrilled that everyone I asked instantly whispered, 'Yes'.

Placing my letter of resignation down next to the four matching pens on John Hemming's desk, however, was not only easy, it was a pleasure. He was clearly blindsided and wanted to know if it was about the pay rise. It seemed unfair not to tell him that it was a huge contributing factor. For the sake of all the women who might go on to sit in my chair down the track, I hoped he would remember that.

Next stop was the office of Sandra Yates. Just how she would take my move to ACP and how much it would interrupt those plans she had for *Sassy* magazine to launch in the US was unclear. When I told her my news, she didn't miss. I had, she said, betrayed her and the company, let myself down, and just made the biggest mistake of what would now be my, undoubtedly, short career.

Hardest of all, though, was saying goodbye to *Dolly*'s readers. But it had to be done.

And so on the following Friday, my last at *Dolly*, I did four things: signed off on the cover of my final issue (another joyous pic of Sarah Nursey, shot by Graham and styled by Pasha, which went on to sell just shy of an astonishing 400,000 copies); wrote, through tears, my final Editor's Letter; chose, also through tears, the final six poems for the next Poet's Corner page; and walked out the doors of 57 Regent Street, Chippendale, for the very last time.

CHAPTER ELEVEN

The Cleo years begin

'You never know how strong you are until being strong is
your only choice.' – Bob Marley

I WASN'T MOVING FAR. The ACP building in Park Street, just across
from the stunning gardens of Sydney's Hyde Park, was only a
mile from the humble laneways and tiny forgotten terrace houses of
Chippendale.

But with its nine gleaming, glass-fronted storeys reaching around
to the city's bustling Elizabeth and Castlereagh streets, my new
workplace may as well have been, as the crow flies, in another century.

Starting life as the home of the *Daily Telegraph* newspaper (before
that was sold off to Rupert Murdoch's *Herald & Weekly Times* by
Kerry's late father, Sir Frank), 54 Park Street was now considered the
pinnacle of Australia's glittering magazine universe.

The basement space – where once huge old printing presses
roared into life seven days a week, flicking out hundreds of thousands
of copies of one of the biggest newspapers in the country – was now
home to the ultra-glamorous subterranean Hyde Park gym, with its
glistening in-ground heated pool and, if you were one of the lucky
few, direct lift access to and from the ACP offices above.

*The Australian Women's Weekly, Cleo, House & Garden, Wheels,
Belle* and the highly influential century-old *Bulletin* news magazine
were all money-minting market leaders, and Kerry, having taken

over the business upon the death of his father in 1974, had steered them all to even greater financial success with his winner-takes-all style of ownership.

But with just 24 hours to go before my first day on the job, there was a party I had to attend first.

'It's on Sunday afternoon,' Trevor told me. 'My wife, Christina, and I are just having a small gathering at our place and I thought it would be nice for you to meet a few of our friends.'

Trevor's 'place' was just five minutes from the cute little apartment Chris and I had finally taken the plunge on. While I would have preferred to spend the afternoon prepping for my first big day at *Cleo*, it was no biggie for us to drop in at Trevor's for 'half an hour, Chris, that's all, I promise'.

But from the moment we were welcomed through the front door of Trevor and Christina's stunning home in Kirribilli, and looked across to the big open verandahs, with the waters of Sydney Harbour lapping at the jetty outside, we could see this was no ordinary Sunday barbie.

As the champagne flowed and waiters in crisp white shirts and sharp waistcoats served sushi and something called duck pancakes, Trevor very kindly took both Chris and me around the room and then outside to introduce us to some of his 'friends': amongst them were Maggie Tabberer, Brian Henderson, George Negus, John 'Strop' Cornell, Delvene Delaney, Max Walker, Mike Gibson, Mike Willesee, and the very intimidating head honcho at Channel 9 (if you didn't count Kerry), Sam Chisholm.

It was like roll call at the Logies and it left me wondering why I had even been invited, until Trevor, with clinks on his champagne glass, called for everyone's immediate attention.

'So lovely to see everyone on this beautiful Sunday afternoon, and I just wanted to thank you all for coming,' he began.

As I looked around the room and tried to avoid making any kind of eye contact with this gathering of TV titans, I was mesmerised by the walls in this exquisite room, covered as they were in the most captivating artwork I'd ever seen. It was something of a distraction until ...

'... And so I would like to toast what both Kerry and I know will be a new era for *Cleo* under Lisa's magnificent editorship. Cheers, and good luck, Lisa!' Trevor said, before everyone, including an equally stunned Chris, joined in: 'Cheers!'

I looked around the room again as everyone, smiling, looked back. So this was all for me?

The message was clear. These are your new colleagues. You're now part of this powerful extended media family.

But even as everyone gave a gentle round of hand-on-wrist applause so as not to spill their champagne, it hit me: just a few weeks into taking out my first-ever mortgage, everything really was now riding on this new job. I had to get it right. Still some haunting thoughts pressed forward. What if I get it wrong? What if *Dolly* had just been a fluke because I'd been a reader ... and any reader, with a bit of common sense, could have done what I did?

The belief was, if you could make it at ACP, you could make it anywhere. But fail there? You'd be falling from such a height your career could be crushed forever after.

The press had been full of stories about this new kid from *Dolly* who was taking over at *Cleo*. The industry was watching – including everyone in this room whose appraising eyes had just fallen upon me.

So, I kept smiling, amidst my new colleagues and their partners. Or was I just clenching my teeth? I was doing both. And then, displaying all the cool confidence I could possibly muster under these ridiculous circumstances, I looked around the room and said, 'Thanks Trevor. Um, thanks ... everyone.'

As Chris and I left that evening and made our way up the garden's wide sandstone steps to our car, Trevor, with the totally charming Christina by his side, mentioned he unfortunately wasn't going to be in the next morning to welcome me on my first day. But he had organised for a woman called Dawn Swain to look after me, so it was best that I go to her office at the *Women's Weekly* first up.

'Dawn will sort everything, and introduce you to the team,' Trevor assured me.

It wasn't until Chris and I had settled back into the quiet of our car, safely out of anyone else's earshot, that we turned to each other and finally breathed out, still not saying a word or daring to believe what we had just come from.

Then, as Chris pulled on his seatbelt and I turned the key in the ignition, my darling fiancé said out loud what we both now knew to be patently clear: 'Jeez, you'd better not fuck this up.'

He laughed. I'm not sure that I did.

*

Dawn Swain, as it turned out, was a fascinating – if somewhat elusive – character in the halls of ACP, despite enjoying, to that point, one of the most illustrious careers in magazine publishing.

Known for assiduously shunning any kind of public profile, and now in her early fifties, Dawn had played a crucial role at the *Women's Weekly* for decades, with many of those years as second-in-charge under Ita.

But in the aftermath of the great 1980 Christmas Eve bust-up between Kerry and Ita, Dawn immediately stepped in to fill the void.

At the time, no-one could imagine the *Weekly* without Ita, who was for years the star of its TV commercials and, seemingly, the personification of all the *Weekly* was, and stood for. Many thought the *Weekly* would crumble in the wake of her departure.

It didn't, in part because in February of 1981, Dawn was handed the biggest gift imaginable to women's magazines: the sudden arrival onto the world's stage of a 19-year-old British kindergarten teacher called Diana Spencer.

Dawn instantly rode the public's insatiable appetite for this beautiful young princess, her somewhat troubled marriage to Prince Charles, and the births of their two adorable royal sons, William and Harry – the heir and the spare.

Dawn knew what Australian women wanted to read in the *Weekly*'s pages, and her complete lack of interest in playing the fame game sat well with Kerry. Her sharp focus on the product took the

Weekly's circulation to well past a million copies every week – its highest ever.

By 1985, though, with Dawn's hands-on editing days behind her, Kerry had repaid that debt of lifelong loyalty by giving her both an Arthur Boyd painting (after apparently asking her what she would like), and a roving brief as 'Associate Publisher' across all the magazines.

Waiting at reception for this first meeting with Dawn felt a lot like waiting to see the headmistress, especially when the young woman stationed at the front desk told me, 'Mrs Swain will see you now.'

But when I entered her light-filled office and leaned across to shake Mrs Swain's spectacularly bejewelled right hand, her flashing green eyes ever so subtly checking out my simple red linen sundress, her charm soon followed, 'Please, call me Dawn.'

And so I did. Dawn wanted to hear what I was planning for the magazine. That, I explained, was still a work in progress, as I was keen to consult with the staff and know a bit more about the current strategy before I made any firm decisions. But, I told her, I certainly wanted to give *Cleo* a shake-up, and one thing was for sure: that centrefold had to go.

While I appreciated the uniquely Australian sense of humour that accompanied the original decision to publish the world's first male centrefold for women – and I loved that comedian Barry Humphries, rock group Skyhooks, actor Jack Thompson, even the Sydney Swans AFL team had all laid themselves bare (each one saved from showing their 'all' by a strategically placed prop) – I explained why I thought its time was done.

'I know it worked well early on,' I said, 'but it's a one-line joke that's been told too many times.'

Dawn looked at me with barely concealed wry amusement before informing me, 'Others have tried, you know?' Then adding, 'And failed.'

'That's OK,' I assured her. 'I've already told Trevor and he's fine with it. And Kerry said he wants me to just get on with fixing *Cleo*. He said he has no interest in the detail of how I do that, or in doing the job for me,' I said, choosing not to repeat the actual words Kerry had uttered on that verandah at Palm Beach a few weeks before.

Dawn raised one of her already sharply arched brows and said with a smile, 'We'll see,' before inviting me to accompany her to the *Cleo* offices on the fourth floor.

'My assistant has already called ahead, so your staff will be waiting for us,' she said.

There was only one problem, and it became pretty apparent soon after the lift doors opened and we arrived at the gleaming gold letters of the *Cleo* logo adorning the front wall of reception. Dawn peered around the corner into what, I gathered, was soon to be my new office.

Far from a room full of employees snapping to attention upon her request for a meeting, it seemed just a handful of the 20 or so staff had bothered to turn up. 'Where are they all? Umm ...' her voice trailed off. Dawn was unused to her orders not being followed and now she wanted answers from the young receptionist whose name she clearly didn't know.

'My name is Pam,' the receptionist offered helpfully, then, 'I told everyone, just as you requested, Mrs Swain. Let me just check and see where they are.'

With gossip columns predicting mass *Cleo* sackings once I arrived, I understood if some of the staff may have been less than enthusiastic about meeting me. I did have some staffing plans, but they could always change. I just wanted to meet everyone first. But right now, I figured the only way I was going to get that whole ball rolling, was to just walk right on in.

For someone who was meant to be running this moment, Dawn seemed strangely uncomfortable, and quickly followed me into the office, along with the remaining staff who were now also making their way in. The word must have spread: *she's here.*

The *Cleo* offices were on the Park Street side of the building, and as soon as I walked across to my new desk, I was immediately struck by the huge windows taking up one entire wall, welcoming in the glimmering greenery of Hyde Park.

Something else I couldn't help noticing was the threadbare carpet just beneath the wheels of my new (make that old) office chair, or the windows' broken matchstick blinds hanging low on one side, or the large crack in the nearby smoky-glass-topped coffee table piled high with dog-eared magazines and ring-folders. The place was ... well lived-in. Perhaps a sign of the long days and nights I had ahead of me. But that was fine. I felt right at home.

The sustained silence in this room was killing me, though. Dawn still hadn't said a word. Was I meant to speak? I simply couldn't leave this awkward moment hanging any longer. 'Hi everyone!' I offered warmly. I looked meaningfully over at Dawn, hoping she would use my words as a cue to start with some proper introductions.

'Team!' she announced finally. 'I'd like you to meet your new editor, Lisa Wilkinson,' before her eyes quickly darted down to her stilettos, and then across to Hyde Park.

Silence. Again! This was becoming excruciating ... and obvious. Just like Pam in reception, she didn't know a single one of the names of these staff members either.

It wasn't a great beginning, but after filling the void with a few words on how much I was looking forward to sitting down with each of them throughout the course of the day, we were done.

I clearly had some pretty serious winning over to do, made apparent in one of those one-on-one meetings that day, when I met the redoubtable Monika, the magazine's spectacularly efficient production manager, whose tenure went back to the magazine's earliest days. A ballsy, blonde American around ten years my senior, Monika told me through half-lidded eyes and with no desire whatsoever to impress, 'Look, I've seen them all come and go, ya know?'

It was true, there had been a few different editors in recent years; and as far as Monika was concerned, I was just another one who would probably be out the door sooner rather than later. And in that exact moment right there, I couldn't have been more grateful to Monika. Because from that day forward, I vowed that I was going to prove her predictions wrong.

I wasn't going anywhere.

*

Despite the awkward start, those early days at *Cleo* flew by. There were some really talented people on staff; some of them admitted they wanted a change and welcomed the chance to head off to work on other titles within the ACP group. Luckily, I was able to fill their places with those I wanted to bring across from *Dolly*, and it worked out perfectly.

ACP did feel like the big league, though, the place where you were only as good as your last set of sales figures. So, the job ahead was huge. Fortunately, within a week, Graham and Pasha were already out shooting all our fashion and covers, and Ron and Pete were redesigning the entire magazine, including *Cleo*'s front cover logo. We also began work on what was to become the last-ever *Cleo* centrefold – featuring Australia's biggest Hollywood star of the day, *Mad Max* actor, Mel Gibson. Clothed.

The photos were by famed US fashion photographer, Herb Ritts, and sure, Mel was lolling around pretty darn sexily in a T-shirt and jeans on a couch, but with the photos fashionably shot in black and white, they were about as far as you could get from the muscled-up, oiled-up, oh-my-god-I-can-see-his-pubes male-model pics the mag had been featuring in more recent times. I wanted something to clearly mark the end of the 'Mate of the Month' era. And this was it.

But, it seems it took a while for word to filter through ...

At no time was this more apparent than on day three of my new role at *Cleo*. As the office newbie, I'd done a big tidy-up of my new digs in those first couple of days; but when I walked in on the Wednesday morning, I arrived to find that the desk I'd left so tidy the night before was now completely covered in envelopes of every size, shape, thickness and colour imaginable. Not at all unlike that very first day at *Dolly*, with all those Poet's Corner submissions. Same, but as I was about to discover, very, very different.

Pam, though, knew exactly what was going on.

'Oh, sorry Lisa. I forgot to tell you. It's Wednesday ... it's a *Cleo* tradition,' she explained. 'Every Wednesday – ever since the magazine started, apparently – the editor always gets to close the door and personally open up every one of the unsolicited naked male centrefold submissions. As you can see, we get a lot!'

I looked at Pam. 'Ever since the magazine began?'

Yep.

And I immediately thought: *Ita Buttrose, you sly old fox ...*

*

Ask any editor, and they'll tell you the day their very first issue comes out is a pretty harrowing one. Is the story mix broad enough and on point? Is the cover sending the right messages? What about the new graphics? What will all the long-time readers who loved it before think of the changes?

Whatever happened, at least the advertisers had responded well to the idea of a new era at *Cleo*, and so the issue was a fat one, chock-a-block with editorial and those all-important revenue-generating ads.

Of course, axing the infamous *Cleo* centrefold was proving controversial. With the magazine focused for so long on sex, sealed sections and that naked guy in the middle, many legitimately wondered if *Cleo* would sell at all without it.

And there were moments, mostly at 2 am as I stared at the cracks in the ceiling, when I started to wonder the same thing. Not that I admitted it to anyone. I was making bold changes, and I still didn't know if they would work. For everyone's sakes, including my own, I had to stay strong.

That resolve proved particularly challenging when I got the call to appear on Ray Martin's *Midday Show* on the Monday that my very first issue was scheduled to hit the newsstands.

Sure, I was glad to have the chance to spruik my reasons for taking these bold steps, but as the show would air during a long weekend, I knew that this holiday Monday viewing audience was going to be much bigger than normal. And now, so was I.

Three stressful months had passed since my first day on the job, most of it fuelled by comfort eating: chocolate during the day, Thai takeaway at midnight, and not a single minute spent in the glamorous Hyde Park gym downstairs. I was working around the clock, and bad old habits during difficult times had kicked right back in. In just over 12 weeks, I had put on more than eight kilograms.

Every new day began with a struggle to find anything in my wardrobe that still fit, and now I was going to have to do the unthinkable: walk out from behind that big velvet curtain at Channel 9 as the lead guest on *The Midday Show*, lights and cameras trained on my every thumping step.

I didn't want to be on TV. I didn't crave fame. I hated red carpets. Nothing annoyed me more than the expectation that I should be fitting into some glamorous, sharp-shouldered, clichéd version of a 'magazine editor'.

Ita was now the most celebrated woman in the country. And while I might have taken over what was once her chair, I was not her, and there was no comparison. Every one of Ita's public appearances was marked by her exquisite elegance. I was going into the office most days in baggy dresses and boiler suits in a desperate attempt to hide my growing frame.

I was working so hard I hadn't been back to Campbelltown since I'd started at *Cleo*. Mum loved Ray Martin, though, and never missed a show. I shuddered to think of her reaction on seeing her girl looking – well, looking the way I was looking – in front of a national audience. *You're so much prettier when you don't have weight on …*

So, I didn't tell her. Or Dad.

God, there were sides to this business I hated. And every morning, as I stood in front of that mirror seeing my ever-expanding reflection staring back, I would punish myself for the sugary excesses of the night before by pinching down hard on those ever-thickening rolls of fatty flesh around my stomach, at the tops of my legs and on my arms, which had all so easily returned. Readers expect glossy people behind their glossy magazines, and I was anything but the public face they would be expecting.

I hated the voices in my head telling me I wasn't good enough. Why, I kept asking myself, had I even taken all this on? So publicly. Who on earth was I kidding? I was a kid from the western suburbs and felt like a complete fraud. I didn't want to be a 'figurehead'. I just wanted to roll up my sleeves, be in my office, work with my team and do my job – *well*. But now I wasn't even sure I could do that.

On this particular Monday, though, I had no choice. Right now, part of my job meant fronting those cameras and selling this big change I was making to one of Australia's most iconic magazines. But wearing what? What on earth could I find to disguise the un-disguisable? How did that fashion advice I'd heard for years go? Keep the lines simple. Don't add, subtract.

One of the few items of clothing I had that might follow that rule (and still fit me) was a man-style satin shirt I'd bought from Sportsgirl. It was a pretty shade of pastel pink, so I teamed it with a simple black pant (the zipper somewhat aided by the large safety pin hidden underneath my shirt), pulled my waist-length straight hair into a ponytail, and asked the lovely Channel 9 makeup woman to please keep the face-paint to a minimum.

And so, just a few minutes before 12, as I stood to the side of the *Midday* stage awaiting Geoff Harvey's band to strike up that familiar lunchtime theme song, I peeked out between the heavy folds of the massive black velvet curtains into the blinding lights of Studio 22 in Willoughby – the studio once so famously occupied by Graham Kennedy, Don Lane, Bert Newton, Mike Walsh and so many other huge names of Australian TV.

Squinting through the lights, I could just make out the audience – an eclectic mix of retirees, housewives, tradies and 20-somethings, all here to see in the flesh the charming Ray, owner of Australia's most-loved dimples. The crowd didn't look too scary – in fact, they were all in a great mood as the curly-headed warm-up guy, Mike 'Shirley' Williams, had them all in stitches with just seconds to go before Ray's arrival, so I simply took a huge deep breath, stepped back into the shadows and waited.

'Lisa, there's a mirror over here, if you want to have a last-minute check,' a young production assistant whispered. I thanked her but said I was fine. Seeing how I looked at that very moment was the last thing I needed.

And then, just as I was patting down the folds of my shirt in a futile attempt to reduce any wrinkles that might amplify my size in front of those unforgiving cameras, and pondering if it would be best to actually cross my legs or keep both feet flat on the floor when I sat down, I heard Ray's warm, familiar voice announce: 'Would you please put your hands together for the brand-new editor of *Cleo* magazine, Lisa Wilkinson ...'

Then, as I walked out to the sound of, thankfully, generous applause to get this thing over and done with, something amazing happened. Somewhere deep inside, that young girl, once so convinced she didn't have what it took to get through difficult times, rose up.

I'd been set a challenge once again, and with every step I took towards Ray and those hot lights beaming down on that chair, something inside me fundamentally shifted ... and, clear as day, I heard my inner voice. Soft at first, then more assured with every inch I moved closer to Ray's welcoming, outstretched hand. The same voice that got me through all those difficult days in the playground at school; the same one that told me to push away the groping hands of Therese's disgusting father; the same one that guided me so well at *Dolly*; the same one that mustered all that courage to go and ask for a pay rise, only to get knocked back and then come back even stronger.

So, with that charming gap-toothed smile on full display, the country's favourite TV presenter invited me to sit down (my feet flat on the floor), and cheekily began: 'Well, Lisa, haven't you got Australia talking? Tell us about your decision to ditch the *Cleo* centrefold!'

I, in turn, took a deep breath, smiled, and just went for it ...

'Look, Ray, it's time. As ground-breaking and cheeky and fabulous a joke as that original Jack Thompson centrefold was, we all got the punchline. We know women can do anything that men can do now. Even ogle at semi-naked members of the opposite sex if they really want to. But it's time to move on.'

And blow me down if the *Midday* audience didn't cheer.

*

It's a weird thing when you come off live TV. Once you go to an ad break, the audience stops clapping and you disappear into the inky blackness backstage – often passing the very next nervous guest in the constant cycle of daily TV. All that is left is the bare, neon-lit confines of the network hallways. Suddenly everything falls eerily silent.

I felt surprisingly confident while I was out there talking, but now there was no-one for me to ask: *Did it work? Did I make that point well enough? Did I smile enough? Will anyone head out and buy a copy?*

Mum. What did she think? Even though I didn't tell her about my appearance on the show, I knew she would have been watching.

As it turned out, so was someone else that day.

Kerry had recently been in the US on business and, the last time I'd heard from Trevor, he was still there. I was keen to hear his thoughts on my first issue and the redesign, but that could wait until his return. However, as I made my way up to the first-floor 'Green Room' at Channel 9 to collect my bag and head back to the office, I was about to find out *exactly* what Kerry thought.

'Lisa, are you here?' I heard someone calling out as I arrived at the top of the stairs just outside the Green Room door.

Looking in, I could see a young producer, seemingly in … was it pain? … with the plastic curly cord of the phone stretched tight from the wall socket in the corner, and all the way across the room to between her firmly clenched thighs. Buried in there somewhere, I presumed, was the handset.

'Lisa!' she shout-whispered, her face drained of all colour. 'It's … it's Mr Packer on the phone. He called while you were on air, and I said you'd call back.' She stopped, drew a deep breath, squeezed down harder on the phone's bulbous mouthpiece just protruding from between her legs and went on, 'But he's rung again! And he wants to speak to you. NOW!'

Gee, the holiday Monday viewing audience that day *was* big. Kerry was known for being Channel 9's most enthusiastic – and vocal – viewer, so hopefully he was happy with what he just saw. But as the producer offered up that rather warm, slightly clammy green handset from between her legs and passed it to me, she added, 'Mr Packer never calls the Green Room ... and he doesn't sound happy.'

Great. Thanks. Just what I needed to hear.

Well, this was it. He wasn't happy, she said. He's called twice, she said. I didn't need the powers of ESP to know this was not good news.

To this point, all my dealings with Kerry had been extremely pleasant. 'Call me Kerry,' he'd said, from the outset. And even though it never felt completely natural, I had.

While both Kerry Packer and his father, Sir Frank, were known for their generosity, they were similarly legendary for their autocratic, capricious style of management, which could mean instant dismissal if you screwed up.

A story that regularly did the rounds at 54 Park Street was one of Sir Frank, waiting impatiently on one occasion for the lift to stop at the third floor after it sped past him two or three times. Suspecting the young man carrying a number of heavy boxes had been the culprit, when he finally emerged through the lift doors, Sir Frank's judgment was instantaneous.

'How much are they paying you?' the gruff, bespectacled proprietor demanded. Then without waiting or even caring for an answer, Packer reached into his pocket, pulled out a huge wad of notes, forced them into the young man's hands and announced, 'That should cover it. You're sacked.'

Now, whether that story was true or not, I didn't know. But when the punchline revealed that the young man was simply a passing postal worker delivering packages to the building – and then hitting the cash jackpot in the process – it became too good not to share. And it did serve as a cautionary tale for the rest of us, lest anyone ever got too comfortable just coasting along in the Packers' employ.

So, I cleared my throat, and put the phone about half an inch from my ear, just in case.

'Hi, Kerry, nice to hear from you. I thought you were overseas?' I began, breezily. But I don't think he heard me. Or maybe he did.

'What the fuck are you doing to my magazine? And who said you could get rid of the fucking centrefold?' Kerry was good at getting straight to the point.

The fact Trevor told me he'd got the OK from the boss to do that from the get-go just didn't seem the right defence in that moment, so what was? Whatever I said to Kerry in this call, I knew it would be my one and only shot at it. If I didn't sound like I believed, if I didn't fight his fire with my fire, if I wasn't prepared to die on this hill, then I knew it was all over for me.

So, I laid it all out once again in pretty strong terms, looking over at the young producer at one point, her mouth slightly agape at what she was witnessing. 'Seriously Kerry, I know what I'm doing ...' And then, possibly pushing my luck, I mocked anyone old enough, grey enough, and still-so-stuck-in-the-70s enough to think that keeping the centrefold was a sane idea. 'Honestly Kerry, whoever it is who's telling you this stuff shouldn't be working in magazines.'

...

...

I wasn't sure if the connection had dropped out. 'Are you still there, Kerry?'

'All I can tell you is ...' his voice now ever-so-slightly more measured – or at least as measured as Kerry was capable of being when faced with the idea that one of his greatest assets was under serious threat – '... you'd better know what you're fucking doing.'

Click.

*

As is typical on public holiday Mondays, the Sydney traffic was light, so the trip across the Harbour Bridge back to the office was a quick one, hastened all the more by my strong desire to find out from Trevor what the hell had just happened in that phone call. He had assured me he would tell Kerry about all my planned changes, including getting rid of the centrefold, so we needed to talk. Now.

I wasn't sure where Kerry had been calling from, so when I arrived in the hushed confines of the executive offices on the third floor and there was no sign of his formidable personal assistant, Pat Wheatley, I figured the coast was clear. Kerry must have called from home.

Trevor, on the other hand, like every journo in the building, was working that public holiday and in residence behind his desk, deep in spreadsheets, when I knocked on his office door. As always he was charm personified, and as I walked in he immediately picked up the copy of *Cleo* on his desk and congratulated me. 'It looks great. Well done. You've got your first one out of the way.'

'Thanks, Trevor. So, you didn't just see me on *The Midday Show*?' I asked. 'Like Kerry just did?'

'Oh. Have you heard from him? He's due in here soon.' Then he looked at me again. 'Didn't like the changes, huh?' appearing to have already guessed the answer from the look on my face.

'One in particular,' I said. 'The centrefold.'

Trevor had known of my intention to drop it from day one, so what happened?

'Oh, I thought I told him,' Trevor muttered, cradling his chin in his hand, before leaning back in his sizeable black leather chair, and adding, 'Actually, when I think about it, maybe I didn't. He's had a lot on lately. What did he say? Actually, don't worry, I can imagine.'

Then, in a moment so very wisely flagged by Dawn just three months earlier, he said, 'You know, a few editors have tried to get that change across the line before. And failed. But I figured this time, with you steering it, he would be OK.'

Leaning even further back in his chair, Trevor added with just the barest hint of a smile, perhaps in a rare personal and professional win against his formidable boss, 'Yeah, I've been telling Kerry for years that its time was done. But he's always been the one who's insisted it stays.

'So good on you. Now you just have to make it work.'

Yeah. I sure did.

*

Eleven a.m. on Fridays was always a slightly tense time at Park Street. That was because, like clockwork, a small STRICTLY PRIVATE AND CONFIDENTIAL yellow envelope would land on the desks of every editor in the building, containing that week's sales figures from newsagents around the country – a report card that would not only determine the rest of your day, but also just how much you could enjoy the weekend ahead.

Not that I was getting a lot of time at home on weekends these days. Chris was used to me working crazy hours, and fortunately he had his own work and friends at the ABC. By now we had a rhythm to our relationship that didn't include a lot of time together, but it seemed to work for us nonetheless.

Ours was a partnership anchored in deep friendship. As a couple in our mid-twenties, we knew that these were our career-building years, so whatever personal sacrifices we had to make now, we were sure they would eventually be worth it. We celebrated each other's wins and were always by each other's side when times were tough.

And the times were certainly starting to get that way. Because, while that first issue with the last centrefold had seen a small lift in sales, the ones that followed showed that our numbers were starting to slip. Far from the intoxicating rise in circulation I'd enjoyed at *Dolly* – and which had seemed so effortless – this *Cleo* audience was proving much harder to get a handle on.

The brighter graphics, the lighter content, the new, streamlined *Cleo* logo we'd quietly changed, and the headline-making messages of less sex and no more centrefolds were all proving to be a lot to take in for those hundreds of thousands of traditional readers who actually didn't have a problem with the *Cleo* of old.

If we weren't a sex-obsessed magazine, then what were we? Readers were confused. I could feel it. And every Friday when that yellow sales envelope arrived, I could see it. In trying to entice all those *Dolly* readers to come with me, had I simply turned off all the 20- and 30-something *Cleo* readers in the process?

There was another problem too. Far too late, I realised that in a genius and extremely expensive marketing move back in 1972, ACP had fitted out, free of charge, every newsagent in the country with an enormous light box–style shopfront hoarding featuring just one thing – the soon-to-be iconic logo of this brand-spanking-new magazine, *Cleo*! Ever since, every one of those hoardings across the country – from Parramatta to Perth, Ballarat to Brisbane, and Darwin to Dubbo – had sat as a permanent all-day, all-night, neon-lit advertisement for *Cleo*, while also providing lighting for the shop. It was a brilliant idea, and one that money could no longer buy.

And yet, here I was, this young upstart who'd gone ahead and completely changed that logo, on nothing more than gut instinct. Oh, and a straw poll of a few neighbours, a handful of women in a cafe in the city one morning before work, and a what-do-you-all-think-guys? session with the *Cleo* team one lunchtime.

Trevor had certainly trusted me when I showed him the logo alternatives, but true to his and Kerry's promise, they were leaving me alone to get it right. No interference. As we'd agreed. (Trevor, too, also clearly forgetting about all those expensive, irreplaceable shop hoardings at the time.)

But there was simply no hiding the facts: those circulation figures were not going in the direction expensive helicopter rides and celebrity-studded waterfront welcoming parties warranted in return.

The panic was starting to overwhelm me, and I couldn't admit it to anyone. Not even Dad. I knew how proud he was of all I'd done to this point, and now I was hiding from him and Mum. I hadn't seen either of them in six months, and my weight continued to balloon.

I had made a terrible mistake. Chris could see I was a mess, and many was a night I would come home from work in tears, exhausted, inconsolable, desperate to find a way out of this very public mess I'd made of everything.

Every day I had to keep fronting up to work, smiling and positive about staying the course; but every night the only thing that would bring some comfort was grabbing the local paper and once again looking in the Women & Girls employment section. Once again for a job as a receptionist. I was a bloody good one after all. I could do it again, I kept telling myself. And I wasn't too proud. Maybe at a local real-estate office. Or at a vet practice. I loved animals.

Besides, I'd only been at *Cleo* for six months. I could just disappear. A failed experiment. They could easily get someone else. Plenty of people would kill for that role. Soon, everyone would forget I had ever even existed. Including, eventually, Kerry Packer. I would just be a tiny whatever-happened-to blip on the media landscape. But I had to get in first before Kerry came for me. In fact, he probably wouldn't even bother. He'd just send Trevor. It would be quick.

Chris would stick by me, I knew that. Sure, the mortgage would be an issue. But, hey, we could sell. We could move to somewhere much quieter, like Tassie. We'd been on a short holiday there once. It seemed nice.

And if I didn't stick my head up and listen to all the negative voices on the way out, it should be pretty painless.

CHAPTER TWELVE

Guess who's coming to dinner?

'All I can do is turn a phrase until it catches
the light.' – Clive James

T HE HEADLINES WERE ALARMING. A little-known virus called
HIV-AIDS was sweeping the world and there was no
known cure. Believed to be sexually transmitted, it was proving
particularly virulent in the gay community, and now one of
Hollywood's leading heartthrobs, Rock Hudson, had announced
he'd contracted it. Just a few months later, on 2 October 1985, he
was dead.

AIDS was initially dismissed as 'the gay disease', and alarmist
misinformation was everywhere. Homophobia was rife. But as more
women and children were being diagnosed, confusion grew, and
reliable information sources were thin on the ground.

In the UK, Princess Diana visited hospitals and shook hands
with AIDS patients, dispelling the myths around transmissibility;
while in Australia, Ita led the charge to demand a government-
funded education campaign. The shift in thinking was seismic – sex
could now kill you.

Where once *Cleo*'s readers were all about the myriad ways of
getting pleasure in the bedroom, the demand now was for trusted,
factual information around safe sex. As the months rolled by and fear
grew, young women were turning to *Cleo* in droves.

Ita was once again everywhere, and in one TV interview she gave about the deadly virus, she was asked what she thought of all the changes going on at *Cleo*, and most particularly, the demise of the centrefold.

'Oh, for heaven's sake,' she started, 'that should have gone years ago. Good on Lisa for having the courage. It was well past time. *Cleo* has a much more important job to do now. And Lisa is doing it.'

Ita. Even though she hardly knew me, there she was again, supporting my work, this time not just privately, but publicly. It was exactly the call to action and the confidence boost I desperately needed. It was a reminder, too, of the crucial role *Cleo* had to play in keeping our readers informed and safe. By early the next year, as we continued to respond to this worldwide health crisis, sales continued to lift.

And with that, all thoughts I had of heading off to a receptionist's desk in the suburbs – or moving to Tasmania – were gone. At least for now.

*

Even though I didn't see Kerry often, you could always feel his presence in the building – or at least see evidence of it in the form of his sparkling silver Mercedes sedan, still sentimentally displaying the personalised 'FP' number plates of his late father and parked just beyond the open door by the security desk in the ACP foyer.

Rare was the editor who, upon arriving at work and clocking in their peripheral vision the steely shadow of the boss's car, didn't sit up just that little bit straighter in their chair that day, knowing that Kerry was in. It was a subtle form of, perhaps unintentional, proprietorial communication, but it worked.

Kerry had other ways of casting his omnipresent shadow around the building each day too. The most anxiety-inducing of them was the 'batphone' – an almost toy-like handset that sat like a bright-yellow beacon on the desk of every editor and senior executive at ACP and Channel 9. It was your own personal direct line of contact with Kerry. And one another.

For all that, I never met a single editor in the building who had any desire to ever willingly make a phone call to Kerry. Kerry, however, would call us, each on our very own allocated number. Mine was 52.

The batphone's distinctive ring set it apart from any other phone in the office – louder, more shrill, more urgent, more like an alarm. On the rare occasions that it did ring, it sent everyone in the office into a complete panic, because it was well known that two rings were the absolute limit of Kerry's patience for a pickup.

If I was a couple of rooms away in the fashion department, not even running through the office at breakneck speed would get me to the handset in time.

Was it Kerry? It could have been Trevor. Or Dawn perhaps. You could never be sure. So, if I did miss one of those two-ring calls, I would always park myself in my office for ten minutes and wait, my hand hovering right by the bright-yellow handset. Just in case he called back.

In the end, I always figured if it was important, I'd hear soon enough. Sometimes that meant Kerry arriving at my office door unannounced, heralded more often by the scurrying of staff overwhelmed by his instantly commanding 1.9-metre presence than the sound of his actual voice at my door, asking – always surprisingly politely – if he could come in.

Then, in an act that instantly reminded us both who was boss, he would make himself right at home in one of the plush apple-green designer chairs on the other side of my desk. I was told these chairs dated back to *Cleo*'s heady (and by the looks of things, pretty darn groovy) launch days. Leaning back in one of them, sometimes with his feet on the desk and gazing over the top of his reading glasses, he would begin: 'So, how is it all going?'

Such was Kerry's arresting charisma, and what felt like an ability to see right through anyone in his presence, that I was never sure if this was a trick question. Did he know something I didn't?

Every time he arrived in my office like that, my mind would race. It was exciting, exhilarating and terrifying all at once. I could never quite get over the fact that he trusted me so much with this title he had so much personal pride and investment in – second only in importance to *The Australian Women's Weekly*, the jewel in the company's magazine crown.

In anticipation of those impromptu meetings, I always did my homework, and made sure I was across the interminable weekly financial P&L spreadsheets that arrived in a concertina-style stack every Friday, along with the yellow weekly sales envelope. Maths was never my strong suit, but with every new issue, as readers continued to warm to our new look and feel and purpose, and advertisers were responding in kind, it had almost become a guilty pleasure being across how well we were doing.

Strangely, though, even when the numbers were particularly good and I would proudly point to them on the pages for Kerry to see for himself, he never peered too closely and checked. It was only years later, when I discovered he suffered from dyslexia, that I realised why. Kerry never read the papers but relied instead on his instincts. Decisions were made not by intellectual process, but by tuning in to the deepest rumblings of his gut. Somehow, despite the extraordinary privilege of his upbringing, and now his life as a billionaire, Kerry still had an almost uncanny ability to read the mood of the average person.

Often, Kerry's chats with me about *Cleo* simply felt like a cursory check-in, because often those conversations would quickly turn to something else: politics, TV shows, cricket, how I thought the other magazines were doing and, sometimes, how totally confused he was by women.

'What is it exactly that you women want?' I was always happy to oblige on that topic. And he was even happier to argue the point. As was I, right on back.

Kerry loved an argument and seemed to enjoy having people around who challenged him. He had his opinion, and in my experience didn't mind having it questioned – but only if you could prosecute a decent case. And for some possibly masochistic reason I quite liked the sport of it.

Such chats invariably left me both energised and unsure as to their exact purpose, but one topic that never came up again was the centrefold. After that one thundering phone call to the Channel 9 Green Room, the subject was never raised again. The rising circulation figures meant I'd won. Which of course meant that, ultimately, Kerry had also won.

Most of those surprise meetings in my office had about a 15-minute time limit, their end signalled by those two gigantic feet coming off my desk, and his larger-than-life figure disappearing out my door. The strangest thing? Whenever Kerry left my office, there was always an immediate vacuum, a strange vortex that marked where he had just been. A space left behind that took some time to fill. And an eerie silence.

Yet, once those lift doors shut, and everyone knew he was safely on his way to somewhere else, the rest of the office would return to its normal busy buzz, before one or another of the team would check in to make sure I had survived the encounter.

Usually it was Pam. 'Everything OK?' she would ask.

Increasingly, it was.

I was really starting to love working at *Cleo* and ACP. In that building, everything felt possible. An intoxicating mix of power and influence seemed to seep out of every office and every senior employee.

At the regular Thursday-night drinks, held in the private dining room on the fifth floor for editors and ACP's chosen powerbrokers, you felt as though everyone you spoke to was on a trajectory to the top.

Tony Abbott, Malcolm Turnbull and Bob Carr, all *Bulletin* columnists, stationed just down the hall from *Cleo*, were three figures already ear-marked for political life. Of all of them, Turnbull, a sharp-eyed, good-looking barrister in his late twenties, was seen as the guy most likely, given his other position as the company's general counsel.

In that atmosphere, for all the pressure and expectations, the adrenaline of work had become my drug of choice. And now, with *Cleo*'s sales figures climbing and readers embracing all the changes, the old me was back. I even started using the gym downstairs, and all that weight I'd put on was finally starting to melt away.

*

Magazine anniversaries were always a great excuse to release special editions: 10th, 15th, 20th, 25th, etc. Anything ending in a 5 or a 0 was considered a legitimate reason to celebrate longevity in the cut-throat world of publishing.

As a marketing device they encouraged feelings of nostalgia. Just like sharing the birthday of a special friend, it was yet another way to cement a reader's ongoing bond with the magazine.

Anniversary issues always sold a motza. Advertisers loved them as well.

So, what to do with a 14th birthday? In human terms, 14 was the age many of us hit peak awkward, so that was no help. I needed a gimmick. I had to find a way to make that number 14 mean something. Something that would also catch the eye of the press and hopefully grab us some free publicity.

I'd read that there were some seriously famous names in town at the time, including legendary British TV host David Frost, and the brilliant expat Aussie documentary maker and scorching BBC TV critic Clive James.

Clive's book, *Unreliable Memoirs*, a portrait of growing up in working-class Sydney in the years after the Second World War, was one of the funniest books I'd ever read. In the 60s he had joined a wave of talented intellectuals, including Germaine Greer, Barry Humphries, Robert Hughes and Geoffrey Robertson, who had gone and reverse-colonised England, and helped place brilliant Aussie minds firmly on the world's map. His razor-sharp observations, writings and TV documentaries had become the stuff of comic legend.

According to Clive, Arnold Schwarzenegger's body was like 'a condom full of walnuts'; romance novelist Barbara Cartland's eyes were 'Twin miracles of mascara, like the corpses of two small crows that had crashed into a chalk cliff'; and of his time as a Sydney schoolchild, 'The whole secret of raising a fart in class is to make it sound as if it is punctuating or commenting upon what the teacher is saying. Timing, not ripeness, is all.' When asked how he managed to so hilariously put into words our unthought-of thoughts, he'd said, 'All I can do is turn a phrase until it captures the light.' Genius.

And now the celebrated raconteur was on one of his regular visits back to Sydney to see his much-loved, aging mum. And that gave me an idea.

Why not throw a dinner party for 14 of the most famous people I could find – starting with Mr James – then invite the press, score some guaranteed instant publicity, and put all the behind-the-scenes moments in the pages of *Cleo*'s 14th birthday issue? We would call it – and I was hoping against hope that it would turn out to be – 'The Ultimate Dinner Party'.

Surprisingly, the fact I'd never even thrown a dinner party before, and was still haunted by that awful moment at my own fifth birthday party, didn't put me off. If I could bring together the right mix of celebrities and have them fire off each other – and someone else was doing the cooking – how hard could it be?

First, though, I had to get Clive James across the line as my bait to lure every other invitee on my list.

Amazingly, one phone call to Clive via a close friend we had in common was all it took, and he was in.

UK TV host David Frost, satirist Barry Humphries (aka Dame Edna Everage), comedian Pamela Stephenson, model Deborah Hutton, radio host Wendy Harmer, artist Ken Done, rocker Angry Anderson and celebrity astrologist Athena Starwoman were all in town, and all on my wish list. And to my utter shock and elation, they all RSVP'd yes.

Of course, with so many huge names attending, there was only one choice for the appropriate Sydney venue: the private dining room of the Sebel Townhouse, which by now was enjoying an even more iconic status, courtesy of Elton John who had famously (and hastily) married his young sound engineer, Renate Blauel, at the hotel just a few years before.

How I gathered the stupid courage to host this extraordinary line-up of bright minds and big personalities on a Friday night, straight after work (with no more preparation than throwing on a black dress and some horrendously bright pink lippie, and quickly running a brush through my hair), I'm not quite sure.

As it turned out, I didn't really have to play hostess at all. The invitation was for 7pm, and despite the light drizzle falling outside, almost everyone arrived right on time, with Clive, David Frost and Barry Humphries immediately taking turns at holding court during pre-dinner drinks, and making everyone (including yours truly) feel perfectly at ease.

This was the celebritocracy in action, because even though a lot of these famous faces had never met before, there was an instant unspoken understanding between them all. I'm a celebrity, you're a celebrity, so, hey, we're practically related!

But by 7.30, with the cameras catching every sparkling guest and every shiny smile from every possible angle, and as we started taking our seats at the superbly set table, I realised that one crucial guest was missing: Pamela Stephenson. And her vacant chair was right next to mine.

I loved the New Zealand–born Aussie comedian's appearances on the BBC's political satire show *Not the Nine O'clock News*, alongside the brilliant Rowan Atkinson, and was hoping to spend at least some of the evening chatting with her. I knew she was staying in the hotel and, having seen reports of her latest pregnancy – which must have been well advanced by now – I wondered if perhaps she was just having a bit of a slow start to the night.

Just as the entrée was being served, the maître d' leaned in to ask if I was still expecting Ms Stephenson, and whether he should take her plate and place card away to take the focus off her absence. Unused to the protocol of such matters, my answer was instant: I simply had no idea.

Then, at 7.45, Pamela Stephenson suddenly appeared, slightly flustered, apologising profusely in that breathy but commanding quasi-British accent she now had, and quickly took her spot right next to me.

It was clear TV simply didn't do Pamela Stephenson justice – in the flesh, she was utterly stunning, as she was on this night in a simple roll-neck black velvet dress, her long blonde hair pulled into an elegant high ponytail, with brightly coloured earrings the only sign of the flamboyant Pamela we were all expecting.

Pamela told me that she had very fond memories of *Cleo*, having been a reader in the 70s during her acting days in Sydney, before she moved to the UK.

'I'm so grateful you could make it. You have lots of mates here, and I know Clive and Sir David are very keen to chat to you,' I offered in turn.

I admitted I was a huge fan of *Not the Nine O'clock News*, and said I was so glad that she and her husband, Billy Connolly, were already staying here in the hotel – you know, being pregnant and all – so at least she hadn't needed to battle through that darned Sydney rain to get here.

'So, when is the baby due?' I added, hopefully further easing her discomfort at being late, and indicating that I was across at least some of the detail of her life. Some of it, but not all, as it turns out.

Pamela looked at me. Then looked down to her black velvet dress stretched tight across her midriff. I looked down, too, and resisted the urge to pat her beautifully rounded tummy. These days, that well-meaning gesture was starting to be regarded as a bit of an intrusive, presumptuous no-no. This was apparently Pamela's third child, and I noticed she did seem to be 'carrying small' as they say.

She lifted her gaze, and looked square into my eyes, before moving her hand to her mouth to cover a small cough and clearing of her throat, before declaring, 'She arrived three months ago. Her name is Amy. That's the reason I'm late. I was upstairs breast-feeding.'

And just like that, I was mouth breathing.

I.

Could.

Have.

Died.

Exactly what happened in the next 30 minutes was lost in a daze of embarrassment, profuse apologies (it was my turn now), and immediately swapping spots with David Frost. I then gave strict instructions to the head waiter to keep the champagne in

Ms Stephenson's glass one millimetre from the rim at all times throughout the night – and in mine too.

Mercifully (the somewhat numbing effects of the champagne aside), the rest of the evening went off without a hitch and at one point, around midnight, I had one of those moments, a pause to take it all in, knowing I wanted to remember this night forever.

There was Clive up one end of the table telling the stunning tale of his last encounter with Margaret Thatcher, as Deborah Hutton and Pamela Stephenson hung off his every word. Meantime, Barry Humphries and Angry Anderson were getting comprehensive horoscope readings from Athena Starwoman, while Ken Done had begun decorating everyone's place cards with miniature Opera House and Harbour Bridge drawings to take home.

Wendy Harmer, never one to miss an opportunity, had cheekily brought along her tape recorder to interview all the guests for her radio show and was going hell for leather with David Frost. Alas, so excited was Wendy, only afterwards did she realise she forgot to press 'record'.

No matter. Waiter! More champagne!

Then, sometime around 1am, final honours for the best story of the night went to David, who pipped everyone at the post with tales of the time he spent with disgraced US President Richard Nixon for the Frost/Nixon interviews.

In the 60s and 70s, Frost had been the golden boy host of such BBC series as *That Was The Week That Was* and *The Frost Report*, satirical news shows that had given names like John Cleese their start. His *Nixon Interviews* series, however, had been a masterclass in unflinching journalistic technique. Nixon simply had no chance against Frost's forensic examination of the facts surrounding the plot to bug the Republican's Democratic rivals at Washington's Watergate building during his presidency.

Nixon was cornered, and after hours of Frost's intense, unrelenting questioning, a depleted Nixon had no choice but to apologise to the American people for letting them down.

Just as Frost was a master interviewer, he also knew how to captivate a dinner party gathering with a compelling story, and everyone in the room that night had questions. I wanted to know what the former president was like when the cameras were off. Was there small talk?

Frost said that Nixon was quite bizarre in that way. Most guests, he said, can be relaxed before going on air, and then freeze once that red light goes on. Nixon was different: uncomfortable with the small talk beforehand, but surprisingly calm once the cameras rolled. In fact, so awkward was he, Frost said, that in the minutes before the cameras rolled, Nixon had turned to him and asked, 'Did you do any fornicating last night?'

As Frost told it, 'Here was this incredible politician, a pro, who had convinced the American people in '72 to vote him back into power in a landslide victory, and yet he'd never learnt small talk.'

On that point, Frost was keen for me to know that the Frost/Nixon series and a long-standing friendship he had with Kerry Packer were actually the reasons he had accepted my invitation to this *Cleo* party. He told me that, without Kerry, those history-making interviews would never have happened. Kerry, he said, had been one of two Australians who had delivered crucial last-minute finance on the series – the other was long-time Packer friend, and now New York–based financier, Jim Wolfensohn.

In a decision Nixon would undoubtedly live to regret, the former president had agreed to Frost's request to front the cameras, but according to David, in order to meet his production costs and get the interviews across the line, he needed a final $200,000. Without the money, the series couldn't go ahead.

Frost was desperate. If it all came off as he hoped, he would be able to sell the series around the world, including to Australia. Packer was interested. And as the British TV host pleaded his case at a dinner in Sydney on the night before he was due to fly to LA for the interviews, Packer told him he was prepared to put $160,000 on the table. Tops. Nothing Frost tried would convince the media owner otherwise.

Then in a last-ditch effort for the full $200,000, and well aware of Packer's love of gambling, Frost had one more go: 'I'll toss you for it.'

With his heart beating hard in his chest, and to Frost's complete surprise, Packer agreed, saying, 'And you can call.'

As Packer produced a 20-cent coin from his pocket, Frost chose tails. Then, in a speedy flash of spinning silver, the coin landed on the back of Packer's left hand, with the other hiding the crucial result.

With an almost imperceptible lift of three fingers Packer announced, 'Tails it is, son. The money's yours.'

And the rest, Frost said as we all leaned in, was TV history ... and some huge ratings for Packer's Channel 9 when the series aired on the network shortly afterwards.

Despite that shocking rookie hosting error with the extremely gracious Pamela (who admitted upon leaving that she had actually found my gaffe quite hilarious), *Cleo*'s 14th birthday dinner was one of the most extraordinary nights of my life. A memory only made better on the following Monday when, as I was heading back to my fourth-floor office at lunchtime, the lift doors opened at Level 2 and in walked Kerry and David, deep in conversation.

Then, as Kerry reached for the third-floor lift button, David looked up, saw me, and exclaimed, 'Darling Lisa!' There was just the three of us in the lift for that brief one-floor journey, so the moment passed in an instant, but Kerry immediately looked at me, smiled, and said, 'I didn't know you two knew each other.'

'Oh my gosh, I've just sent you flowers,' David continued. 'Thank you so much for Friday night. It was fabulous!'

And as the lift doors opened once again, David quickly leaned over and gave me a warm hug.

As I looked over at the boss, just before he and David walked out into the third-floor corridor, Kerry muttered, 'I'm not even going to ask.'

CHAPTER THIRTEEN

A New York state of mind

'I myself have never been able to find out what feminism
is; I only know that people call me a feminist whenever
I express sentiments that differentiate me from a
doormat.' – Rebecca West

H E WAS LOUD, HE was gauche, he was filthy rich, and Donald
Trump was standing right next to me here in the magnificent
marble foyer of New York's stunning Plaza Hotel.

With just 48 hours' notice, Trevor had sent me to the US to
check out the market viability of *Ms.* magazine, a title Kerry was
considering buying. He'd long harboured ambitions to get into the
US publishing scene, and for the next four weeks, Trevor told me, I
would be working out of the magazine's offices in Lower Manhattan.

This was all moving so fast, and I could hardly believe it as I
farewelled Mum, Dad and Chris at Sydney airport, and boarded my
flight for snowy New York, knowing I was about to spend a month
working alongside *Ms.* magazine's legendary founder, editor and
feminist hero, Gloria Steinem.

Right now, though, here at the glistening Plaza Hotel reception
desk, I was alongside this guy, Donald Trump, a second-generation
multi-millionaire property developer whose showy, headline-
grabbing antics were rapidly making him the poster boy for the
'greed-is-good' 80s. It struck me in that moment that if ever there

was an inverse and opposite to Steinem's learned, wise, trailblazing activism for women, Donald Trump was probably it.

Stories of Trump's womanising ways, growing property portfolio and sheer overwhelming arrogance were the talk of the Big Apple and perfect ongoing fodder for the pages of one of my favourite US magazines, *Vanity Fair*, with its ability to speak biting truth to glossy power.

And Trump was all about glossy power. Not enough that just around the corner on Fifth Avenue he had already constructed a 58-storey luxury apartment complex and monument-to-self, Trump Tower, where celebrities like Michael Jackson, Sophia Loren, Liberace and Steven Spielberg had already taken up residence. Now, The Plaza, this exquisite turn-of-the-century hotel, setting for one of my all-time favourite 60s rom-coms, *Barefoot in the Park*, and about to be my home for the next month, was also rumoured to be on his property hit list.

From the way he proprietorially snapped his fingers at the two young bellhops nearby as I stood there waiting for my room key and continued to shake off flecks of powdery snow from my jacket, I wondered if in fact he already owned the place, such was his air of imperious command.

Like everyone else in this foyer, though, I just couldn't look away. There was something mesmerising about him, as he took off his huge black coat and threw it at the head of another young bellhop, almost swallowing him whole in the process, until ... he caught me watching all this gross behaviour at close quarters.

He turned, smiled and winked at me. What was that smell? Was it the heady scent of the massive floral displays throughout the foyer that had suddenly hit my nostrils, or an overly generous, industrial-grade dousing in Giorgio Beverly Hills For Men by the man now just inches away from me? Possibly both.

He looked me up and down before saying 'Hello', his eyes finally settling on my breasts. The fact they were completely hidden under the many layers of clothing I was yet to remove didn't seem to deter him. By the look in his steel-grey eyes, he'd removed a lot more layers than that in his time. Ugh.

So, with my room key now in hand, I thanked the receptionist, turned, shook my head in Trump's direction and headed for the lift, in the absolute knowledge he had no interest in me whatsoever. But as a female in my twenties – with a pulse – he obviously just needed to tick me off his list.

I knew guys like that always tended to implode as they worked their way through marriages and divorces, houses and mistresses, and I took comfort knowing that with every new wife, and every new ten-carat diamond engagement ring he handed over, eventually Trump would end up a bitter, lonely old man. He was a property developer spiv to beat them all, and I'd seen interviews where he, strangely, talked about one day running for US President ... But hey, as if ...

Anyway, I had much more important things to do, like get upstairs to my room, jump on my bed and squeal because ... I was in New York! It had finally happened. I was on my first big trip overseas!

Sure, it wasn't Europe like I'd planned, it wasn't with a backpack, there were no beach sunsets in Manhattan, and Moroccan boys were well and truly off the list now. But my room was on the tenth floor, directly opposite Central Park; and when I drew back the heavy, mushroom-pink velvet curtains, those tall windows either side of the fireplace revealed the most superb snow-covered wonderland just across the road, extending as far as the eye could see across the park's bare treetops, branches bending under the picturesque burden of a week's fresh powdery fall.

Just below, the lanterns of clip-clopping horse-drawn buggies were disappearing into the romantic darkened maze of the park's meandering pathways, and nearby I could hear the incessant blaring horns of yellow cabs nudging their way down Fifth Avenue; while above, the twinkling lights of row-upon-neat-row of apartment blocks marked the clear demarcation of the park's rectangular perimeter and served as an added reminder of the bustling lives being lived on every square inch of this heaving metropolis.

New York, New York. No bloody wonder they named it twice.

I had all of Sunday free before I started work on Monday at *Ms.*, and the possibilities of how to spend my first full day in this incredible city were endless. The Statue of Liberty? The Museum of Contemporary Art? Barneys Department Store? The Dakota building, where, just six years before, John Lennon had so tragically lost his life? Wall Street? Times Square? Greenwich Village? The World Trade Center?

Yes! The World Trade Center. Everyone said that no trip to New York would be complete without visiting these two stunning buildings, their combined 220 floors standing as identical matching monuments to the city's position at the centre of the world's financial markets. I'd caught sight of them in the distance as I'd flown in to JFK airport – brilliant beacons reaching up out of the inky blackness of the Hudson River, high into New York's phosphorescent night sky.

But where there is light, there is also darkness, and right now, for all its gloss and glamour, New York was going through a difficult period with crime at an all-time high. The crack epidemic surged, gun crime was rampant, and the city's mafia bosses went about their business largely unchecked.

The strong advice was don't walk the streets, but if you have to, keep your head down, don't look anyone in the eye, and always have a set of keys splayed between your fingers, hidden in your pocket and ready to strike (a problem when all I had was my single hotel key, but at least it was a big one). The city's famous subway was a no-go zone, as was Central Park (unless it was daytime, and with someone you knew), and muggings were commonplace. Most important of all: don't even think about going anywhere on your own after dark.

Trouble was, by the light of day, this city completely drew me in, and when I ventured out that next morning into the clear bright sunshine of a mid-winter Manhattan day, I soon broke that promise to myself to only walk a couple of blocks.

The Plaza sat on the corner of 59th Street, and once I turned right and started to head down the famed shopping strip of Fifth Avenue, looking to hail a taxi to get to the World Trade Center, all good sense left me. I just had to walk, and I certainly wasn't looking down.

First, a little wander past the beautiful blue windows of Tiffany's where once Audrey Hepburn had stood, croissant in her gloved hand for those iconic scenes in *Breakfast at Tiffany's*; then watching as families lined up for their turn on the ice at the Rockefeller Center, while skaters of all ages squealed with delight beneath the waving flags of the United Nations; then back across the road for a little sneak peek into Saks Fifth Avenue; and down a few more blocks through the neon lights of Times Square and into Broadway.

It was only when I arrived at the Empire State Building and realised I'd just walked 25 blocks that I finally grabbed a taxi to the giant doors of the World Trade Center in Lower Manhattan.

This city had it all, and now I was catching the express lift all the way up to the 107th floor of the South Tower's public observation deck, directly across from the famed Windows on the World restaurant in the North Tower, to take this whole city in from a bird's eye view.

My god, did birds even ever get this far up? Four hundred metres above the southern tip of Manhattan, right where the Hudson meets the East River, everything below seemed so tiny and distant. The Statue of Liberty, the Brooklyn Bridge, the magnificent Gotham City–style architectural lines of the Chrysler Building – all glistening, all right there in front of me.

Heights have never been my strong suit, so it took me a while to gather the courage to make my way over to the giant walls of glass that allowed you to take in the full extent of the cavernous view straight down or, if I kept my eyes straight ahead, 80 kilometres in every direction.

My hands now clammy as I held on tight to the cold stainless-steel safety railing, I simply couldn't shake the uncomfortable feeling in the pit of my stomach imagining what it would be like to fall 107 storeys. I'd read that a total of 60 workers died in the construction of the two towers before their combined opening in 1973, and felt sick at the idea of what an awful death it would be to plummet from this height.

I had to get away from those windows, but somehow felt compelled to stay for a while and take everything in. I had no idea when, if ever, I would get back to this extraordinary place, so I got some quick happy snaps to prove to everyone back home that I'd actually been here, grabbed one of the giant pretzels (slathered in mustard) from the cafeteria everyone said was a New York must, and parked myself for two perfect hours on one of the scattered bench seats to watch it all from a comfortable distance ...

The shifting shadows across the city as the sun's orb began to slowly fall behind the Manhattan skyline and cast its last golden rays over Brooklyn. The occasional puff of a passing cloud, so close I felt I could almost reach out and touch it – much like the North Tower, sitting so separate, yet so inextricably linked to its southern twin, where I was perched. The jet planes regularly making their way across the sky's superhighway in and out of JFK in the near distance seemingly at the same soaring height as us.

It was a moment in time to savour.

*

The next day would be a big one, and my instructions from Trevor were to be down at the *Ms.* magazine offices at East 32nd Street at 9.30am to meet with Gloria Steinem and the team.

I was excited. I knew that much of the life I was now living was largely made possible by the bravery of women like Steinem who had for decades, despite enormous pushback, been taking on the patriarchy and working hard to help redefine modern womanhood.

Under Steinem's leadership, *Ms.* was the first US magazine to demand the repeal of laws that criminalised abortion, and the first to: advocate for the Equal Rights Amendment; rate presidential candidates on women's issues; put domestic violence and sexual harassment on its cover; fight to close the gender pay gap; conduct a national study on date rape; and blow the whistle on the undue influence of advertising on journalism. As a writer, academic and activist, Gloria Steinem was a force to be reckoned with. And the ripple effects of her advocacy and activism were felt around the world.

One of her most celebrated pieces of writing came in 1963, when Steinem was employed as a Playboy Bunny at Hugh Hefner's New York Playboy Club. She then detailed the exploitative working conditions experienced there as well as the sexual demands made upon the women.

In a semi-satirical essay she wrote for *Cosmopolitan* magazine, titled 'If Men Could Menstruate', she imagined a world where – of course – periods would be a badge of honour for men.

She was a fierce and vocal opponent of the Vietnam War, and had put Wonder Woman on the cover of the very first issue of *Ms*.

I loved her already.

Our first meeting was about to be brought forward, though, because there, waiting on my bedside table when I got back to my room, was a handwritten note from Gloria herself, welcoming me to New York and inviting me to dinner that night with someone called Elaine.

'We'll be there to pick you up from The Plaza foyer at 7pm. Dinner at Elaine's. See you then. Gloria. x'

'They,' I discovered, were Gloria and her boyfriend, Mort. And 'Elaine's' turned out not to be a 'someone', but a chichi restaurant where 'someone who was anyone' ate in New York.

Both Gloria and Mort were warm and welcoming from the outset and keen that my first dinner in New York be a memorable one. Mort was in fact quite the man about town, a Canadian billionaire who had made his fortune first as a magazine editor and now as an investor. Gloria was as whip-smart and gracious a woman as I had ever met. She also shared over dinner that she had recently been diagnosed with breast cancer, but was fighting it hard and optimistic that all would be OK.

We talked at length about publishing, and about the history of *Ms*. and its crucial place in improving women's lives. I assured her that I would do all I could to support the magazine before I reported back to Kerry in a month.

Then, something truly weird happened. I had already clocked as soon as we arrived at Elaine's that over in the corner, not three tables away and all in black, was the supremely elegant figure of former US First Lady, Jackie Kennedy, and by the door, actor Robert De Niro, both of whom had nodded warmly and waved to Gloria and Mort. Right now, though, the small greying form of a somewhat dishevelled, curly-headed man in spectacles, a crumpled shirt and baggy pants was approaching the table.

It was Woody Allen. Not with his partner, actress Mia Farrow, but a stunningly beautiful young woman, perhaps 20 years or more his junior whom I didn't recognise. They appeared to be close.

The actor, renowned for his awkward demeanour, had an obvious affection for Gloria and Mort, and after a warm exchange of words, Gloria introduced me to Allen and his companion as her 'friend just arrived from Australia'.

'Uh-strail-yuh! I wanna go there one day. You have some fabulous actors coming out of there I wanna use in my films,' he said.

That was great to hear, I said. 'Which ones?'

'I love Judy Davis; she's so talented. I'd love to work with her. And there's another one, a young redhead. I can't remember her name, but someone sent me a movie she was in. She's really got something.'

It was only later, after they had said their goodbyes and headed out into the freshly falling snow of 88th Street, that I wondered if the 'redhead' he was talking about was Nicole.

'I thought he was with Mia Farrow?' I whispered once they were gone, clearly exposing my knowledge of celebrity pop culture way more than was probably cool in this moment. I was sure Gloria had no time for such mindless trivialities, and I instantly regretted appearing to gossip so soon after Allen had left the conversation.

But Gloria, with her eyebrow raised, was totally up for it.

'I know,' she said. 'He and Mia have this interesting relationship where they both keep apartments on opposite sides of Central Park, and I get that. I think a lot of relationships would work better that way. She has this huge heart and lots of kids – some of them adopted – but I don't think he's that much into kids.'

Turns out Woody was often seen out with young starlets, just like the protagonists in the plotlines of his own movies, a good number of which involved Allen falling in love with inappropriately young women – or them with him. 'He's a brilliant filmmaker,' Gloria said, 'so he seems to get away with it.'

*

It had been an exhilarating two weeks. By day I was working with the small, committed team at the charmingly chaotic *Ms.* offices on 34th Street, led by Gloria. While the content for the magazine was much heavier and more hardline than I was used to, I could definitely see various ways forward to drive sales – one of Trevor's key requests of me during this month-long sabbatical. And Gloria was open to it all.

By night, she continued to show me the best that New York had to offer, including a trip to the famed Studio 54, and what was now the city's newest, hottest club, Nell's, co-owned by and named after Aussie actress Nell Campbell.

Nell was famous on so many levels. First, as a feature character in her father Ross's gently satirical *Women's Weekly* column about Aussie family life in the 50s and 60s. Then, in 1975, the 22-year-old Nell had tap-danced her way into cult film history as the top-hatted Columbia in *The Rocky Horror Picture Show*.

Now, as the co-owner of the trendiest club in New York, she was playing the real-life role of 'mine host' every night in the club's darkened, slightly decadent interior, with its beaded chandeliers and rich velvet sofas. Nell herself was in the middle of it all, with her flaming red Cleopatra bob, flapper-like fashion style and penchant for, on occasion, tabletop dancing.

Nell's was the favoured nightspot of Mick Jagger, Jerry Hall, Debbie Harry, Calvin Klein and the famously reclusive Prince. In recent weeks, the club had only grown in infamy with word that it was the last nightspot famed 60s pop artist Andy Warhol had visited before his untimely death. And on the night we were there, it didn't take long for Nell and Gloria to plunge into animated conversation.

Everyone loved Gloria. Her fast-paced New York world, mixed with the long hours we were putting in at the office every day, was an intoxicating combination for me. Often, when I got back to my room at night, I would lie there staring at the ceiling, studying its delightfully pretty turn-of-the-century cornices and listening to the muffled sounds of life on 59th Street – there was *always* life on 59th Street – rising up from below, still not quite believing my extreme good fortune in having these once-in-a-lifetime experiences.

Every time I tried to describe some of the latest amazing things that had happened when I called Mum, Dad and Chris back home, I would pull back on the detail, lest they thought I was getting too carried away by the glamour of it all.

'Look, I'm just enjoying it while it lasts. I know it will all come to an end soon,' I would say. But every night as I closed my eyes, I was willing myself to never forget these days.

Unfortunately, these days and that end would come sooner than I was expecting. By that third weekend, I got a message from Trevor. Both he and Kerry were in New York for a few days, and they wanted to meet me for dinner in Kerry's suite at the Waldorf Astoria over on Park Avenue.

That night they told me that Kerry's financial team had done the books and, in the end, it didn't matter what I thought could be done editorially. Much as Kerry was keen to get a foothold into the US market, they just couldn't see a way to make it work financially. *Ms.* was not going to provide the opportunity he'd hoped, and it was time for me to pack up and head home.

It was hard to farewell Gloria that next day. Kerry had already called her with the news that we were pulling out, but she insisted on us both having lunch before I headed to the airport. I felt like I'd let her down, but she assured me there were no hard feelings. Kerry had been absolutely charming and she had, she said, faced much tougher battles over the years – this was just one more. And I knew that was true.

Gloria was a warrior to beat them all, and so much of what I'd learnt in those two weeks came from simply observing the courage, humility and grace with which she went about her work and lived her life. Her commitment to the cause of bettering the lives of women right around the world was lifelong and unwavering, and I was so much the richer for having been in her incredible company.

It had been an unforgettable experience, I told her, as we said goodbye on the steps of The Plaza before I jumped in my cab for JFK.

And then I suddenly realised: I'd never thought to get a single photo with this woman it had been such an honour to work alongside.

'Would you mind if I got a photo?' I asked. And with her typical generosity, Gloria said, 'I insist.'

With that, I passed my camera and a ten-dollar tip to the closest hotel doorman, no doubt well used to these types of requests from excited tourists, and he took the snap of Gloria and me I knew I would treasure forever.

Back home, I could hardly wait as I left the half-dozen rolls of film of my New York adventure for processing at the local chemist. Four days later, they were ready. The pics I'd taken of that incredible view at the top of the World Trade Center, the one I captured of me sitting on the edge of my bed before the dinner at Elaine's with that clever time-lapse button on my camera ... and of course, my much-anticipated picture on The Plaza steps with Gloria.

But it seems my doorman wasn't quite as adept at taking pictures as I'd hoped because when I excitedly pulled that photo, the last one on the roll, out of its bright yellow Kodak envelope, I discovered it was completely out of focus. A total blur. Much like my entire, unreal, unrepeatable New York experience itself. How very appropriate, I thought.

As for *Ms.* magazine's future, just months later, Australia came knocking on Gloria's door once again. This time, it was in the shape of my former colleague at *Dolly*, the redoubtable Sandra Yates. As well as being interested in buying *Ms.*, Sandra was now just months away from finally launching *Sassy* magazine into the US market as planned. And *Sassy* was about to get herself a big US sister.

CHAPTER FOURTEEN

Saved by the bachelors

'A strong woman looks a challenge in the eye and
gives it a wink.' – Gina Carey

So, THE CENTREFOLD WAS gone, and while its removal had ultimately worked, a few years on I still felt we needed something in its place – something we, and most importantly our readers, could have fun with. With just a minuscule annual marketing budget for TV and radio ads, whatever this new thing was needed to be something that would guarantee us free publicity. Something so irresistible, so tantalising, that TV, radio *and* newspapers would just *have* to talk about it.

While *Cleo* was serious about encouraging women to forge an independent, fulfilling life with or without a man, and safe sex remained a crucial pillar of our editorial as the world continued to deal with the AIDS crisis, I still felt there was room for a bit of cheekiness when it came to blokes.

I had an idea. As we headed towards the late 80s, the world had become obsessed with lists. The Most, The Best, The Funniest, The Sexiest, The Richest, The Hottest of anything and everything were all suddenly big talking points. So why not start a list of our own? And so began *Cleo*'s annual List of Australia's 50 Most Eligible Bachelors.

While I may have been known to some as the killjoy who had so heartlessly removed a dozen nude blokes from the pages of the magazine every year (mostly, as I discovered, to the great disappointment of our gay readers), I was now giving back 50, albeit with their clothes on, and with lives and careers and passions that went well beyond what they might look like covered in fake tan and baby oil, with their genitalia hidden behind a strategically placed prop.

It wasn't a bad job instruction to give my mostly female, largely single, *Cleo* staff either: get out there and keep an eagle eye out for straight, eligible bachelors leading interesting lives with no 'significant other' to speak of. And make sure they're *nice* blokes. The sort of guys you'd recommend to your closest girlfriends.

But there was a caveat: the sort of guys I wanted for our annual list of 50 were the very type that I hoped *wouldn't* want to be on a list like this. A no-dickhead policy, if you like – a little bit of humility being one of the most attractive qualities of all.

It set quite the challenge for Deborah Thomas, my new beauty and lifestyle editor. But she was up for it. Deb was a former model who'd graced the European catwalks for every top international designer early in her career and was settled back in Oz as a budding writer and stylist when she came to work for me.

Deb was superbly hooked in with the business, arts and social scenes in Sydney and Melbourne, and proved pretty quickly she could nail any task I set her, including the annual Bachelor List.

And if that list was going to perform its intended PR job, we needed to convince a number of high-profile names to take part, and there were very few Deb couldn't get over the line. INXS lead singer Michael Hutchence; successful Bondi surf shop owner David Gyngell; up-and-coming author Tim Winton; and one of the coolest actors around, Ben Mendelsohn were all reluctant to appear, but Deb's charm managed to talk every one of them around.

Sure enough, the media loved it, as did our readers, and every year we were inundated with suggestions for future bachelor inclusions. We became pretty good at weeding out the pushy self-promoters and the cheeky gay guys for whom, we discovered, it was a badge of honour to sneak their way onto the list. We also had to make a lot of awkward 'backgrounding' phone calls … which sometimes resulted in last-minute changes before we went to press.

Each year, as soon as the list came out, everyone had an opinion on who had and hadn't, should and shouldn't have made the list; and once or twice, we heard from disgruntled exes. And disgruntled 'currents'. On one notable occasion, a fiancée emerged who begged to differ as to the said bachelor's 'availability'. Somehow, he'd forgotten to tell us about his forthcoming wedding. But she fixed that problem pretty quickly. Before the day was out, the engagement was over, and he was indeed now fully single once again.

By any measure, I was loving my time at *Cleo* and, once again, just like at *Dolly*, I was surrounded by a hugely talented, hard-working team. The hours were long, but the work was a joy.

Planning meetings in my office were a hoot ... especially when it came to talking through ideas for relationship articles. Egos had to be left at the door, and strict Chatham House rules applied as every sexual vulnerability was laid bare, every crazy fear exposed, every embarrassing bedroom experience shared. It was all fodder for stories and nothing – at least in those meetings – was off limits.

Close friendships in the office were common. I was working with a group of people I really liked – which now included Kerry's daughter, Gretel, whom I'd first met at Palm Beach on that fateful day a few years before. Kerry told me she'd developed a huge interest in the magazine side of the business, and he wanted me to teach her all I knew.

While I was flattered by Kerry's request, I also knew it was a double-edged sword. Gretel joined as the lowest-paid, most junior person in the office – but I didn't want anyone to feel that the boss's daughter was about to take their job.

I needn't have worried; Gretel got it. Far from presenting as the privileged one, the softly spoken Gretel quickly became known in the office for her strong work ethic. From taping the soles of shoes for fashion shoots and making coffee, to answering phones and doing hours of research down in the ACP library, Gretel was keen to prove she had zero interest in any free ride. Her title was editorial assistant, and with her desk right next to reception, that often meant welcoming visitors, which sometimes included her own dad when he came to see me. I know it took both of them enormous restraint not to greet each other with a kiss on those occasions.

Kerry utterly adored Gretel, and soon so did the entire *Cleo* staff. Everyone could see she was working doubly hard to prove herself. And now, just six months after she had joined *Cleo*, all 20 of us were opening up the stunning, personally monogrammed invitations we'd received to attend her 21st birthday party at the Packer family compound in the city's Eastern Suburbs.

It was one of the biggest parties Sydney had ever seen, and for many of us, it lasted well into bacon and eggs the next morning. But despite a very foggy head, there was one thing none of us would ever forget from that night: it doesn't get much better than John Farnham doing a ten-minute version of 'You're the Voice' live on stage *right there* at your friend's 21st while you and everyone else 'make a noise and make it cleeeear' at the top of your lungs.

*

I don't think I'd ever seen Dad work so hard. There was so much going on at rugby headquarters in the city as the Wallabies prepared for the '91 World Cup in England the following year. After 18 months of complicated negotiations, Dad had finally managed to secure an Australian tour by Russia's national side – one of many such tours scheduled for the intense lead-up to the UK World Cup. Much as Dad was absolutely loving his job as a rugby administrator, the Russian tour had been a mammoth task, and I could see how exhausted he was.

The last game at the Sydney Football Stadium of the six-match tour was a particularly tough day for Dad. He was feeling poorly and the game itself was proving vicious. The Russians were being trounced by the Sydney side, and with the score at 35–4, captain Nick Farr-Jones had to be helped from the field with a suspected broken jaw after being targeted in a king hit from behind by one of the Russian forwards. It was described as one of the dirtiest matches ever played on Australian soil.

Dad, too, tried to hang on until the end of that game. Along with Farr-Jones, many of his favourite players were on the field that day, including Tim Gavin, Phil Kearns and, in the number-5 jersey, a guy called Peter FitzSimons. But Dad was having real trouble breathing there on the sidelines after being diagnosed at Christmas with pleurisy. His long-time doctor had assured him it would clear up in a few weeks. It was now April.

'All those years of smoking have caught up with you, Ray,' Dr Gardiner had said. I took heart from knowing that, after a shocking case of the flu a decade before, Dad had given up his two-pack-a-day habit cold turkey and hadn't had a single cigarette since.

But as the final whistle blew and he was taken from the Sydney Football Stadium by ambulance to Royal North Shore Hospital that night, the pleurisy diagnosis changed. It had moved to emphysema, an incurable lung disease with a life expectancy of around five years. The doctors told us that early detection was key, however, and, with treatment, that prognosis could be extended.

Nothing could have prepared us for that news. Five years. How could that possibly be? I tried to imagine a life without Dad in it. I simply couldn't.

Even though Chris and I had been engaged for a few years, we'd never really talked about an actual wedding. Should we now? For Dad? What about grandkids? The idea that he would never get to see his own grandchildren grow up, and they, in turn, would be robbed of his beautiful presence in their lives was just too much to contemplate.

But I was racing too far ahead. The doctors assured us that Dad could still live a normal-ish life. There would be drugs, a need for regular oxygen-assisted breathing, and they were looking at other treatments that might help.

The timing of the diagnosis couldn't have been worse. Chris and I had long ago booked a mid-April holiday in Italy, and I was positive we should cancel. Mum assured me Dad would be fine, and Dad made me promise we would still go. He just needed to take it easy for a while, he said, 'And then when you get back, I'll be right as rain.'

But when they both came to the airport to see us off a few weeks later, Dad suddenly looked decades older than his 68 years. Where once he would have insisted on walking with us to the gate to say our farewells, today he apologised: he wasn't feeling quite strong enough. Instead, we hugged goodbye at the check-in counter. And as we wrapped our arms around each other, we both held on far, far longer than usual. I didn't want him to see my tears, but when I saw his and Mum's, I knew. We were all scared.

*

I had never been to Venice before; and while I was checking in with Mum by phone every night to see how Dad was doing – her answer was always the same: 'He's fine, darling, he's just taking it easy' – Chris and I tried as hard as we could to make the most of our holiday in this fairy-tale city with its romantic waterways, cobblestone streets and gondolas gliding under endless bridges that linked this ancient city back to itself.

Everywhere I looked was a photo waiting to happen, and with my growing love of photography and brand-new camera with its telephoto lens at the ready, I started taking pictures for *Cleo* of the stunning street fashions the women of Venice wore so effortlessly. Seriously, what was this trick Italian women had for arranging a scarf *just so* that instantly made any outfit exquisite?

It was the Easter weekend of 1990 and we were loving it, but just one week into our Italian holiday, Chris and I decided it was time to head home. Dad was in hospital once again after taking a turn for the worse. Mum tried to tell me it was just for some more tests – they were being cautious, she said – and we should really stay and finish off the last week of our holiday, but I could hear the fear in her voice from the other side of the world.

Then, when Chris and I emerged into the Arrivals hall at Sydney airport on that Sunday night and unexpectedly saw the lone figure of Kyle waiting for us, I knew it could mean only one thing.

The diagnosis, he said, was wrong. Doctors had tried to find the primary cancer. It was probably in the lungs, they thought, but by this stage, there was no telling where it had begun. It was too far advanced. Too unforgivably late. Dad's entire body was now riddled with it.

It took me 36 hours to find the courage to stand at reception in Royal North Shore Hospital and ask for Ray Wilkinson's room in the Oncology ward. Kyle had already warned me that Dad had lost a lot of weight and was looking much the worse for all the drugs and painkillers they were using. Then I realised, I'd never really seen Dad in pain before. I didn't want to start now, but I had no choice.

I steeled myself. But when I arrived at his room, Dad was nowhere to be seen. In fact, in this shared ward for four, there was just a blank space where his bed should have been.

'He's just off having radiation,' one of the other gentlemen in the room said, perhaps seeing my sudden look of panic. 'You must be Ray's daughter, Lisa. He said he was hoping to see you today.'

It was no surprise to me that Dad had already made some friends here in hospital. Four men, whose lives had never intersected before, were now inextricably linked forever by their cancer diagnosis and shared fate.

While the two other gentlemen in the room slept, Geoff, who looked to be in his mid-forties, introduced himself. And in a soft voice, so as not to wake the others, he said, 'Your dad is struggling a bit with the radiation. He's been gone a few hours.'

I took some solace from that. Radiation. That had to be a good sign. At least he wasn't on heavy-duty chemotherapy. At least we weren't at that point yet.

And here was Dad in his bed, being wheeled in now. Almost unrecognisable, with oxygen tubes, drips and beeping monitors everywhere.

'Oh look, Ray. You have a visitor. Now, this has to be your daughter!' one of the cheery nurses said, as they positioned Dad back by the window, next to all those machines, before double-checking the drip connections and his blood pressure. Dad was only just awake. 'I think your dad is finding the radiation a bit much. Doctor wants to talk to the family about whether it's still worth putting him through this.'

I looked over at Dad. He was drowsy, but tears were rolling down his cheeks. It clearly wasn't worth it.

And with one, final heart-wrenching meeting with doctors the following day, there was no more pretending. Dad was coming home to die.

*

No-one could tell us how long Dad had, not even the lovely visiting area nurse Julie, whom we took aside in the kitchen every day, just out of earshot of Dad, and asked that same question. She simply didn't know.

'Just make the most of the time you still have with him,' she would say, before administering the sort of end-of-life care and kindness that went way beyond anything medicine could possibly do.

Every afternoon, it felt like an angel had walked through the door as she cheerily chatted to Dad, gave him back massages, monitored and administered his pain relief, helped us bathe him and, without fail, told us what a wonderful job we were doing. We knew that nothing we did changed a jot the inevitability of what was happening; but those encouraging words from Julie mattered and always kept us going for another 24 hours, until her next visit.

Meantime, we tried to make Dad as comfortable as possible. Kyle organised a recliner chair and set it up in the lounge room so Dad could watch his beloved rugby games on TV; both of us took turns helping Mum. She was being so incredibly strong. But we were all fretting about Brett, who had been travelling through Europe for the last six months. Now backpacking his way home via the remote beaches and jungles of Thailand, he hadn't called for weeks and we couldn't contact him. He had no idea Dad was dying.

Apart from those few rugby games on TV, if there was one bright spot for Dad over those weeks, it was when I read out for him anything rugby-related in the papers. In particular, he was loving the writings of one of the *Sydney Morning Herald*'s newest columnists, and current Wallaby, Peter FitzSimons.

One in particular – about a call he had taken out of the blue from ocker advertising guru John Singleton – actually made Dad laugh. And for me, the story hit very close to home as I read it to Dad ...

'Hello, Fitzy mate?' (This from a man I'd never met or talked to in my life.)

'Er, yes?'

'Mate, ha, ha, ha ... you sure looked pretty buggered running around on the box the other night ... ho, ho, ho ... I wasn't sure if you were going to make it, ho, ho, ho ...'

'Yes, uh, John, ha (?), ha (?), ha (?), I sure was buggered ...'

On it went. Somehow, after 20 seconds we were speaking with the familiarity of old friends. A minute passed and we were like brothers. After two minutes I had the distinct impression that if my mate Singo had come by the knowledge that I needed a kidney transplant, he wouldn't have hesitated more than a split second to give me one of his – under the auspices of the Really Old Mates Act. Call me a gullible fool if you like, but it was 'male bonding' over the phone par excellence, with all the work done by him, and when the time came I was more than primed for the kill.

'So anyway, Mate, we've been approached by *Cleo* magazine – on a non-commercial basis – asking us to try and sell the advantages of being a househusband, and we needed the ugliest mug we could find, so I immediately thought of you ... ha, ha, ha.'

What this 'thing' for *Cleo* magazine involved was for me, a fairly scarred footballing type, to dress up as a caricature of a housewife, with apron and curlers and the whole deal while they took photos of me from every angle bar up my left nostril. For publication in a national magazine.

Could anything be more excruciatingly embarrassing? 'Sure, John, mate, if I can help you out in any way I'd be very happy to.' (What could I do? I knew full well by this time the guy would have kicked in a kidney for me if I'd needed it, so what was a little photo shoot in return?)

'Great, Fitzy, our people will be in touch to organise times and dates. Thanks. Bye.' Click.

Uh, who was that masked man anyway?

How could it be that on the strength of a three-minute phone call, I'd readily agreed to do something so contrary to my real wishes it was breathtaking?

Well, he was John Singleton after all, and he was an Old Mate …

Was this the quintessentially Australian way of doing business? To create in two minutes a strong atmosphere of Old Mateship, and then quickly invoke the Old Mates Act, before signing off with a quick slap on the back?

It was devastatingly effective. It took a good six hours of rational, analytical and logical progress, step by step in my head, to make headway against the overwhelming feeling that I couldn't let down such a tried-and-true Old Mate. Finally, I decided I really didn't want to be photographed in such a fashion.

Even then, it took three schooners and a lot of anguish before I worked up the courage to totally betray ol' Singo and make the call to renege on my promise.

I still hate myself for doing it to him and I know I'll never be able to look him in the eye again. But I have every confidence that Singo will go a long, long way, regardless. Even on one kidney. He's a good 'un alright, my mate Singo. A real good 'un.

It was lovely hearing Dad laugh.

CHAPTER FIFTEEN

Good night, sweet prince ...

'You – you alone will have the stars as no-one else has them.
In one of the stars I shall be living. In one of them I shall be
laughing. And so it will be as if all the stars were laughing
when you look at the sky at night. You – only you –
will have stars that can laugh.'
– Antoine De Saint-Exupéry, *The Little Prince*

IF THERE IS A marker for that moment in the silent watch of the
night when one day has truly passed, and another sits ready to
begin, it is at 3am. And on this cool mid-May morning, as Chris
and I lay in Mum and Dad's bed, trying to get some rest between
Dad's four-hourly morphine doses, it didn't take much for me to
wake as the bedside alarm clicked over to 3.00.

Had I even slept? The past three weeks had felt like I was
moving through a strange, shadowy twilight where everything was
not quite real, and the best way forward was to lightly skim over
the surface, hoping perhaps that I would soon wake from this awful
nightmare and Dad would be OK.

As I gently moved the sheets aside, I momentarily looked over at
Chris, his face just discernible in the glow of the streetlights outside.
Dad had been like a surrogate father to him for the eight years we
had been together, and Chris, too, was struggling.

As I looked at him again, I took a deep breath and tried to draw some strength. Bleary eyed as I was, there was a job to be done – administering that next crucial dose of morphine to ease Dad's pain. Yesterday had been a particularly bad one for Dad, and now that things were nearing the end, I wondered if Julie, who had been so good at keeping our spirits up for those hour-long afternoon visits, had increased the intensity of the dose as I had heard so often whispered when cancer patients are in their final days. Did I want that for Dad? Did I want the end to be hastened if it lessened the agony for him?

As I pulled on my dressing gown and made my way into the lounge room, those thoughts no longer mattered when I saw Mum. She hadn't left his side all night, and now she was rocking back and forth, tears falling onto Dad's left hand as she kissed it, desperately, softly, repeating the words, 'I love you. I love you. Ray, I love you ...'

I raced over, knelt down next to him and gently lifted his right hand into mine and gave it one long, lasting kiss. The hand that had once played so exquisitely his beloved double bass. The one responsible for the most beautiful, sweeping handwriting I'd ever seen, the same handwriting that had imparted so much wisdom to so many over the years. The hand that would have patted my tiny forehead on the day I first entered the world.

But now, his hand felt different. There was no response.

Through her tears, Mum was still repeating the words, 'Ray, I love you,' while Kyle was now rubbing her back. It was 3.01 and I could see on the small side table, next to the ever-present box of tissues, that the morphine vial was still full.

The next dose was a minute past due, but as I looked at Mum and Kyle wondering why, I knew. There was no point. The cycle of life was now taking over and applying its own, ultimate pain relief.

It was time.

And with that, I dared to glance up to that beautiful face I loved and trusted and utterly adored: suddenly all the pain and the years were starting to disappear. I wanted to tell Dad it was OK. To let go. But I just couldn't find the strength. And I wouldn't have meant it anyway. I simply wasn't ready. Just one more day. Please, just one more day with this beautiful man. The deep, aching hurt was like nothing I had ever felt before. No, please, not yet. I'm not ready.

'I love you, Dad,' was all I could manage.

And then, with one last gentle, almost imperceptible shallow breath, everything stopped.

Dad was gone.

All that kindness, all that wisdom, all that gentle love, just gone. Gone. Forever. It was as final a moment as I have ever experienced.

Somehow though, none of us could bring ourselves to acknowledge what had just happened in the minutes that followed. Instead, we sat there talking to Dad, his presence still strangely in the room, repeatedly telling him the depths of our love, hoping that wherever the winds were taking him, he could hear us.

I felt a hand on my shoulder. It was Chris. Without a single word, he had seen it all.

I turned, not daring to move from Dad's side, and finally said the words I never thought I would.

'He's ... gone.'

Chris leaned down towards me, wiping away his own tears, and kissed me gently on the forehead, just like Dad used to. 'I know, sweetheart, I know.'

I looked over at Kyle. Was this really the day Dad was meant to go? Why did it all happen so quickly? He's only 68. He's too young. He can't go now – Brett doesn't even know he's sick. How on earth can we track him down? Nothing was making any sense.

Because when you lose someone you love so unconditionally, so completely, and who loves you in a way you know no other man ever will, not only does your heart break, but your sense of meaning does, too. All the comforting clichés, all the stories we tell ourselves about how strong we are, and how we want the pain to be over for them, they all melt away in the face of complete and permanent loss.

Mum and I sat there, not daring to move, holding Dad's now lifeless hands, still telling him all the things we felt needed saying. Kyle bent down and kissed Dad, a long, beautiful kiss, as gentle as it was final, and silently stepped outside into the chilly darkness. I looked again at the clock: 3.15am. In just three hours, the sun would come up on a world that, for the first time in my life, no longer offered my father's embrace.

As Kyle stood under the porch light, his head bowed, I wondered if he had prepared for this moment. I had no idea what we were meant to do now. I looked up into the leaves of the giant camphor laurel trees outside the lounge room, glowing transparent green through the streetlight. There was not a breath of wind. Nothing was stirring. The only sound, the occasional faint call of the pre-dawn curlews.

I looked down once again at Dad's limp body, Mum still unable to leave his side. I suddenly felt four years old again, lost in a crowd, not recognising anyone or anything, desperately searching for Dad's gentle, familiar figure. Then, willing myself, I remembered in a warm rush what it was to see his smile, feel his comforting hands reaching out for me and scooping me up in his arms, knowing everything would be alright as I nestled my head in that perfect space made just for me in the cradle of his neck.

But nothing would ever be alright again. I closed my eyes, but the ache, deep in the pit of my stomach, was overwhelming. How is the human body meant to withstand this? My whole world felt like it had just disintegrated like burnt paper between my hands.

Then I heard Kyle in the hallway, on the phone to the funeral home. Chris at some point had quietly slipped away, and three tangled, impossible hours by Dad's side had passed in mere minutes. Now the first fingers of dawn's light were reaching in to the lounge room as if to make real, the unreal. Just as I wanted to run away, Kyle had stepped up for both me and Mum. An undertaker would be here shortly.

With that, I kissed Dad's cheek and softly stroked his hand for the last time, and apologised to Mum. I hated myself for being so weak, but I was woefully unprepared for what was about to happen. As I saw that van turn up and Kyle went out to open the gates, I quickly dressed, gave Mum the longest hug and left my mother and father alone, for their very last moments together.

As I walked out the gate, I saw the faces of the two men who would be taking Dad. I wanted to say 'Please be gentle', but I didn't.

There was no point. It felt like there was no point to anything anymore.

Except anger. Why on this day, of all days, was the sun shining? Why was life everywhere appearing to carry on as it always did. I wanted everything to pause and be still. Instead, commuters were still rushing to catch the bus. Kids in uniforms were still heading to school. Packed buses were still heading towards the city. Life was still going on. Just like any other day. It was all so utterly normal. And so unspeakably cruel.

*

Funerals are strange things. Just when you want the world to go away, the world comes rushing right at you, demanding your attention. There are so many people to contact … and readings and music and photos and food and speakers and eulogies and beers to organise.

And exactly what grain of wood would you be after on Dad's coffin, do you think? What about the handles – traditional brass, or maybe something in black iron? A lot of families feel that's more masculine for Dad.

I wondered if maybe it was all an unintended side benefit of funerals – to keep you so busy and distracted with detail in the days following your loss as to momentarily push all that grief aside.

Even still, it took me three throat-burning shots from an all-but-forgotten bottle of Dad's 25-year-old Johnnie Walker just to have the courage to get in the car taking us to the service at Northern Suburbs Crematorium that morning … and I could have done with three more when our first-day-on-the-job funeral car driver got completely lost on the way.

By the time we arrived, the chapel was completely packed out – with just as many outside as in. Simply hundreds of people, whose lives Dad had forever touched, turned up to pay their respects. From rugby clubs right across the state to current and former Wallabies; Lions Club members and presidents; charities and community groups he'd worked with; all his old colleagues from Cyclone; band members from his muso days. And of course, Campbelltown turned up in force. Everyone was in shock at the speed of Dad's death and wanted to bid farewell to a man it was impossible not to have loved and learnt from.

As Kyle, Chris and I took our places in the front pew, with Kyle and me seated either side of Mum, I was once again struck by her incredible strength. After 40 years together, and at the age of just 61, she was now a widow, as the one man who had never let her down was gone.

Together we listened to story after story of Dad's countless kindnesses, of lives he quietly guided and of lessons taught when he thought no-one was watching. How Kyle then gathered the strength to deliver the eulogy – so beautifully – I will never know.

One thing I did know was that life, for me, would never ever be the same.

*

Trevor told me to take off as much time as I needed before heading back to work. But after a week, I was ready. I'd read, I'd walked, I'd cried, I'd gone on long drives, I'd sat with Mum, I'd cried some more. Brett had finally rung, and he was heading home. For all of us, the aching, the yearning for Dad was unbearable. But now I needed to get busy and find a way to climb out of this deep well of sadness.

Our latest issue was hitting the stands on Monday, and there was a request for me to appear on the *Today* show over at Channel 9. I really liked the hosts, Liz Hayes and Steve Liebmann, as they'd always been so kind to me in the past, and even though smiling for the cameras was the very last thing I felt like doing, I knew Dad would want me to get on with my life. Work seemed like the easiest way to get back on the horse.

I was scheduled for a 7.40am appearance, so I set the alarm for 5.45am, allowing plenty of time for the poor Channel 9 hair and makeup team to try and put my sad, puffy, pillow-marked face into some sort of presentable order for the cameras.

I woke early that morning and lay there for what felt like hours, staring at the ceiling, feeling every one of the slow beats of my broken heart. I looked over at the bedside clock. 5.40am. God it was early. How do breakfast hosts do this every day? I wondered.

Chris, beside me, was still fast asleep. I turned the alarm off so as not to wake him, and pulled the doona just a tad higher for those last few minutes. The chill of the approaching winter was settling in, and our little house was freezing cold. As Chris and I continued to work hard and save hard, we'd made the leap from our apartment just up the road, to this 1920's 'renovator's delight' right opposite the ferry wharf in Neutral Bay.

Sure, there were leaks in the roof, we never could quite get that funny old Kookaburra gas stove to work properly, and the 'lockup' garage on the street had recently collapsed during heavy rains ... but one day we'll renovate, I thought. And we'll put in that fireplace I'd talked to Dad about. Dad loved our house, and was excited for Chris and me, and our plans.

'Hi Lisa, thanks for coming, I'll take you straight through to hair and makeup,' the *Today* show producer said, as we made our way from Channel 9 reception through the endless maze of hallways, storerooms and prop bays backstage. No matter how many times I came to this place, these back-of-house areas always felt like I was just one wrong turn from finding myself somewhere I really shouldn't be.

That Monday morning traffic had been bad, though, and I only had about 20 minutes before going on air, so the producer was more than apologetic when she found that there was no spare chair when we arrived in hair and makeup.

'Sorry, we've just finished,' said one of the young makeup artists, as the producer guided me over to the still-occupied chair.

'That's great. Thanks Sal. Oh, hi; it's you, Peter!' she said as 'Peter' began to lift himself up and out of the chair.

'All good,' he said. 'I'm done,' before laughing and adding, 'Or at least as "done" as anyone is going to be able to make me.'

'Thanks, Peter, you're on after Lisa, so we just need to get her straight in the chair. Actually, not sure if you two know each other – Peter FitzSimons, this is Lisa Wilkinson. Lisa, Peter,' she said as this mountain of a man extended his big bear-like right hand towards me and continued to get up … and up … and up … and up. My god, he was huge.

'Hi there. Nice to meet you, Lisa,' he said as our hands met. What a lovely firm handshake, I thought, not too hard, not too soft, just … warm, as I looked up at his face and huge beaming smile.

That name, why was it so familiar? And then, suddenly his grip completely softened.

'Lisa … Wilkinson? You're not Ray Wilkinson's daughter, are you?'

Oh no. Please, no. Please don't mention Dad. Please don't know Dad. Please— And then I realised. *Peter FitzSimons.* The byline from the *Sydney Morning Herald.* Those articles I read Dad just weeks ago that had given him so much pleasure.

It was him. He was a rugby player. What do I say? Bloody hell, he was tall. I tried to look him in the eye, just as mine started to well up with tears.

'Everyone was so sorry to hear about your dad's passing. Ray Wilkinson was an amazing man. In fact, he organised a rugby tour I went on to Italy and France that completely changed my life. I hope you're OK …'

If only he knew. I was wearing the aftermath of a week's worth of tears, every lost hour of sleep, every ounce of my exhaustion raw on my face, so maybe he did. And now I was starting to cry. I just wanted to get into that makeup chair and work out what the heck I was going to say once I hit the bright lights of the studio.

'That's very kind. Thank you,' was all I could manage before I turned and slipped into the chair.

What a nice man, I thought, as I wiped away the few tears that had annoyingly escaped, and the producer handed me the list of things Liz and Steve wanted to discuss.

The makeup artist certainly had her work cut out for her now. 'You OK?' she asked, before handing me a tissue. I was – just – and thanked her. But now I had to concentrate. I had to get back to work.

CHAPTER SIXTEEN

An ending ... and a beginning

'Don't hold on to things that require a tight grip. Including thoughts, expectations, and even people. When you let them go you create space ... and in that space will flow the things that naturally fit.' – Mark Groves

SPRING FELT LIKE IT had finally arrived on this Saturday, as I sat in the reflected warmth of the September sun streaming through the big sliding timber windows in the front room at home. Many a time I'd tried to open those windows to try and catch the breeze off the harbour, but at some point in our old home's life, they'd been painted shut.

But no matter. This sunroom was enough. Its pretty views through the palm trees across the road down to the ferry wharf steps and the filtered phosphorescent shimmer of the water beyond was what sold it to us in the first place. On any given day in recent months, if I wasn't at work, this cosy spot was always where you would find me.

On this particular morning, I was doing what I so often did on weekends – working my way through the pile of accumulated paperwork I just couldn't quite get to during the week. There was a speech to write, feature stories to read and edit, and the *Cleo* 'grid' to play with – the giant monthly planning map of what went where in the next issue.

It was always a delicate balancing act trying to get those ratios of editorial to ads, fashion to features, and everything in between, just right. It determined the energy and the mood of every issue, and the uninterrupted hours I had at home always gave me plenty of time to work on that mix.

Work was proving a great way of keeping me occupied after Dad's passing. As a family, we felt in many ways that we had lost that crucial glue that had always held us together, and each of us was coping as best we could.

Chris, too, had struggled without Dad … and as he walked into the sunroom that morning, I could still see it. But there was something else. He looked concerned and asked if we could talk.

Chris wondered what I saw in our future. It was a big question for a Saturday morning and it momentarily threw me, as I looked into his eyes wondering where this was going. Did I see us together in ten years' time? he asked. Did I still want to get married? What about kids? I had to be honest. I wasn't sure I saw any of it in our future. Right now, I was just taking it one day at a time.

The truth was, though, after a short break-up four years before, Chris and I had never quite settled back into each other. I wondered if that wasn't just the way all relationships evolved over time: into a nice, warm, but ambivalent, companionship. There were worse scenarios.

But our lives were so separate now; and despite the laughter, the friends, and the tender memories we still shared, we had become not much more than caring flatmates. Our relationship – or at least the relationship we'd once planned for – was over. We both knew it, but that didn't make it any easier.

Chris and I had grown up together. He'd shown me a world I had never known. A world filled with Vivaldi's 'Four Seasons', the songs of Edith Piaf, the joy of foreign films, the ridiculous brilliance of Charlie Chaplin and the stunning writings of Pauline Kael; and he made me appreciate more than ever just how lucky I was to have known the security of two parents whose marriage, while not perfect, had endured even through difficult times.

Did I really want to lose this man who had so cherished my dad as if he were his own? Who knew better than anyone on the planet the deep and bottomless chasm losing him had created? As Chris said to me on more than one occasion, if you could choose a man to guide your path through life, you would always choose Ray. Chris understood how unique Dad was, and I loved him for knowing that.

I wondered if there was perhaps a world where Chris and I could not spend every day together but still co-exist, still care for each other, still check in, still be there in the tough times? Then I realised, we'd been doing that for years.

A life without Chris seemed unimaginable ... but so, too, did a future together.

Chris said he would move out the next morning. I couldn't stand being around to watch him pack, so I went to the gym, and by the time I got back, he was gone.

*

So, this was what a panic attack felt like.

It had been less than four months since Dad died, and not yet 24 hours since Chris had left. But as I lay in bed on this Monday morning, trying to will myself to get up and ready for work, something was wrong. I couldn't move. I was utterly terrified of getting out of bed. The world outside felt cold and dark; my internal world similarly bleak. I was suddenly acutely aware that I was now alone. Truly alone.

The two men who, just six months before, I knew would have laid down their lives for me, were both gone. I felt completely vulnerable and exposed to anything the world had to throw at me. How would I pay my mortgage if I got sick? Or lost my job? Who would I turn to? Who could I rely on now to tell me it would all be OK?

I was a strong woman, I knew that. I'd been running teams at work for more than a decade, and I could hold my own in just about any situation. It didn't matter. Because so much of that strength – that wind beneath my wings Bette Midler sang about –

came from the love I was surrounded by *outside* of work. I knew that if I ever did fall, there were two wonderful men right there ready to catch me.

It was well past 11 o'clock before I finally made it to the shower, and almost midday by the time I got out. Showers always made me feel better, and the water had run cold by the time I finished.

When I walked back to the bedroom I could see the red light flashing on the answering machine. It was Deb Thomas from work checking to make sure I was OK. After a couple of memorable overseas trips on photo shoots for work – most recently to Mexico and New Orleans – Deb and I had become great mates, and she was now my deputy. Deb knew I'd been having doubts about my future with Chris – tequila shots and tacos at 3am in a Cancun bar will do that to you – and I'd called her the night before to let her know what had happened.

'Don't worry about coming in, I've got everything under control. I just wanted to make sure you're OK,' she'd said in her message.

And with that, for the first time in my life, I gave myself permission to take a full-blown 'sickie'. I'd never done it at school, I'd never done it at work, and I'd certainly never done it as a boss. Lisa – always the 'good' girl, never wanting to disappoint.

It was a beautiful day, so I walked down to my favourite spot down by the harbour. Being lucky enough to live in this part of the world was never, ever lost on me; and looking at the water, seeing the ferries effortlessly slicing through the swell, watching young mums with their prams and kids on trainer-wheeled bikes thrilling in their first tentative moments unaided, just reminded me that life goes on.

Those questions Chris had asked about what I saw in my future – questions I'd never really considered or, or more likely, was avoiding – came back to me. I really wasn't sure what my future held. Less so now than ever. I'd turned 30. I suppose that window for having kids was starting to close. I wasn't even sure I wanted to have them anyway. And I certainly wasn't brave enough – or even sure I was capable enough – to have kids on my own.

I was far from ready for another relationship, too. If I was going to be single, this had to be the moment to wipe the slate clean, to spend more time with girlfriends, start work on that gnarly, unloved old garden at home – maybe even finally get to Morocco liked I'd once promised myself.

To this point so much of my self-identity had been tied up in my relationship with others. Someone's daughter, someone's partner, someone's employee, someone's boss. Without those definitions, I wasn't exactly sure who I was. It was as if for years I had been in a boat that had no oars, happily being carried by the ebb and flow of the current, just enjoying the view.

Maybe it was time I discovered the value of having an oar. And putting it in the water and steering myself. I wanted to create space for the new. In whatever form that took.

*

My personal life wasn't the only thing in a state of flux. The winds of change were rolling through ACP, too. After surviving a massive heart attack that had left him clinically dead for seven minutes (thereafter declaring he'd 'been to the other side and there's nothing'), Kerry was, on doctors' orders, scaling back his work schedule and encouraging his son, Jamie, to step up.

By 1991 there was also a new breed of management arriving at 54 Park Street. To the disappointment of every editor in the building, the much-loved Trevor had resigned to team up with Malcolm Turnbull as part of the Tourang consortium in an attempted takeover of Fairfax newspapers. Working on behalf of Kerry, the bid failed spectacularly, bitterly and publicly – and with it, a close personal and professional relationship of almost two decades was over. For all three.

To replace Trevor, at least in the magazine arm of the business, Kerry had hired Richard Walsh, a charming, cardigan-wearing, book-loving, former 60s wunderkind of the political satire magazine, *Oz*, and a Sydney University contemporary of Clive James.

Meanwhile, at 23, Jamie Packer had become James Packer, and a new CEO was appointed – a mentor to James, hand-picked by Kerry, who came with a ready-made reputation for ruthless cost-cutting. His name was Al 'Chainsaw' Dunlap. Known as a 'turnaround management specialist', he was said to delight in his long history of mass lay-offs at companies he'd 'turned around'. With his strong New Jersey accent, pinstripe suits and pocket kerchiefs, he looked and sounded more like a mafia don – which was probably the point, because he terrified everyone.

My one and only close encounter with him took place over a lunch, requested by James, so Dunlap could get to know some of us. Eight editors were chosen from the dozens in the building, and then put into groups of two to attend one of four lunches with Dunlap down at Circular Quay – the biblically ominous choreography of doing it all 'two-by-two', *by the water,* not lost on any of us. I was happy to be paired with Shona Martyn, the sharp-as-a-tack editor of *GH* magazine for what we'd both nervously speculated could have been our last supper. By the end of the mercifully short meal, an $800 bottle of wine, and a lot of boasting about the cost-cutting he was planning (which presumably, didn't include his own expensive bottles of wine at lunch), both Shona and I were scratching our heads as to the point of it all.

But soon after, Dunlap himself – live by the chainsaw, die by the chainsaw – was 'moved on', and eventually replaced by John Alexander, a former *Sydney Morning Herald* editor with elbows as razor-sharp as his instincts, and who himself became known as 'the dark prince of Park Street'.

With Trevor gone, Kerry and James were increasingly keen for me to meet the new management arrivals. My instructions were always the same: to acquaint whomever it was with all I knew about the magazine side of the business, and thereafter be someone they could call on should they need to.

By this stage, I was pretty good at knowing how to play the various personalities. But sometimes there are men – and the occasional woman – you come across who just make you shudder. Our eyes peel, and our backs straighten. I've always been pretty good at identifying the type and steering clear, but sometimes they're impossible to avoid. Particularly when your boss asks you to have lunch with one of them in ACP's fifth-floor dining room, a location of long legend at Park Street.

But on the day of our lunch, there was a last-minute change of venue to Tre Scalini, a bustling Italian restaurant just a short walk from the office across Hyde Park, which had quickly become a favourite of Sydney's Eastern Suburbs set. The lunch was set for 1pm; but when I arrived, so too did a beautiful young female reporter from one of Channel 9's new lifestyle programs. We'd never met before, and when we were both escorted to the same table for the same lunch, to be met by the same smiling middle-aged executive we'd also never met before, it was clear he had a different kind of spreadsheet on his mind.

At one point, when our host ducked out to the bathroom, the young reporter asked me if I had any idea why she had been summoned to lunch. This show she had just joined was her big break and she knew this guy had the ear of the Packers, mostly because he kept telling us that. How much lip service did she have to pay, she asked, when he was so clearly making a play for her?

'Leave it with me,' I said.

So, when he returned to the table and began telling her she should stop hiding that fabulous body of hers and start wearing bikinis – the teenier the better – when she's out shooting stories, I did the only thing any self-respecting member of the sisterhood would do in the same situation: I started asking him lots of questions about his wife and kids. I knew enough to do a little homework before the lunch so I just went for it: 'And did I hear you have another one on the way? Congratulations! How many does that make now?'

As she left to head back to Channel 9, the young reporter leaned in and whispered, 'Thank you. I owe you one'.

The walk back to ACP across Hyde Park with Mr Bikini Man was uncomfortable. Over the course of the lunch, he had asked me exactly nothing about the magazine business, but for some reason needed to tell me at great length about the mansion he was currently building by the harbour. Whatever. Then, as we stood at the lift back in the foyer at Park Street, he told me he had something he needed to get off his chest.

As the lift doors opened and we stepped in, he turned to me. 'You're single, right?' he asked.

'Ah, yeah.'

'Own your own place, right?'

'Well, not really, the bank owns it, but I'm working hard trying to pay it off, yeah.'

'And I think we all know you're ambitious too, aren't you?'

Clearly this was not a quality he was particularly used to in a woman.

'Well, yeah, I love my job, and I'm ambitious for the magazine's success, so yeah, I suppose, I don't know. Why?'

'Well, look at you, I mean you're pretty and successful and all that, but you'd scare any bloke right off. Blokes need to feel needed. You don't need a man. If I was you, I'd get used to being single.'

I'll never know if that was some sort of payback for thwarting his chances with our lunch companion, but with that parting shot, the lift doors opened and, without even bothering to turn his head in my direction, he said, 'Thanks for lunch,' before wandering off to do whatever the hell it was that he did.

Whoa. Silly me. Here I was thinking I was finally settling into singledom, living my best life. I was 31. Had the occasional quite nice date. Some hits, some misses. Chris and I agreed that I would buy his share of the house, and even though I knew it would once again be a huge financial stretch, I just didn't need another upheaval. I was paying it off on my own. I was proud of that. But according to this guy, that was a major turn-off for blokes. Really? And was *that* how the world saw me? Ambitious and scary?

I was completely thrown, despite trying really hard not to be.

*

Somehow, Liz Hayes and I just kept running into each other. We discovered we had a number of mutual friends, and every time we connected up, the friendship grew. Liz was the undisputed queen of breakfast TV, and at the time was married to one of Australia's highest-profile 'rogues' – adman John Singleton.

For better or worse, Singo was the personification of the ocker bloke, but despite his old-school ways, he had a history of being attracted to strong, successful, intelligent, beautiful women, and Liz, wary of his reputation, took some convincing before they quietly eloped.

Many thought it was an odd fit – just about every bloke in the country (and not a few women) had a huge crush on Liz. Did the hard-living, beer-swilling, many-times-married Singo really deserve the love of Australia's favourite sweetheart?

I, too, wondered about the connection, but John was an absolute charmer, and every time I saw them together, it was clear he adored her, and the attraction between them was obvious. The gossip columnists had a field day whenever they were seen in public together – which was not often. Despite their huge public profiles, both hated the attention.

But for all the highs with John, the lows eventually became too much, and when the marriage quietly came apart a few months later, I asked Liz if she'd like to move into my place. It was a long way from the Ritz, but it was cosy and private, and much as I was loving living on my own, I knew we were going to have a ball together.

*

The Bachelor List was now, by any measure, a raging success. Every year that issue was a sell-out. It generated year-round publicity. And advertisers were lining up with their chequebooks to get a piece of the 'Cleo Bachelor' action. So, to get more bang for those advertiser bucks, we held a big annual event in Melbourne towards the end of 'Bachelor month' to name the Bachelor of the Year.

I knew that Sydney media loved a freebie trip to Melbourne, and Melbourne media loved it when a Sydney-based brand brought the love and national attention to their city. It was a no-brainer, and every invitation sent came back a yes.

Our very first event was held at that Bourke Street institution, Florentino's restaurant. Melbourne's finest turned out in full force, as did the media. TV crews were wall to wall, and first up for an interview was an old mate of Chris's from the ABC, Mark Llewellyn, now a gun reporter at *A Current Affair*.

Also amongst the gathered media that day was an enthusiastic young reporter from Channel 10 called Eddie McGuire. Two or three of his mates had made the list that year and wanted to make sure I knew of Eddie's existence. By the end of the lunch, how could I not? I could have wallpapered my lounge room with the number of Eddie's business cards his mates handed me that day. Eddie certainly had an undeniable charm, and was quickly rising through the ranks at Channel 10, but he was breaking the cardinal rule I had about the list: if you're desperate to be on there, then I don't want you. But there was something about Eddie ... and the following year I couldn't help but put him on.

The criteria for what constituted the title of Bachelor of the Year was always left up to the judges, and we certainly managed to secure an impressive bunch: Liz, actor Rachel Griffiths, comedian and writer Gina Riley, and actor Deborra-Lee Furness all took on the challenge – and had a ball doing it.

Deborra-Lee was one of the country's most accomplished actors, and her flatmate, filmmaker Mark Pennell, was one of my favourites on the list that year. Talented, intelligent, funny, as nice a guy as they come ... and when I found out they lived together I wondered if he and Deborra-Lee were quietly an item. But one of the other judges set me straight: 'They're long-time besties but that's all. Deb is one of the best women you'll ever meet, and whoever she finally ends up with is going to be one incredibly lucky guy.'

Within a few years that incredibly lucky guy turned out to be a young, up-and-coming actor called Hugh Jackman, and Mark played the role of Deb's best man at their wedding.

Comedian, writer and former Triple M newsreader Jane Kennedy was another who agreed to judge the Bachelor awards. Jane was part of a cohort of comedians to come out of Melbourne in the late 80s who were kicking goals with every new project they took on. Magda Szubanski, Glenn Robbins, Steve Vizard, Jane Turner,

Gina Riley, Tom Gleisner and Rob Sitch were just some of those stars Australia was falling in love with, and that year, Rob was not only on our list, he was my firm favourite to take out the Bachelor of the Year title.

Not only did Rob tick all the bachelor boxes (nice guy, super talented, smart-as, hilarious and, at least *initially*, didn't want to be on the list), but I also knew that once we hit the publicity trail upon his announcement, every radio station, current affairs program and newspaper writer in the country would want to cover it. I thought Jane would agree wholeheartedly, but as each of the judges cast their vote, and Rob was looking the clear winner, Jane made it clear in turn that she didn't agree.

'I'm sorry, Rob can't get it ... he's just not the right fit,' she announced. I wondered if she knew something about Rob we didn't, and it was only when I quietly pulled her aside, after a stalemate between the judges that lasted almost 20 minutes, that I got it. He and Jane were an item and had been for some time, but very privately. Putting Rob out there as 'available' to the women of Australia was an issue Jane didn't particularly want to deal with.

Fair enough. So, we did a deal. I would make him runner-up, but on the condition that Rob came with me on the publicity rounds and agreed to do any of the interview requests that came in ... along with the guy who would now be our default winner.

Of course, Rob was the only one anyone in the media wanted to talk to, and he stole the show every time he got in front of a microphone. He totally took the piss out of the whole exercise and I loved it. Unfortunately, I don't think our poor winner – a lovely, shy art director from the ad industry – got quite the look-in he was hoping for, or deserved, and I don't think I ever properly apologised. Sorry about that, Graham Smith.

*

It wasn't the easiest of days. Chris and I had finally signed the last of the paperwork transferring full ownership of the house into my name, and he'd come over to gather the few remaining boxes of his things stored on the back verandah. We were now done. He was in another relationship, and I wished him well.

Then, just when I wasn't looking, someone came into my life. He was tall, charismatic, charming, and the chemistry between us was undeniable. This was a guy who was used to being the centre of attention in every room he entered, and we met at an industry function.

He wasn't my type, or at least wasn't the type I'd dated before. Truth is, my dating experience to this point had been pretty limited. I knew I could cut it in professional relationships in boardrooms, but when it came to personal relationships that ended up in bedrooms, I was still a novice after all those years happily ensconced with Chris. What even *was* my 'type'? I wondered.

But as the night we met wore on, the booming music was making conversation impossible and my attempts to grab a drink from a passing waiter proved fruitless, so I headed to the bar. There, right next to me was that guy, and as we both jostled for attention to place our orders, he said something that made me laugh.

He suggested we find a quiet corner away from the noise and, within an hour, and against all my better judgments, we were both pouring out our most intimate life secrets. He was, he told me, heartbroken. His partner of many years had just moved out, and with her went their young daughter. He said he didn't know why he was telling me all this, but it was like we'd known each other for years. Strangely, I felt the same. I ended up dropping him off at his apartment, and after asking for my number, he promised to call.

Sure.

But the next day he did. And every day after that for a week.

The conversations were always easy. There was laughter too, along with an unending stream of compliments. He knew I was resisting taking things any further, but eventually his smooth lines during long, languid late-night phone calls won me over.

What followed was a head-spinning love bubble. He said I was different to every girl he'd ever dated. He told me he was in deep, and I believed him. But always, bubbling just beneath the euphoria, was an uncomfortable feeling that this was a guy who was high on the thrill of falling in love.

Chaos quickly governed our relationship. He would often inexplicably cancel plans and go away for work at the last minute. His ex-girlfriend and daughter would sometimes turn up on his doorstep, and according to him, he just had to let them stay.

Like a fool I would always tell him I understood. There was a child involved, and I tried to convince myself that that care he had for his daughter was a beautiful quality, and one day if we ever did have kids together, surely that was a plus? I put him on a pedestal, too high for me to reach. When we were apart, I was riddled with insecurity, and before long a crippling internal monologue began to play. Was I pretty enough? Skinny enough? Smart enough? Exciting enough? Glamorous enough to keep him?

Sometimes he wouldn't call for days. The excuse always involved one drama or another and he would apologise profusely; there were even tears. He knew exactly how to play me. Often, he would leave lovely messages on my home answering machine during the day while I was at work. Which only confused me more. Why didn't he call and speak to me there?

And yet at night, when I listened to those messages, I had hope once again that we were meant to be together. Some nights I would play them over and over as I went to sleep. I was in love. Or at least it felt like it. He even invited me to Italy to go sailing with his parents on their yacht. Maybe this really *was* getting serious now?

The romantic thrill of it all quickly dissipated, though, once I arrived in at their place in Rome. For the life of me, I couldn't work out how he had described me to his parents, and exactly where I fitted into his life. I couldn't help feeling I wasn't exactly the first girl he'd taken sailing on the Mediterranean with Mum and Dad.

How on earth had I got to this point? In order to make this relationship work, I had slowly, almost imperceptibly, made my needs irrelevant in a desperate effort to be the always malleable, always understanding, always available one. He constantly told me I wasn't like those other girls he'd dated: so needy, so demanding of his time, so difficult to talk to. I was special.

But he also told me that having a kid was complicated, and it was difficult to commit. He needed time to trust. Or something. And yet, I was determined to be there when he was finally ready.

Girlfriends couldn't understand why I kept waiting and hoping. Deb even took me out for some good old 3am tequila shots to try to talk some sense into me. 'It helped last time,' she said. I loved her for that. This time I just got a hangover.

In the end it all came to a head one sunny Saturday. After four days interstate for work, he'd planned a romantic dinner together at our favourite restaurant. But at midday, he called to say he was unwell. He sounded terrible on the phone and upset that this very special evening now couldn't go ahead.

So, what's a girl to do when her man is feeling so very poorly? It was obvious. I decided to surprise him later that afternoon with the biggest bunch of lilies I could find, hoping they would brighten his miserable day. Lilies were his favourite, so the look on his face when he opened the door surprised me. Were the white ones I'd chosen too funereal? I knew immediately that I should have grabbed the pink ones – dammit, they would have been so much more cheerful.

'Hi!' I chirped, suddenly noticing how beautifully dressed he was in a crisp white linen shirt and pants. He smelt and looked fresh out of the shower, with a lock of wet hair falling ever-so-enticingly forward in a way that I had to physically stop myself from gently caressing it back behind his ear where it belonged. He was clearly feeling much better because that familiar twinkle in his eye I knew and loved had returned.

'Wow, you look great,' I said. 'I thought ...'

And then I saw her. Just over his shoulder, as I looked through to the lounge room from my spot at the front door, *there* was the reason he was feeling better: a stunning blonde perched on the couch, obviously leaning into our conversation. She, too, was in white linen – how cute – a little off-the-shoulder number, her hair cascading over just one of those perfectly tanned bare shoulders. And there wasn't a runny nose in sight.

The letter I wrote to him that night was a doozy. I didn't hold back. It was a character assessment for the ages. I finished by wishing him the very best of luck in life, but suggested it might not be a bad idea if he stopped fucking up other people's. Not quite Shakespeare, but it was exactly what he deserved. And I needed.

He didn't even have the decency to write back. Instead, he got mutual friends to tell me he was heartbroken. I didn't believe it for a second.

I had dodged a relationship bullet. And he couldn't have done me a bigger favour.

CHAPTER SEVENTEEN

'If you don't want him, I'll have him ...'

'At the end of the day, it's about who you want to
own a dog with.' – Author unknown

B Y DECEMBER 1991, *CLEO* had become the number-one selling
women's lifestyle magazine per capita in the world. Life, on all
fronts, was good.

I loved my funny old ramshackle house, and I particularly
loved sharing it with Liz. Our days quickly fell into a comfortable
rhythm – she was off to Channel 9 every morning well before I got
up, and then had the house to herself until I came home, usually
around 7 o'clock, when we would make dinner together and chat
about our days, before she headed to bed for that crazy early alarm,
and I more often than not stayed up and read, or worked, or just
rediscovered the joy of stillness.

I was loving the freedom of single life – heading off on
weekends away on a whim, borrowing movies from Blockbuster I'd
long wanted to catch up on, staying late at work without apology to
anyone, dancing to Madonna's 'Vogue' on full volume in the lounge
room, and eating Tim Tams and takeaway in my PJs with Liz. Who
needed men anyway? I said to Liz on more than one occasion.

I think she forgot that last bit, though, one night as we were sitting in the lounge room – her going through the briefs that had just been delivered for the next morning's *Today* show, me watching TV and simply breathing out after a big day at work.

'Do you know a guy called Peter FitzSimons?' she asked. 'He's just started as a part-time reporter at *Today*. He's a Wallaby, and I figured, with your rugby connections through your dad, you might know him.'

'He's a great guy,' Liz said. 'Anyway, he's having a Christmas dinner party for a bunch of us at the show, and he asked if I'd like to bring someone. Want to come as my date?'

It was that same guy from the Channel 9 makeup department who'd said all those kind things about Dad. I told Liz the story, and of the columns I'd read to Dad in his final days. 'Perfect!' she said. 'And so typical of Pete to say that. He is just lovely. It's Thursday week at his house in Annandale. I'll pick you up from work on the way through.'

The only problem was, 'Thursday week' turned out to be 12 December, Mum's birthday; and when Liz called me that morning to check I was still good for 'dinner at Fitzy's' that night, I realised I'd double booked. This was only Mum's second birthday since Dad's passing, and I didn't want her to spend it on her own. Liz totally understood.

When I arrived home that night sometime around 10 o'clock and heard the phone ringing, I was concerned. No-one ever called after 8 o'clock at night – 8.30 if you absolutely must. Anything after that had to be an emergency.

It was Liz. 'Oh good, you're home! Hope it all went well with your mum. Look, the night is still young and someone here wants to speak to you,' she said. But before I could say anything …

'Hi there. I was really sorry you couldn't join us tonight, but if you jump in the car, you can still be here in time for dessert.' It was Peter. What had Liz been telling him?

As lovely as the invitation was, the night with Mum had been difficult. She told me she'd spent the last few weeks going through the mountains of memories still in storage at the house and was missing Dad terribly.

I apologised to Peter and said I'd just had a bit of a tough night and had a big day at work the next day and needed to get to bed.

He said he was sorry, but understood. 'Maybe another time?'

'Of course,' I replied.

I felt bad. He did seem very sweet, but I just wasn't in the mood. I was worried about Mum. She kept insisting that she was doing fine, but so often when I tried to call her, she was out, trying as best she could to get on with life without Dad, which usually meant taking the train to Circular Quay and randomly catching one of the many ferries to wherever they and the harbour breezes took her, and then back again. I'd tried to get her an answering machine, but she kept forgetting to turn it on, so our catch-ups always had to be in person. Now birthdays were just a reminder to her that another year had passed without her beloved Ray.

I woke late the next morning with the summer sky already blasting light through the old leadlight windows in my room. But as I lay in bed, for just 30 more seconds thinking about last night's conversation with Mum, I could see a shiny white envelope sitting on my dressing table.

On the front it said, 'Lisa', in Liz's writing.

Dearest Leese,

You missed a great night. Fitzy is such a sweetheart. He's a fantastic host, has this cute little house in Annandale he's renovating, he's a brilliant cook, speaks fluent French and Italian, and I swear, probably sews his own clothes!

He was really disappointed you couldn't make it last night.

Call you later this morning,

Liz.xx

PS. If you don't want him, I'll have him!

If you don't want him, I'll have him? One thing was for certain: if this Fitzy guy needed an agent, he certainly had one in Liz.

And when my private line at work rang at 11 that morning, I knew it had to be her. I was ready for a laugh, but also wanted to know, how on earth had she managed to get home so late, and out the door again at some god-forsaken hour for the *Today* show, yet *still* have time to write that letter for me?

'OK, so how much is this guy paying you?' I asked as I picked up the phone.

'Hello? Sorry, I was hoping to speak to Lisa Wilkinson ...'

It was him.

Liz had struck again and given Peter my private number. And, despite last night's dessert knockback, here he was again. This time, much as I was happy to chat, I explained I really only had a few minutes as I was just in the middle of putting together my always-overdue column for the next issue and had a bit of a writer's block.

'Too easy. Give me a hard one. Why don't you read some of it out to me? Maybe I can help ...' he said in what I suspected was possibly a very Fitzy way of dealing with any problem he ever came across. *Here, hand it to me and let's see if we can't solve this together.*

I don't know how, but almost half an hour passed before I looked at my watch. We were on deadline for the next issue and there was now a line-up outside my office of people needing answers on all manner of last-minute decisions before we could go to press. I apologised to Peter and told him I had to go.

'Look, before you do, I hope you don't mind me asking, but I have another dinner at my place tonight. It's for all the guys I work with at *Wide World of Sports*, and I was wondering if you'd come as my guest?' he asked.

Oh dear. I couldn't. Again. Deb Thomas and I were going to have drinks with Nicole Kidman who was back in town to spend Christmas with her mum, dad and sister, Antonia.

Nicole's acting career had certainly taken off since we'd done that *Dolly* cover all those years ago. Her roles in the brilliant mini-series *Bangkok Hilton*, and then *Dead Calm* with Sam Neill, had brought her to both the world's, and Tom Cruise's, attention, and this was her first trip back since their wedding the year before. As was typical of Nicole, despite now being one-half of the hottest couple in Hollywood, she was having a small gathering for everyone back in Oz who'd been so supportive of her over the years, and both Deb and I had been invited.

But how could I explain to Peter that yet again, I was knocking him back? I just had to say it straight. I had something else on.

His response was immediate. 'No problem. I get it. I totally understand. Look, it was nice to chat. I'll let you get back to it …'

Oh no … I'd hurt his feelings. He sounded so nice, but I really did have something on, and he thought I was just making excuses. I had to think quickly.

'But look, that's OK. Liz and I are having an afternoon tea at our place on Sunday with a bunch of friends. It's only small, but I'd love you to come if you're free?'

He was. And he said he would love to. 'I'll bring a bottle of red.'

'Great, how does 3 o'clock sound?' I said before giving him my address. 'See you then.'

My next phone call was to Liz.

'Hey there, we're having an afternoon tea on Sunday …'

*

It was just a few minutes before 3 and, somehow, I was really looking forward to properly meeting this guy Liz was so convinced I would like. 'Honestly, you two are going to get on like a house on fire – and if nothing else, he'll certainly make you laugh.'

We'd managed to quickly throw together about a dozen people for our afternoon tea, and the first of them should have been arriving shortly. But just as I was putting out the last of the plates, the phone rang. I couldn't believe it: out of a clear blue sky, it was my Ex. It had been months since we'd last spoken and I'd sent him that pretty full-on farewell letter. Why on earth was he calling now?

His voice was soft. Deep. Apologetic. All these months on, he wanted me to know how sorry he was for all the upset he'd caused. He had, he said, acted abysmally. I deserved so much better, and even though he didn't ever expect me to forgive him, he wanted to make it up to me.

In his hand, he said, were two tickets to Thailand, and one of them had my name on it. A beautiful suite was booked for seven days just after Christmas on an island off Phuket, where, he promised, he would explain everything.

My heart, despite all the reserves of strength I had mustered in recent months, instantly melted. Finally, the words I once would have given anything to hear. And he wanted to take me on a romantic holiday. To Thailand.

'I love you,' he whispered, 'and I know now that I've been a complete idiot.' Well, that last part was certainly true. He said he'd finally seen the light and was convinced that everything that had gone on was simply a test that proved we could get through tough times.

So apparently, we were now 'through the tough times'? And he says he loves me? He mentioned nothing of the girlfriend who had cast such a long shadow over our relationship … if that's what you'd call the time we'd spent together. Where was she? I wondered. Had she, too, finally had enough? Was I now just the fallback?

'Lisa, I mean it. You are like no woman I've ever met. I love you.'

Aaaaaaaargh. Why now?

But just as I could feel my resolve and all that history of heartbreak starting to disappear, something twigged. Did he say he'd bought a plane ticket and it already had my name on it?

Was he really *so* sure that this invitation, this single phone call, would result in a yes, that he'd gone ahead and, without checking, put *my name* on a plane ticket? With an actual date he had decided I would be available. Presuming I had just been sitting around for the last six months waiting for his call. I simply had no idea what to say.

And then the doorbell rang. I looked at my watch. It was 3 o'clock on the dot.

Suddenly, everything he'd put me through came flooding right on back. The arrogance was breathtaking. This time, that smooth voice and his long list of promises just weren't going to cut it.

'Are you still there, Lisa? What do you think? Will you come with me to Thailand?'

I had to do it. So, I took a deep breath and …

'Look, that's a lovely offer, thanks so much, but there's a guy at the door who I think I'm going to marry, so a trip to Thailand right now probably wouldn't be appropriate. I'm sure you'll find someone else. Maybe you could take your kid? I reckon she deserves your time more than I do. Bye.'

And with that, I put the phone down and punched the air. I did it!! OK, sure, that might have been a slight fib – alright, total fib – to say I was going to *marry* anyone … But hey, details. At least I knew that those would probably be the last words my Ex and I would ever exchange.

As I walked towards the frosted glass of my front door, I had a huge smile on my face, which I tried to pull back. How could I possibly explain to whoever was at the door what had just happened?

Through the glass, I could see the shadow of a ridiculously tall figure dressed in … Was that a yellow shirt? It had to be Peter. How funny. And he was holding something. When I opened the door, I could see that it was the largest bottle of red I'd ever seen.

I needn't have pulled back on my smile, though. Because his was even bigger.

*

It had only been two weeks, but here I was sitting at the FitzSimons' family dinner table on Christmas night sharing in a magnificent spread of leftovers, and meeting for the first time his five wonderful brothers and sisters, their spouses and kids, and Peter's lovely mum and dad.

Their home was a small orange and veggie farm up at Peats Ridge on the Central Coast, but this was the family's timber beach house just near the sands of Newport on Sydney's Northern Beaches. Peter's grandfather had built it way back in the 1920s, and it was the place in which every one of the FitzSimonses had woken up every Christmas morning of their lives since. They were as close, humble, welcoming and joyous a group of people as I had ever met.

In my family, the 25th of December was always strictly reserved for close family only, so I was unsure whether this invitation to Newport on Christmas night was really appropriate. Pete assured me, though, that he'd already warned his parents that things were pretty serious between us. And he wasn't wrong. From the moment he'd arrived for afternoon tea that Sunday a fortnight before, we'd hardly left each other's side.

I now knew why it had never worked out with anyone else. Pete was a complete one-off. And the most positive, generous, funny, fascinating person I had ever met. We had fallen instantly in love and would talk for hours into the early morning, on long drives to nowhere and back again, and on the phone when we were apart. Our lives, our loves, our dreams, our disappointments.

We'd grown up on opposite sides of Sydney – him the rough and tumble farm boy who'd rarely worn shoes until the age of 11; me the ballerina in the crisp white tutu with big dreams of one day wearing 'points' on stage. Him the boisterous baby of seven, desperate just to get a look-in; me the well-behaved middle child, desperate to never be any trouble. Him learning the poetry of Banjo Paterson with his dad as he packed tomatoes in the farm shed; me the kid buried in the pages of *Archie* comics and *Dolly* magazines in my bedroom. Him the rugby player who'd wandered the world hitchhiking and playing rugby throughout his twenties; me the conscientious career girl who'd spent most of *her* twenties in boardroom meetings and shoulder pads. I told him about my struggles with bullying; he told me about the tragic death of his brother Martin at the age of 11. We both laughed at anything by Robin Williams, and then cried over *Dead Poets Society*. He introduced me to Bob Dylan and Leonard Cohen. I introduced him to Van Morrison and Nina Simone.

After five years living and playing rugby in France and Italy, he was now settled down back in Australia, working full-time for the *Sydney Morning Herald*, but somehow also squeezing in stories for the *Today* show and *Wide World of Sports*, and writing his second book. Pete's thirst for everything that life had to offer was insatiable and infectious. And while he'd represented his country as a Wallaby seven times (or as he would go on to describe it, he and David Campese had represented Australia 108 times between them), that was the last thing he wanted to be defined by. What he wanted more than anything was to be a working author, telling stories 'my way'.

Some thought we were an odd fit. Mum included. She also thought it was all moving too fast. We didn't. And whatever differences we did have just made it a whole lot more interesting …

I was in awe of his drive. His unshakeable belief in the goodness of people. His intellectual curiosity. And his ridiculously huge heart, which seemed to know no bounds.

Was this, I wondered, the boy I had been thinking of all those years ago as I watched those taillights on a Sunday night disappearing up the hill to St Greg's from my bedroom window back in Campbelltown?

*

We couldn't *wait* to tell everyone. But for the time being, our news would have to wait.

Pete's beautiful dad had been found between the fourth and fifth rows of his much-loved orange orchard at the farm at Peats Ridge. It happened in an instant. And when Pete and his brother Jim got the call from their mum, who'd found him just minutes before after she called him in for afternoon tea, they raced straight there.

Peter FitzSimons Snr had died with his boots on and, as requested, the undertakers left him in that same spot until all his children arrived, just as the last light of the day was fading on the farm, in time to say their goodbyes.

It was Monday, 16 March 1992. Even though we had barely been together three months, the night before Pete had asked me to marry him … and as silly, and fast, and crazy as I knew it would seem to everyone else, I immediately said yes.

Pete was sad he'd never got the chance to tell his dad about our plans of a life together, but he wondered if maybe there was something significant in that timing. The last of Peter Snr's children had now chosen their life partners, and were starting families of their own, and after years of health worries, his work here was now done.

We decided to wait until after the funeral to share the news of our engagement. We figured plenty would wonder exactly what the hurry was. But when you can so clearly see what you want the rest of your life to look like, you can't wait for the rest of your life to start happening.

The date for the wedding was set for Saturday 26 September – the first weekend after Pete's rugby season finished for the year. It also gave me just enough time to get the 20th anniversary issue of *Cleo* off to the presses. And organise a wedding. And a honeymoon. And a huge party to celebrate *Cleo*'s 20th birthday just two days after we got back.

The November anniversary issue of *Cleo* was one of the thickest we'd ever produced, and I was ambitious for it to be a worthy celebration of an incredible two decades for the magazine. We'd started work on it six months before. Unfortunately, though, simultaneously organising the 'simple' wedding we both wanted – with dresses, cars, venues, guest lists, menus, speeches, flowers – was an accident waiting to happen.

So no-one was at all surprised when I fainted in the *Cleo* art department two days before I was due to walk down the aisle. Like a lot of brides-to-be, I'd simply done that old trick of being too busy to eat, or at least, that's what I told Pete when he came to collect me. Much as I'd tried to kill off those old weight demons from my teenage years, every so often they would rise up again. And now that I had to fit into a wedding dress and pose for photos to hopefully last a lifetime, the insecurities were back.

Pete became aware of my 'weight issues' early on, after he'd made what he thought was a compliment about my generous curves and how much he loved them. But that wasn't what my head heard. I was completely inconsolable. He'd never seen me so upset. He simply didn't understand that, for me, comments about my weight lay deep down in rejection. Straight away I heard Mum's voice reminding me that with fat came failure. Was this the coded moment he too was telling me that the way I looked wasn't good enough?

Nothing he said made me feel better. And by Pete's own admission, being the big strapping rugby player he was, he was the last one to talk. For him, weight had nothing to do with *anything.*

'You just don't get it, do you?' And with that he cupped my face between his hands and looked me square in my tear-filled eyes. 'What you don't seem to understand yet is, I would love you if you were a hundred kilos! That would just give me more of you to love. And by the way, I also reckon you're still about thirty years off your prime. So just be warned, when you're in your sixties, you're not going to be safe,' he laughed.

I did too. And I knew he meant it.

*

Despite the murky grey skies and imminent threat of rain, there was something magical about waking up on the morning of 26 September. I was marrying my Pete – with Liz, Deb and Tia as my bridesmaids – and I had never been more sure of anything in my life.

By mid-afternoon, the skies had cleared just enough to hold the promise of a beautiful pink sunset … something I probably shouldn't have even been aware of given our scheduled 4pm start. But between a bit of a timing miscalculation on hair and makeup back in the city, some shocking traffic on the Pacific Highway on the way to the church at Wahroonga, and the lack of one of those new-fangled mobile phones in our old vintage car to warn anyone about our delay, I arrived more than half an hour late.

It was then that I saw that poor Pete must have got a little panicky as the minutes ticked by and, with no sign of his bride, had snuck out the back with his best man, Nick Farr-Jones, to share a nervous cigarette. I couldn't help but wave as soon as I saw him, and immediately cursed the tall, strappy stilettos I'd chosen for the day. Forget walking down the aisle. I wanted to run towards him, so excited was I for what was about to happen.

If there was one brief moment of sadness, it was standing at the door of the church on my brother Kyle's arm. As I looked around at all the happy faces smiling in our direction, and then saw Mum, I could feel a lump rising in my throat. More than anything I would have loved for Dad to have been here for this. I could feel the tears welling and me willing them not to fall as the first stirring chords of the bridal march started to play.

'Ready, Leese?' Kyle asked as he squeezed my hand, feeling just as keenly, I'm sure, the absence of Dad.

'As I'll ever be,' I whispered.

And as I took those first steps down the flaming-red church carpet, rose petals marking the path to my beaming husband-to-be, the Wallaby, standing next to Nick, who not 12 months before had held the Rugby World Cup aloft for Australia, I looked to the heavens and thought of my rugby-loving Dad.

Maybe he was here, after all.

CHAPTER EIGHTEEN

Hello Jake, goodbye Cleo

'Your children are not your children. They
are the sons and daughters of Life's longing for
itself.' – Kahlil Gibran, *The Prophet*

OUR HONEYMOON BY THE beach in Noosa was perfect. It passed by in a delirious week-long cocoon of late mornings; long, long breakfasts lasting well past lunch; a mountain of videos from the local Blockbuster; and regret that we couldn't stay longer.

But I had no choice. I had to get back for *Cleo*'s 20th anniversary party at the recently opened Museum of Contemporary Art down at Circular Quay. There was something more to celebrate, too, as we'd just got news that the previous September issue had hit sales of 400,000 for the very first time. It was a figure we once would have thought unimaginable.

By now, *Cleo* parties had gathered quite the reputation; just about every celebrity, advertiser, media writer and industry heavyweight we'd invited had accepted ... including Kerry Packer and Ita Buttrose. I had no idea how that would work out because, as far as I knew, the two hadn't crossed paths, let alone been in the same room together, since their very public parting of the ways back in 1980. But how could I not invite the two people who had given birth to this iconic magazine, which had now surpassed all expectations of success?

Kerry arrived at my door on the Monday morning after I returned from my honeymoon, wanting to have a chat. I was glad to see him, too, as he and Ros had sent the most exquisite wedding gift the week before of more crystal glassware than I knew what to do with. Maybe he already knew of Pete's somewhat clumsy tendencies around anything delicate, and was future-proofing? Either way, I figured we now had enough glasses to ensure we would still be drinking from at least some of them at our 50th wedding anniversary.

I wanted to say thank you; he wanted to talk about the *Women's Weekly*, and when I would start taking seriously his offer to take on the editorship. Kerry had mentioned this idea before, but I'd always told him I didn't feel ready. Or old enough. He was sure, now that I was married, I would want to make the move. I promised to think about it. The timing couldn't have been worse, though: Pete and I were hoping to start a family as soon as possible.

Then, just before he left, he had a quick question about the 20th anniversary party – more specifically, who was coming. Not minutes before he'd arrived, Ita had called asking the same question. My answer was the same to both of them: yes, the other was coming.

And sure enough the following night, with a swarm of TV cameras and newspaper photographers going crazy, Ita and Kerry politely chatted for the first time in 12 years, in full public view, as the magazine that had played such a significant role in both their lives turned 20.

*

There was no mistaking that solid pink line. Four months after walking down the aisle, and just a few weeks after my first official Fitz Christmas at Newport as a family member, we were definitely pregnant.

Not much more than a year prior, I thought I would probably never get around to having kids. Yet once I met Pete, I couldn't imagine a life for us without them. I certainly could have done without this rotten morning sickness, though, that was actually going 24 hours a day, seven days a week.

We tried to keep our news secret at first, but more than once in those early months I had to disappear to the loo in the middle of meetings, using everything – from last night's dodgy Thai takeaway to hangovers and migraines – as excuses for the constant vomiting.

That 'nesting' instinct everyone talks about during pregnancy kicked in big time, too. When it came to where we would live, we wanted to start afresh, so we let go of both our places and were soon settling into our first home together, this time in Mosman, not far from Taronga Zoo. The old house had plenty of work that needed doing, but we were up for it and excited to make it our own. There was a small backyard and even a little granny flat upstairs, so Mum – who was over the moon at the idea of becoming a grandmother – could stay over once the baby arrived.

I'm not saying giving birth for me was an easy process. But I was strangely relaxed at the prospect – mostly because I just wanted this wretched morning sickness to stop. And when I called my old friend Michelle who'd recently given birth herself to a beautiful daughter, Emma, her perspective was illuminating: what's a few hours of hell in a single day when you get to spend the rest of your life with the greatest joy you'll ever know? I held on to that.

Most nights I would fall asleep reading *What to Expect When You're Expecting*, keen to know what extraordinary things this little person and I had been busily creating that day. If Pete and I ever had a disagreement, it was a running gag between us that I now held the trump card: 'Look, I've been busy making a spleen and a set of lungs today, so unless you've got something better, I win!'

We dutifully attended all our birthing classes, although there was one class towards the end I wish I'd taken more notice in: the one on caesareans. As the midwife out the front noted, one in three of you will be having a caesarean, and most of you won't have planned for it. And I hadn't.

But here I was, in the birthing suite at the Mater Hospital, 41 fully cooked weeks' pregnant, almost 17 hours after my first contraction at 3am (what was it about that time of the day that just kept coming up in my life?), and the baby simply refusing to move. There was nothing regular about the contractions and, despite a pain that felt like the hammers of hell when I did have one, I was only two centimetres dilated.

It was a Sunday night and *60 Minutes* was on the TV, featuring a story predicting Bronwyn Bishop as the politician most likely to be our next prime minister. Directly below the TV was a beanbag, in case I wanted to give birth kneeling on all fours, or just to relax in. Right now, Pete was fast asleep in it.

In nearby rooms I could hear the tortured wails of other women as they went into labour, and then the cries of their newborns. Since arriving, I'd heard maybe four brand-new lives come into the world. And here I was, tossing, turning, grimacing and, still … nothing. The entire night was frustrating, slightly comical and terrifying all at once.

By 5am the call went out. Our baby was in serious distress. They'd tried forceps. Three attempts at an epidural had failed. My blood pressure was through the roof. This little one wasn't going to be able to do this thing alone.

Then, at 5.15am on 20 September 1993, after an emergency caesarean under general anaesthetic, our son, Jake Raymond FitzSimons, was born. A tad misshapen, a little worse for wear – much like his mum at this point – but he was here, and he was healthy, and he was ours!

Six days shy of our first wedding anniversary, a whole new chapter in our life as a family had begun. For the first time, I completely took my hands off the tiller at work and left it to the team. I didn't want to miss these early days with our precious baby boy, so I took four months' maternity leave, and then planned to ease back part-time.

After two years as my trusted deputy, Deb had moved on to become editor of our sister fashion magazine, *Mode*. I was thrilled for her, and now had a new deputy, a seasoned women's magazine editor just arrived from the UK, so I knew *Cleo* would be in safe hands. I was looking forward to the time I would have at home with Jake, and even wondered how I would fill my days. How much work could a newborn really be? I didn't wonder for long.

After a couple of debilitating bouts of mastitis, a fairly foggy head from the after-effects of that general anaesthetic, and the unique torture of sleep deprivation that comes with a baby who wants to feed every three hours, Jake and I *eventually* settled into a rhythm.

Most days I was a sloppy mess, but a happy sloppy mess. I relished all the wonderfully simple joys of motherhood: bathtime; the first smile; taking him for long walks in his pram around our new neighbourhood, pointing out puppies and butterflies and sparrows and rainbows; dipping his tiny toes in the water's edge at the beach; and sometimes after a feed, lying in bed, just him and me, watching him sleep. If his smiles were anything to go by, his favourite thing of all was to sit in a nearby park, watching, mesmerised, as I fed the pigeons. He was discovering all the easy pleasures of the world, just as I was savouring them anew.

One of the greatest joys of all, though, was seeing Mum with Jake. Her first grandchild. Their bond was instant. And the sight of her singing to him one night not long after he was born stirred beautiful memories in me.

When I was little, Mum would often sing me a soothing lullaby at bedtime. Over and over she would caress my forehead and softly sing, until I drifted off ...

Singing too-ral-li, oo-ral-li, addity,
Singing too-ral-li, oo-ral-li, ay,
Singing too-ral-li, oo-ral-li, addity,
And we're bound for Botany Bay.

As I got older, there were many things I was too cool to receive from Mum anymore – hugs in public, fashion advice, and any guidance whatsoever about sex – but that song was never one of them. Early in high school I remember having a really bad toothache and, lying in bed dosed up on painkillers, Mum came and sat next to me and started ...

Singing too-ral-li, oo-ral-li, addity,
Singing too-ral-li, oo-ral-li ay ...

I fell asleep within minutes.

When I was pregnant with Jake, I would sometimes rub my growing belly, and without even thinking, start softly humming that tune to him as if stirred by ancient maternal awakenings. Now, he had both his mum and his grandma singing it to him.

Once, when Jake was still very young, he found an injured baby starling he immediately named Affi and declared as his best friend. Shortly after, as his tiny feathered buddy was clearly dying, Jake asked me if we could sing that lullaby for him and maybe that would make Affi feel better. So we did. It didn't. But the fact he thought it would meant everything.

My mother's lullaby was far more than a song to sing, far more than something I used to calm my child before he fell asleep. It was a soothing melodic vibration sung with love and tenderness and intention, now passed down through the voices of three generations. It also helped me as I navigated this scary new path of motherhood. I was forever grateful to Mum for giving it to me.

*

There was something about going back to work that terrified me. I'd jumped off that ridiculously fast-moving corporate merry-go-round; and now – as I started to emerge from the gentle joy of the baby bubble I had so happily wrapped myself in – it seemed to be spinning a whole lot faster than I remembered.

Technology had hit the magazine business in a big way, and change was happening across the board. Every stage of production and communication was being done on the computers we now all had on our desks. I much preferred the old way of doing things – face to face – and while I knew this was the way of the future, I wondered if in fact that lack of personal contact might mean that, ironically, we would all start to lose the very art *of* communication.

There was another problem. And it involved penises. *Cleo* had a long history with penises … one that mostly, courtesy of the centrefold, involved hiding them. We'd had fun with hiding them too.

Most recently, Deb and I had come up with a fun idea to capitalise on the new 'scratch-off' printing technology that had become available. While our sister mag, *Woman's Day*, under the venerable Nene King, was using it for scratch-off lotto tickets to entice readers, we came up with something much better – and much more *Cleo* – after finding a photo of Arnold Schwarzenegger from his early 'modelling' days, flexing all his 'muscles'. The coverline read 'Scratch Off Arnie's Undies'. The issue was another huge seller, as readers were invited to scratch off the raised, silvery, underpants-shaped paint our printers had carefully applied to the page.

I will go to my grave neither confirming nor denying whether I knew that our paper stock was never going to survive the rigorous scratching our readers applied to the page in their hunt for what lay beneath that paint, but suffice to say, for anyone who tried, we managed to keep Arnie's dignity intact.

It was funny to think of all the copies of *Cleo* that would end up in doctors' waiting rooms and corporate reception areas across the country, with the Arnie page bearing a hole, right in the crucial middle bit. No doubt those casual readers would either laugh or feel robbed. Either way, no harm done. It was a fine line taking *Cleo*'s cheeky personality right to the edge, and then knowing exactly when to pull back. Mostly it was a simple case of just listening to my gut, as it had always served me so well.

But it was while I was away on maternity leave that my penis problem arose, after a decision was made to run a story on the benefits or otherwise of circumcised versus uncircumcised penii. Opening the story were two in-your-face, full-page, full-colour, close-up photos of penises, showing an example of each. It was graphic and confronting; and in one fell swoop, four of our biggest-spending, most prestigious advertisers withdrew every one of their significant dollars, declaring they would not be coming back.

Of all the hills to die on, the penis hill would not have been my choice. So, just back from maternity leave, I had a lot of work to do to get things back on track.

*

It was an offer I just couldn't pass up. The editorship of *New Idea* was about to become vacant, and its boss, Dulcie Boling, wanted to fly me to Melbourne to discuss the possibility of me taking over. *New Idea* wasn't where I saw my career heading at all, but I certainly couldn't resist meeting the other half of one of the greatest rivalries Australian magazine publishing had ever seen.

Dulcie was the *New Idea* equivalent of the *Women's Weekly*'s Ita, fronting, as she did, the magazine's weekly TV advertisements. Her great rival, though, was not Ita, but *Woman's Day*'s wildly successful editor, Nene King. Nene had once been Dulcie's deputy, and many (including Nene herself) believed that she was in fact the reason for all of *New Idea*'s success at the time. Now, five years after taking over at *Woman's Day*, Nene had leap-frogged Dulcie's sales and taken the crown as queen in the weekly women's magazine market. Dulcie was now Nene's arch enemy.

In the TV ads, Dulcie appeared warm and softly spoken, but her reputation was formidable. She was now executive director at News Corp, as well as one of Rupert Murdoch's most valued board members. Dulcie was also the final word in who got her old job. It takes a particular kind of cold-eyed calculation to edit those weekly tabloid magazines, and a certain casual attitude towards fact-checking. It helps, too, if you have no particular care for the effect you might be having on the lives of those you are writing about.

I just didn't have any of that stuff in me, so I was honest about my low level of interest. Pete meanwhile was anchored to the *Sydney Morning Herald*, so there was very little chance we would be moving our young family to Melbourne.

'No problem,' the go-between I was dealing with said. 'If this works out, we could always find a spot for Pete in the company. We could make him editor of *Aussie Post*.'

Aussie Post was about as blokey and old-school a magazine as you could get, and as far from something Pete would be interested in as ever there was. A favourite of barber shops across the country, *Aussie Post* was probably best known for its bikini-model cover girls, and legendary for the thrilling moments it provided inside its pages for so many young Aussie boys sneaking their very first pubescent peek at women's nipples at the local newsagent.

Amusing employment offers for Pete aside, there was another reason I wasn't looking for a new job. Unbeknownst to anyone, I was actually two months' pregnant, and hoping to fully wind down my work for a while once baby number two had arrived.

But here I was in Melbourne anyway, about to meet Dulcie Boling in a private executive space on one of the top floors of the Grand Hyatt hotel. Right on time, a young woman ushered me into the room and introduced me to the strikingly slim, utterly polite 'Mrs Boling', dressed in a perfectly neat pastel-pink suit, the exact image of the woman I had seen on TV. I could see immediately why Dulcie Boling and the bolshie, boisterous Nene would clash.

I'd been assured that this meeting was her idea, but from the outset something told me she wasn't completely comfortable in the company of other women in the same line of work. I was happy to answer questions, and Dulcie Boling had plenty. What magazines did I read? What's Kerry Packer like to work for? How involved does he get in the running of the magazine? How was my bottom line going? All of which were easy to answer. Then the tricky ones came ...

What did I think of *New Idea*? How would I improve it? Did I read it? The next one, though, was something I definitely wasn't expecting ...

'Editorially, I'm wondering where you would want the magazine to go? The royals for example. They're big sellers for us. What do you think of Fergie? *New Idea* readers don't like her at all. But they just can't get enough of Diana. And how would you deal with a story on, say ... Prince Philip?'

Prince Philip? Even with my limited experience at this end of the magazine market, I was pretty sure Philip was as far from a 'big seller' as you could get in the royal family.

She continued. 'Say, for example, you came into possession of a tape. A tape of Prince Philip talking to a woman on the phone that made it absolutely clear that the Prince was having an affair behind Her Majesty's back. A long-standing affair.'

'But how would that even happen? And how could you prove it was him?' I asked.

'If you could prove it – and let's just say you could – would you publish it?'

'But, Mrs Boling,' I responded, 'recording someone without their knowledge is illegal. Not to mention publishing the transcript. Do you actually have a tape like that?'

And with that, Mrs Boling looked at her watch, and explained she had to get back to the office.

Then I remembered, a couple of years before, Murdoch's *Sun* newspaper in the UK had published a tape of Princess Diana talking in excruciatingly intimate detail to her then-lover, James Gilbey, in what became known as the Squidgygate tape scandal. It sold newspapers by the truckload. It rocked the royal family to the core and was the final straw for Her Majesty, who ordered Diana and Charles to immediately separate. Within weeks the Queen, in her annual Christmas message to the Commonwealth, described 1992 as her 'annus horribilis', coming as it did on top of the recently announced separation of Andrew and Sarah, the Duke and Duchess of York.

But there was worse to come. In January of 1993, it was Prince Charles's turn with a similarly private conversation recorded between the future king and his long-time mistress, Camilla Parker Bowles. The rather icky, very personal fantasies of living life as a tampon inside his lover immediately branded the Prince a 'lavatory-minded adulterer'. This time, however, the transcript wasn't published in the UK. It instead made its way to Australia and in a world exclusive was published by *New Idea*.

Within hours of publication, Clive James was on the phone to me from London. It was 2 o'clock in the morning in Old Blighty, and he said he just couldn't wait until the morning. 'Have you seen it yet?' he asked me. 'The issue of *New Idea*? We can't get it over here, but if you get a copy, can you fax it to me?'

New Idea became the most-talked-about magazine in the world. Dulcie Boling had doubled the print run; and with every last copy becoming a 'collector's issue', *New Idea* sold a whopping 1.3 million copies that week alone.

Royals, caught on tape, inappropriately having affairs, and all published for the first time in News Limited publications on the opposite side of the world. Questions were being asked: what was going on in the Murdoch empire with these recordings?

An editorial in the Fairfax press underlined the perceived sleight of hand involved in the *New Idea* 'scoop': 'It has been suggested that the transcript was published in Australia in an attempt to avoid the scrutiny of a British government fast losing patience with that country's tabloids. How better to circumvent such scrutiny than to have the story bob up in the "colonies" and then [*The Sun*] report on that report?'

A public statement issued on Rupert Murdoch's behalf said he had 'no knowledge of negotiations to buy the tape, nor that *New Idea* had it or had published it. Any suggestion of "collusion or conspiracy" between companies in which he has an interest is totally without foundation.'

Asked by the world's press why she had decided to publish the tape – particularly in a magazine the very proper Dulcie Boling always took pride in declaring as one based in 'family values' – she simply replied, 'I agonised over it.'

That fierce circulation war between *New Idea* and *Woman's Day* (which just months before had published, in their own world exclusive, the infamous toe-sucking photos catching out Sarah Ferguson) was never more fierce. And for a brief period, Dulcie Boling was the new victor.

None of it was for me, though.

Two years on from those scandals, did *New Idea* really have another tape, this time of Prince Philip? Would she publish it? I really didn't care.

As I left that meeting, I politely indicated to Dulcie Boling that this was a corner of the media in which I just didn't belong. And I have no doubt that she agreed.

*

With a second baby on the way, I was already eyeing that September 1995 due date as a time to reassess everything.

More and more, it was feeling like a jumping-off point for me. I'd had more than ten years in the chair at *Cleo*, and I figured it was time to bring in new energy and a fresh perspective for the magazine. I'd hired a crop of brilliantly talented new recruits in recent years who were quickly rising through the ranks and on a path to becoming editors themselves.

For a long time in my early days at *Dolly*, I could never quite understand why I had been given so many incredible opportunities at such a young age. I was a kid from nowhere who knew nothing and no-one. But I'd prospered because people believed in me. Every day, as I sat on those old red rattler trains from Campbelltown on my way to work, I always wondered, why me?

But it didn't take me long to work it out. You get given that stuff for a very real and precious reason – to pay it forward yourself. Because when you learn early on what it is to be encouraged and supported, to be given opportunities to shine, to take risks and see how far you can go, then it's only appropriate that you pass that same joy on to others in whose eyes you can see that same passion.

By this stage, Deb Thomas had moved from *Mode* to become the highly successful and respected editor of *Elle*; and Mia Freedman, who had arrived four years before as a chatty, hard-working and talented work experience girl of 21, was now one of those in the running to be my successor. Paula Joye, our beauty editor, and Rebecka Delforce, our picture editor, were two more I knew for sure would soon be full-blown editors themselves.

Lifelong friendships had been formed in that office. Together we had achieved more with *Cleo* than any of us could have ever imagined possible. I knew I would be leaving the place and its people in great shape.

And so, after more than ten years of watching so many seasons pass in the changing leaves of those big old trees in Hyde Park I could see from my office window, it was time to pass the baton on.

CHAPTER NINETEEN

The times, they were a-changin'

'Becoming who we are is an ongoing process, and thank God! Because where's the fun in waking up one day and deciding there's nowhere left to go?' – Michelle Obama

LOUIS MCCLOY FITZSIMONS WAS clearly in a big hurry. After the marathon that was Jake's arrival, his little baby brother had decided he wanted to get this thing over with *and* do it on his big brother's 2nd birthday, too.

I'd always heard that every pregnancy, every birth and every child is different. And yet, this pregnancy had once again been a nightmare of nausea. The birth, though, *was* different: natural, and over in less than an hour. This baby was definitely different, too. Where Jake had been a pretty good sleeper, Louis rarely slept for more than 45 minutes at a time.

It stretched me and my reserves of patience, as my new life at home as a full-time mum unfolded, surrounded by nappies, nipple pads, toys and *Thomas the Tank Engine* on repeat. It was an emotional roller-coaster, and there were days when, if I didn't laugh, I cried. Yet, even on the tough days and during the exhausting nights, I was grateful for the two healthy babies we were lucky enough to have.

It did take some adjusting, though. And at least one colleague doubted the wisdom of my decision. Just before I'd left *Cleo*, I'd run into one of ACP's high-profile editors in the lift who, on hearing that I was leaving, asked me if it was true that I was giving up such a prestigious job. When I confirmed it was, she was shocked.

'So, you're just going to leave? You don't have anything else to do?' she asked.

'Nope, nothing,' I happily replied. 'I've worked hard for a long time. I'm looking forward to concentrating on being a mum for a while.'

She then leaned in and said something that would forever after stay with me.

'But what about all the invitations and the glamorous first nights? All that stuff will dry up, you know. I mean, who will you be if you're not the editor of *Cleo* anymore?'

I was, very happily, about to find out.

Pete was working flat out now with the paper, as well as writing his eighth book, doing a weekly TV show in New Zealand, and in demand as a guest speaker. I, meantime, wanted to pull back. I wanted to know who I was without that job title. I'd worked hard and saved hard for a long time. I'd given everything to my work, but I knew I would only ever get this one chance to have this precious time in my little babies' lives. And I was taking it.

*

A call from Brian Walsh came out of the blue. I'd been mates with Brian since his old PR days at radio station 2SM in the early 80s, and then as the genius publicist behind the careers of *Neighbours* stars Kylie Minogue and Jason Donovan. Now, he was heading up things at the newly opened Foxtel pay-TV service, and he was calling with an idea.

'Mate, do you remember the show *Beauty & the Beast*? Four women, bombastic male "beast" in the middle, reading out letters from viewers that the female panellists then comment on?'

Did I know it? I'd only recently deemed myself recovered from the pretty ordinary experience of being on the show with Clive

Robertson on Channel 10 more than a decade before. Not that I told Brian that.

'Sure,' I said. 'My mum used to watch it back in the days before I even started going to school.'

Great, he said, because he was bringing it back for a 13-week series, starting in September, and he wanted me to join as a regular panellist.

TV? Really? I'd done plenty of interviews for both TV and radio over the years on a bunch of different subjects relating to *Cleo*, but looking down the barrel of a camera into a black hole, as if I were having a casual conversation with an actual person, was a whole different ball game. But maybe that was a good thing: a new skill to learn during this in-between time before I went back, eventually, to work in magazines.

'Sure, Brian, why not,' I said. 'It could be fun. Just one thing, though: who have you got as the Beast?'

'Oh, he's going to be great, Leese,' he said. 'Do you ever listen to talkback radio on 2UE at night?' I didn't. 'His name is Stan Zemanek.'

I was horrified. 'Hang on, Brian, you're not talking about that right-wing shock jock that calls everyone a goose, are you? If you are, then I think you'll find we'd clash.'

My naïvety was embarrassing. As Brian said, why did I think he even wanted me?

My first time on set for that very first show was completely daunting. I was surrounded by Australian TV icons. To my right was former Gold Logie winner Jeanne Little, best known for her many years on the *Mike Walsh Show* and her knack for turning garbage bags, bottle tops and sausages into 'wearable' fashion.

Opposite was another multi-Logie winner, Anne Wills. Anne was a TV institution in her hometown of Adelaide, and in fact the record holder for the greatest number of Logies ever awarded to a woman. Nineteen, at last count.

Next to her was Maureen Duval, a former Miss Australia, who for many years had her own morning show on Channel 10. 'Mawsy', as we called her, was old-fashioned, and sweet, and big-hearted, and everyone's favourite.

TV veterans all. Between them, they had something like six decades of on-camera in-studio experience. Stan and I had exactly ... none.

So when Brian came down to the studio floor to see how everyone was feeling just before we started recording, the collective enthusiasm from the other three women was palpable. 'Oh, daaaaaaaarling,' Jeanne started, 'I can't belieeeeeeve it but today is the 22nd anniversary of my first-ever appearance on TV. I feel like this is meant to beeeeee!'

Mawsy and Anne were similarly thrilled, and grateful to Brian for giving them another chance in this fickle business. Gigs on television for women over the age of 50 were rare, yet Brian wanted to embrace and celebrate all that wisdom and experience on the show. All three women were primed, pumped and ready to go.

And then there was Stan and me. We just sat there in tense silence, feeling like the complete TV amateurs we were.

'What's wrong with you two?' Brian asked, before lifting his arms and pointing to the huge bank of studio lights beaming down from above and the four big cameras on the floor ready to capture us from every possible angle. 'This is television, guys! Where's your energy?'

I looked at Stan as he looked at me, and then we both looked back at Brian.

'Sorry, but I've never done this kind of TV before, Brian,' I said, before Stan added, 'Yeah, I'm actually really nervous.'

Brian then looked over at the other panellists watching this at close quarters with knowing eyes.

'Oh, for fuck's sake, can you two get over yourselves? It's only television! And besides, it's pay TV. No-one's watching anyway!'

It was the best advice I could have possibly been given. Brian was right. It *was* only television.

*

Our 13-week season for the show had been deemed a success, and Foxtel decided to make *Beauty & the Beast* a permanent part of the schedule. Somehow, my little part-time TV stint in between magazine gigs had just got a whole lot more long term, at least in the short term.

Each week, we recorded five shows in a single day, and it still gave me every other day at home with the kids. As a part-time job, it was perfect, and I was learning a lot; while the boys were thriving and, as partners in crime, getting more mischievous and boisterous with each passing week.

One year in, Louis's sleep patterns had finally settled down, and after those pretty tough early months with him, so had I. He was now the most beautiful ball of pudge – a bumper car in nappies with a seemingly indestructible Pete-like quality when it came to falls and knee scrapes.

Meanwhile Mum had sold her house and was living with us in the granny flat upstairs, helping out with the kids on those days I was at work. She was an ongoing and absolute lesson in patience to me, and the boys adored being with their grandma who was now, sadly, their only surviving grandparent.

When Jake was just nine months old, Pete's beautiful mum, Helen, the heart and soul of the FitzSimons family, who had so quickly welcomed me into the fold, suddenly passed away from bowel cancer. Even though I only knew her a short time, Helen, and her parenting ways, left an indelible mark on me. A woman from wealthy Wahroonga, Helen had returned from serving as a physiotherapist in the Second World War in love with a soldier of much-lesser means, Peter FitzSimons. They soon married and moved to a humble two-room cottage on that farm at Peats Ridge where they'd raised seven children, of whom my Pete was the youngest and biggest.

Pete's brothers and sisters had shared plenty of stories with me about growing up with the loud, rambunctious, big-hearted Pete. Once, according to family folklore, when Helen was said to be at the end of her tether with a young Pete, she turned to his older brothers and sisters and said, 'You're going to have to help me raise this one.' And they did.

Hers had been a particular way of raising children that I tried to learn from. Helen wanted magic and fantasy in her children's lives, and when Pete had once asked her to share the logistics of arranging 'Santa Claus' to visit the house in Newport so groaning with children, she was appalled at the very question and refused to answer it. (And to Helen it made no difference that at that point Pete was already old enough to have not only played for the Wallabies, but also to have been sent from the field against the All Blacks for violence!)

And she was earthy, too. Helen didn't quite believe in headaches, so her children never got them. She certainly didn't believe in colds, so her children rarely got them either. Tummy-aches? She mostly ignored them, as did her children ... but right there was the problem. What took Helen in the end was ignoring the tummy-ache that was in fact the first symptom of the bowel cancer that was ravaging her.

In her final days, we all gathered at the farm, knowing the end was near. When Pete's sisters, Cathy and Trish, helped her to the bathroom on the day before she died, Cathy gently asked, 'Mum, what's been the best thing in your life?'

'What?' Helen groaned as she struggled through her pain.

'What's been the best thing in your life, Mum?' Trish repeated, this time a little more loudly.

There was a momentary pause. And then, in a voice as clear as day, 'Oh. Sex with your father!'

It was an impressively honest answer from a woman who Pete told me had barely acknowledged the *existence* of sex to that point, and forever after the entire family cherished her answer.

Easing her passage out were her children – David, Andrew, Cathy, Jim, Trish and Pete – gathered around her bed to sing her favourite hymns, prefacing what turned out to be some of her last words on this earth. Rousing herself, Helen opened her eyes, looked around at her beloved offspring, including her one tone-deaf son, and gasped out what needed to be said: 'Pete! I've told you before, please stop singing!'

For more than 50 years, Helen FitzSimons had been a pillar of the local community, and the memorial service five days later at the farm saw no fewer than 300 people turn up, such was the legacy of this amazing woman. Even after her death, she has remained a daily presence in our family, with Pete and his brothers and sisters constantly citing her wisdom. In the face of upset, they would quietly note, 'It will pass.' When it came to sharing food or drink, 'Of a little, have a little, and be thankful, too.' In life, 'Friends will come and go, but family is forever.'

Of all things, that last one was the chief belief of the FitzSimons family, and I felt not only grateful to be part of it all, but blessed that my own children would be raised on those values, too.

*

We just had one last Christmas Eve episode of *Beauty & the Beast* to record, and our first season would be done.

One of the great things about the show was the adrenaline that came from the fly-by-the-seat-of-your-pants nature of it. Apart from Stan reading out the viewers' letters and questions, everything we did was totally unscripted and Brian's instruction to us was to always just be ourselves. 'The camera doesn't lie,' he would say. 'If you try and be someone else, the audience will know it instantly.'

So when Stan asked me during that final show for 1996 what I would be doing over the Christmas break, I was honest.

'Heading for the usual Fitz family Christmas get-together, and hopefully spending a lot of time making baby number three!'

Sure, we would be six couples with a plethora of kids between us squeezed into a small four-ish bedroom beach house with lots of sleeping bags on the floor – but, hey, where there's a will, there's a way.

*

We'd just turned on the radio news, but surely the announcer had it wrong.

Pete, the kids and I were driving back from our regular Sunday morning coffee and play on the swings down at Balmoral Beach when we heard that Princess Diana had been involved in a serious car crash in Paris with her boyfriend, Dodi al-Fayed.

Just days before, the tabloid press had been filled with photos of the princess kissing her new boyfriend on a luxury yacht in the Mediterranean. The romance took the world by surprise, but Diana looked happy and had described it to her biographer, Andrew Morton, as her first serious relationship since the divorce. Her life was taking a new direction.

Dodi was the son of Egyptian billionaire and Harrods department store owner Mohamed al-Fayed. There were whisperings that the royal family, despite never being able to escape the spectre of its own unsavoury historical Nazi connections, was none too pleased that the mother of its future king now had a new beau who was Muslim. Could this mean Prince William and Prince Harry may one day have a Muslim stepfather?

By the time we arrived home and turned on the TV, with every network taking the story live out of the UK, Dodi al-Fayed had been pronounced dead, while Diana, her condition unknown, was in a Paris hospital.

I stayed watching in disbelief, as rolling coverage showed the mangled mess of their black Mercedes at the crash site, and years of familiar footage of the princess's roller-coaster public life was played over and over and over again. I found it all quite upsetting – perhaps because, at 38 weeks' pregnant with baby number three, I was feeling desperately sad for those two young boys whose mum was now reported to be in a critical condition.

After putting my own boys to bed for their afternoon nap, I decided to have one myself. Until …

'Darling.' It was Pete. 'Diana's dead.' It was the strangest of news to wake up to. It was as if I had just been told that an old friend had died. Diana and I were close in age and, even though she only existed for me in magazines and on the nightly news, she had inserted herself so completely into the daily culture of our lives, it was as if we all knew her. The wedding, the babies, the divorce, the outfits, the shy smiles, the frailties, all those very human, joyous moments as a mum – willingly or not, she had shared it all. Diana was always so alive, and now it was completely shocking that she was dead.

I wondered how Clive James was coping with the news. Clive and I had continued to stay in touch over the years and occasionally caught up for coffee when he returned to his beloved Australia. I had seen photos of him with Diana sometimes appearing in the press, and he confessed to an insatiable crush on the Princess, a woman he described as 'like the sun coming up, giggling'. They were coffee mates, too, and she regularly sought his counsel as she navigated the press and paparazzi, and her divorce from Charles. Even though Clive had strongly advised her not to take part in the infamous *Panorama* TV interview, he'd agreed to help her on some of the more difficult topics he warned her would inevitably arise.

Clive's tribute to Diana in the *New Yorker* magazine in the days after she died was, like all his writings, simply superb …

> She had a remarkable capacity to do exactly the opposite of what she was notorious for: far from being obsessed with her own injuries, she would forget herself in the injuries of others. It was the secret of her appeal to the sick and the wounded. When she walked into a hospital ward, everyone in it recognised her as one of them, because she treated them as if they could have been her. They were her. She was just their souls, free for a day, in a beautiful body that walked so straight and breathed so easily. The sick, she would often say, were more real to her than the well: their guard was down, they were themselves.

Those words helped to consolidate the belief Clive had also lent a helping hand in the extraordinarily eloquent eulogy delivered by Diana's brother, Charles Spencer, at her funeral.

Whether he did or not, I never found out, because when next we met, it was something he just couldn't talk about. All he would say was that he and Diana had an agreement: you tell me what you can't tell anyone else, and I'll tell you what I can't tell anyone else, and then neither of us can tell anyone else about what we said.

And, as far as I know, he never did.

*

My girlfriends were convinced I was having another boy. As one of them pointed out, 'Just look at Pete! As if there's an ounce of oestrogen in that footy-playing body?'

Nevertheless, on 16 September 1997, our little girl, Billi Mariah Sofiah FitzSimons was born. Her middle names – pronounced Mah-rye-ah Sah-fye-ah – were courtesy of her great-great-grandmother on Pete's side, whose no-nonsense reputation was the stuff of legend in the family. Billi's due date was also 20 September, so we had been expecting a triple whammy of birthdays on the same date; but the fact that she arrived four days early indicated to us that maybe that matrilineal DNA had already kicked in – our girl wasn't sharing her birthday with anyone, especially not with a couple of boys!

We were a pretty busy household by now. As well as *Beauty & the Beast*, I'd started doing a bit of consulting work back at ACP; and Pete, along with everything else, was now co-hosting a drivetime radio show with Doug Mulray on 2WSFM.

Pete's thirst for life, and people, and work, and family, and charities continued to amaze me, but that sometimes meant he had a tendency to take on a bit too much. And when time allowed, I would pick up the slack … which had now extended to filling in for him two days a week on radio. Doug's breakfast show on Triple M had been number one in Sydney right throughout the 80s and early 90s, and it was an absolute treat just to be in the same studio working beside him and trying to learn as much as I could.

I realised just how much I had to learn on one particular occasion that would take years for Doug and the bosses at 2WSFM to recover from. It was during an interview we were doing with John Blackman from TV's *Hey Hey It's Saturday*. Doug and John were old mates and the chat was going brilliantly. But five minutes in, I simply hadn't managed to get a word in. John was bagging Doug over something or other and I wanted to ask John, 'Can't you see it's a bad idea to have a go at Doug?'

Sadly, the moment I chose to break in was just as the two were momentarily drawing breath, and the only word I managed to get out was 'Can't ...', before Doug started talking again.

The look on Doug's face as he continued to banter with his buddy, while simultaneously registering his shocked dismay that his female co-host had just uttered – *live, on Sydney's family-friendliest radio station* – the most horrendously offensive word in the English language ... would take me years to forget.

It was a crucial lesson for me to learn in this business of talking live on air: timing is everything, and, oh yeah, don't say the 'c-word'.

Doug taught me, too, the importance of team chemistry. Without that mutual support, without that teamwork, without the whole crew enjoying each other off air and loving putting the show out, it can't prosper. As Doug put it: 'If it ain't happening in the corridors, it don't go up the stick.'

How prescient those words would prove to be in the years to come.

*

Brian was on the phone. 'We have Pauline on the show tomorrow!'

'Pauline' was the newly minted federal politician Pauline Hanson. Her controversial maiden speech in parliament and many interviews since had guaranteed her single-name-needed-only status, and in almost record time, she had completely divided the nation. Amongst other things, Hanson contended that the country was in danger of being overrun by Asians, immigrants generally were destroying it, and that Aborigines had a history of eating their young.

Everywhere this former fish-and-chip–shop owner went, every TV show she appeared on and every newspaper interview she gave, headlines followed. So, always with a mind to publicity, Brian had organised for this most-talked-about woman in the country to appear as one of the panellists on the show. Brian was ringing to tell me that I would be on the panel with her, figuring that Pauline and I would have somewhat differing ideas on quite a few topics.

By now we had quite an eclectic mix of panellists each day: from Ita Buttrose, Gretel Killeen, Johanna Griggs, Julia Morris, Rebecca Wilson and Indira Naidoo, to transgender cabaret performer Carlotta and Jan Murray (best known for revealing to the nation that she had once left her post-coital panties in the ashtray of her politician husband's ministerial desk).

As far as Stan was concerned, Jan covered 'the loony left', while sitting way out there to Stan's right was a former editor of *TV Week*, Prue MacSween. A busty, bolshie blonde, she was now working in PR. Prue loved a shoulder pad, a drink, her mum Lol, and attacking me on camera.

While Stan and I often clashed – just as I had predicted to Brian – it was never nasty or personal. He would even sometimes check in with me during the ad breaks to make sure he hadn't gone too far. If he had, he said, he would pull back.

That was never the case with Prue. Prue just went for me. I think it was an attempt at 'showbiz'. I always tried to laugh it off, or reason with her, or if the issue was a political one, I'd just try to put my case forward and move on. But one day she went too far. I'm not sure why I reacted the way I did; maybe it was echoes of the years of bullying at school when I felt I had no voice. Now I did.

Prue had never hesitated to include Pete in her attacks on me, but this time she pointed out that he was away from home a lot and that *had* to be 'for a reason'.

The on-air abuse had been going on for too long, and I was sick of it. And what she had just implied was outrageous. So I sat there, patiently waiting for her to finish, and delivered a line to Prue (who was herself in a de facto relationship at the time) that I just didn't know I had in me: 'Well, at least mine married me.'

It was cheap, nasty, undignified, sexist, judgmental and beneath me. And I regretted it as soon as I said it. (Although I'd be lying if I didn't say my 16-year-old self was cheering.)

As regular *Beauty & the Beast* panellists went, though, nothing compared to the 'big ticket' inclusion of Rose Hancock-Porteous, widow of mining magnate and Australia's richest man, Lang Hancock. Rose was becoming legendary for her kooky TV appearances, extravagant lifestyle, multiple homes, flamboyant designer fashions, and always travelling with something of an entourage. She also insisted on having her own separate Hollywood-style 'trailer' outside the Foxtel studios, rather than mixing it with the rest of us in the little shared changerooms upstairs. Rose was … larger than life. But when she was on screen, you simply couldn't look away. As she said herself, 'I used to be the housekeeper, now I keep the houses.'

Rose was of Filipino descent, and therefore more than likely one of those Asians Pauline Hanson was feeling swamped by. So, when it came to choosing which two other panellists to have in the mix for that 'Pauline' episode, Rose was a no-brainer, with the dazzling Jeanne Little along to provide some comic relief … Between us all, we were quite the picture of Australian womanhood.

From the moment I arrived at the Foxtel studios by the water in inner-city Pyrmont that morning, I knew this day would be different. The press had turned out in huge numbers, with news crews from every free-to-air channel, and more photographers than I'd ever seen at one event crowding the entry. Security guards were everywhere. Pauline had received death threats since she first hit the headlines, and as keen as Brian was for our little show to make some noise, he didn't want it to get too silly.

While the show itself was pretty fiery and, not surprisingly, Rose and Pauline had a ding-dong battle over Asian workers (most of which I found bloody hard to make sense of), it was the show that happened afterwards that was the one to watch.

It had been many, many years since Rose had been in a room with cameras and journalists where she wasn't the centre of attention. Everyone wanted a piece of Pauline; no-one had any interest in the rest of us. It was a little too much for Rose to take, though, and despite the fact we still had four more shows to record that day, Rose suddenly retired to her trailer. Sort of.

With Pauline gone, and just a few straggler camera crews packing up, Rose, always one with an eye for 'the photo op', decided that this was her moment. So, she donned her fluffy white 'Rose' robe, parked herself in her 'Rose' director's chair just by her 'Rose' trailer door and, with her lengthy Hollywood-style cigarette holder in hand, against the magnificent backdrop of Sydney Harbour ... lit up. The exquisitely perfect curls of white smoke trailing upwards and then disappearing in the light of the midday sun were alone worthy of documenting.

But to Rose's no doubt great disappointment, not a single photographer turned their head, nor appeared to even vaguely care. Such is the ephemeral nature of fame.

CHAPTER TWENTY

Tough times

'You can't skip chapters, that's not how life works.
You have to read every line, meet every character. You
won't enjoy all of it. Hell, some chapters will make you
cry for weeks. You will read things you don't want to read,
you will have moments when you don't want the pages to
end. But you have to keep going. Stories keep the world
revolving. Live yours, don't miss out.'
– Courtney Peppernell, *Pillow Thoughts II: Healing the Heart*

THE BUSH LINING THE route of the old Wakehurst Parkway was
alive with the song of summer's cicadas, and it reminded me
of all those trips to Wollongong, sitting in the back of the family
Holden when I was a kid. Except now, I was one of the parents up
the front, excited, as our family of five headed to Newport Beach
in a car loaded to the gunnels for the annual Fitz family Christmas
holiday.

This year was going to be a big one. There had been a serious
baby boom amongst Pete's brothers and sisters in recent times, with
eight little ones arriving in quick succession. Together with our own
kids, they formed a good chunk of the fifth generation of Fitzes to
walk the old floorboards at Nantucket, as the house was named.

And if it takes a village to raise a child, then there were no fewer
than 26 villagers about to bed down for Christmas Eve, sleeping

variously in bunk beds and collapsible cots, on couches, in sleeping bags on the floor, on blow-up beds in the garage, and – most excitingly of all for the littlies – in tents on the back lawn.

It was always a mystery how Santa was going to be able to identify which of the many sleeping kids was which, as he delivered presents into the empty pillowcases left out the night before, with the only certainty being that wherever The Big Guy in Red found Jake, he would also find his cousin Freya.

The two were born just four months apart, lived 100 metres from each other, and were just about to start kindergarten together. They were inseparable – not just cousins but each other's best friend and protector, and like all the cousins, beside themselves at the prospect of once again sharing two weeks of non-stop backyard cricket, board games, boules on the back lawn right by the clothesline – always groaning under the weight of a constantly changing patchwork of washing – and, of course, more trips to the beach than anyone would care to count.

Those beach visits had now become quite the exercise as our ever-expanding mob traipsed barefoot en masse across the council car park, laden with towels, buckets, spades, umbrellas, nappies, litres of backup sunscreen and – somewhat optimistically – books, before settling down on the sand.

At the beach was where our 'village' really came into its own, as every parent remained on duty, keeping an eagle eye out for potential drownings, sunburn, blue-bottle stings, and the really little ones eating too many fistfuls of sand, all while grabbing snatches of conversation (*'Yes darling, that IS a big sandcastle – well done!'*) with one another and catching up at the end of what were invariably busy years for all of us.

I loved watching how this family worked. Twenty-six humans sharing a small cottage, with one bathroom, an outside shower and loo, a tiny kitchen, and four bedrooms rotated between six families each year – with one bedroom so small it became known as the dog-box, so named because it wasn't even big enough to swing a cat in. It was a bit like National Fitness Camp meets *National Lampoon's Vacation*, but it worked, as everyone rubbed along together in the manner their late parents had always taught them from day dot: 'share and share alike', 'of a little, have a little and be thankful too', and 'FHB' for 'Family Hold Back' when any – and there were many – visitors dropped in and there wasn't enough food to go around.

Sharing was the base principle of everything the Fitzes did. Every evening, one of the six families was in charge of providing dinner for all – with spag bol, leftover Christmas ham, and sausages on the barbie being regular staples – while another family would be on washing-up duty. Then it was kids down before we adults could breathe out and sit up talking and drinking wine until late into the night on the back verandah. The best thing? Knowing that the next day, we would be doing it all again.

As the years passed and some of the older cousins mastered various instruments, 'Grandma's Good Time Band' was formed in honour of Helen. This musical ensemble involved everything from guitars, a French horn, harmonicas, toy tambourines and raucous singing ... to Billi (sort of) beating time with a wooden spoon on the back of an old saucepan.

For all of us, the favourite was a song the family had embraced when their grandmother died, Chrissie Hynde's anthemic 'Hymn To Her', which promised never to forget a beloved family member, even long after she was gone – for she would always carry on.

When my own mum visited, she was always warmly welcomed and included, but I could see she often felt overwhelmed. This was 'family' like she had never experienced before. And while I knew she loved her grandchildren being in the middle of such a large, loving mob, I often wondered – as she sat in one of the old cane chairs in a far corner of the backyard, and tuned out of the noise of Nantucket and in to the world of her much-loved talkback radio – if she was comparing these Christmases to those she had known in her own childhood.

That trip on the Wakehurst Parkway each year meant driving right past the gates of Dalwood Children's Home at Seaforth, the very gates she had passed through as a little girl with her somewhat indifferent mother on that Christmas Eve all those years ago, leaving her Shirley Temple doll and so much of her innocence behind. One year, I asked Mum if she would prefer I took a different road to Newport, but she said no. I'm not sure why; maybe she drew comfort from that stark reminder of her own grandchildren enjoying a deep and wide love the younger Beryl never knew.

Mum had been born into a difficult family at a difficult time, and whether she would ever give herself the credit she deserved or not, she had done the very best she could with the very little she was given. She had made some smart choices along the way – most particularly in the man she married – and with Dad gone, I hoped these holidays with her three beautiful grandchildren were helping to provide happy times and some long-deserved balm for her soul.

*

'Do you want to go again?'

Well, we were at Nantucket, and it had proven to be a pregnancy good-luck charm for us in the past, so despite the fact we had the 'dog-box' that year, why not give it one last try? We couldn't believe how easily we'd been falling pregnant, but as I headed towards 40, we knew if we were going to go for child number four, we had to do it soon.

I won't lie: the thought of four kids did feel a little daunting, but Billi had been the easiest of all the babies, and when you're in the zone and your kids already outnumber the two of you anyway ... well, in for a penny, in for a pound. With each child I could feel my heart grow bigger and stronger – and I realised when it comes to children there is no limit to how much, or how many, you can love.

Sure enough, by late January, the nausea was back, and a visit to the doctor confirmed that baby number four was indeed on its way. Hilariously enough, this one was also due on 20 September. Yep, Nantucket was certainly lucky for Pete and me.

The early stages of this pregnancy were going to be a little harder to conceal, though. *Beauty & the Beast* had just been signed to the Ten Network, and the shows were now one hour long, so ducking out to the loo to relieve the shocking nausea was tricky. I had tried everything: copper bangles, ginger tea, sea sickness tablets, scratching and sniffing the peel of lemons, vitamin B6, minuscule bites of dry toast, drinking water, not drinking water, drinking only tiny sips of water ... but I simply couldn't keep anything down.

I had precious little appetite for anything, except occasionally biting Pete's head off. Still, the nausea counted for nothing against the rainbow waiting for us at the end of it all. A little brother or sister for Jake, Louis and Billi.

*

It was just like any other Saturday, and just like any other day of being pregnant for me. At 11 weeks, bed was the only place I wanted to be, and weekends always brought the sweet relief of knowing I didn't have to hide from anyone at work just how shocking I was feeling. The kids knew Mummy had a little baby in her tummy, but what the kids (at five, three and one) knew more than anything was that Mummy wasn't much fun right now, and Daddy was taking them to the beach to get ice-creams *a lot*.

Sometimes, in those times between babies, I would look back at the nausea, and try and minimise in my mind the appallingness of it all, or project forward and remember those words I heard so often: 'every pregnancy is different'. But here I was yet again. I seemed to only have one kind of pregnancy. I just had to keep counting down the days.

Crazily, in the middle of all this, we'd just moved house again, this time into what we hoped was our forever home, just around the corner from the apartment Chris and I first owned. I knew the neighbourhood well. It was a house I used to pass by on walks and for some strange reason, it had always intrigued me. I wasn't sure if it was the falling-down fences, the gnarly old garden full of camellias and roses, or the small glimpses of the house I could see, with all its quirky, weatherboard, weather-beaten charm, that drew me in.

The whole place looked to be completely frozen – if not a little forgotten – in time. As we soon discovered, it was. In a hundred years it had only ever been home to two families, neither of which appeared to have ever put their mind to such modern concepts as renovation. The old, widowed doctor who owned it was now in his eighties and he told us that, with his kids grown up and with families of their own, it had all just got too much for him to care for on his own.

The place certainly needed a lot of work, and while we figured it may take us another 50 years to finish it all, our little – and growing – family were up for it. But as I lay there on that Saturday morning in our new, old bedroom and looked out through its quirky circular windows, trying to ignore the sill's peeling white paint and instead watching the passing clouds beyond, something was wrong. There was blood. Not a lot, but enough that I called down the stairs to Pete.

I'd 'spotted' twice with Louis, and there had been no issue; but, just to be sure, we decided to leave the kids at home with Mum and head to the hospital.

I wasn't nervous as I lay on the bed in the radiologist's office. I'd done this so many times before and was used to the routine.

But something made me shiver. Maybe it was the sudden chill of the gel she smeared on my tummy as she began to take measurements on the screen. Or maybe it was when all her friendly questions about work, and life, and how many other kids we had fell away to nothing.

'How many weeks did you say you thought you were again?'

Or maybe it was that moment. Now I was shaking. And I couldn't stop.

As Pete squeezed my hand just a little bit tighter, he said in as confident a voice as he could muster, 'We're eleven weeks.'

Or maybe it was the moment she said she just had to go and check some things with the senior radiologist.

*

It is a strangely cruel thing to leave the very hospital where you had only known the joy of taking home three healthy babies, and now walk through those same sliding doors with arms – and your own body – completely empty.

The house was quiet when we returned. Sleep came and went, as I drifted in that strange twilight that lingers in the days after a general anaesthetic. Outside I could hear the faint, delighted squeals of all three kids with Pete on the trampoline.

My doctor had told me I was just fitting in with the statistics.

'At your age, one in four pregnancies ends in miscarriage. This is your one in four,' she'd said, just as I'd been wheeled into the white light and cold stainless-steel surrounds of the operating theatre to finish what nature had already begun.

I took comfort in those numbers – this was my one in four. Pete was heartbroken, but also his typically optimistic self – never failing to find a way, in difficult times, to steady the course for both of us.

'We'll try again,' he said. 'This little one just wasn't strong enough for the world.'

The one saving grace was that we'd still only told a few close family members. And once I explained to the kids that our little baby was now with the angels, their only concern was if that meant they couldn't go and get ice-creams anymore.

And sure enough, ice-creams were back on the menu just two months later when, unexpectedly, we'd fallen pregnant again. Our doctor had said I should give my body a rest and wait three months before trying again. But sometimes the universe just makes these decisions for you.

This pregnancy did seem different, too. Mercifully, I was finally having a pregnancy where the nausea wasn't quite so bad. I was thrilled. Until, again, at 11 weeks something was wrong. The pain was unbearable. It was like an unholy storm was moving through my body. I was miscarrying at home.

But how could that be? I'd had my one in four. We were falling pregnant so easily. My body knew how to do this. Now it was betraying me. Why couldn't I hold on to these babies?

I ached for the bliss I'd once known: of not knowing what this pain of loss felt like. I was so sad I could hardly breathe. I couldn't look at pregnant women or babies in prams. I wanted to be happy for them, but I was consumed with being unhappy for me. And overwhelmed with guilt because of it.

I was so grateful to already have three healthy children, but had I not been grateful enough? I lashed myself for all those times I'd complained about the nausea. Why hadn't I listened more closely, been more sympathetic when friends had talked of their own fertility problems? How could I have been so consumed by my own issues, and so blind to the stories of others? Yet, they didn't seem to be living under the same cloud of grief that I was ... or were they, like me, desperately trying to keep it all together in front of others for fear of completely falling apart?

I had been so busy with life; had I cherished enough all those unique joys that only come from the extraordinary wonder of creating it? Did I remember clearly enough all the firsts with my babies? Those first flutters at 18 weeks as your baby truly makes its presence felt inside you. Then that moment when one becomes two, they're placed on your chest, and you look into the eyes of this little human for the very first time. That intoxicating smell of newborn skin. Those games of peek-a-boo during nappy changes.

Had I marvelled enough as my body burned to do what it was designed for in the reproductive cycle of life: to twist itself completely out of shape, drink itself dry of nutrients and place them all in the future of this little human ... or was I too darn busy just trying to get to the end of each day? I didn't know. I just knew we had to be patient, wait three months as the doctor had ordered, and try again.

*

It was parent–teacher evening – our first – as Pete and I sat there in those little plastic chairs meant for five-year-olds and looked around at all the brightly coloured children's paintings hung from fishing line across the room. I tried to concentrate on the teacher's comments about Jake. He was, she said, happy and doing really well. But I was not. We were finally pregnant again, but at nine weeks, I was crippled by cramps and it was becoming impossible to hide the pain.

I was grateful for the box of Lego that took Jake's attention away from our tears that night at the hospital. As he sat there on the floor, in his still-far-too-big school uniform, and I lay there on the radiologist's bed once again desperately staring at the screen for signs of something – a pulsating anything – Pete held my hand. There was no heartbeat.

And as we headed home that night, without saying a word, Pete and I knew we were done. I couldn't do this anymore – *we* couldn't do this anymore. A fourth child just wasn't meant to be ours. We had been blessed three magical times, and right now, and in the days and weeks and months that lay ahead, we had to hold on to that … and heal.

And right on cue, from his booster seat in the back, Jake – our precious, perfect, first-born boy – without even realising, started that process.

'Mummy, you never come for ice-creams with us. Can we go and get one now? Please, Mummy?'

And we did.

*

It was early morning, but the soft, grey haze outside made it look like dusk. Getting out of bed was going to be hard, but I had to get moving, as Johanna Griggs and I were flying to Melbourne at 10am to film a pilot for a new afternoon talk show, based on the wildly successful American show *The View*, anchored by the legendary Barbara Walters. Brian was convinced that the country had moved on from the male-dominated cast of *The Midday Show*, and there was a growing hunger for a live daytime talk show 'manned' exclusively by women.

A warehouse in Richmond had been converted into an apartment-style studio for the day, and Julie and Paul, the clever duo behind the day-to-day success of *B&B*, had gathered together a great line-up of guests for Jo and me to interview, including – be still my beating heart – Sherbet lead singer, Daryl Braithwaite.

At one point on a previous episode of *B&B*, Stan has asked us who had been out biggest teen crush, and I'd confessed all about my love for both Garth and Daryl. Things had stalled a little for Daryl after the crazy, heady days of Sherbet's success in the 70s, but he was now enjoying a major reboot with a string of hits, including his version of the Rickie Lee Jones classic, 'The Horses'.

'We've probably got about ten minutes for the interview with Daryl,' Julie told me. 'But I need you to do me a favour. We're having some technical issues with the feed going back to Sydney, and I need you to take care of him for about half an hour, otherwise I think we may lose him.'

Fill half an hour 'taking care' of Daryl Braithwaite? And you call this work? Give me a tough one, Julie.

In person, Daryl was just as lovely as I'd hoped. And for my sins, I couldn't help confessing my rather intense teenage crush and the role Sherbet had played in my high-school years ... including that awful day at the oval. I was probably well and truly over-sharing, but Daryl didn't seem to mind. He appeared genuinely touched, too, when I mentioned I still had all the scrapbooks I'd lovingly pasted together over the years, and the old vinyl Sherbet albums – admittedly a little scratchy by now, but still playable.

Maybe that was why, just as he was leaving, he invited me 'and a guest' to an invitation-only turn-of-the-millennium Sherbet reunion concert that was happening the following month, to be aired at midnight on New Year's Eve. I was thrilled; that meant I would get to see my biggest crush of all, Garth, performing live – though I didn't tell Daryl that.

Pete knew about my teenage Sherbet obsession, but it was one that escaped him growing up, so it took a bit of convincing to get him to come along.

The venue was the ABC TV studios in Sydney and, to my surprise, as soon as Pete and I arrived to check in and join the studio audience, we were told Daryl had invited us to the band's dressing room for a pre-show drink. My inner teenage self couldn't believe it. A drink ... with Sherbet! Oh, my lord, I really was going to finally meet Garth! But as we made our way backstage, I wondered: did Daryl realise I was bringing my husband? Did I even mention I was married? Was this about to get very awkward?

We arrived at the dressing-room door and I peered in. Sure enough, the first face I saw was Garth's, who was standing just near the doorway – instantly recognisable and completely unchanged from the one I knew so well, bopping behind the keyboard all those years ago. Those long blond curls were somewhat shorter these days and, dammit, he was even more handsome because of it. I tried not to stare.

Strangely, Garth looked up and smiled in my direction. Huh? But I'd never even met him before … and this was no ordinary smile. He was absolutely beaming and, embarrassingly, clearly thrilled to see me. It was just like I'd dreamt all those years ago: Garth Porter and I were having, I kid you not, a 'moment'. From just outside the doorway, I smiled right on back, trying to silently communicate that I was feeling everything he was feeling – and had for a long time – but look, our lives had gone in different directions (because, you know … husband). I didn't know how he knew me – maybe he'd seen that episode of *Beauty & the Beast* where I'd confessed my love? Still, how sweet for us to meet just this once, and for both of us to acknowledge what might have been …

But hang on, what about my other crush, Daryl? I looked around, and there he was, sitting in a far corner chatting to the band's drummer, Alan Sandow. He looked up and smiled, too. I smiled back.

The room was small and I wasn't sure what to do next. I wondered if I should go in, but Daryl immediately got up and started to walk towards me just as Garth began to do the same. They were both heading right for me.

Oh, dear God, after all these years of Sherbet worship, had it really come to this? Did I now have to choose between the two? And what was I going to do about the husband I had chosen years before who was still standing right behind me watching this fight for my affections about to unfold? And should I give them fair warning that on the rugby field he had once been sent off for violence against the All Blacks?

So I closed my eyes for just an instant to take in this surreal moment and let destiny take its course.

And then I heard it.

'Peter FitzSimons! What a pleasure to have you here. I'm a big fan of your work. Love your books and your columns!'

I opened my eyes to find Garth completely bypassing yours truly and instead warmly shaking Pete's hand, followed by Daryl doing exactly the same thing. And Pete was pumping theirs in turn, my husband suddenly pretty darn pleased to be here and hear how much these two pop legends loved his work.

Oh, the treachery! It was over between Garth and me before it had even begun. And Daryl, too. Turns out I had been right all along about pop stars: your affections are just wasted on them!

CHAPTER TWENTY-ONE

Reach out for the sunrise

'Your past does not define you. It prepares you.'
– Author unknown

I T WAS THE YEAR 2000, the Olympics were finally coming to 'Syd-er-nee', and while the Foxtel afternoon talk show that Julie and Paul had planned never did quite get off the ground, something else did: a morning show on Channel 7 I was asked to co-host.

Seven was the Olympics rights-holder, and they were beefing up their year-round morning schedule. Starting February, we would follow their breakfast news bulletin, called *Sunrise,* anchored by Mark Beretta and Georgie Gardner, at 9am.

The producers said our show, *The Morning Shift*, would probably only run for the year of the Olympics; but once again, I took the same attitude I'd adopted since those very first opportunities I'd been given at *Dolly*: why not give it a shot? I could be terrible at it, but as Brian Walsh had so wisely told me, 'It's only television.' The difference this time was, a much bigger audience would be watching.

It was going to be a bit of a juggle, though. Doug Mulray had decided to take another break from radio so the show on WSFM had come to an end, but I was still consulting at ACP two days a week, now as editor-at-large of the *Women's Weekly*.

Kerry had approached me again to take on the job of editor and, as flattering as his invitations always were, I had to decline. If I ever

My dad, Ray, bottom left, with his beloved double bass – and his jazz band, Jack Allen & The Katzenjammers, playing the Hydro Majestic, in the New South Wales Blue Mountains, 1948.

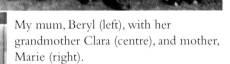

My mum, Beryl (left), with her grandmother Clara (centre), and mother, Marie (right).

Mum and Dad, newly engaged, and planning a life together, 1950.

Mum, Brett (age two), me (four) and Kyle (eight), on holidays on the south coast.

On my beloved Cyclops tricycle, age five, on the verandah at our house in Sturt Street, waiting for Dad to come home.

Two of my great loves: our boxer dog, Heidi, and ballet. Here I am, age eight, in my tutu, about to head off in the family Holden for yet another joyous performance.

Lunchtime with some of our group in the playground at Campbelltown High, 1974. Left to right: Sue, Julie, Michelle, me and Chris.

School was finally over, and it was time for a new life and a new me. And that started with chopping off my waist-length 'Marcia Brady' hair and getting a 'pageboy' – everyone's favourite style of the day ...

With some of my *Dolly* team in 1982, including Ron and Pete, who came with me to *Cleo* three years later.

At Sydney airport with Dad as I headed off to New York to work with Gloria Steinem, in 1987.

At my desk at *Cleo*, in 1988, and loving it.

Another year, another *Cleo*'s List of Australia's 50 Most Eligible Bachelors, which in 1991 included Channel 10 reporter Eddie McGuire (back left) and AFL player Dermott Brereton (bottom left).

The night in December 1991 I had to choose between drinks with Nicole Kidman, now a major Hollywood star, and an impromptu first dinner date with Pete. Drinks with Nicole (and Deb Thomas) won … but within days Pete and I had fallen hopelessly in love.

Cutting *Cleo*'s 14th anniversary cake with Barry Humphries and Clive James, two of the huge names attending what we called 'The Ultimate Dinner Party' at the Sebel Townhouse in 1986.

Hosting Kerry Packer and Ita Buttrose at *Cleo*'s 20th anniversary party, 1992. It was the first time they had seen each other in 12 years.

Beaming on our wedding day, September 1992, nine months after we first met.

Pete and me at Newport, Christmas 1992, about to find out that we were pregnant for the first time.

One of the many changing lineups at *Beauty & The Beast* as we made the move to Channel 10. Left to right: Johanna Griggs, Prue MacSween, Jan Murray, Stan Zemanek, Maureen Duval, Ita Buttrose and me in 1999. *(Courtesy of Foxtel)*

The happiest and craziest of times as I tried to juggle work and home life, 1998. Left to right: our constant saviour, Mum; Billi, age six months; Jake, four; and Louis, two, in the kitchen window at our first house.

Growing up fast. A Fitz family picnic, Clareville Beach, Christmas 2003.

Karl Stefanovic and me at our first photo shoot, just days after I joined the *Today* show, May 2007.

Karl and me at the Melbourne Cup, 2008, with our *Today* show executive producer, Tom Malone, who played such a significant role in building the success of the show and keeping me on track as I was learning the ropes of breakfast TV.

The day in June 2010 that Julia Gillard became our first female prime minister, Karl and I broadcast non-stop for 11 hours. It was a moment that, as a little girl, I never thought I would see in my lifetime. This photo is from an interview for *The Project* in 2018.

Outside Mawson's hut in Antarctica, January 2011, on the family trip of a lifetime.

When it comes to pinch-yourself moments, singing 'back-up vocals' to Daryl Braithwaite on 'The Horses' was right up there. This was during the Sydney Children's Hospital telethon in 2013 and, despite my singing, we still managed to raise a bucketload of money! *(Brad Hunter/ Newspix)*

With a bunch of Channel Nine legends: Ken Sutcliffe, then-Nine-CEO David Gyngell and the wonderful Brian Henderson, 2014.

One of my favourite photos of Karl and me. On the road again (as we so often were) with *Today,* this time at Uluru, 2015.

Meeting Prince William and Catherine, the Duchess of Cambridge, at the Australian War Memorial in Canberra on Anzac Day 2015, while my husband, the Chair of the Australian Republic Movement, hid.

What 4.30am used to look like for Karl and me in 2016.

Celebrating on the day we found out we had finally won the breakfast TV ratings in 2016. Left to right: Richard Wilkins, *Today*'s executive producer Mark Calvert, Karl, me and Sylvia Jeffreys.

Receiving the Order of Australia with Pete and the kids at Government House, 2016. One of the greatest honours of my life.

Three generations, three vastly different sets of experiences as women … but all of us with so much hope for the future. Billi, Mum, and me having a girls' get-together in 2016.

The blouse with the 'strategic cut-out above the bust' that caused all the controversy when I had the audacity to wear it twice in the space of just four months!

At the Logies in 2017 – a rare moment for Karl and me with our opposite numbers at *Sunrise*, David 'Kochie' Koch and Samantha Armytage.

With Sylvia and Karl on my 10th anniversary at *Today*, when we took the show to my hometown, Campbelltown, in May 2017.

The 'toilet race' that took place in the main street of Winton, Queensland, in May 2017 – an event that made me wonder whether my future really was still with *Today*.

That fateful appearance on *The Weekly* with Kitty Flanagan and Charlie Pickering, in May 2017. Charlie's questions started a chain of events that became impossible to ignore.

Renewing our vows for our 25th wedding anniversary, surrounded by all those we loved, Saturday, 7 October 2017. Just ten days later, my world was turned upside down.

How Sydney's *Daily Telegraph* reported my defection to Ten on 17 October 2017, the morning after the Night of the Long Knives. *(News Ltd/Newspix)*

My first night on *The Project*, 28 January 2018, with Peter Helliar, Hamish Macdonald and Rachel Corbett.

What a difference a year makes. On the Logies red carpet in 2018 with my *Project* buddy, Carrie Bickmore.

The moment Pete crashed my interview with Celine Dion in Vegas, 2018 ... and Celine decided to answer the call.

When *The Project* sent me on a round-the-world trip in 2018 to interview David Beckham in London, Bradley Cooper in New York, and Jon Bon Jovi (seen here at the Four Seasons Hotel in LA), guess which one was my favourite?

Just some of the Fitz clan gathered in the backyard at Newport for the annual Fitz Family Christmas holiday.

Besties Deb Thomas, Jen Byrne, Mia Freedman and Gretel Packer. I treasure these women who have seen me through so many of the highs and lows … and still love me anyway. As I do them.

On stage just after I introduced Brittany Higgins at the March 4 Justice rally in Canberra, 15 March 2021, exactly one month after our interview went to air. More than 100,000 people marched across the country that day calling for action against gendered violence. Women had finally had 'Enough!' *(Photo by Mike Bowers)*

was going to do that job, it certainly wasn't now – so soon after the miscarriages, with three little ones and the start of renovations at home making for a slightly chaotic household. I did, however, agree to being involved on a smaller basis if they took my strong advice and appointed Deb Thomas as the editor. Deb had been kicking goals everywhere she went and was the smart choice for the job. And sure enough, my great buddy and I were now back working together again and loving it.

This time, I wasn't doing the crazy hours I'd known during my *Cleo* days. There is nothing quite like juggling school pick-ups, day-care schedules, tradies and family dinner-time to focus the mind, and for the first time in my magazine career, I was out the door on the dot of 5pm. The show on Channel 7 was on air for two hours, Monday to Friday, but we recorded all five shows over two intense days each week, so the balance between work and home suited me well.

The producers, Bob Campbell and Des Monaghan, were convinced we would be able to knock off Bert Newton over on Channel 10 from the number-one spot within a few months.

The set design was borrowed from the recent changes at the NBC *Today Show* in the US with its much-talked-about 'window on the world' outside. That show had New York's famed Rockefeller Center visible in the background, with its busy forecourt full of tourists and shoppers. We had something slightly less busy: the deserted daytime sidewalks of Sydney's Darling Harbour, with our studio in a couple of vacant shops in the middle of the newly built shopping centre there.

Now, we just needed to find me a co-host. Initially Bob and Des wanted Pete and me to front the show together, hoping to mimic the huge success of a husband-and-wife team in the UK who were baring the inner workings of their marriage for all to see – and judge – on a daily basis. That was an easy 'no' for us.

The auditions for a co-host went on for weeks, and included the charming and accomplished Mike Willesee Jnr, and a former Olympic gold medallist at the '88 Games, Duncan Armstrong. Bob and Des made the call that Duncan was the one, his Olympics experience giving him the edge over Mike.

Also on the show was a young entertainment reporter, Jackie Last. Jackie was best known as Jackie O, co-host of Triple M's wildly successful night-time show, the *Hot30 Countdown* alongside her husband 'Ugly' Phil O'Neil. That marriage – and on-air partnership – had recently broken down though, and Jackie was now looking for a new radio co-host.

At just 25, Jackie was a huge star on the rise – Bob and Des had also signed her to host a new 'reality' show of theirs, *Popstars* – and since her marriage had ended, she was being relentlessly chased by the paparazzi. Wherever she went, there they were, with their rapid-fire clicking cameras, hoping to catch Jackie off-guard so the tabloids could put whatever spin they wanted on whatever pics they had. I'd never spoken to anyone who'd been through that experience before, and it was clearly terrifying for her. And she was dealing with it while trying to find her new radio partner.

Backstage at *The Morning Shift*, Jackie would sometimes share with me how it was all going. It wasn't good. They'd auditioned lots of potential DJ partners for her, but Jackie felt that none of them were the right fit. Jackie's bosses were losing patience and decided to give a relatively unknown music announcer from Triple M in Brisbane called Kyle Sandilands a shot – no audition, just straight to air.

Jackie was convinced it was never going to work. But her male bosses were convinced it would. And so was Kyle. So much so that, as the weeks went by and the chemistry between them started to settle and quickly build, the subject of their salaries came up.

Jackie told me that Kyle was horrified when he discovered he was earning more than three times Jackie's 'phone girl' (as she'd been known in her radio partnership with Ugly Phil) salary. Kyle knew that even though their styles were very different, that was one of their strengths, and as a duo it just worked. In the blokey world of FM radio at the time, though, female presenters were rare, and as far as management was concerned, women were really only there as 'support' to the male stars.

Kyle would have none of it. Jackie said he went straight to their bosses, demanding that what they were doing was completely unfair and, as they were a partnership, he and Jackie should be on equal pay.

The result? Jackie's pay was immediately raised to match Kyle's. And I was seriously impressed.

The rest became history. As did *The Morning Shift*. We had taken the show to number one, just as Bob and Des had predicted; but the bosses at the network had other plans for the slot, maybe involving that *Sunrise* news show before us. But, hey, that was television. I was grateful for the experience and felt like I'd learnt a whole lot about what it took to host a TV show. It was just another one to tell the grandkids about one day.

*

By 2003 life had settled into an enjoyable, if always busy, rhythm. The kids were all now in school and going well, work at the *Weekly* with Deb was a joy, and I'd returned to doing a couple of episodes a week of *Beauty & the Beast*.

Jake and Louis were playing something that looked a bit like rugby on Saturdays – although whenever Louis got the ball, he did have a tendency to just charge, resisting all calls from Pete on the sidelines to pass it on. It would be safe to say that a love of rugby didn't exactly get passed down through the family's DNA, as the boys' enthusiasm for the game appeared to be lukewarm at best. But every week Pete, God love him, was still out there enthusiastically coaching them and their teams on Tuesday evenings, confident that, if not in rugby, they would eventually go on to find and forge their own paths.

Billi, meantime, was loving spending her Saturday mornings in ballet classes at the local church hall just across the road from school. I cried the first time I dressed her in her tiny pink leotard, put her hair in a bun and helped tie the soft satin ribbons on her little shoes. It felt like it was just yesterday I was lacing up my own pointe shoes.

With Sundays reserved for Nippers down at Balmoral Beach, and Wednesday nights for Cubs at the local scout hall, our family had a full dance card.

The biggest thrill of the week, though, was saved for Thursday nights, when each of the children would take it in turns to have a sleepover at grandma's new place just down the road from us. It was a little one-bedroom apartment with a huge view of Sydney Harbour. Mum was always drawn to the water, and she forked out every cent she had to ensure she could have it in her life every day. For a little girl who had spent so much of her childhood in a dark place, Mum loved her light-filled home and being able to provide such happy times for her grandchildren.

This was the night they each got Grandma all to themselves. More than anything, they loved that their 'bed' was Grandma's lounge and they got to fall asleep watching the ferries come and go on the water ... and probably eat more lollies than their mum would say was OK. I kind of loved that; this was their relationship to have. And, I figured, what happens at Grandma's stays at Grandma's.

The kids were the joy of Mum's life, and my joy was seeing her receive all that unconditional love in return.

*

Things were changing in breakfast TV. It turned out that the Seven Network did, indeed, have plans for that *Sunrise* news bulletin, and in the space of just 18 months, they had turned the timeslot on its head.

Georgie Gardner was gone, and in her place was the largely unknown but hugely likeable newsreader Melissa Doyle, along with trusted finance journalist David Koch. Together they had become known as 'Mel-and-Kochie', and along with Natalie Barr on news, Mark Beretta on sport and Grant Denyer on weather, they were giving the breakfast TV ratings a red-hot go.

Behind the scenes was Adam Boland, one of the hottest young TV producers in the country. He was executive producer of *Sunrise*, and he was now on the phone to me. Adam told me he was a long-time fan of *Beauty & the Beast*, and was keen for me to become a contributor on the show.

With the growth of so many new forms of communication, such as emails and SMS, Adam's vision was to break down the walls of TV and actually make the audience a part of the show, where viewer feedback would drive much of the content.

To demonstrate the show's strong commitment to that vision, Kochie had a whiteboard he regularly wheeled in to write down requested story ideas live on air, and he updated it each day. As issues were doggedly pursued, dealt with and wiped off, new ones would be added. Then there was the Joke of the Day, submitted by viewers ... often, the more politically incorrect, the better. Adam's instruction to everyone on air was, 'If it comes into your head, say it. I'll deal with the fallout later. I want you to speak like Australia.' The format relied less on scripts and more on talking points. Chemistry was everything, and this team had it in spades.

Adam was all about trying new things. If it hadn't been done on breakfast TV before, he was prepared to give it a go, adding and subtracting as he went. His philosophy was simple: 'If it doesn't work, dump it, move on and try something else that will!'.

Rising politicians Kevin Rudd and Joe Hockey became 'Brekky Central' regulars in their Friday-morning slots, appearing for all the world to be such good mates it sometimes seemed implausible that they sat on opposite sides of the chamber. Adam even talked them into performing in rap-style videos. They looked daggy, uncomfortable and silly – and both proved so popular they were soon pegged as future prime ministers.

In a post–September 11 world, with the threat of terrorism on the rise and Australian troops in both Afghanistan and Iraq, *Sunrise* was all about finding the positive spin, allowing viewers to wake up each day to happy news ... and their growing audience was absolutely lapping it up.

The *Today* show over at Channel 9 now had its first real competition in years, and the very stable and trusted team of Tracy Grimshaw and Steve Liebmann was under attack.

Pete and I had been long-time, rusted-on *Today* show viewers, due in no small part to the role it played in our romantic beginnings, but also because Pete had once actually hosted the show alongside Liz on the morning the Sydney Harbour Tunnel opened just weeks before our wedding in 1992.

It would be fair to say it was not his finest performance. A natural ad-libber, Pete discovered live on air that squeezing him into a collapsible director's chair and asking him to read an autocue was, as he would later describe it, more like a hostage situation. But Liz kindly nursed him through the entire morning and, typical of her on-air generosity, declared to Pete at the end of the show, 'You did great!'

But for all that, it was getting hard to take our eyes off *Sunrise* as we woke up each morning. There was just something mesmerisingly raw, hokey and unpredictable about it.

Pete held tight to his *Today* show loyalties, though, and was convinced *Sunrise*'s appeal was just a passing fad. And he decided to tell his old rugby mate Kochie exactly that when we ran into him at the annual Andrew Olle media lecture that year.

'David,' he said, refusing to buy into the nickname almost all of Australia was now using, 'all this sunshiny optimism you keep trying to push down our throats at breakfast? Your "good news Fridays"? You're embarrassing yourself. Don't do it, mate. It's not going to last.'

David was unfailingly gracious and, knowing Pete and his straight-talking ways as he did, copped it on the chin. Possibly because the ratings were heading skyward and doing the talking for him. There was now no stopping these new kids on the breakfast block.

None of that must have been reported back to Adam, though, which was evident when he rang me. Because it wasn't just me he was interested in; Adam was calling to see if both Pete and I would join the show for a regular weekly spot. He wanted both of us to bring some of that off-script energy to a new segment he was introducing pitting two 'social commentators' against each other each morning to talk about the breaking news of the day. We would be one of five rotating duos each morning.

I had to admit to Adam I didn't know what a 'social commentator' was, and that Pete and I really weren't into having disagreements in front of the cameras.

'We save all that good stuff for behind closed doors,' I laughed, before adding that I did know someone I would be happy to argue the issues of the day with in the Seven studios – the father of Billi's ballet buddy and best school friend, Lucy: radio host Steve Price.

It didn't take much to convince Adam and, thereafter, every Tuesday at 7.15am, Steve and I would battle it out on set while Mel and Kochie, well, refereed.

*

At last, we were ready.

With renovations on the house underway, we'd finally got around to rebuilding the old falling-down fence, so we could now get the puppy we had long been promising the kids. And not just any puppy. I'd often told them about the cherished memories I had of Heidi, the beautiful 'red' boxer of my childhood, and I wanted one exactly like her for them, right down to the four white paws.

Even a few years before, finding such a specific kind of puppy would have been a major exercise, but not now. For the first time, we decided to try and find something we wanted to buy on the internet.

While I looked over his shoulder, Pete went to the *Trading Post* website, typed in 'red boxer, four white paws, Sydney', and in an instant the phone numbers of six breeders popped up. The first two he called had already sold, but the third breeder had exactly the little one we were looking for, and we arranged to head there the following day to pick her up.

Pete put the phone down, and we looked at each other, a bit stunned. From deciding to buy a puppy of such a specific description, to finding her and doing the deal had taken three minutes. We both recognised the moment that, even if we were behind everyone else, we had truly arrived in the age of the internet.

Pete also recognised that if we could find what we wanted so easily from the 'net, things had to be looking grim for the very model his *Sydney Morning Herald* lived off – the famed 'rivers of gold' of classifed advertising, the very same place where I had found that first job of mine at *Dolly*.

Our world was changing rapidly.

'Princess', as the breeders had temporarily named her, was the runt of the litter and the only one of their puppies that hadn't found a home by the time we came calling. 'She's not strong,' they'd warned us.

But as soon as Pete, the kids and I all piled out of the car and saw her, we knew she was the one. In our eyes, she was perfect. And as soon as she laid eyes upon us, she seemed to indicate the same, as she performed the first of her many 'happy dance' greetings that would never fail to make us smile.

At my behest, we called her 'Scout', after my favourite childhood character in *To Kill a Mockingbird*. Pete had never been a 'dog person', and yet on that first night, as Scout whimpered on the back verandah of her new home, he grabbed a blanket and a pillow and spent the whole night with a reassuring hand upon her, simply to let her know that we were her new family now. I loved him for doing that.

For us, Scout was a cure-all. Having a bad day? Go and spend some time with Scout. Mum and Dad on your case? Scout will give you a cuddle. Kids driving you nuts? Scout again. She never took sides. She was just there. And always, always happy to see us.

She was meant to be an 'outside dog', but whenever Pete and I weren't around, the kids would quickly sneak her in and they'd all snuggle up together on the big comfy lounge in our kitchen. I always knew when that had happened, because our old much-loved red-and-white quilt that always sat on that lounge would have the tell-tale signs of Scout's hair.

Occasionally I'd rouse on them, but mostly I turned a blind eye. And sometimes when neither Pete nor the kids were around, I'd do the same. It was our little secret. We *loved* our girl, and she loved us.

The only one Scout possibly loved more than us was 'Grandma'. Mum and Scout formed an instant, deep bond. When Pete would go and collect Mum to bring her over for lunch or dinner, and the kids would shout 'Grandma!' as she and Pete pulled into the driveway, Scout was instantly up and out, excitedly waiting at the passenger door, so Mum could bathe our girl with love.

It was a beautiful thing to see and reminded me of a conversation I'd once had with Dad many years before. At a time when I was no doubt being a difficult teenager, and Mum and I were having a tiff, I'd noticed her unfailing warmth and kindness to Heidi and wondered why she wasn't always like that with us.

'It's simple, darling,' he said. 'Heidi will never hurt your mum. There's no judgment, no rejection, just unconditional love.'

A beautiful thing indeed.

*

It was a Boxing Day tradition in the Fitz family. While Nantucket was two weeks for the immediate Fitzes, Boxing Day was a day for the wider family.

And right now, well over a hundred of them were on the front lawn as Pete and I took our turn on the rotating roster to host everyone back at our place for the 2004 gathering. My mind was admittedly elsewhere, though, because the following day I was starting a fortnight of filling in for Mel, hosting *Sunrise*.

The show was now firmly number one in the ratings, finally overtaking more than two decades of the *Today* show's breakfast TV dominance. While I'd done a couple of very last-minute hosting spots that year when both Mel and Nat were away, this was the first time Adam had asked me to host for such a continuous stretch.

I confessed to being a little nervous. The *Sunrise* audience really had taken complete ownership of the show, as Adam had wanted, and were quick with feedback on every aspect – including if the usual team weren't in their rightful positions each morning. Someone was away? The audience demanded to know why. The upset was so strong that Adam found the only way to deal with it was to run absentee info as breaking news on the 'ticker' that ran across the bottom of the screen for the duration of the show: 'Mel is off sick. Nat is hosting today.' Or: 'Mel is on holidays. Nat is sick. Lisa is hosting today.' It seemed bizarre, but it also seemed to calm the farm. Basically, as long as the audience felt they'd been consulted, it was OK and we could carry on.

Adam assured me I had nothing to worry about. The *Sunrise* audience had been slowly getting to know me with the regular spots I'd been doing with Steve, he said; besides, that fortnight between

Christmas and the first week of January was always quiet, and we'd mostly be filling the three hours each day with a whole lot of year-end wrap-ups and 'best of' packages – the best interviews, the best movies, the biggest news stories and the like – and they were already in the can.

'It'll be an easy transition for you into longer-term hosting, Leese,' Adam said. 'Just relax and be yourself. Also, don't forget we have the conference call every afternoon at five-fifteen where we go through the whole rundown so you know exactly what we have planned for the next day.'

So, with lunch already cleared on this Sunday afternoon as a flock of Fitzes played games on the lawn, grazing on cake and leftovers, I excused myself and headed upstairs to the relative quiet of our bedroom to punch into the 5.15 conference call. But as my line dropped in, it seemed things were already underway …

'… I don't know, they're saying maybe as many as one hundred dead, but it could be much worse …'

'I just saw a report on the BBC that it's probably going to be at least two hundred …'

'Did you see the Maldives could be affected as well? But there's still no word out of there yet …'

'There would have been plenty of Aussies already on holidays over there …'

I had no idea what anyone was talking about.

'Hey guys, it's Lisa. Sorry, have I missed something? What's happened?'

The reports were sketchy, and there were still only a few shaky videos out of a resort in Thailand to look at, but that morning, a 9.1 magnitude earthquake lasting up to 10 minutes had jolted awake the sea floor off the northern tip of Sumatra in Indonesia, unleashing a massive tsunami right across the Indian Ocean. The devastation was likely to be on an unimaginable scale, affecting millions along the coastlines of at least a dozen countries and thousands of tiny islands.

'Guys, this is going to be huge,' Adam cautioned. 'Get ready for a big week, Lisa.'

So much for that soft introduction to breakfast TV I'd been promised.

I immediately turned the TV on to CNN, staying glued to the rolling coverage for the rest of the night. With so many mobile phones now also mobile cameras, holidaymakers who'd managed to scramble to safety and survive the horror were sending through terrifying footage of unstoppable walls of water smashing through whatever stood in nature's way. The death toll was growing exponentially as each hour passed.

By the time I arrived at work the next morning, bleary-eyed from just a few hours' sleep but full of adrenaline and clutching notes I'd been taking all night as I'd tried to get across as much of the detail as possible, the death toll was expected to be in the many thousands. I took a deep breath as I entered the Channel 7 car park at the back of Sydney's Martin Place, knowing that I was about to undergo an initiation by fire in the arena of live, breaking TV news.

'You'll be fine, Leese,' Adam assured me. 'Kochie and I have got your back.'

By the time Kochie and I took our seats in the studio, we knew that at least 14 countries had been hit, more than 10,000 people were dead, and millions of people were in the affected areas. New details and new footage were coming in every few minutes, every new frame making it clear those numbers were only going to continue to rise sharply. Adam was constantly in our ear from the control room, 'More details coming out to you in just a sec, guys. Meantime, just talk to the pictures, guys, just talk to the pictures …'

All morning, shocking new images came rolling in. Each one more unbelievable, more heartbreaking than the last – raw, hastily recorded grabs on phones, as tourists and locals from across the region shared the moment of impact from every devastating angle. Horrific scenes of people walking oblivious one moment, being washed away the next, debris smashing into anything in its path, screams of terror as relentless waves of water kept pushing further onto land, homes simply disappearing, whole buildings being engulfed … while Kochie and I kept the information coming. At times, I struggled to deal with what I saw on the screen, and each time Kochie saved me.

What neither Kochie nor Adam knew on that day, and what made it all the more daunting for me, was that no-one had ever actually sat me down and taught me how to do any of this. And I'd certainly never hosted live, commercial-free breaking news before. The logistics of it all were overwhelming.

All those episodes of *Beauty & the Beast* were pre-recorded. Sure, I was hosting on *The Morning Shift*, but we were never live so there was never any breaking news, and a lot of the processes that now applied had never come up.

As the hours rolled by and Kochie and I continued to introduce new footage, throw to the news, and cross to interviews as they became available, I also couldn't help wondering what on earth all those strange words were in the autocue, between all the words we were actually meant to say out loud. What the hell did SOT and GRAB and VOX and LVO mean? And all those frantic hand signals silently delivered by the floor manager – is that chopping one he's doing indicating I've got 30 seconds or 15 to go?

I lashed myself. Why had I been so afraid to ask for help those last couple of times I'd hosted? Why had I been too scared to admit I didn't know what I didn't know? It seemed, quite reasonably, that everyone just assumed I knew what I was doing. Did I really need to panic anyone *right now*? Besides, what sort of idiot would place themselves in such a ridiculous dilemma as the one I was currently in?

But somehow – miraculously – by listening, watching, not speaking unless I had new information or something to offer, and observing the very relaxed way Kochie approached things, I got through that first confronting day without screwing up.

The 'Boxing Day tsunami', as it became known, proved to be the deadliest in recorded history and killed more than 230,000 people across 14 countries. It was a natural disaster and humanitarian crisis on an unprecedented scale.

By the end of my hosting stint, I had interviewed my first prime minister in John Howard as well as Foreign Affairs Minister Alexander Downer, and spoken to countless families waiting for word on missing loved ones. It was an initiation into breakfast TV like no other.

The privilege of being trusted to report such vital information on a story that broke the world's heart, and the huge responsibility that came with always getting it absolutely right, was not a career turn I was expecting to take, but in those two weeks, breakfast TV had just got into my bones.

CHAPTER TWENTY-TWO

Movement at the station

'Don't run from a challenge. Instead, run towards it, because the only way to escape fear is to trample it beneath your feet.' – Nadia Comaneci

THE SHIFTING SANDS OF breakfast TV was now the favourite topic of media columnists around the country. Sticking the boot into *Today* and speculating on line-up changes had been easy pickings for almost a year. At Nine, fingers were being pointed in every direction as to who and what was to blame for the show's ratings woes. With a constantly rotating roster of producers, and myriad conflicting ideas from management as to what the show needed to get back on top, everything was in a state of flux.

The old *Today* show set was considered passé against *Sunrise*'s shiny, new, glass-fronted studios in Martin Place, which mimicked perfectly the NBC *Today* show's vibe in the US. Every day, viewers at home bore witness to the huge crowds waving and cheering for 'Mel-and-Kochie!!!', a constant subliminal reminder of the ever-growing enthusiasm Australia had for the *Sunrise* brand.

So, with a new *Today* show set in the style of a loft apartment under construction at Nine, the entire team had decamped to the 'penthouse bar and nightclub' on the 32nd floor of the Intercontinental Hotel in the middle of the CBD. The exact reason for that locale was never clear, and rumours of it providing an unlimited supply of alcohol for the Nine executives in which to drink their ratings problems away were, I believe, untrue.

Sadly, Nine's troubles also meant that on 11 February 2005, that glitzy bar provided the backdrop for the much-respected Steve Liebmann's very last show and his farewell immediately afterwards. After two decades at the helm of the iconic show, and enormous success, the veteran broadcaster, with impeccable timing, had announced he'd had enough. Pete and I felt honoured to be invited, courtesy of our shared history with the show (and to be fair, Pete was a past host after all), to help celebrate Steve's unmatched tenure at Nine.

But from the moment we arrived we could both sense the unease in the room as TV writers, notepads in hand, circled conspiratorially around a handful of small, splintered-off groups amongst the 60 or so invited guests. Steve had made it clear that leaving was his choice, hastened somewhat by the heart attack he had suffered just a few months before, but there was little doubt that the main topic of these whispered conversations had to be, *Where was Steve's replacement?*

Fortunately, the first face we saw was that of the kindly Ian Ross, the former long-time newsreader on the *Today* show, but now the reigning king of 6pm news over on Channel 7. Ian was probably the happiest person in the room that morning. Life at Seven, he said, was great, especially now that he no longer had to obey that early *Today* show alarm. And nothing, he said, would have kept him from being here to honour his great friend Steve. Also in the room were former *Today* weatherman Monte Dwyer and his replacement Sami Lukis, as well as former *Today* newsreader Sharyn Ghidella and her replacement Leila McKinnon, and of course Steve's co-host of more than eight years, Tracy Grimshaw.

MC for the morning was Nine boss David Gyngell. After calling the room to attention to usher in a moving speech from a clearly emotional Tracy, we all looked to the large screens and watched as an impressive ten-minute montage of Steve's years on air played out.

Then there were the warmest of messages from those who couldn't be there in person: his very first *Today* co-host Sue Kellaway, the now-retired Brian Henderson, Liz Hayes sending her love from a *60 Minutes* shoot overseas, and former Prime Minister Bob Hawke. It definitely was the end of an era. And Steve richly deserved the sustained applause that followed.

Humbled by the warmth in the room, his thanks in response were brief and heartfelt, and as he returned to his tight group, including his wife, Di, and two sons, I was struck by the familial feel he also had with his agent John Fordham, also there with his entire family, including sons Ben and Nick. John Fordham had risen to prominence as the agent of John Laws, Alan Jones and Australian cricket captain Mark Taylor, but his genuine care of Steve on what must have been a deeply difficult day was tangible. Especially with what was just about to happen.

By the time Gyng took the microphone again to wrap things up, there was just one last item on the agenda: introducing the person about to take Steve's much-prized place on Australian TV.

'Well, I suppose you're all wondering what happens on Monday morning when we head back to our brand-new studio?' Gyng said as he looked around at the gathered faces. It was as if a giant gust of wind had suddenly blown this entire media mob forward, as every person in the room leaned in.

'Look, we're very excited by the new set. It's a really comfortable new home for the hosts. They'll be able to make their own toast and coffee and stroll out to the apartment's balcony for a view of the suburban skyline. Tracy is even going to bring her dog in each day,' Gyng announced.

Yeah, yeah, but what about the new host everyone was waiting for?

'As it happens, we have that very person here with us right now, and I hope you will put your hands together to congratulate – just over there in the corner – the new host of the *Today* show, Karl Stefanovic!'

Everyone turned their gaze to the far corner Gyng had indicated and there, by the room's heavy black curtains well away from the morning's proceedings, was a lone figure. A young guy, possibly half Steve's age.

Who? Where had he come from? Who was this young gun Nine had just declared it was pinning all its *Today* show ratings hopes upon? The polite applause was somewhere between muted and confused.

What was clear from the look on this young guy's face was that if the ground could have opened up and swallowed him whole right there and then, he'd have welcomed it.

My only thought? You poor bastard.

*

While I was enjoying breakfast TV and those weekly segments with Steve Price, I was realistic enough to know that my future still lay in magazines. Besides, all the hosting roles at *Sunrise* – and the order of any hosting line of succession – were already well and truly sorted. As far as I could see, Mel had a job for life, and should she ever decide to move on, the much-loved Nat would be her replacement. Viewers would demand it.

So, I continued to work part-time at the *Weekly* with Deb, while Paula Joye and I had launched a brand-new magazine, *Madison*, aimed at a slightly older, slightly edgier audience than *Cleo*.

Madison was an immediate success, but that was our problem. It was a joint venture with the Hearst corporation in the US, and the bosses there had plans to soon launch it Stateside as well. But too late, Hearst decided it would eat into the readership and ad revenue of some of their existing titles, and so internal politics made *Madison*'s long-term future less assured. The editor, Paula, and I were keen that the magazine have a simultaneous presence on the internet as well, but that too was a problem for management, particularly John Alexander, who was running both ACP and Nine at that point. Why give away for free, he consistently argued, what advertisers and readers were still lining up to pay real dollars for?

Much as we tried to convince management of just how crucial an online presence would be for the future viability of *Madison* – and every title in the group – they wouldn't shift. These brands had the potential to be huge assets in a digital world. But Alexander simply couldn't see the dollar return. The short-sightedness of it all frustrated the bejesus out of Paula and me.

Meantime, Adam had a plan. He told me he'd been eyeing off the weekend breakfast TV timeslot for a while now, and despite a new host at *Today*, *Sunrise* had continued to soar in the ratings. So his mission now was to have viewers waking up to *Sunrise* seven days a week.

Peter Meakin – for decades the guiding force behind the success of news and current affairs at Nine with shows like *60 Minutes*, *Sunday* and *Today* – had moved to Seven a few years before and become something of a mentor to Adam in the process. Meakin had clearly brought that same brilliance to Seven which, for the first time since the 70s, was now dominating news and current affairs at both breakfast and 6pm. In commercial TV, that's everything.

Meakin and I were also long-time mates, having both been part of the Nine/ACP family, so I was thrilled at the prospect of working with – and learning from – both him and Adam. Meakin was on board with the idea of a Sunday version of the show, but remained unconvinced there was an audience for both days. For *Sunrise* viewers, he said, Saturday mornings were filled with kids' sporting commitments. He spoke from experience, too, having been burnt in the ratings by a similar attempt at a Saturday version of the *Today* show a few years before.

'Let's take this slowly. First, we take on the *Sunday* program,' Meakin said. 'We know there's already an audience switching on their TVs at that time, so let's just see how those numbers go first.'

It was a significant call for Meakin to make, having worked so closely for so long with the team at the iconic multi-award-winning *Sunday*. But his departure from Nine had come after a major falling-out over editorial independence with the then-recently installed CEO, John Alexander, who, for all his acknowledged brilliance as the former editor of the *Sydney Morning Herald*, had not achieved an equal level of respect in television in which he had exactly no experience. That continued interference explained a lot about Nine's and the *Today* show's woes. So in many ways, for Meakin, this was personal.

Sunday was often referred to as 'Kerry's TV baby' – a politically powerful current affairs show with star reporters like Jennifer Byrne and Sarah Ferguson that, journalistically, offered a credible alternative to the ABC's *Four Corners*. Kerry's health, however, had been failing in recent times, and much of the available energy he did have was now focused on the Crown Casino side of the business. A couple of major heart attacks and regular dialysis after a kidney transplant (that organ donated by the very same pilot who had choppered me up to Palm Beach to meet Kerry all those years ago) meant that Kerry's usual eagle eye was off his much-loved Nine and it was left in the hands of others.

According to widespread reports, Nine management was at war with itself. And now, the hugely respected Gyng, a close friend of James' and son of the first man to welcome Australian audiences to TV back in 1959, had had enough of Alexander's interference, too, and walked out on his post as CEO.

'We're going to smash this!' Adam said, when he took me out for coffee to talk about the idea of the weekend show. I would be hosting alongside Chris Reason, the former host of weekday *Sunrise* who, after a cancer diagnosis (from which he was now fully recovered), had been permanently replaced by Kochie. The bad news? In that Sunday-morning slot, we would be up against *Sunday*'s formidable host, Jana Wendt.

I was daunted. Why would anyone – and particularly a complete novice like me – want to put their career on the line by going up against possibly the most iconic female news and current affairs host Australia had ever produced?

But Adam was good at selling an idea, and those ideas and his enthusiasm were completely infectious, and I finally agreed. So, on 10 April 2005, with all the overnight footage from the wedding of Prince Charles and Camilla beaming in from the UK, Chris Reason and I welcomed the *Sunrise* audience to the very first episode of *Weekend Sunrise* – so named in Adam's clear anticipation of eventually getting his much-hoped-for seven days of *Sunrise* to air a week.

*

The last time I saw Kerry was in the foyer at Park Street in about July of 2005. He was moving slowly, and his normally robust frame was diminished. Kerry was always immaculately dressed when in the office, but today his suit seemed loose, and as we chatted, his breathing was laboured.

His ill health was no surprise. Kerry's addiction to junk food was legendary and had not changed a jot despite being diagnosed with diabetes – just as he continued to smoke despite six coronary procedures. When a specialist at New York's Cornell Medical Center gave him the rounds of the kitchen about his unhealthy lifestyle, Kerry replied, 'All right, son, you've given me the fucking lecture. Now, are you going to fucking fix me up or aren't you?'

I don't know if Kerry was aware the end was near, but he was particularly warm to me, saying how happy he was with how the *Women's Weekly* was looking, and very kind, too, about having seen me on *Weekend Sunrise* a few days before. He then added, 'What are you doing on Seven anyway? I don't remember approving that. You should be hosting the *Today* show, not that bloody upstart *Sunrise*.'

As we parted that day, and just before he headed through the foyer door to his waiting silver Mercedes with the FP numberplates, Kerry gave me a warm hug, not something he was normally inclined to do. I think the only other times were at Gretel's 21st, and then again at her wedding at the family home in Surrey in the UK – at the big life events.

Maybe he did know.

The announcement came just before 9am on Boxing Day, 2005.

'Mrs Kerry Packer and her children, James and Gretel, sadly report the passing last evening of her husband and their father, Kerry. He died peacefully at home with his family at his bedside. He will be lovingly remembered and missed enormously.'

Few Australians had lived a life as large as Kerry Francis Bullmore Packer. As a boss he was loud, brash, demanding, uncompromising and, at times, terrifying. He could also be warm, generous, persuasive and utterly charming. And in many ways, he changed the course of my life.

*

It was hard to believe that our eldest, Jake, was heading to high school. Where had all those years gone? We were a busy household, and with Jake's new school an hour away on a good day, 90 minutes on a bad one, we were about to get even busier.

Pete had big changes afoot as well. He was going back to radio; this time in the highly competitive breakfast slot on 2UE, co-hosting with his mate, the brilliantly acerbic Mike Carlton. Together, they would be going up against Pete's former Wallabies coach and, latterly, the long-time king of this very same breakfast radio spot, Alan Jones. A few years before, Jones had decamped to 2GB in one of the biggest radio deals ever done, a move that saw 2UE immediately falter and scramble to gain back the significant chunk of audience that Jones had taken with him. Steve Price had had a go but, as he was a Melbourne identity, Sydney just didn't respond.

For both Pete and Mike, though, this battle had some added layers. In Pete's case, he and Jones had had a bad falling-out back in the 80s over – amongst many other things – Jones's desire for the Wallabies to tour South Africa, thereby breaking Australia's firmly held sanctions with the country over apartheid. It was an issue I remembered that Dad, during his days at Sydney Rugby Union, had also clashed with Jones over.

Pete was the only Wallaby to publicly break ranks with Jones on the issue, and it was the first of many occasions that the two would find themselves on opposite sides of the political parapet, firing furiously. During that time, with Jones as coach, Pete's Wallaby career was put on hold, and he would not make his way back into the green-and-gold jersey again until Jones eventually lost his position as coach.

The executive producer for *The Mike and Fitz Show* was a hot-shot young journo who'd quickly risen from work-experience kid to cadet to gun reporter, and now at just 26, Tom Malone was running two of the biggest, most opinionated A-type personalities in Sydney: Mike, the slightly grumpy, brilliantly funny, politically astute journo with 40-plus years' TV and radio experience to draw from; Pete, the dishevelled columnist and author, who didn't mind a chat, a laugh and playing rapid-fire with Mike.

Mike was in a particularly happy place at the time as he had just become engaged to the talented ABC producer and investigative journalist Morag Ramsay, who was already racking up awards for her breakthrough stories. More and more I was realising that this world of media was a small one. By April, Tom had been headhunted by Nine to become a senior producer at the *Today* show. And that world was about to prove even smaller still when I ran into a mutual friend at Mike and Morag's engagement party that same month.

Mark Llewellyn and I had first met way back in my *Dolly* days at Friday night drinks with my ex, Chris, while both were working at ABC Radio in the city. Since then, he'd made the jump from one of Aunty's junior reporters to commercial TV, and every so often we would run into each other, including that time he interviewed me for *A Current Affair* during our first-ever *Cleo* Bachelor of the Year lunch in Melbourne.

Mark was now head of news and current affairs at Nine, a position reserved for only the toughest and smartest in the business. He'd been appointed the previous November by the network's gruff and headstrong CEO Sam Chisholm, who had rejoined the network for a short time to fill the significant void left by the departure of David Gyngell.

In Sam's place in the Nine management mix was the fast-rising, ambitious Eddie McGuire, who had come a long way from his days as one of our most enthusiastic participants in *Cleo*'s Most Eligible Bachelor list. Eddie was now happily married to his wife, Carla, dad to two young sons, president of his much-loved Collingwood Football Club, the successful host of both *Who Wants To Be a Millionaire* and *The Footy Show* ... and the newly appointed CEO of Nine.

Mark said things were ... complicated at the network. He also agreed that we'd been too long between drinks, and insisted we rectify that over lunch down at the Bathers' Pavilion at Balmoral Beach in the coming weeks.

The 9th of June, 2006, was a stunning day, and Mark and I had lots to catch up on. As we sat down to lunch, Mark looked exhausted, but I wasn't surprised. He'd just spent much of the previous month consumed by the Beaconsfield mine disaster in Tasmania, a story that had completely gripped the nation for 14 continuous days and nights as two workers lay trapped in the collapsed mine one kilometre below the earth's surface. Another, Larry Knight, was believed already dead. Mark had been on location the entire time, working around the clock, helping behind the scenes on *Today*'s daily broadcasts with Tom Malone, along with *A Current Affair*'s night-time coverage of the event.

Mark admitted, as we made a toast to old friendships over lunch, that he was shattered.

He had turned up late to our lunch, and, beyond his obvious exhaustion, seemed slightly distracted, apologising that there was a lot going on back at Nine's Willoughby headquarters and that there was a call he was expecting and would need to take as soon as it came through.

Once we'd covered where life was up to for the both of us, the conversation quickly turned to the success of *Sunrise*. Mark was extremely complimentary about the way Adam had turned the traditional breakfast TV game upside down and so masterfully taken on *Today*. I told him I was loving my time there, learning so much from Adam and Peter Meakin about the very tricky nuances of the timeslot, and their constant striving to do better.

As to *Weekend Sunrise*, Mark admitted that the speed with which we'd taken the show to number one at the expense of the *Sunday* program had caused some significant angst at Nine. But with Kerry now gone, James in discussions about selling 50 per cent of the Nine business, and the executive structure at Willoughby 'still settling', there were bigger issues he was dealing with behind the scenes. Exactly what those issues were, he didn't say.

He wondered what I thought of the pairing of Karl Stefanovic and his new co-host Jessica Rowe, and on that I had much to say. Jessica had been an excellent newsreader at Channel 10 and had, in many ways, been placed in an impossible position. After a year with Karl, the incredibly popular Tracy had moved to *A Current Affair*, and Jessica was installed in Tracy's place to go toe-to-toe with the virtually unstoppable freight train of success that was Mel and Kochie. Or, as everyone now knew them: 'Melandkochie'.

One word. An indivisible, much loved, strangely-cool-yet-family-friendly trusted Australian 'brand'.

As anyone in the industry knows, breakfast-show chemistry is a mysterious and inexact science that can sometimes take years to get right. From Jessica's very first day she had been up against it. No-one had given her or Karl a chance to settle into each other. It was going to take time, and no-one was giving them any. I told Mark how much I admired Jessica for her grace and professionalism in dealing with the negativity, and just getting on with the job.

Mark wanted to know if I was happy at Seven. 'Absolutely,' I said. It was a privilege to be learning from two of the best in Adam and Meakin, and now with a new young executive producer called Michael Pell. I had no reason to go anywhere.

'But surely with your history with the Packers you would be much more at home at Nine?' he added. 'Would you ever consider coming over?'

Oh. Was there something in particular he had in mind? He said there was nothing specific ...

Mark's phone had been lighting up with texts ever since he sat down and right then, just as our meals arrived, it looked like that call he'd been waiting on was coming through.

'I'm so sorry, I have to take this. Please start without me, Leese,' he said as he disappeared out to the picturesque pathway overlooking the waves of Balmoral Beach. One thing I knew for sure as I watched Mark talking animatedly into his phone while he paced up and down for ten minutes in the sunshine, past the mums with prams, and little kids on their brightly coloured scooters, was that TV is a brutal game.

When he finally returned to the table, ashen-faced, his meal already cold, Mark again apologised profusely. Something big had blown up at work and he had to go. Now. Could I take a rain check on lunch?

Sure. And he was gone.

When I picked up the papers the next morning, and quite a few mornings following, the detail of what had been going on was laid bare. Mark had been at war with Eddie over his pay. He'd been asked to take a significant pay cut; or – in the words revealed in an affidavit from Mark as he departed Nine and took legal action against the network – he'd been asked 'to eat a shit sandwich', by having his pay cut virtually in half. 'That's quite a shit sandwich,' he'd apparently replied.

There was talk of Jessica's future too, with a new word entering the lexicon that many had to check the actual meaning of. The talk was that Jessica was going to be 'boned'.

Yep, a brutal game.

More than ever, I was very happy to be where I was.

CHAPTER TWENTY-THREE

'I wake up with Today'

'Be around the light bringers, the magic makers, the world
shifters, the game shakers. They challenge you, break you
open, uplift and expand you. They don't let you play small
with your life. These heartbeats are your people. These
people are your tribe.' – Author unknown

I F THERE IS ONE room you don't want to be in when your name is
on the front page of most newspapers in the country speculating
that you're about to sign on for the most-talked-about job in TV –
co-host of Channel 9's *Today* show – it's the Palladium Room at
Crown Casino on Logies night.

And you certainly wouldn't want to be sitting on the
Channel 7 table opposite Mel, Kochie and your boss, Adam. But
that is precisely where I found myself on this Sunday, 6 May 2007 –
smack-bang in the middle of the Australian television industry's
buzzing night of nights, all black ties, flowing gowns, and frenzied
waiters trying to keep up with the demand for champagne and
more wine!

The formal offer from Nine had only been made a few days
before, and I was still trying to decide whether I really did want
to take on the seemingly poisoned chalice many thought the role
had become. If I took it, I would be the fifth successive woman in
18 months to sit at the *Today* show desk next to Karl Stefanovic.

It had been almost a year since my lunch with Mark, and while he had moved on from Nine, as had Jessica — happily, leaving to have her first, reportedly much-longed-for baby with her husband, Peter Overton — the press continued to examine the fortunes of *Today* with an eagle, if not vulture-like, eye on an almost daily basis. Post Jessica, Sarah Murdoch (the former host of *Next Top Model*, and wife of media scion Lachlan) and Nine newsreader Kellie Connolly had both sat in the chair, with Nine consistently saying no decision had been made on a new, permanent female host.

The *Today* show offer was meant to be highly confidential, but that leak to the papers meant someone was trying to force my hand. Just like that time at *Cleo*. And this Logies night was made all the more awkward because Adam had made me an offer of his own just a week before: a morning show, called … *The Morning Show*.

Nine o'clock chat shows and their hosts had come and gone, Adam said. Bert Newton, Maureen Duval, Kim Watkins, David Reyne, Kerri-Anne Kennerley, hell, even me … but according to Adam, no-one had done it the way he was planning. 'Think Graham Kennedy,' he said, where the advertorials were totally integrated into the content. 'That's what the audience wants now. Think authentic, think real, think Graham's labrador weeing on the carpet during the PAL dog-food commercials.'

Adam said he already had the perfect male host, Larry Emdur. 'I know, you're thinking game-show host. But Larry can do it all. He's a fully trained journalist. You two will be brilliant together.'

Adam said he could see it now: '*The Lisa & Larry Show*.'

The thing about wonderful leaders is that you want to follow them. Particularly ones with a clear vision and who say they believe in you. If Adam thought this show was going to be a winner and it really would be different, then there were plenty of reasons to jump on board. I liked Larry, too. I hardly knew him, but I did know he could turn his hand to pretty much anything on TV.

Trouble was, I'd been bitten by the breakfast TV bug. There was just something special about that timeslot, something about the honour of being invited into viewers' homes each morning during their most raw, chaotic and unshowered moments that was never lost on me. Nor was being part of a team that was first to share all that had happened in the wider world overnight and in our own world right now. It offered the opportunity to hold politicians to account in a live environment and, if you did it well, help to set the agenda on issues that really mattered. There was an adrenaline to that breakfast slot that morning TV simply didn't offer.

While the call I got from Eddie saying he wanted to talk to me about the *Today* show role was a flattering one, and I was thrilled that Tom Malone had now risen to become *Today*'s executive producer, I was far from convinced that it was actually going to happen.

One thing was for sure, though: I knew and liked too many of the people involved at both networks to make this decision on my own, so I needed to step back from the negotiations and, for the first time in my career, find myself an agent to manage all this. But who?

This almost exclusively male club was the stuff of legend in media circles and I had no idea where to start. And then I remembered Steve's farewell and his manager, John Fordham. I'd met the entire Fordham family that day at the Intercontinental and was impressed both by their unwavering loyalty to Steve and their own tight connection to one another.

As I was married to two metres worth of former footballer with a lot to say, I was, now, well used to being in crowded gatherings and having men gravitate to Pete, keen for a one-on-one chat. I won't say I was ever actually elbowed out of the way, but on many such occasions I could easily become invisible when blokes decided they wanted to bend Pete's ear about one topic or another.

In those moments Pete would always either immediately draw me in and introduce me, politely shut down the conversation, or I would simply find someone else to chat to. I was used to it. No biggie. Really.

But at Steve's farewell, it was completely different. Even though John, Nick and Ben were all rugby men through and through, it was almost as if Pete didn't exist. I chatted to the three of them for ages, while Pete did the same with John's wife, Veronica, who I got the distinct impression was in fact the heart, soul, and real boss of this family. And I liked that. Maybe John would be interested in being my manager?

Just to have a point of comparison, though, I did check out one other high-profile agent who'd recently made quite a few headlines for some big-name deals he'd done. But when he proceeded to spend our entire lunch together telling me the salaries of just about every client in his stable, followed by his less-than-flattering opinions of everyone they all worked with, I figured he was not for me. So, the Fordhams – with John and son Nick working in tandem – it was.

The timing couldn't have been better. My two-year contract with Seven had run out just as we were negotiating for *The Morning Show*, so we were free to talk with Nine. I was genuinely torn on which job to take, and neither network knew I was talking to the other. But Adam was getting impatient. He wanted an answer.

I wanted to stick with breakfast TV, but did I really want to go up against *Sunrise*, the hottest show in the country, and the genius of Adam? He had, in the space of four years, taken a small news bulletin with 60,000 viewers to, on some days, well over 500,000 people tuning in. The *Today* show was hovering around 220,000.

I really wasn't sure about Karl, either. Everyone said he was a bit of a loose cannon and I'd already seen one interview with him saying his clear aim was to move on to *60 Minutes*. Exactly how committed my potential co-host would be was an unknown. Eddie, meanwhile, assured me Karl wasn't going anywhere. He said Karl was dreaming, and had given Eddie an iron-clad long-term commitment to the show.

I told Eddie I needed until Monday – the day after the Logies – to make my decision.

As the wine flowed and the awards were given that night, Mel and Kochie (both of whom were nominees for Most Popular Presenter) couldn't have been nicer. Which just about killed me. They said they didn't know if the rumours were true but congratulated me if they were. At one point, Mel, knowing all too well by now the peculiar level of scrutiny that comes with breakfast TV, even said to me, 'I know this sounds bizarre, but you and Karl are just the right height for each other. It shouldn't matter but, I promise you, to the viewers it does.'

Mel was right. I hadn't really thought about it before, but always in those times when I had hosted next to Kochie, Adam would always insist that I stand on a box, so the height difference didn't become a 'thing'. I thanked her, but assured her I hadn't yet made any firm decisions.

This was my very first time at the Logies; and for an event I'd been really looking forward to just a month before, the whole night had now become deeply uncomfortable. My aim was to remain as inconspicuous as possible, and I spent most of the evening glued to my seat, not wanting to draw any more sets of eyes my way than were already upon me.

About two-thirds of the way through the night, though, just after the lovely Kate Ritchie (who I'd recently found out had grown up in the house across the road from us in Sturt Street) got up on stage to accept her Logie, once again as Most Popular Actress for *Home and Away*, I took the opportunity to head out to the bathroom. The problem with Logie-night loo visits is if you aren't super speedy you can easily get caught behind long queues of women struggling to get in and out of all manner of tulle and sparkles and sequins and Spanx. Take too long and those big Palladium Room doors will slam shut once the show is back on air, and it's a long wait until the next ad break to get back in. But after spending much longer than I'd anticipated struggling to help a slightly sozzled *Big Brother* contestant get her boobs back in her dress, getting locked out of proceedings was exactly what happened to me.

The trick then was to find a friendly face amongst the similarly locked-out guests propping up the foyer bar while we all waited. Sure enough, there by the bar was one very friendly face indeed – Larry Emdur was looking right at me.

What to say? There was a major elephant in the room for both of us, because even though there was some chance we might be about to work together, we'd had no contact since Adam had offered me *The Morning Show*. I knew that he knew, but I didn't know if he knew that I knew.

True to his reputation as one of the truly nice guys of TV, as soon as I approached the bar Larry immediately broke away from the conversation he was in and, with a big smile, motioned to me to come on over and join him.

'Hey, Leese ... well, aren't you the talking point tonight!'

'Hey, Larry,' I said. 'So lovely to see you. Look, I feel really bad that we haven't spoken, but I don't know, it's all been a bit rushed, and ...'

Before I could go on, though, Larry walked a few steps back to the bar again and said, 'It's absolutely fine. It's TV. I figured we'd speak at some point, and besides there's someone I want to introduce you to.'

With that, Larry slapped the tuxedoed back of the guy he'd just been talking to, inviting him to turn around, and said, 'Lisa Wilkinson, I think it's probably time you met Karl Stefanovic!'

And with that, a dark-haired guy, not a whole lot taller than me, did indeed turn around, also with a huge smile on his handsomely boyish face, and said, 'Wow, this is awkward ... Great to meet you.'

Two commercial breaks came and went over the next 20 minutes as the sparkly and increasingly raucous hordes poured past the three of us continuing to chat there at the bar. Karl and I knew exactly what we were doing. It was speed dating TV host–style. Did we get on? Did we make each other laugh? Could we each give the other as good as we got? Were there awkward moments or, from a standing start, was there plenty to talk about?

Was it a little weird that I was doing this quasi-audition in front of my other potential on-air husband? Yes it was. But as I was learning, there is a lot about TV that's weird, and in the end, that conversation was crucial in helping me make my decision.

Karl and I immediately clicked. There was an undeniable chemistry there that was hard to ignore, and even Larry gave us his seal of approval. 'I don't know if you two have thought of this, but you really should work together!'

We all laughed, said our goodbyes, and headed separately to our tables, me keeping my eyes down, trying hard not to meet the gaze of any of the Seven executives.

I'd done some research on Karl, and for all the tomfoolery he'd become known for, he had some seriously impressive news reporting credentials. He'd done award-winning work covering the Childers backpacker hostel fire, as well as a vast array of big, on-the-spot, breaking news stories, and been the 6pm newsreader at Ten in Brisbane as well as doing a stint at TVNZ. He totally lapped me when it came to on-the-road news credentials, but I hoped that our differences, and what I brought, could make for a great combination. I liked him too, and for me, that mattered.

Then, just as I was about to take my seat back at the *Sunrise* table (feeling a whole lot like I'd just been sleeping with the enemy), a familiar face appeared in front of me. It was the *Today* show's weather presenter, Stevie Jacobs, and he grabbed me by the hand and whispered, 'Lisa, I really hope the rumours are true … tell me you'll come over and play!'

How could I possibly say no now?

*

Pete was convinced I should say yes to the *Today* show from the start. He thought it just made so much sense: him doing breakfast radio, me doing breakfast TV – the synergies couldn't have been more perfect. We would both be on exactly the same timetable.

There was another reason, too.

'You'll probably only get offered this once in your life, darling. This is your chance,' he'd said. And while that was what Pete said, I also knew what he meant.

There wasn't exactly an abundance of women over the age of 40 on Australian TV at that time, and I was now in my late forties. Yet no-one at Nine seemed to think my age was an issue. The topic simply never came up. Presumably, their intention was for this to be a long partnership and, if I took it and it worked, I was hoping for the same.

There was just one more hurdle to jump: the kids. Ultimately, if I was going to do this job, the family were going to be doing this job, too. The hours would be brutal. After almost 18 months of watching Pete do the same punishing 3am starts, I'd seen up close what that kind of exhaustion looked like – and what it sounded like if the house wasn't absolutely quiet after 8pm: 'QUIIIIIIEEEEETTT!!! I'm trying to sleep!' Pete wasn't really at his best when he was tired. For him, it was at least seven hours of sleep or forget it.

I could survive on less. Maybe that came from all those sleepless late nights breast-feeding three babies.

I did wonder, though, if the kids – at 13, 11 and 9 and barrelling towards those tricky teenage years – really deserved to have two potentially grumpy, sleep-deprived parents. When we sat them down to talk them through what was happening and hear their thoughts, they all said they really didn't mind. Although a small alarm bell rang when I saw Louis's big brown eyes light up as he asked if that meant Grandma would be getting them off to school. For Louis, that immediately translated into unlimited time on the Gameboy (*you-beauty!*), something we had banned before school but their soft-touch grandma would probably have struggled to enforce. I told him I was on to him and that was a definite no. We would have to get ourselves a nanny just for those hours before school, because Dad and I would be leaving at 3.30 each morning in the dark.

Billi wanted to know if I would still be able to do canteen duty at recess (with the usual guaranteed treats for her and all her friends, courtesy of yours truly). I had to gently tell her that that, unfortunately, was going to be tricky. 'Maybe I can talk to the lady who runs the canteen, sweetheart, and see if I can still do it but start a little later? The good news is, I'll definitely be there to pick you up in the afternoons now. So that will be great!'

With the prospect of fewer raspberry Icy Poles in her life, Billi now wasn't so sure about this new job. I suddenly started feeling it: the struggle to juggle it all had begun. Like so much of this big change, I told them, there may be a bit of a wait-and-see element to it all.

The guilt I already felt before I'd even started, knowing I wouldn't be there for them as they headed off to school each morning, would take quite a while to get used to. I knew Pete just didn't feel it the same way. Most men don't. But mother guilt is real. That's the trouble with this whole parenting caper: there is no book that tells you if any of this stuff you're doing is working. Only time tells you that. There are no hard and fast rules, no guaranteed safeguards, and every kid is different. Like every marriage. How we would navigate it all as a couple was also an unknown. I knew we wouldn't get everything right, but we vowed to be kind to each other, knowing our patience may, at times, be a little stretched.

In the end, we were just putting one foot in front of the other and trying not to trip. Kids are often more resilient than we give them credit for, and we figured that as long as they felt safe and seen and heard, then that was the very best that we as parents could do.

Now, there was just one last thing. This decision also meant that for the first time in almost three decades, I would no longer be working in magazines. At least for now. If TV didn't work out, perhaps I could always go back? Magazines were in my blood, after all.

But TV? Who knew?

*

With the decision made and the *Today* show contract signed, there were two people I needed to see before they found out from anyone else. Adam Boland and Peter Meakin. I was so grateful to both of them for the chances they'd given me, and I really wanted them to know that.

When I saw them in their offices in Martin Place, it would be fair to say they weren't thrilled. They were genuinely surprised I would want to go from the number-one show at breakfast, to one that possibly had its best days behind it.

There was little I could offer by way of explanation other than, I just didn't want to die wondering. And as a 'westie', I'd always been pretty partial to being the underdog. That was the case when I took over at *Dolly*. *Cleo* was on a downward slide when Kerry asked me to take the reins there. And at *Today*, I knew we had a huge job ahead of us to re-engage with the audience, but I was up for it. I'd always loved a challenge – and being underestimated. It gave me something to aim for.

I also came with sincere thanks and peace offerings that day. To Adam, a bottle of Grange, because … Grange. To Peter, a hardened newsman with a legendary feel for television, a framed letter promising that if all of this didn't work out, I would come grovelling back and he could say, 'I told you so.'

*

'What's wrong with your voice, Leese?'

It was Tommy on the phone, checking in to see how I was feeling ahead of my first day on the *Today* show. But on this Sunday afternoon, with less than 24 hours to go, my voice had inexplicably disappeared. I had no idea why. I wasn't sick. My throat wasn't sore. I didn't have a fever. I just … didn't have a voice. I had a squeak.

Sure, I'd had a full Saturday of racing around with the kids. Early ballet for Billi, a judo tournament for Louis, then a lunchtime rugby match for Jake – and yes, I may have done some polite cheering from the bitterly cold rugby field sidelines, but that was it. Just normal weekend mum life. Certainly nothing to lose my voice over.

Maybe the universe was trying to tell me something. Or was this actually my way of saying something to the universe? It would be fair to say that this new job had all come about so quickly; I really hadn't had much time to think too long and hard about just how much life might be about to change, and on so many levels. But the truth was, come Monday, there was a better than even chance that I was going to completely blow it. Freud would have had a field day prising meaning out of someone whose job was now to talk out loud, suddenly, without explanation, finding themselves completely unable to talk out loud.

Tommy wondered if I wanted to take the day off? I didn't mean to, but I laughed. Not that he heard me.

'How bad would that look …' I squeaked. Five women in 18 months, and I couldn't even turn up for my first day. That chair would start to look like it was jinxed.

…

…

'Sorry, Leese, did you say something?'

I did, but had made little sound. This really was getting laughable. At that point, I handed the phone to Pete, who was sitting nearby.

'Don't worry, Tommy,' he said, having seen the words I'd just mouthed. 'She'll be fine for work in the morning.'

My first show now had the potential to be a complete disaster. But, hey, in the words of Brian Walsh: it's only television.

*

Oh, god, how had I let it come to this? I'd had all year to get on top of these bloody Maths equations. Why hadn't I listened in class more closely and done more of my homework? There was a time when I was good at this, when I was in Third Form and I had that great teacher – what was his name again? But how could I be so stupid not to stay on top of this? I was looking at all these numbers and letters and they may as well have been hieroglyphics. Sixth Form was killing me, and my HSC mark was now doomed. I was a failure, and how would I even get a job now? ...

Brrrring-brrring. Brrrring-brrring ...

'Shit!' What was that? Oh ... the alarm. It was 3am on Monday, 28 May 2007. God, it was dark outside. And I wasn't doing my Sixth Form final Maths exam at all. Dammit, I was having that bloody nightmare again, the same one I'd had for 20 years after I left school, usually in moments when I was feeling under pressure. But I hadn't had it for years.

I looked over at Pete, a veteran of this god-awful early alarm. Somehow, even though it had been going off for 18 months right next to me, on those mornings I did wake, there was never a more delicious sleep than the one I quickly returned to, knowing that I wasn't the one who had to jump out of bed in the complete darkness and head to work.

I had never been a morning person, so this was all so unnatural. It felt for all the world like I had only put my head down an hour before. But I'd been good – after tucking the kids into bed at 8, and Jake and Louis promising lights out no later than 9, I'd headed to bed myself – just as everyone I knew who'd done these hours recommended, including Pete. This was my new life from here on, and I had no choice but to start getting used to it. Even now as I stood in the shower, hoping that warm flow of water and the last of those news headlines I was catching on the radio would both take the edge off this foggy head, I was calculating that I had exactly two years and 364 days to go on that contract I'd signed.

Even though Nine had been going through some tough times recently, it was somehow, of all the free-to-air networks, 'Still the one!', best known for its power to sprinkle magic dust on a presenter's career. This was the network over which Kerry Packer had wielded his immense power. A place where, under Kerry's rule, 'near enough' was never even vaguely good enough.

And as I wandered into Channel 9's reception that first morning, grabbing the papers at the front desk on the way through to the makeup department, my hair still wet from the shower, I felt waaaay out of my depth. There, hung on every available wall, were huge glossy reminders of the never-ending list of Nine's iconic shows – *60 Minutes*, *Hey Hey It's Saturday*, *Burke's Backyard*, *A Current Affair*, *Sale of the Century*, *Wide World of Sports* – and the mega-watt smiles of its unmatched line-up of stars: Graham Kennedy, Daryl Somers, Don Lane, Brian Henderson, Jana Wendt, Bert Newton, Liz Hayes, Tracy Grimshaw and Ray Martin. Wander these corridors and you've reached the summit. After Nine, so the legend went, there was nowhere else to go. What on earth was *I* doing here?

As silly as it sounds, I'd already planned well ahead what I was going to wear on my first show. A simple, inoffensive white short-sleeved blouse. I knew from experience that audiences at breakfast take a lot of notice of what the hosts wear – sorry, what *female* hosts wear – and of the many, many things I could possibly get wrong on my first show, I at least wanted to get that one right.

That particular Monday was a busy news day, too. Tommy came to see me before the show, somewhat relieved when he could hear that my voice was at least partially back and we went through the show's rundown.

A federal election was coming, and if Prime Minister Howard's worst fears were realised, Coalition numbers in the House of Reps would be halved and the PM, Treasurer Peter Costello and Minister for the Environment Malcolm Turnbull would be amongst 13 members of the Cabinet to lose their seats.

Meantime, the almost pop-star-like popularity of Opposition Leader Kevin Rudd, or 'KEVIN07' as the T-shirts all described him, continued unabated.

The baffling case of missing three-year-old Madeleine McCann while on a family holiday in Portugal was now into its third week, and fingers were still being pointed at the toddler's British parents, even though there was mounting evidence that the entire case had been woefully mishandled by Portuguese authorities.

And the children of the accused terrorist, Australian David Hicks, were making headlines after they had appeared on *60 Minutes* the night before with their mother, saying they forgave him for fighting with the Taliban.

We certainly had plenty to go on with. And now, as the clock ticked over to 5.30am and that familiar music started to play, it was time.

Right on cue, Karl sat forward in his chair, turned to me, and warmly introduced me to the *Today* show audience ...

'Hello to you all, and a very special welcome to you, Lisa! Welcome to our little family. How are you feeling?'

'I'm feeling fabulous,' I croaked, extremely politely, 'despite the fact that after standing on the sidelines of our son's rugby match on Saturday ...'

And we were away. Who knew for how long?

CHAPTER TWENTY-FOUR

Something's gotta give

'OK, for this to work, then *we* have to work. We are the
core. We have to do good work and support each other,
and all the rest will sort itself out ...'
– Karl Stefanovic to me, 2007

O N WEEKENDS, AS I tried to catch up on precious sleep, even 9am
felt early, and phone calls at that hour were never welcome.
But this one was different.

'Did you see the ratings? We won!'

It was Easter Saturday, 2008, and Karl was not so much on the
phone as he was bursting out of it. He was beside himself with joy,
as was I now, to hear this amazing news. For good reason. It was the
first time in years *Today* had beaten *Sunrise*. Sure, Mel and Kochie had
had that Good Friday off, and sure, the overall numbers were small
as Aussies took the chance for a bit of a sleep-in themselves on this
holiday weekend, but we'd done it! After almost a year together at the
Today show desk, Karl and I were seeing the first signs that this combo
was working and we were starting to close the gap on our opposition.

As Karl put it that night at an impromptu and very boozy
celebratory dinner down at the Bathers' Pavilion restaurant with his
wife, Cass, and my Pete, 'They can say what they like, but they'll
never be able to take away from us the fact that, one time, we beat
Sunrise!'

Karl was now into his fourth year of these early mornings, so it's fair to say he knew better than anyone how significant this win was for us as an on-air duo. We knew our chemistry was working. We could feel it. And behind the scenes, we had the sharp news sense and steady-as-she-goes team-building abilities of the always wise Tommy. It was just as Doug Mulray's sage words had foretold – at Today it *was* now happening in the corridors, and it *was* now going up the stick, and our viewers were responding in ever-greater numbers.

We had a long way to go, though, and I knew I still had a lot to learn; so every day after the show, Tommy would sit me down and go through, chapter and verse, what I'd got right, and what needed improving. He didn't pull his punches, either. That whole thing of blowing smoke up the arse of TV presenters just to keep their egos puffed up? Tommy didn't subscribe to that idea at all.

He was particularly tough on me about our regular Friday political interviews with Deputy PM Julia Gillard, and Shadow Cabinet Minister Tony Abbott: 'No "Dorothy-Dixers", Leese. Keep your questions tight, and to the point. Your job,' he said, 'is to move them through the subjects that count, and get them off their prepared "talking points", so we can generate news.'

'Also,' he added, 'in the range of topics we have to cover every day, when you're going from the tougher subjects to the lighter ones, you need the audience to come with you, so you need to work on those gear changes. Anticipate them and work out ahead of time what you're going to say. Otherwise, it's like hitting a brick wall. Get to the next subject smoothly, but quickly. Same thing when you're farewelling a guest. Hurry it up and move on. Don't linger. It slows everything down.'

Tommy was gentle and encouraging, but firm.

'If I don't tell you, Leese, the audience will. Or worse, they'll change the channel. And by then it's too late.' So I took it all on board, grateful for the advice and *trying* really hard not to take it all personally.

Karl and I had come a long way, and that Easter Saturday dinner at Bathers' was the perfect time for us to reflect on all that had happened in our first of, what we both hoped, would be many years together.

Before anything else, though, I wanted Karl to know that there was something he'd done early on that had left an indelible mark on me. It was generous and thoughtful, and I wanted to sincerely thank him.

It was a passing moment at the end of our very first week together, and by then, I could really feel the energy drain of a whole week's worth of 3am starts. Just before the 7.30 news, as I was checking scripts in the ad break, I'd had a quick scan of the viewer emails on our shared computer there at the desk. One of them stopped me in my tracks.

'Tell that fat hag Wilkinson to go back to *Sunrise* where she belongs and bring that lovely Sarah Murdoch back instead.'

It was like a punch to the stomach. And a good morning to you, too! With 30 seconds until we were back on air, I slumped. I didn't mean to, but Karl noticed.

'You OK? What's wrong?' he asked, before looking down and seeing the email still open and in full view. Karl was now a veteran of this kind of nasty, unfiltered vitriol, and immediately closed the email, grabbed my hand, and looked me square in the eye.

'OK, for this to work,' he said wildly pointing at both of us, 'then *we* have to work. We are the core. We have to do good work and support each other, and all the rest will sort itself out so long as we remain strong together and make good television. So, forget all that shit. Let's just focus on us, and the rest will come.'

He was right. And it had. From that moment forward, I told him, I knew that he really did have my back. And tonight, as we celebrated our win and he ordered more champagne, I proposed a toast to that.

It had been a big news year, dominated by the federal election, as the almost record-breaking run of Prime Minister John Howard came to an abrupt end after he and the entire Coalition were comprehensively run over by new Prime Minister Kevin Rudd's 'KEVIN07' train.

It meant we'd done plenty of political interviews, including one morning with Prime Minister John Howard on the subject of him possibly losing his seat to the ALP candidate, Maxine McKew.

Even though Mum was a dyed-in-the-wool Liberal voter, I was still proud enough of the interview that I rang her that morning when I came off air wondering if she had seen it, and if so, what she thought. It would be the first of many times I would make such a mistake, but it was also a salient reminder of the lens through which many of the audience would view me at breakfast as the years rolled on.

Yes, Mum said she had seen it; and while she was fairly nonplussed at my line of questioning, there was something else that bothered her much more: 'Darling, I'm just really not sure about the way they're doing your hair at the moment. I don't know if you've got someone new, but I wouldn't have them do it again.'

I couldn't work out if I should laugh or cry ... so I took it as a comment.

Meantime, viewers were loving Karl's cheekiness more than ever and, in those early months, his efforts at losing weight after one of our regular guests, Dr John Tickell, came on to spruik his latest diet and fitness book. In the space of around ten weeks, with weigh-ins on the show every Monday morning, he'd gone from a strapping 93 kilos, down to a lean, mean fighting machine of just 82. Karl had become the hot young dad of breakfast TV, and the fan mail flooded in.

As for me, along with Mum's comments on my hairstyles, the biggest audience reaction also seemed to centre around the visual – most particularly, just as I'd expected, what I was wearing each day.

I liked fashion, but the volume of the feedback on this topic amazed me. Something Karl never had to worry about – another navy-ish/grey-ish/black-ish suit, a change of tie, and he was done.

I'd learnt early on in my *Beauty & the Beast* days, too, that it's true what they say about TV: 'the camera adds ten pounds'. And while the weight battles I'd had in my younger days were now pretty much under control, it was taking a while for me to feel completely at ease under the almost microscopic scrutiny of those cameras. We all wake up some mornings and have to suffer through 'fat days'. I now had to get used to battling mine in front of the nation.

Most of the women I was surrounded by at the various networks were much taller and slimmer than me, so that's what viewers were 'visually' used to. I had generous curves that started with my boobs, and without careful dressing, I could easily become horribly self-conscious about them, like the morning I wore a flesh-coloured blouse with what I thought were two pretty harmless-looking chest-high pockets at the front, each with a decorative gold button attached. I really liked it, until it was pointed out to me that those buttons looked exactly like two nipples, and every so often when I shifted to a certain angle, they were catching the studio lights and it looked for all the world like my breasts were winking at the audience.

The reaction to that blouse would compare as nothing, however, with what happened after I sat down at the desk one morning in what I thought was a perfectly chic, dusty-pink blouse with three decorative feature bows down the front. I should have known I was in for it from the moment Tommy said to me from the control room, 'Leese, is that what you're actually wearing this morning?'

I said it was. 'Do you like it?'

He was treading gently, but said he wasn't sure if it was quite right ... and that there was still time to change if I'd like to.

I don't know if it was Tommy's request that I might like to have a bit of a wardrobe rethink that made me dig my heels in, but I genuinely thought the blouse was lovely, and anyway, he was a bloke. A bloke best known for his extensive wardrobe of puffer vests. What would he know about fashion? Perhaps not a lot, but Tommy certainly knew a whole lot about the tastes of early-morning TV audiences.

By 7am, there was no stopping the flood of viewer comments.

'Now, we'll get to the government's economic stimulus package in just a moment,' Karl said, as he looked down at the now tsunami of emails before him. 'But the thing that is on everyone's mind this morning is Lisa's shirt! Our inbox has been inundated. INUNDATED! This one is from Chris: "Hey Lisa, just wondering if your propellers spin?"'

I told Chris that they did, but only for very special people!

The emails on that blouse literally lasted for days.

And even though Tommy clearly thought that I must have won (or perhaps lost) some sort of bet by wearing it, he ended up loving that blouse for the reaction it generated. The fun we'd had with it was, according to Tommy, breakfast TV gold. It was all about having a laugh at ourselves and breaking down those walls of mystery that TV often puts up.

Indeed, ways of communicating generally were beginning to shift across the board. Everything in the media was becoming less formal, more relaxed, more personal ... and more social. Reality shows like *Big Brother* and *Australian Idol*, along with a series about a family of women in the US called the Kardashians, were now the biggest franchises on TV. Audiences wanted authenticity more than anything (which was no small irony when it came to the Kardashians), and that shift coincided almost exactly with something called social media taking off in a big way.

Over dessert, Karl, Cass, Pete and I laughed about what was probably our most embarrassing – for me at least – interview of the year.

The former US vice president and now documentary-maker Al Gore had come to town to promote his film *An Inconvenient Truth*, a film about the devastating effects of climate change. There was always a chance that it wasn't going to end well when Gore's PR team demanded Karl and I submit our questions ahead of the interview – something we would never normally agree to do – but they said it was a deal-breaker, and as we worked to rebuild the show, Tommy felt that securing such a big name was a great 'get'.

I tried hard to stick to the script, really I did. But towards the end of our allotted seven-minute interview, I just couldn't stand it anymore. If there was an opposite to inspiring, Al Gore was it. Maybe it was his pomposity that I lost patience with, but I swear I could almost hear the TV sets around the nation switching off in unison. So, I decided to go just a teeny bit rogue and ask him if his environmentalist beliefs extended to his toilet habits.

There was a pause. Al Gore blanched and stared back at me.

His minders grimaced. The full-on security detail he arrived with did not reach for their guns, but their expressions said they would probably like to. The hell with it.

'Do you use recycled toilet paper at home?' I asked.

It was clear he had no idea what I was on about. To be fair, Karl probably didn't either, but I dared not look to my left to find out.

It seemed like a reasonable enough question to me, but the interview pretty much ended there. Right after the bit where I suggested that maybe he didn't know because, like a lot of men, he probably had one of those magical 'toilet-paper fairies' at home who did all that stuff like changing the empty toilet-roll holder for him.

OK, I admit, I probably should have given him a leave pass, seeing as not that long before, he'd been only a heartbeat away from the presidency and all. But, hey, I gave it a shot and it didn't work. I could tell because he only just stayed around for Karl's thankyous.

My biggest lesson from that day? Never interview anyone who can only stick to the scripted questions ... and try to avoid anyone devoid of a sense of humour.

I also had to learn in that first year how to keep my emotions in check when, mid-interview with a guy attempting to do 52 jobs in 52 weeks, I had to break off and announce that, at 8.43am Sydney time on Wednesday, 23 January 2008, the actor Heath Ledger had been found dead in his New York apartment. I knew there was a good chance that many of his wide circle of Australian friends, and possibly family, could be watching. His breathtaking performance as The Joker in the newest Batman movie had not yet been released, but all the talk was that it was yet another Oscar-worthy performance. I tried to stop the tears from welling up, but I'd interviewed him once and was really struck by his gentle ways. The fact he was gone, and so young, just got the better of me.

Another challenge was one Karl, Tommy and I faced together early on, and that was dealing with 'the third floor' – that fabled level atop Channel 9 where management resided – on the future direction of the show. Tommy mostly kept that stuff from us, but one morning there was a request from one of the news bosses for a meeting in his office to discuss that very topic. This particular executive was known for a rating system he used when it came to on-air female talent at Nine after telling one well-respected reporter that 'in this business you have to have fuckability'. So I was already wary.

We tried to understand his directive after we all took the glass lift to Level 3 and gathered for a good half-hour to hear his thoughts on *Today*. But maybe his best days were behind him, because it was all just a little … vague.

According to him, when he turned on the *Today* show in the morning, he wanted it to feel like he was opening the *Daily Telegraph*. OK, we all said, but in practical terms, what did that look like for the show? What did that mean for content? What did that mean for Karl and me and how we did our job? The answer wasn't absolutely clear.

What was clear was just how clinical this hardened newsman could be when he quickly moved on to tell us about his long career in TV news, which included a stint at *60 Minutes* at a time when *Alf*, a family-friendly sitcom about a sassy, fluffy alien, became the first to win against the previously unassailable '*60*', as everyone at Nine called it.

He said the *60* team had tried everything against 'that fucking puppet', but then in 2001 the world changed forever with the terror attacks in the US, and along with it, the fortunes of *60 Minutes*.

'Thank Christ for September 11,' he said.

I couldn't believe what I'd just heard, and I could tell from the looks on both Karl's and Tommy's faces that they couldn't either. Almost three thousand lives had been lost in those horrific attacks, including ten Australians, and yet to this guy they were all just ratings points.

The comment was so appalling that, as the three of us left his office shortly after, we couldn't even bring ourselves to discuss it, let alone repeat it, trying to pretend, I suppose, that he had never said it. Fortunately, I never had to deal with that executive again.

Around the same time, former Channel 9 CEO David Gyngell had finally been lured back to the network, and I wondered if Gyng's return might have had something to do with the news chief's departure.

Something else I'd learnt that year was that no matter how ideal Pete's and my matching early-morning work hours appeared to be on paper, the whole dual-breakfast-hours experiment was not going well. Six months in, we knew it couldn't continue. There was no escaping the fact that one of us was going to have to give up our gig. Every day, when we came home looking for sympathy and support in order to keep going, neither of us had any energy or patience left for the other – and more importantly not enough between us to go around amongst three children who needed it most.

As a family we needed one of us at home to act as the buffer, to soak up the challenges that come with doing shift work. Add to that the public scrutiny we were both under and, hey, fun times! The kids weren't prospering, and our jobs were causing such a blur of fatigue that, come the evening, Pete and I were on our last reserves of energy ... and equanimity.

In the race to bed, Pete usually won. His strong view was that it was crazy for us to put our energies into cleaning up after dinner and putting on loads of washing when what energy we did have should go to the kids. And getting to bed. Pete always argued that we were paying the nanny to also clean up in the three hours she had before the kids woke up, so why on earth was I breaking my neck to do it before I went to bed?

Maybe it was a female thing harking back to my childhood conditioning, but I always felt like I was failing if I didn't have the house at least presentable for her when she arrived. I didn't want to be judged. So I ended up trying to do both. And it was proving to be a disaster.

I told Pete I just couldn't keep this up anymore – I was going to leave *Today*. Sure, in the short term it might be a bit embarrassing, but in the end, what's one more new host in that *Today* show chair next to Karl, against the kids and our marriage?

But Pete insisted: he wanted me to stay at Nine. He would leave radio. It was a big call on his part. Radio was something he'd always dreamt of doing, and both he and Mike had developed quite a loyal following. At their best they got to within four or five points of Alan Jones on 2GB, but as he wrote to his bosses at 2UE at the time: 'Lisa and I have discovered that while it is possible for a family to cope with two parents getting out of bed in the wee hours, it cannot prosper. And as we want to prosper, I herewith tender my resignation …'

So at least now, one of us was back at home in the mornings. Pete was doing his best with the housework and even sometimes the cooking, though the kids couldn't wait to report back to me on his attempt one night at a chicken salad when I was interstate with the show. Inexplicably, it included mango, orange, white onion and … ice-cream. I was sure the kids must have been imagining things.

'Are you sure Daddy didn't … I don't know … have the bowl of ice-cream next to the salad, and you got mixed up?'

'No!' they said. When I managed to get to the bottom of it all – ever so delicately trying not to look like I was sitting in judgment when Pete was, um, trying so hard – it seems the original salad was so appalling and the kids so intent on not eating it, that Pete's solution was to throw ice-cream on top.

The arguments reportedly went on for so long that the resulting meal became a chicken, mango, orange, onion and melted ice-cream soup. When they still refused to eat it, Pete ate the entire thing himself, just to prove to them that it was edible. It was months before he would confess to me (but never the kids) that the after-effects of that meal on him lasted for days.

So I had to learn, at certain points, to turn a blind eye and let certain things go. Chicken and ice-cream soups aside, though, having Pete at home in the mornings had eased a lot of the night-time pressure on me.

But try as I might, I still found it hard to get to bed at the same time as the kids each night; more often than not, it was somewhere nearer 10pm before my head hit the pillow. Part of it was the constant fear I had that I might not yet be fully up to speed with the day's news before the next one dawned. So, once the busyness of after-school activities, dinner, homework and goodnight kisses were all done, I would take a moment to breathe out, and then do all my own homework.

Some nights, ahead of big political interviews, it was even later. Pete thought I was nuts, convinced that that time was much better spent getting some shut-eye so I was fresh to do my research in the morning. It was just the way I did things, and if I didn't, I knew I wouldn't sleep. I lived in dread of sleeping through the alarm, so I had to wake up knowing I was fully prepared. I lost count of the number of times we had that argument.

On the issue of sleep – or lack thereof – I more than had an ally in our newsreader, Georgie Gardner, who'd been on maternity leave with her second child when I first started at *Today*. She was now back at the desk with a still-settling young one at home, who had no regard for Mum's gruelling hours. Many was a morning when, during ad breaks, we would swap sympathetic notes on the kinds of pressures that came with the different stages we were both at as mums. Together with Karl, we each had young kids and marriages to sustain beyond the demands of the job, and there was always a great sense of camaraderie between all of us as fellow sufferers of sleep deprivation, sharing stories of our various struggles at home, before the show went on …

'Welcome back! Good to have your company, on what is a beautiful day in most parts of the country. We'll get to Stevie's weather shortly, but first to some breaking news …'

… Always, the show had to go on.

*

I simply didn't see it coming. Karl was in talks with Channel 7, and the first I knew of it was a report in the *Daily Telegraph* – one of the very newspapers that was sitting on the reception desk as I walked through the Channel 9 foyer on this cool September morning in 2008.

I read it closely, as I did all the papers each morning, while the wonderful Channel 9 hair and makeup fairies did all they could to turn my tired face and sopping wet hair into something presentable for the cameras. Usually, I would chat to them and various producers as they came and went between reading articles and all the briefs for the show, but on this morning, there wasn't a lot of talking in that room. Most of us were shocked to read Karl's news. And I felt just a little bit stupid because I'd had no clue.

It had been just six months since that great dinner at Balmoral Beach with Karl and Cass, and since then our numbers had continued to rise. Occasionally, we were even getting close to that magical figure of 300,000. But now Karl had been in talks with Channel 7 to leave?

The report quoted a Nine spokesperson as saying that there had been at a dinner at Seven boss David Leckie's house, courting Karl to become the new host of *Today Tonight*. But Seven refuted the claim, saying there was no dinner, but that Karl had come to them seeking an exit from Nine and the *Today* show by February, and if he stayed at Nine, he wanted Tracy Grimshaw's chair at *A Current Affair*. He'd even gone so far as to sign an agreement on terms with Seven, which Nine then matched.

Karl had released a statement in response which read, 'I find it hard to see the positive in talking about this publicly, so I'll be brief. Seven made a great offer, but ultimately I am loyal to Nine and Gyng. I'm more than happy here. It's as simple as that.'

Seven responded in kind with the following statement:

Karl wanted to come to Seven. He expressed his desire to join us in a private meeting with David Leckie. He signed an agreement on terms. Nine matched that offer. We have moved on. Quickly.

Karl saw his future being at Seven. There was no dinner meeting. There was a meeting one morning two weeks ago to discuss and agree on Karl leaving Nine.

The issue for Nine is to meet Karl's career objectives – objectives he clearly expressed to us and which indicated a desire to not be in breakfast television or at Nine past February next year. This raises a number of issues for Nine's management of its people and its news and public affairs programmes, including *Today* and *A Current Affair*.

Karl didn't say a word to me about the story before the show or at the desk that morning. And I had no idea how to broach it. It was like it never happened.

While it was of course his business, it was hard to carry on knowing he had wanted out. And while pledging his loyalty to Gyng was great PR for their relationship, I really wasn't sure where that left ours.

*

Deputy Prime Minister Julia Gillard described it as a tragedy beyond belief, beyond precedent, and really beyond words.

'The seventh of February 2009 will now be remembered as one of the darkest days in Australia's peacetime history,' she said, her voice choked with emotion as she offered Parliament's deepest and most sincere condolences to suffering families and Victoria's lost communities in the Black Saturday bushfires.

The fires began on a day when the temperature in Melbourne reached 46.4 degrees Celsius, the highest ever recorded in the city. As I watched the rolling coverage on Sky News on that Saturday night, the reports were still sketchy.

Worryingly, communication lines in many parts of Victoria were down. By the next morning, as news crews from around the country started to arrive and feed pictures out, it became clear why. More than 400 fires, fanned by scorching northerly winds, described as being like blasts from a foundry furnace, had moved through the state. Tommy called to say he was sending us to host the show from Whittlesea, right next to one of the many devastated fire zones.

From the air, through breaks in the thick pall of smoke above Melbourne, the extent of the devastation was almost impossible to comprehend. Whole towns looked to have been wiped out. What once were forests had been stripped of all living things.

Locals talked of 120-kilometre-an-hour winds that for many, even those fleeing in cars, were impossible to outrun. The death toll was expected to reach more than 100, and amongst them a much-loved familiar face to Victorians, Channel 9 newsreader Brian

Naylor, and his wife, Moiree, at their Kinglake West home. What was left of the Kinglake area defied description. The landscape, with its trees now turned into bare, blackened stakes in the ground, looked more like a moonscape, the fire having cleared everything in its path.

It was the first time I had covered a major disaster on the ground, and it was a steep learning curve for me. No comfortable studio. No helpful autocue. No neat scripts. Just rolling coverage as it happened, from where it happened. Each day the alarm went off at 2am before we drove from our small motel in Eltham, 40 minutes away from the Whittlesea footy oval, where a makeshift relief centre had been set up and most of the nation's media had gathered.

After the show each day, when authorities and rescue teams permitted, we visited the affected areas to film, hear the accounts of shell-shocked locals who had survived, and help tell the heartbreaking stories of those who had not. We heard of firefighters whose own homes had burnt to the ground while they defended the lives and homes of others; and saw the incinerated shells of burnt-out cars by the side of the road, the fate of their drivers more often than not unknown.

Flowers marked sites where people had lost their lives, as everything, everywhere, constantly brought home the human cost.

Fires continued to burn in the area for a total of ten days, and by the time Karl and I were back at the studio desk in Sydney the following week, an estimated 450,000 hectares of Victoria had been razed to the ground, 173 people had died, more than 3500 homes and buildings were destroyed, and 5000 firefighting personnel had become the nation's heroes.

It was as moving an experience as I'd ever had as a journalist. And yet ...

And yet, when I opened the paper that following Monday morning, it was to see a report assessing the performances of all the journalists who had been there on the ground that week. Which was fair enough, I thought. Until ...

I was accused of looking too pretty, being 'choppered' in every day from Melbourne for the show, and admonished for not having my hair in a ponytail. Exactly what my hairstyle and face had to do with the worst bushfires in Victoria's history, I had no clue. But the chopper accusation? A complete and utter lie.

When I confronted the writer in question, she admitted she was wrong and had actually got me mixed up with another journalist, but she insisted that what I looked like and the lack of a ponytail mattered.

I left it. But it was a lesson that, when you're female and in the relentless spotlight of breakfast TV, sometimes you just had to suck it up and carry on.

CHAPTER TWENTY-FIVE

Well, good morning to yoooouuuu ...

'Trust me, you can dance.' – Vodka

THE 2009 LOGIE AWARDS marked the second anniversary of that fateful night Larry Emdur had introduced Karl and me at the Crown Casino bar, and we had much to celebrate. *Today*'s numbers were continuing to move ever upwards, to the point that if we stood on our tippy-toes, we actually could see *Sunrise* from there.

On the night, *Packed to the Rafters* took the gong for the most popular show on TV, scooping the pool with an incredible 12 awards, including the Gold Logie going to the woman who was the heart and soul of the show's success, Rebecca Gibney. Rove McManus once again picked up the Silver Logie for Best Presenter, legendary movie man Bill Collins was honoured in the Hall of Fame, and an emerging young actress from *Neighbours* called Margot Robbie was just pipped at the post for Best New Female Talent by the *Rafters'* Jessica Marais.

As is so often the case on the Sunday night of the Logies, once the broadcast is over at around 11, it's party time, as each of the networks hosts their own invitation-only shindigs. And as the late night turns into early morning, those rules do tend to loosen a little with plenty of network cross-pollination.

As the host broadcaster, Nine's party was considered the best one to be at, and it was always a treat to be able to say hello to someone from another network who'd managed to talk their way in and whose work you've admired over the years. It was a pity that admiration usually had to be yelled directly into their earhole over 'Disco Inferno' or 'Dancing Queen', but that's just the way it worked on Logies night. A little bit loud, a little bit crazy, a little bit loose.

All good common sense told me that I should probably skip the party and grab at least a few hours' sleep before that 3am alarm for Monday morning's show broadcast from the hotel's foyer at Crown. But Logies was the one night of the year when this married mother of three got to kick off her heels and hit the dance floor for a few hours. I was also sure that if I *did* go to bed and get a few scant hours, once I woke it would become more about the sleep I'd missed rather than any sleep I'd actually had. So, for one night of the year, I just kept going until that second wind kicked in and got me through. And, heck, it was the Logies for heaven's sake. After growing up watching this show, I still couldn't believe I actually got invited. I always figured I can sleep when I'm dead!

So, just before 3 o'clock that morning, as the dance floor was starting to thin, it was time to retrieve the long-discarded stilettos I'd stashed behind the bar, pick up my dress train (always the worse for wear after being trodden on more than once throughout the night) and hotfoot it back to my room for a shower. It was only as I was putting my room key in the door that I remembered I had 48 buttons securing the back of my dress, and no-one around to help undo them. Fortunately, a lovely housemaid was passing by right in my moment of need. I was apologetic but she told me that this was nothing for a Logies night.

'I see celebrities doing the walk of shame every year. Some of them don't even bother to get dressed before they head back to their room. It's the best night of the year to be working!'

God it was a relief to get out of that tight dress, but as I was about to learn, getting those buttons undone would prove to be the least of the challenges I was to face on this particular morning.

The post-Logies episode of *Today* each year was a pretty laidback affair. It was, essentially, a celebration of the very big night before and, as a Nine-owned event, we had access to all the international guests (provided they weren't still asleep). Unlike *Sunrise*, we could also replay every big moment – the great and not-so-great speeches, the funny sketches, the glitches, the celebrations of industry titans and colleagues lost, as well as all the red-carpet hits and misses.

For all the morning-after fun, though, Tommy always took the day's news component very seriously and insisted our half-hourly bulletins came with all the available resources of the Nine Newsroom, rather than trying to make do from the slightly more chaotic foyer of a casino. Georgie had the morning off, so it was Mark Ferguson on duty that day and joining us down the line from the Sydney news desk. That put him close to the news action, and us dangerously close to the many random strays still wandering home via the shiny black marbled foyer of Crown.

The problem we had on this morning, though, was that there was one particular stray no-one could find. Karl was missing. He wasn't answering his phone. Repeated text messages had drawn no response. And with the broadcast about to start, I wondered if I might be hosting the next three and a half hours solo … or at least until someone could summon hotel security to open Karl's door and get him down here. If that was indeed where he was.

'Mark, it could be just you and me doing this down the line today,' I said, only half joking.

'I'm up for it, Lisa. We've certainly got plenty to work with!' he said, also only half joking.

But with minutes to go, my AWOL co-host was sighted. There to the side of our set I could see a slightly dishevelled but very happy-looking Karl, makeup hastily being applied, surrounded by a swarm of our techies quickly getting his microphone, battery packs and earpiece in position.

Then, with the opening strains of the *Today* show theme going to air around the country, I felt the brush of a rush of air and people as Karl moved in beside me.

'Hey, darl,' he offered from behind one of the sound guys.

'Hey, Karl,' I said in return, just as they all moved away, our microphones were turned up and the red light came on.

The funny thing about that moment was, after two years together, Karl and I were getting very used to each other's personal rhythms and body language. We could tell, almost without even looking, when the other was about to speak, so we each knew when, in turn, to pull back. And right then and there, I noticed that Karl was leaning in.

'Hah-low and welcooome too yooouuu ...'

What. Was. THAT?

I tried not to turn my head. I tried not to look surprised. I tried not to engage. Truth is, I was barely breathing.

And then I remembered someone at the Nine party saying something around 1am about the last time Karl had been sighted. Karl had apparently declared he was heading to Lachlan Murdoch's room. Something about a bottle of tequila. Something about doing shots. Something about ...

Surely not. Surely Karl wasn't?

With the clock showing we were only five seconds into a broadcast that still had 3 hours, 29 minutes and 55 seconds to go, I had no idea if Karl was still on his way up the side of this alcohol-fuelled mountain or, please dear God, on his way back down. Then again, maybe he was right now at the top, and peaking right here as he sat next to me, live, on national television.

Oh, god, no. He's opening his mouth again ...

'How good does Lisa Wilkinson look on zero sleep?!

'Look. *Look* at you! Look at you in that little monitor there ...

'I applaud you, I salute you, and I praise you. Didn't she look beeewwtiful last night? Look at that smile!'

He was as happy, and polite, and inoffensive a drunk as you could ever imagine. But he was hosting a news and current affairs program, and none of us knew where this was going to end up, apart from every Best of TV Bloopers reel for years to come.

Tommy was in my ear. 'Just hang in there, Leese, you're doing great.'

At one point, there was an attempt by Karl to read out the weather around the country, but he only got two states in before he lost interest. And then the emails started flooding in.

Is Karl drunk?

This is disgusting.

Love it. How much has he had?

What's he on?

Karl is hilarious, keep it coming!

Get him off!

In the first ad break, I asked him if he was OK. 'Oh, babe, it's been a huuuuge night!' he snorted, smiling, clearly still high on the memory.

By the time we got to the 6am bulletin, Fergo just couldn't hold it in any longer, and he did something I simply didn't have the courage to do: he took the bull by the horns and (if you'll excuse my mixed animal kingdom metaphors) live on air, with a twinkle in his eye, addressed the elephant in the room.

'Karl, despite what many of the emails are saying,' he purred, 'I think you are doing a terrific job this morning.'

Oh, lord. We all froze. How would Karl respond to Mark being so … honest? It was now out there. We were being inundated with calls to the Channel 9 switch, Twitter was going off and the emails just didn't stop.

I stared resolutely at Mark's image in the monitor. There was an uncomfortable, momentary pause from Karl. The floor crew, the camera guys, the sound team, the producers to the side of the stage, and more than likely everyone watching around the country waited to see what would come next. Was this car crash about to become a train wreck?

'That's nasty, Fergo,' Karl said mildly, 'that's really nasty.'

'I'm sorry,' Mark offered, not sorry.

'I'm trying, mate,' Karl shot back. 'I'm really trying.'

'I know,' Mark said, the smile never leaving his face. 'You are doing your very, very best.'

In that small moment Karl took to pause, though, I sensed that Fergo's gentle message might have got through. Like a small splash of cold water on his face, I could feel Karl pull back *ever* so slightly; enough that I had some hope we would get through the rest of the show relatively unscathed, and Karl would get to sleep off the rest of that tequila – or whatever his poison of choice had been that night. I estimated we probably hit peak 'beeewwtiful' at around 6.15am, and sure enough as the morning wore on, the alcohol was wearing off.

Was I offended at Karl turning up drunk? Not particularly. And if the worst he did that morning was to tell me, again and again and again, that I looked good, did I really have much to complain about? (Although I was sure there would be some at home convinced that if Karl thought I was 'beeewwtiful', then he *had* to be drunk.)

As we were wrapping up the show that morning, I wondered exactly what the ramifications would be for Karl. We all knew the story of a very giggly Mike Willesee hosting *A Current Affair* back in the 80s after a veeeery long lunch. It had caused a scandal. But it had been a long time between drinks (on air) for audiences, so who knew? It was up to management to decide.

What I did know was, had it been me who'd been drunk, the chances I would have been allowed to stay on air past 6am would have been just about zero. My reputation would have been destroyed. A drunk father of three hosting a news and current affairs show was one thing, but a drunk mother of three? I shuddered to think.

The moment we were off air, Karl bolted. I wasn't sure if he was feeling a bit sheepish, or very possibly unwell, but when I spoke to Tommy after the show to ask about the reaction from viewers, he told me it was 'mixed'.

'But we got through it,' he said. 'Well done for soldiering on.' He also told me that Karl had headed off on a pre-planned two-day *60 Minutes* shoot.

Rumours abounded, though, that Karl had been taken off air for a couple of days to have a good long think about what he'd done. Whatever it was, those two days did give us a welcome chance to let a little bit of the heat out of the story, and for Nine management to decide how they would play it. They decided pretty quickly.

'Karl was tired, yes, but drunk, no. Emphatically!' a Nine spokesman said. 'Nine supports Karl to the hilt.' Denials didn't get any more full-on than that.

Until ... Channel 7, perhaps with a small sting still in its tail after their recent negotiations with Karl had come to nought, decided to lead the Wednesday night edition of *Today Tonight* with a story examining Karl's whole post-Logies episode. A reporter wandered the city streets at lunchtime, computer in hand, showing footage to passers-by of some of Karl's 'happier' moments from Monday's show, asking whether he was in any shape to host. 'He's pissed!' was the almost unanimous verdict, and just about every one of those asked found it amusing. It was a pretty comprehensive stitch-up and included other famous drunk performances across the TV and radio years: Willesee, US actor John Stamos on *Mornings With Kerri-Anne*, and Molly Meldrum on Kyle & Jackie O's program. One thing they left out of their story though, as a number of TV writers subsequently pointed out, was that our ratings over the last 12 months were now a lot closer to *Sunrise*.

But if Seven was out to get Karl and *Today*, the whole exercise totally backfired. They couldn't have done him a bigger favour. Far from shaming him for unprofessional behaviour, they had just gone and made Karl a national hero. The feedback we got at the show after *Today Tonight* went to air was pretty clear, and best summed as ...

'He didn't hurt anyone.'/'Lisa didn't seem to have a problem with it.'/'Geez, if I got to go to the Logies, I'd get drunk too.'/'Good on him for showing up the next morning.'/'Leave the poor bloke alone.'/'How good's Australia?'/'GO KARL!'

By the Thursday morning, Karl had, as Tommy predicted, returned to the desk and, at 8am, when viewership was always at its highest, he delivered a heartfelt apology.

'Yes, it was a very big Logies night,' he said, 'probably a little too big ... I didn't feel drunk when I woke up the next morning, otherwise I would not have gone on ... I like to think that I am professional enough to have made that decision, but clearly from the vision I have seen, I wasn't at my best. I want to apologise to anyone who was offended by my behaviour on Monday morning.'

Well, now our viewers really were outraged!

Why on earth was Karl apologising? For what?

Who made him do that? He was just having a good time.

Leave him alone. I'll have a beer with you Karl!

Karl was now, officially, every Aussie bloke. The guy you could have a good old laugh and get pissed with. Leeeeggggeeeeeend!

Who knew that getting drunk would turn out to be one of the best career moves he ever made?

*

Gordon Ramsay really was the hottest thing on TV. The hard-swearing, hard-living Brit was spearheading the whole 'celebrity chef' phenomenon, and *Ramsay's Kitchen* was one of Nine's top-rating shows. The great news for us was that he had just arrived in Australia and agreed to an interview on *Today*.

There was just one proviso. Well, two, actually. Firstly, fronting up to the studio at 7.15 didn't work for him, so we had to do a live cross to the Sydney Good Food & Wine Show he was appearing at over the weekend and wanted to promote. Secondly, no questions about his private life. The previous year it was alleged that Ramsay had been in a seven-year affair with a woman called Sarah Symonds who had penned a book entitled *Having An Affair: A Handbook For the Other Woman*, but Ramsay categorically denied Symonds' claim. It put something of a dint in his previously picture-perfect, happily-married-father-of-five reputation. Ramsay had become 'lean-forward' television, though, mostly because you could never be quite sure what the somewhat hyperactive star would do or say next.

Sure enough, within the first minute of our 'good morning's, Ramsay had already dropped the 's' bomb, before getting away all the plugs he needed for his various appearances around the country, and of course his show on Nine. Then, just as we came close to wrapping the interview, I decided to have a bit of fun and ask about recent reports in the tabloid press that after a trip to the US he'd emerged looking a whole lot more 'refreshed'.

It seemed ludicrous to me that a guy like this, whose raw appeal rested in being rugged and raffish, would ever give in to Botox, but the before-and-after photos doing the rounds were pretty compelling. This was his opportunity to set the record straight.

Gordon was clearly not happy.

'Now, Lisa, you're a smart girl, right?' he said, leering down the barrel of the camera. 'I saw you first thing this morning ... honestly I got my 6 o'clock rise, straight up.'

Did he just ...?

Throughout the interview the sound quality in my earpiece had not been great, and there was a slight delay, so I really wasn't sure if what I thought I'd just heard him say was what he'd actually said. I froze for just a moment hoping I'd heard wrong, kept smiling and tried to carry on, but when Karl collapsed into laughter and buried his head in his hands, I knew. Gordon Ramsay had indeed just told our viewers that he woke up at 6am, saw me on the screen and ...

And then he continued, 'Are you stupid?'

'Does he look like he's had Botox, Lisa?' Karl asked, obviously trying to indicate that he was on Gordon's side. I kept smiling.

'Stop fucking around with me ...' and with that Gordon Ramsay walked off and the interview was over.

'Gordon, great to see you,' Karl said. 'Enjoy your time in Australia!'

So, in the space of one breakfast-time interview, with families tuning in around the country, we'd had one 's' bomb, one 'f' bomb, and the mental image of an excitable Gordon Ramsay first thing in the morning ...

What could I do? There was only one thing to do. I threw to the 7.30 bulletin. 'Georgie, what's happening in the news?'

*

That night, there was Gordon Ramsay again. This time he was being interviewed by the excellent Tracy Grimshaw on *A Current Affair*. I watched closely as they exchanged banter and, at one point, when he complained that the *ACA* studio was cold, he inexplicably followed it up by asking Tracy, 'What turns you on?'

My Nine colleague quickly moved the discussion on, gently asking him about his recent financial woes. Tracy wondered if the cause could have been that 'you'd become a little arrogant or stretched too thin? Do you think maybe you'd become too much celebrity, too little chef?'

A great question and superbly delivered in kid gloves as only Tracy could. Ramsay didn't react too badly, simply claiming that he was the hardest-working chef in the industry, and Tracy must not believe what she might have read, because that kind of stuff just comes with extreme fame.

'You become fodder, whether it's front-page news in the tabloids ... you get caught in the realms of this sort of, you know, celebrity sort of dog fight so you just take the blows ... But I have the right to a private life.'

That Tracy had dared to question his behaviour had rankled, though, for as the interview was drawing to a close, the abrasive Englishman suddenly turned.

'What's that on your face?' he sneered, making reference to a tiny mole on the side of Tracy's lip. No matter that whatever he was pointing out was so microscopic that it had escaped the attention of the rest of Australia over her 30-year career, Ramsay now referred to it as 'a wart ... a cyst ... a fucking Mount Etna'.

Tracy, never precious, always gracious, laughed along with Ramsay at her own expense, who then grew ever more impressed with his own cruelty as he continued to drag the 'joke' out. She didn't appear offended, so he just kept it coming. Just boys being boys, having a little joke, you know?

But there was a theme building here. Just as he had shown us that morning, it was becoming clear that, for Ramsay, a woman's appearance was easy pickings for always making sure he was in charge in any situation.

Compliment (if that's what he thought his comment to me was) or insult, it didn't matter. Just as long as he got to take control. And whatever you do, don't show any offence, because, hey, what's your problem, lady? No sense of humour?

But the saga was only just warming up. Because the next day in front of several thousand people at the Melbourne Good Food & Wine Show, Ramsay completely disgraced himself, first, in what appeared to be a homophobic slur, calling the beloved *ACA* host 'a lesbian', before showing an image of a naked woman on all fours, breasts hanging down and with the face of a pig.

'That's Tracy Grimshaw,' Ramsay told the audience. 'I had an interview with her yesterday. Holy crap, she needs to see Simon Cowell's Botox doctor.'

This, from a man who the day before had been talking to both Tracy and me about his problems with media intrusiveness, the whole tabloid culture of making up lies, and the sanctity of his private life.

The whole affair exploded over the next couple of days, as photographers followed Ramsay across the city – in every frame looking extremely pleased with himself and absolutely loving the attention, as he continued to feed the story with yet more vicious comments on the Sunday and Monday.

All eyes turned to Tracy. How would she react? Some said that it simply went with the territory of being a female journalist. She had asked a couple of difficult questions, so she had it coming. Others noted that Ramsay's show had made a lot of money for Channel 9, so she was unlikely to damage such a key asset. Still others thought she would decide not to engage. Why give him what he obviously always wanted: publicity?

One way or another, huge numbers of Australians tuned in to *ACA* on Monday night to find out. There was Tracy, and she did indeed have something she wanted to say. It was as if the camera lens had crosshairs on it, and somewhere in Australia a soon-to-be quivering Gordon Ramsay was in her sights.

'Now, this is not a business for wimps,' she began, 'and I am not one. I think I've got a reasonable sense of humour. On Friday when Gordon Ramsay made fun of a little mole on my face in a taped interview, I laughed along and was happy to see it go to air.

But that was nothing compared to the attack he unleashed on me the next day in front of three thousand people who'd come simply to see him cook.

'I have no idea what prompted his outburst, which continued yesterday and again today. We've not spoken and I have not responded ... until now.'

At home, we leaned in closer, as Tracy noted that she had always treated the visiting chef with respect.

'It appears with Ramsay that respect is a one-way street. On Saturday he launched a series of unprovoked public attacks against me. I'm not going to pretend that his comments didn't hurt. I was absolutely miserable when I found out late Saturday afternoon. He says it was a joke – well not to me, or to anyone who cares about me.

'Truly, I wonder how many people would laugh if they were effectively described as an old, ugly pig. How is that funny exactly? Worse, it's not even witty. I spent all yesterday considering how to respond and I honestly thought about saying nothing at all.

'But we all know bullies thrive when no-one takes them on, and I'm not going to sit meekly and let some arrogant narcissist bully me.

'Gordon Ramsay made me promise not to ask on Friday about his private life. He then got on stage on Saturday and made some very clear and uninformed insinuations about mine.

'Obviously Gordon thinks that any woman who doesn't find him attractive must be gay. For the record I don't. And I'm not.

'But I'm not surprised by any of this. We've all seen how Gordon Ramsay treats his wife and he supposedly *loves* her. We're all just fodder to him.'

BOOM!

I was in awe. It was so pointed, so powerful. And so completely appropriate.

Like the rest of Australia, I was on my feet cheering. Loudly. I felt strengthened, knowing women like Trace were in this industry. And being heard around the country. It was a reminder, too, that I still had a lot to learn about how to handle the subtle, it's-just-a-joke misogyny that can so easily undermine a woman's confidence. Often, without us even realising.

While Ramsay's comment to me wasn't remotely as bad, he clearly thought that I would be excited about him getting an erection after seeing me on air. I wasn't. I was repulsed, and I was kicking myself for just smiling through it all, not wanting to rock the boat.

Tracy's grace and precision demolition of Ramsay, on the other hand, simply couldn't be underestimated for the powerful message it sent to every woman watching, and every man who was smart enough and enlightened enough to take pause.

Tracy had shown the way. And I resolved to follow her lead the next time I had the opportunity.

CHAPTER TWENTY-SIX

And the winner is ...

'If you ever feel like giving up, just remember there
is a little girl watching who wants to be just like you.
Don't disappoint her.' – Author unknown

COULD AUSTRALIA REALLY BE about to get its first female prime minister? Could the relationship between Kevin Rudd and his own party have reached such a low point that a coup was happening right now in the prime minister's office?

The word came through just after 7.30 on the night of 23 June 2010. Numbers were starting to firm, and the strong belief was that Deputy PM Julia Gillard was going to challenge after a series of government U-turns had seen KEVIN07's support plummet just ahead of an election in which they were expected to be wiped out.

We already had a busy show planned for the next morning, with former *60 Minutes* reporter and mad soccer fan George Negus coming in to talk us through a crucial World Cup game for the Socceroos against Serbia happening while we were on air. But as the evening wore on, it was looking increasingly likely that we might need to call on George's vast political experience to do double duty in the morning.

In the wee hours, Tommy called it. The challenge for the prime ministership was ON and Karl immediately jumped in his car and drove with a camera crew straight to the lawns in front of Parliament House, while I stayed to anchor from our Sydney studio.

I didn't end up sleeping that night. Sky News stayed with the story until 1am, and I spent the remaining couple of hours before I headed to work researching and getting across every possible detail. I figured if I could pull an all-nighter for the Logies, then I could certainly do it for what might be a landmark moment for women and for Australian history – a moment that for a little girl growing up in Campbelltown in the 60s would have seemed close to unimaginable.

It was one of the coldest mornings of the year in Canberra, and Karl arrived at Parliament House with just minutes to spare. Back in the studio, George took us through the Socceroos' triumphant 2–1 performance with the brilliant Tim Cahill delivering a trademark 'header' goal ten minutes before the final whistle. Sadly, it wasn't enough to get Australia through to the next round, but no matter, because the situation out of Canberra was continuing apace.

'George, thank you, but as we follow these fast-moving developments out of the nation's capital, we would love you to stay right where you are,' I said, and he did. I then threw to what turned out to be one of our last commercial breaks for the rest of the broadcast.

Our usual end time of 9am passed by almost unnoticed as Graham Richardson, former Hawke and Keating government minister and legendary Labor powerbroker, joined George and me in the studio. Richo told us he was already convinced Rudd was gone.

All eyes remained trained on the glass corridors of Parliament House as our cameras caught occasional glimpses of various ministers and backbenchers moving furtively in small groups between offices. Behind the scenes, 'numbers men' Bill Shorten and Mark Arbib were doing their counts, shoring up support and negotiating across the factions, until word of a decision finally came through.

Kevin Rudd's reign was over, and he would step down rather than face the humiliation of a party ballot. Julia Gillard had been elected unopposed by the party room and would shortly be declared as the 27th, and first female, Prime Minister of Australia.

Then, as we continued to take live every frame of this extraordinary, unfolding saga, a devastated Rudd faced the cameras in front of a huge press pack with his family by his side. The now-former prime minister spoke for 20 emotion-charged minutes, many of them punctuated by long pauses, as his wife, Therese, stayed ever-smiling and supportive by his side, and he listed the things of which he was most proud, including his landmark 'Sorry' speech to the Stolen Generations, before declaring through tears, 'I have given it my all.'

Shortly afterwards, a completely glowing Julia Gillard, who in 1998 had come under attack for being single and childless – or 'deliberately barren', as Senator Bill Heffernan had sneered – stood before that same press pack.

The country's newest prime minister made it clear how truly honoured and humbled she was. She spoke of the values she cherished in Australians. She spoke of hard work, of loyalty and of service. She made it clear that she accepted her fair share of both the achievements and disappointments of the Rudd government as it had moved the country through the devastating Global Financial Crisis.

She said, too, that she knew she had not been elected prime minister by the Australian people, and promised that rather than move into The Lodge, she would remain in her own home in South Australia and ask the governor-general in the coming months to call a federal election so that 'the Australian people can exercise their democratic birthright and elect their next prime minister'.

It was a measured, humble and extremely dignified speech, after what must have been a brutal 24 hours behind the scenes. Then, in a nod to the younger generation watching, she had an important side note ...

'If there is one girl who looks at the TV screen over the next few days and says, "Gee, I might like to do that in the future," well, that's a good thing.'

Yes, it certainly was, because despite women making up 50.2 per cent of the population, the Australian parliament could still only count fewer than a third of its parliamentarians as female. Maybe this was exactly the kind of boost needed to inspire future generations towards a more equal representation. Only time would tell.

Karl and I finally concluded our broadcast at 4pm that day, throwing to the newsroom to take over after a marathon 11 continuous hours on air, most of them commercial-free. I hadn't been to the loo or had a break of any kind in nine hours – or slept in 37. And yet, my first words to Tommy when he told me we were all done were, 'Why are we stopping? We should be going all the way through to 6pm!'

The adrenaline of live TV can be a bit addictive like that sometimes.

*

Ever and always, in that hurly-burly of live television where you had to move fast and make decisions on the run, mistakes could be made as to exactly where the line should be drawn between my professional and personal lives.

One morning, a poor unsuspecting Billi was at home having her cereal before heading to school, with the *Today* show on in the background, when she heard her name from the TV. She leaned in close.

Karl and I were discussing the growing popularity of online shopping and I happened to mention that 'Just last week, my daughter, Billi, asked me if I could buy some bras from the Victoria's Secret online store for her.'

Billi froze.

(OH DEAR GOD, NO, MUM!)

I explained that I was wary about handing out credit card details online, though, 'So I insisted we go to David Jones to get her chest fitted properly by a professional. I mean, having one of those women at DJs squeeze your teenage boobs into a bra is a rite of passage, after all.'

(PLEASE! SOMEONE! MAKE HER STOP!!!)

'So we got her bust measured and Billi now has her very first bra,' I shared.

At that moment, I am told, a primal scream rang out from somewhere just north of the Harbour Bridge.

It was probably not the wisest of parenting decisions for the mother of a then-moody 13-year-old awkwardly going through puberty – and Billi and I, ummm, *discussed* it at some length that afternoon when she got home from school.

(Thankfully, by Christmas, she was speaking to me again ... but even then, only just.)

*

Icebergs, off the starboard quarter! Whales to port! And Antarctica itself, now starting to appear just over the bow.

As parents with jobs as demanding as ours, Pete and I always knew that the kids paid something of a price for our busy lives. Try as we might to keep the impact of our work on them to a minimum, many were the times we both felt we just weren't up to the mark. Particularly once I joined the *Today* show.

More than once, I missed one or another of the kids' school concerts (and when I was there, the desperate need to stifle yawns and momentarily close my eyes for a quick zizz in the darkened school halls when no-one was looking was often overwhelming). I never did quite manage the amount of canteen duty I would have liked, and I fought with the constant guilt of that as I tried to manage the juggle of involved parenting with one eye still focused on the fast-moving news cycle my job demanded.

So, every year, to try and go some way towards making up for all that, Pete and I promised the kids we would take them on a big trip to somewhere amazing. Somewhere we would all remember forever. This time, it was Antarctica.

It was early January of 2011, and with Jake, Louis and Billi all now in their teens, and Pete well and truly launched on his latest book, this time on the great Australian Antarctic explorer Sir Douglas Mawson, we had taken to the high seas and headed south on the family trip of a lifetime. It was one of the lovely side benefits for me and the kids that as Pete's list of books delving into Australian history grew, so too did the experiences we got to share in as he did his research.

We had already been to 'Ned Kelly country' in Victoria to see where the legendary bushranger had made his last stand at Glenrowan; tramped the trenches of the Western Front where the

Diggers (including my beautiful grandfather, 'Bappy') had made their charge at Villers-Bretonneux in France; and hosted Australia's most decorated war heroine, 93-year-old Nancy Wake, for dinner at our home. Nancy's amazing stories of fighting for the French Resistance in the Second World War had certainly left the kids hellishly impressed, but that was nothing compared to the moment they discovered she had also gone to the very same school as them, just a few blocks away, no less than 85 years earlier.

On this latest adventure, we were retracing the heroic footsteps of the legendary Mawson all the way to Cape Denison on the shores of Antarctica, lying six days' fast sail below Tasmania. If the conditions were right and luck was on our side, the specially designed ship we were on would be able to make its way through the broken ice and arrive just a few hundred metres from the door of the fabled Mawson's Hut. It was the exact spot where the explorer and his team had been based for two years while trekking all over this part of the still mostly unknown continent in 1911.

On the way, the delights and new experiences of this trip just kept on coming. We watched stunned (and rather awkwardly with the kids), as huge male elephant seals had their wicked way with seemingly distressed female seals during a stop-off on the shores of Macquarie Island. We visited the vast penguin colonies of Enderby Island, and then dared each other into doing something called the 'polar plunge', which saw us all briefly jump off the back of the ship into the freezing waters off Antarctica. It was high summer and, at that time of year in these parts, the days stretched on forever, while 'night-times' consisted of nothing more than the sun gently touching the horizon before bouncing right back up again like a magnificent game of nature's handball.

The most amazing thing of all, though, was landing at Cape Denison's Commonwealth Bay, and entering the perfectly preserved Mawson's Hut – an extraordinary wooden structure frozen in time, and fundamentally untouched since the day Mawson and his team had left it.

Our Billi, at the age of 13, was told she was the youngest person to have ever gone inside the hut. Almost in disbelief, we looked around to see such things as a slab of frozen seal meat still on the bench ready for cooking, an opened tin of flour ready for baking, and the very same navy-and-white-striped pillow that Mawson himself had laid his weary head upon a century before. The entire experience for all of us was simply extraordinary.

There was a wholly unexpected but completely welcome bonus to this trip, too – the almost complete lack of internet access. This isolation from the rest of the world was proving a great way for all five of us to remove ourselves from the hyper-connected lives we were now living. The world wide web certainly had its advantages, but if there was one argument we were now having more than any other as a family with three teenagers, it was the one we had over time spent on our computers. 'Screen-time' had become the bane of our family existence and the central theme of far too many arguments. And, for Pete and me, navigating our needs as journalists to be on our computers, while simultaneously telling the kids to get the hell off theirs, was a constant challenge.

Social media was adding to the problem. I'd always thought that Twitter was an indulgent waste of time, but Tommy had insisted that I join for work purposes, and once I did, I realised he was right – with selective use, it was a great tool for plugging into the latest news each day. But of course, while for me it was research for work, all the kids saw was Mum on her phone.

So, as we sailed on the high seas along the coast off Antarctica, we may as well have been on another planet, with the only internet access available via the ship's limited, horrendously expensive (and even then, less-than-reliable) satellite system. And we were happy with that.

The only way to find out what was happening in the news back home was via a daily two-page printout of the main stories from the previous day's *Sydney Morning Herald*, which arrived without fanfare along with coffee and cake at morning tea.

And by day six of our trip through the Southern Ocean, we discovered there was *a lot* happening in the news back home. Queensland was experiencing its worst rains in 50 years and a state of emergency had been declared, with an estimated 90 towns and

200,000 people affected. Lives had been lost, and the Brisbane River and entire CBD were unrecognisable.

Channel 9 was now all-hands-on-deck around the clock, with every available host, reporter and producer recalled from holidays and sent to the flooded frontlines. I, meanwhile, was in the middle of the Southern Ocean, with absolutely no means of getting back. It was the biggest news story since the Black Saturday bushfires, and it was impossible for me to return.

But Karl certainly did, and when I finally made it back home, by all reports he had done a great job. He'd demonstrated that while he was the guy who could probably drink you under the table – and then go on to co-host three and a half hours of live TV – he was also one of the best live-from-the-scene journos in the country. His compassion, news sense and unquestionable work ethic when it actually mattered were on full display there in Brisbane, and viewers absolutely loved him for it.

Fortuitously, the timing of it all couldn't have been more perfect when it came to deciding who Channel 9 would back for the Gold Logie that year. Karl was the obvious choice, and with the Logies voting period falling just weeks after he returned from the flood zone, he looked like a shoo-in.

For blokes, he was the guy next door you'd wanna have a beer and a laugh with. For women, he was the cheeky, handsome, super-fit family man who adored his wife, Cass, and three young kids.

The network came out all guns blazing. Every network host was asked to record promos and put up social media posts. Of course, we were happy to do anything we could to help get our boy over the line. I even asked Hugh Jackman to record a special Vote-For-Karl pump-up, and he did it instantly. It ran across the network for weeks. When it comes to personal endorsements, you don't get much better than that.

The Logie wheels were now well and truly in motion. Australia started voting and word was coming back that Karl had it in the bag for the Gold at the big night on 1 May.

First, though, we had to head to London as a certain young royal couple were tying the knot in that last week of April. To celebrate what was predicted to be the 'Wedding of the Century', Tommy had organised to take the entire *Today* show team to London for the week leading up to the big day, including Stevie, Georgie, Richard Wilkins and our newest addition to the desk, Ben Fordham.

Karl and I had been asked to host Nine's live coverage of the wedding on the Friday night as well, so we knew it was going to be a huge week, filming stories during the day for the show, and then putting the show to air until midnight London time each night. An unprecedented worldwide audience was expected to tune in that Friday, desperate to see a happy new chapter begin for the handsome Prince William, as he finally married his long-time girlfriend, Kate Middleton, in Westminster Abbey.

Just about every television network on the planet was covering the nuptials, and with Wills and Kate now topping the charts as everyone's favourite royals, it was never going to disappoint.

No fewer than 8000 TV, newspaper and radio journalists were descending on the UK, Karl and I just two amongst them.

Nine had scored one of the prime studio positions in the purpose-built three-storey broadcast centre directly opposite Buckingham Palace on the edge of magnificent Green Park. The whole impressive-looking structure had gone up in just a week; painted a discreet shade of Wimbledon Green, it matched the surrounding trees perfectly.

The broadcast centre's tightly packed tiers of box-like studios were tiny but practical, each with their own all-important wall of glass looking directly across to that famous balcony, ready and waiting for that first, highly anticipated royal kiss.

The rain that fell in the days before the wedding, though, told the real story of the speedy build, as leaks started to appear above the common walkways, and slippery, sodden boards presented wobbly hazards for those of us silly enough to be in high heels. On one occasion, when I was there for a quick rehearsal and headed out to the nearby Port-a-Loo-style toilets common to all the studios, I found myself in conversation with the legendary US anchors Barbara Walters and Katie Couric about how easy it would be to slip from the open external hallways and fall straight onto the hard-packed dirt of the park below.

The winner of the best loo chat, though, came just before the live broadcast, while I was standing waiting with yet another icon of the business, Diane Sawyer. Both of us were sure we knew who would get the nod as the chosen designer for Kate's dress. I was convinced it would be Alexander McQueen. Sawyer had her money on the idea that, as a sentimental nod to her late mother-in-law-to-be, Kate might choose Diana's wedding dress designers, the Emanuels.

We would soon see, because at exactly 11am London time (8pm back home where, in true Aussie style, many were donning Will and Kate masks and hosting bouquet-throwing parties) on Friday, 29 April 2011, the British set out to prove once and for all that when it comes to combining pomp and pageantry with royalty and romance, they do it better than anyone else in the world.

Beyond the formalities of the impeccably choreographed ceremony full of ancient customs mixed with some more modern moments (a royal bride who wasn't going to 'obey'), there was a lot to cover, as Karl and I took viewers through every made-for-television moment.

From the moment the whole affair got underway, there was plenty to talk about, as wave after rainbow-coloured wave of invited guests began arriving, and we all caught our first glimpse inside the Abbey. There, waiting for all 1900 of them, was a space now transformed into a fairy-tale forest of flowers – £1 million worth, to be exact – along with four tonnes of foliage, and an entire avenue of gigantic potted trees.

There, too, was Elton John with his partner, David Furnish. Here was a heavily pregnant Victoria Beckham teetering in sky-high Louboutin heels with her husband, David. Tony Blair, the former prime minister who had said such powerful words in the hours after the death of Diana, took his seat with his wife, Cherie. On and on they came: comedian Rowan Atkinson; Guy Ritchie (understandably) sans ex-wife, Madonna; singer Joss Stone; Mario Testino, the photographer who had taken those last, now-infamous black-and-white photos of Diana for *Harper's Bazaar*; and Prince Albert of Monaco with his strangely unhappy-looking fiancée, Charlene Wittstock, ahead of their own wedding in just a few weeks.

Nearly two decades on from her toe-sucking scandal, the Duchess of York, Sarah Ferguson was missing, while her daughters – in some pretty mind-blowing hats – were hard to miss. There was an Aussie contingent, too, led by swimming star Ian Thorpe; and Prime Minister Julia Gillard, along with 'first bloke' Tim Mathieson.

Karl and I had done well to spot them all. But with no official guest list released to us, and neither of us completely across every one of the legion European royals and lesser-known foreign dignitaries joining the congregation, we struggled at times for faces we could identify. At one point it had become like a game of 'I spy with my little eye' between us. The first one to shout it out won.

Minutes were passing, with not a single face ringing a bell ... until ... I looked ... I leaned in ... and looked again ... and then, tragically, in a moment I would forever after live to regret, I spoke ... out loud.

'Gee, Karl,' I started, 'now there's a sign that maybe, in the spirit of this glorious day and the healing of old wounds, the royal family has extended an olive branch to the al-Fayed family. I think that might be Dodi al-Fayed just making his way into ... oh ... I'm ... I'm so SORRY! Of course, I mean his *father*, Mohamed al-Fayed. Owner of Harrods. Who, as we all know,' I continued, without-drawing-a-single-breath-hoping-that-the-more-words-I-uttered-and-the-further-I-got-away-from-this-shockingly-insensitive-misdemeanour-the-more-everyone-would-forget, 'has had a troubled relationship with the royals since the death of his *son* Dodi al-Fayed in that dreadful crash in Paris alongside William's late mother, Princess Diana.'

What the hell had I just said??? In my head (as Karl looked at me with disbelief and, thankfully, resisted all temptation to laugh), I momentarily blamed my monstrous mistake on my shocking tiredness. That day, I'd been up since 4am (after finishing the show at midnight) to pack for the flight home before going into hair and makeup and arriving at 7am to try and beat the crowds ahead of the broadcast. I was counting on adrenaline to get me through.

And yet, I was still confused. What was Dodi's father doing here, anyway? Fortunately, I chose not to say that bit out loud, and soon after, the riddle was solved. According to royal columnist James Whitaker who, along with Dame Edna Everage and UK-based Aussie humorist Kathy Lette, was helping out with some of the commentary, our mysterious doppelganger was, in fact … the King of Tonga.

When I checked later, the likeness between the two men was uncanny, but right now I had no choice but to hate myself, and just push on …

Finally, there she was. And as Kate left the Middleton family's five-star bolthole at the historic Goring Hotel on her way to the Abbey, we got our first peek of her … Alexander McQueen dress. Take that, Diane Sawyer! (And in case you're wondering, no, I didn't say that last bit out loud either, but in my head I was certainly taking any win I could at this point.)

Unlike the Queen, Prince Philip, and various other top-tier royals already on their way to the Abbey in magnificently decorative official carriages, Kate made her pre-wedding journey nestled into a 'commoner's' Rolls-Royce alongside her father, Michael, her gentle, royal wave from the wrist already perfected. Younger sister and maid of honour Pippa followed close behind.

At the centre of it all, that ring: Diana's stunning 12-carat Ceylon sapphire and diamond engagement ring, originally valued at £400,000 when Charles first placed it on Diana's finger in 1980. A piece of jewellery now of incalculable value. And on this day, more than ever, it was yet another reminder that there was one very important person missing: Diana.

But Harry was there. William's best man. His brother. His lifelong confidant. As he and William, touchingly, stood shoulder to shoulder and Kate walked down the aisle towards them, the world watched with bated breath. Then, as she arrived, William, the future king, the little boy whose every major milestone we'd all borne witness to, took a single step towards his life with her, his future queen.

*

With the official broadcast over and not one, but two, highly anticipated Palace balcony kisses sealing the deal in front of a worldwide audience of three billion people, Karl and I raced straight to Heathrow. As always in this job, no sooner was one extraordinary experience over than the next one beckoned. Right now, we had to catch our Friday night flight back home to arrive in time for Sunday's Logies broadcast.

It had been an amazing week, and we were both looking forward to a big sleep as we stepped aboard QF2. But things were about to get a whole lot more amazing because we'd just discovered that we'd been bumped up to First Class. As I looked again at my ticket to see if there had been some mistake, I heard one of the extremely welcoming Qantas flight attendants ask, 'Can I get you both a glass of champagne as you settle in, Ms Wilkinson and Mr Stefanovic?'

We were both absolutely exhausted, but there was also so much to celebrate (mistaken Mohamed al-Fayed sightings aside). As we waited for the champagne to arrive, Karl came and sat with me before a single drop of alcohol had touched his lips. He had something he wanted to say, and as he looked me in the eye, it was clear just how heartfelt this was going to be.

'Darl, what a week. We did it! Well done. But I just want you to know that the next few days might get a little crazy. I don't know what's going to happen at the Logies, but there is absolutely no way I would be in this position, or up for the Gold, without you. You do know that, don't you?'

Our partnership, he said, had changed everything for him at the *Today* show. I was really touched. His work during the floods had showcased Karl the journalist, at his best. If he did get the Gold, he deserved it.

And with that, our champagne arrived and we drank a toast to crazy times.

The first leg of that flight was a blur. The last thing I remembered was seeing Karl fast asleep before take-off, and me ordering post-take-off a delicious-looking lamb pie from the flight attendant.

According to Karl, he woke a few hours later to find me still upright, open-mouth snoring, my right hand for some reason immersed in the middle of the now-cold pie. Figuring the position of my hand indicated I still had something of a sleepy ownership over the pie, he decided to leave me be.

*

Arriving on the red carpet that Sunday night, the normally camera-shy Cass looked stunning in a custom-made, strapless, red satin number, dripping in Logies-appropriate diamonds. With Karl proudly by her side, the paps went wild, as everyone presumed Karl was a sure bet for the Gold.

He was up against some tough competition in actors Asher Keddie, Rebecca Gibney and Jessica Marais, along with ABC host Adam Hills, and Ten's Chrissie Swan. But it was pics of Karl and Cass that the paps were after. Cass had always been very happy for Karl to be the one out the front shining in their marriage, so photos of them together were rare. The paps didn't want to miss a moment of it. I think they also figured, given Karl's Logies history, he might get a little loose in the lead-up, but Karl vowed he wasn't going to touch a drop of alcohol that night until the big announcement.

And sure enough, a few hours later when the evening's host, comedian Shane Bourne, opened the envelope, my very sober co-host heard the words we had all hoped for: 'And the winner of the Gold Logie for 2011 is ... Karl Stefanovic!' The room went wild.

Cass and I were sitting either side of him on the official *Today* show table, and after a hug from both of us, Karl leapt to his feet and headed to the stage. On the way, though, it was clear he had left his biggest hug for younger brother Pete, who had returned especially for the occasion from his stint in London as Nine's highly respected European correspondent. Neither of them could have been more proud of the other.

Finally, the rousing cheers and applause abated, the room leaned in ... and Karl began.

'I would like to thank my wife, first and foremost. She's a beautiful woman and the first person I pay tribute to tonight. She had a promising career of her own at the ABC, and she gave up everything for me. She gave up everything to raise our three beautiful kids. So, Cass, this is yours as much as it is mine.

'She is sitting next to Richard Wilkins, who at times in his life has been untrustworthy, but I absolutely trust him like a brother … and he said, to me, "Mate, a quick speech is a good speech, especially when there is something waiting for you at the bar" … and I know he didn't mean a drink. But Dickie, thank you very much, mate, for all of your support over the years. In all seriousness, you have been a wonderful, wonderful supporter. And you are one of the hardest-working men in this business still to this day, and I appreciate your support.

'I want to say a big thank you to a man who is not here tonight, and that is David Gyngell, who is the best TV executive in this country. Now here's a mental image for you, I know he's probably at home sitting there with his Homer Simpson underwear on, possibly scratching himself, whatever he does at home, by himself, watching the TV … I love you, mate, I love you as a boss but also more importantly as a friend.

'We have got some wonderful people at Channel Nine. Despite what anyone says, whatever is written about us, we have got the best people in the business. Michael Healy, Jeff Browne, you all are amazing. Heidi and Corey, who helped co-ordinate this campaign. Well done to you. Whatever it was, um, the campaign. I want to say thank you to the other nominees who have been absolutely wonderful.

'I never ever ever in my life as a journo thought that I would be standing up here in front of this crowd on this stage, with this thing in my hand … hah! … especially with the class of nominees. Rebecca, Jess, I love your show, and I know it's not politically correct to say that because it's not on our network, but I love your show. And I cried like a baby when Zoe died. No more deaths though, OK? No more deaths. And Asher … Asher was amazing as Ida. Also Chrissie, I just love you, Chrissie. She's just a wonderful person and she's got a lovely soul. And Hillsy, mate, we all know if you weren't at the ABC you would have won five of these things, brother. That's the reality … that's the reality!

'On a personal note, I want to thank a couple of friends, Robyn Gillespie and Jerry Gillespie, our great mates in Brisbane. I also want to thank my mum and dad. Mum has such a beautiful soul, and my dad has such charisma and intelligence, both of which I missed out on. Thanks for the male-patterned baldness though, big fella.

'My sister, Tissy, who is upstairs with her husband, Marcus, we love you guys, and my two brothers, Tom and Pete, who I love more and more each day and I'm so proud of them, doing such amazing work overseas … and thank you to everyone in the business who has surrounded me throughout my career.

'They haven't been easy years the last couple of years, certainly when I started with the *Today* show, but there have been some really important and strong people who have stuck by me through all of that.

'And when I saw Laurie Oakes before give the most amazing speech, he is the reason why I'm in this business, and why I want to be in this business as a journalist for the rest of my life.

'So … I'm going to the bar, thank you!'

It was absolutely classic Karl. Cheeky bordering on ribald, a Dickie joke, a mental image of our boss in his underpants. And the crowd loved it.

CHAPTER TWENTY-SEVEN

The Trump card

'Your work will never be finished. Your inbox will never be
empty. Your body will never be perfect. Your striving will
never end. Don't race life. Walk it. Enjoy it. Breathe.'
– Author unknown

I‍T WAS THE BIG Apple from a perspective I never could have
possibly imagined.

I was high atop Trump Tower in New York, being shown
around Donald Trump's gleaming three-storey penthouse by none
other than the former model Melanija Knavs, now better known as
Melania or Mrs Donald Trump III.

Below us, the full expanse of autumn's stunning effect on
Central Park was evident. Every possible shade of gold leaf – much
like every surface here inside the apartment – was unfolding across
the mushrooming treetops of the sprawling parklands, and from this
vantage point I could almost count every one of them.

It was now more than 25 years since I'd first walked past this
building's gaudy gold façade, near where I'd had that fleeting
encounter with Trump in the foyer of The Plaza Hotel. Now I was
here in New York working once again, this time for the *Today* show.
Tommy was trying to get us out of the stuffy, windowless surrounds
of our Nine studios hidden away in suburban Willoughby, and take
us out on the road so we could meet the ever-growing number of

viewers who were making the switch and 'waking up with *Today*'. From a standing start back in May 2007, when *Sunrise* was literally doubling our numbers every day, we were now beginning to win whole weeks in the ratings. We could all feel that the hard work was paying off.

Mostly, those on-the-road trips were to wonderful holiday locations around Australia; but on this occasion we had taken over the Times Square studios of our US sister program, *Good Morning America*, right in the middle of bustling Manhattan, for a whole week. And right now, I was wandering through Trump's triplex high above Fifth Avenue, so the billionaire's wife could tell me all about the 'Melania' range of costume jewellery and watches she was selling on Canada's home shopping network – all while our cameras rolled.

But the woman herself and her ideas on anything? I had no clue. She seemed so unknowable. Every question about life with Donald was deflected, and seamlessly turned back to her jewellery, which began at the low, low price of just $30. By interview's end, I wasn't getting any sense of the woman in front of me.

Still, there were two things I'd seen that afternoon that probably told Melania's story better than she herself ever could have. Ironically, they were the only things in this space that were out of place.

One was a painting I spied as I stood by the kitchen doorway, waiting for a glass of water Melania had asked one of the maids to fetch me. But this wasn't just any painting. It was one of Pierre-August Renoir's most famous, 'Two Sisters on the Terrace', and I was standing just inches away from it.

I was so taken by it that when I got back to the couch, as Melania's makeup artist was doing the last of her touch-ups, I had to ask, 'I just saw your stunning painting by the kitchen doorway. Is that an *actual* Renoir?'

I don't know if she was offended (which would have been fair enough) … or if perhaps she didn't actually like the painting (in which case I was offended on behalf of one of the greatest painters of all time), but her response was remarkable.

'Oh, that,' she said, as her head turned towards the doorway by the kitchen. 'I don't know. It's Donald's.'

That it was possible to be so rich as to be unmoved by a Renoir blew my mind ... and I instantly felt sad for her, and for the painting itself as this masterpiece sat so unappreciated and forgotten.

The second item that, to my eye, sat out of place here in the Trump apartment was a small, exact replica of a Mercedes convertible belonging to Melania's only child and Donald's fifth, Barron. It was sitting right next to a set of marble steps on one side, and a glass-topped coffee table adorned with what I'm sure must have been priceless ornaments.

There was nowhere here for a five-year-old kid to get up a head of energetic steam and play with it. Indeed, despite its personalised Barron numberplates, it looked like it had never been used. Not a bump, not a scratch, not even a sticky fingerprint to indicate that it had ever brought that little boy with the famous last name a single moment's joy.

I came away feeling more than a little empty. Certainly many people coveted their kind of lives, but seeing it up close was just sad.

*

The rumours had been around for a while, but none of us at *Today* believed them. It had to be just silly scuttlebutt that Mel Doyle was leaving *Sunrise* and being replaced by Seven's Samantha Armytage.

It just didn't make any sense to break up what we all thought was the unbreakable bond of Mel-and-Kochie. They were the mum and dad of breakfast TV. Whereas Karl and I were probably seen more as its slightly brash, somewhat mouthy, and certainly more risqué kids.

Mel's warmth, intelligence and empathy had been such a crucial part of *Sunrise*'s success. The viewers loved her and had been with her every step of the way through her two pregnancies, the kids' missing teeth and first days at school. Adam Boland had always said that Mel and Kochie were an indivisible duo; you simply couldn't separate them. Sam, too, seemed an unusual choice when it was always presumed that the much-loved Natalie Barr would be Mel's natural successor.

Sure enough, though, on 20 June 2013, Mel – with a somewhat shell-shocked looking Kochie and Nat by her side – announced on the set of *Sunrise* that she had been offered an opportunity by the network to move on to 'bigger things'. Typical of Mel, she was pure class in her exit from the show, and the first thing I did when I heard the news was to send her a text. During my time at *Sunrise*, I'd learnt so much, observing at close quarters the way she'd navigated the tricky, sometimes shark-infested waters of the breakfast timeslot – both in front of, and behind, the cameras. I told her that I hoped that she was indeed moving on to something wonderful, which was exactly what she deserved. Her upbeat reply gave away nothing to indicate this move was anything other than her choice. I really hoped that was the case.

*

One of the great joys of hosting the *Today* show was the crazy range of topics you got to cover and the vast array of people you would encounter on any one morning. From the growing list of prime ministers and the biggest stars on the planet, to the many hundreds of stories of real-life Aussies we met who made us proud, broke our hearts, rallied us to causes and pulled on our heartstrings – we engaged with them all.

Every day, the amazing moments just kept on coming. On one occasion, John Travolta took me for a joy ride to Wollongong in his private jet, and I pointed out to him from the cockpit the very beach where I'd spent so many happy summers on the shoreline as a kid. On another, I flew to London to interview Nobel Peace Prize laureate Malala Yousafzai. I was greeted by a super-talented 14-year-old kid from Canada called Justin Bieber as he skateboarded towards me with a 'Hi, Lisa!' just as his fame was exploding; was serenaded by Michael Bublé; reminisced with Sir Bob Geldof about Live Aid; talked exercise videos and the Vietnam War with Jane Fonda; shared a stage and momentarily a microphone with Taylor Swift; hosted a 50th anniversary reunion with every one of the Von Trapp children from *The Sound of Music*; and caused an uproar with the members of One Direction when our conversation – in front of a live studio audience of screaming teens – turned to cooking. I suggested that when making cakes, one of them was probably a 'bowl-licker'. That didn't seem to be what they heard, though. It must have been my accent. (My daughter, Billi, was lucky enough to be in the audience that day, and when the director cut to her for her reaction, it seems maybe it wasn't my accent at all but just her mother being 'embarrassing'.)

Then there was a bright-eyed and super-chatty Kim Kardashian, who won me over forever by quickly whispering just before we came back from an ad break, 'Lisa, your fly is undone'; and film legend Sophia Loren who, much as I tried to win her over, made it clear she didn't want to talk to me at all; and fashion makeover queens, Trinny and Susannah, who decided that a rather lengthy feel of my boobs halfway through their segment was what was needed to work out the most flattering fashion shapes for my figure.

The Spice Girls' Geri Halliwell was an absolute sweetheart, as was the very cheeky Robbie Williams. Pink simply had it all, after the two of us chatted about shoes backstage, before she came out and blew us all away with 'So What!' in front of a packed-out studio audience – all of whom she was happy to chat with long after the lights went down.

I got to sing 'Horses' with the lovely Daryl Braithwaite (and yes, all was forgiven after that night at the ABC back in the late 90s), and on one very special morning I got to co-host the last hour of the show with the wonderful Hugh Jackman.

But for every 50 family-friendly guests like Hugh, there was one Borat ... or should I say Sacha Baron Cohen – or, on this occasion, Admiral General Aladeen from the fictional country of Wadiya. Sacha's latest satirical character was loosely based on a mix of murderous, real-life dictators Idi Amin, Muammar Gaddafi and Kim Jong-il.

Karl and I were already huge fans of Sacha's edgy 'truth-telling' mockumentaries, and happy to play along with the scripted questions he'd supplied, knowing he would bring it all home with his particular brand of comic genius in the answers.

But when, in the opening seconds of the segment, the Admiral General turned to me and said in his thick mock-Arab accent, 'G'day, Sugar Tits', before purring, 'By the way, you must come to my palace. No sleazy stuff, just a bit of touching. Don't worry, I won't touch your malawah ...' Karl and I both started shifting uncomfortably.

'I don't know what that is,' I said, 'but I'm nervous.' He then offered to show me right then and there.

In what Karl probably hoped would be a chance to pick up the tone, he asked the Admiral General if he had some advice for our politicians, starting with Prime Minister Gillard.

He did, as he was of the firm belief that she needed to surround herself with people she could trust. 'For example, I have 25 female virgin guards who protect me at all times,' he said, pointing to the two stunning mini-skirted women in khaki and red lips behind him. 'I know that they are virgins because I check their virginity every night with the head of my penis.'

It was 8.10 in the morning, and I suddenly had visions of viewers with their kids, freezing mid-spoonful over their muesli. I knew it was satire, and I knew it was making a statement about the disgusting behaviour of so many male dictators around the world – for whom misogyny was merely a starting point – but boy, we were on the edge.

And it just kept coming ...

'You know [recently discredited Labor politician] Craig Thomson? When you pay for hookers, don't use the government credit card! Always cash, cash, cash! I know it's tempting to put it on the card because of the air miles ... but you have to do what's right!'

The entire floor crew fell about laughing, and he had just made a very good point, so I forged ahead: 'General, it's an honour to have you here,' to which he replied, 'It would be an honour to have you ...

'You have a husband?' he asked.

'I do,' I said, knowing now that there were no safe answers to any of these questions.

'I will negotiate with him. He will agree. Or he will have an accident.'

That was funny. It was black, but it was funny.

When Karl asked him to describe his new film, he said it was 'a lot like many of the other classic movies from my country of Wadiya, *When Harry Kidnapped Sally*, *You've Got Mail Bomb* or the family film *Planet of the Rapes*'.

At that point, we all went quiet. It had gone too far, and perhaps even Sacha himself knew it did, too ... as he asked the question that, right now, we all wanted to know the answer to: 'Breakfast TV, why you have me on? I know you are thinking about that!'

We were. And our time was up. Almost. Because as Karl thanked the dictator, there was still time for Admiral General Aladeen to get in one last shot at me.

'You come with me now or I fly you over later?'

'Do I have a choice?' I asked, never more excited to throw to a commercial break in my life.

'Ah, no! Don't worry, it will be painless! You will be unconscious ...'

*

When the email arrived, I was sitting at the kitchen table at home preparing for the next day's show, and Pete was working on his next column for the *Herald* while simultaneously writing his latest book. I never quite knew how he did that, switching so seamlessly between the two.

Pete had been working from home for years and had three main 'work spots' around the house he called his own. Every week or two he would move to the next, a bit like a dog marking his territory, but in Pete's case the 'mark' came in the form of endless research papers, historical photographs, pens, computer cords, USBs, documents, earplugs and teacups. Pete had recently given up alcohol after embracing our eldest son's dictum that 'While it's a better Saturday night with alcohol, it's a better life without,' so always there were teacups.

Then, after a fortnight or so, bored with that spot and with another 20,000 words or so written, Pete would pick (almost) all of it up and move it to the next spot in the house. His justification was that it was all about a change of scenery.

One of those spots was at his desk in the study, another by the bay window in the lounge room, and the last was here opposite me at the kitchen table. Although the latter was never a good one if we both wanted to get some solid work done because, invariably, we just couldn't help ourselves – one of us would find something we wanted to share and chat about to the other and, before we knew it, half an hour had passed.

Right now, though, I had something I definitely didn't want to share with Pete. It was an email from the head of the ABC, Mark Scott, with an invitation for me to give the annual Andrew Olle Media Lecture later that year in honour of the late and truly great former ABC journalist's life.

It was an event that Pete and I had been attending since its inception, partly because in the last few years of Andrew's life, we had become quite close to him and his wife, Annette. Andrew had died of a brain aneurysm in 1995 just a couple of weeks before his 48th birthday, and the Olle lecture, raising money for brain cancer research, had become an annual fixture in our diaries.

Everyone from Lachlan Murdoch to Jana Wendt, Laurie Oakes, Ray Martin, David Williamson and Kerry Stokes had all been so honoured, and all had given brilliant, deeply thoughtful orations. If I accepted, I would be the only female journalist since Jana Wendt, 16 years before, to stand on that podium.

The role of the lecture, delivered in front of possibly the toughest crowd anywhere in the country – a room full of my journalistic peers – is to focus on the role and future of the media, and to add new ideas to the national conversation. It was as completely daunting a prospect as it was an absolute honour. And it was one I knew straight away I simply wasn't up to. What on earth could I say that hadn't already been said before?

There must have been some mistake. Mark must have been meaning to send this to someone else. I read it again. And again. And again. And just as I was about to read it out to Pete, I stopped myself. I knew that if I told him the contents of the email, he would be over the moon for me. Pete had always been my greatest supporter, and so often in moments when I feared I was well out of my depth, he was always right beside me, cheering me on.

But this was different. This was on a whole other level for me. How could I tell him in one breath what I'd been offered and then insist on refusing it in the next?

So, I didn't tell Pete – or respond to Mark's kind offer. For a week. And then, one morning, as I was standing in the shower just after 3am, I started mulling over what I would have said on that stage if I'd been silly enough to accept the invitation.

Well, I could start by questioning how it was that I was only the second female journalist to be asked in 16 years. And thinking more about it, why was it that in a profession dominated by women at the lower levels, the chain of command became ever-more male-dominated at the executive level? Why were there so many stories of men in newsrooms around the country being paid so much more than their female colleagues?

And when it came to the portrayal of women in the media, why was our own Prime Minister Julia Gillard constantly judged on her looks, her voice or, God help us, the size of her backside? Why did the weekly 'women's' magazines choose to so often delight in pitting women against each other, inciting jealousy, envy and division?

Dammit, I actually had a lot to say that hadn't been said on that podium before. Standing in the shower that morning, I decided I had to give it a shot, sure in the knowledge that I may well fail … but, at least this way, I wouldn't die wondering.

And as the months rolled on, new material just kept presenting itself. By the time I took to the stage in late October 2013, seven months after the invitation from Mark Scott had arrived, Australia had had three separate prime ministers. We'd begun the year with Julia Gillard who – despite presiding over a hung parliament and successfully passing more than 500 pieces of legislation through it during her term – had been deposed by her own party for the very man she had replaced, Kevin Rudd. Then, just months later, after an election campaign as dirty as the country had ever seen, the man Julia Gillard's famed misogyny speech had been aimed at in our federal parliament, Tony Abbott, became prime minister.

That speech made headlines around the world, and more examples of Tony Abbott's long history of misogynistic behaviour became widespread, including the moment he stood outside Parliament House, entirely untroubled by supporters right behind him holding placards with the words DITCH THE WITCH and BOB BROWN'S BITCH on them, aimed directly at Julia Gillard.

Upon announcing his first-ever Cabinet of 19 newly minted federal ministers, the new PM chose just one woman. To top it off, in recognition of his now much-talked-about 'women problem', he also installed himself as the Minister for Women.

Yes, those few stray thoughts in the shower had certainly begun to form around a consistent theme: the place of Australian women in this second decade of the 21st century.

Though nervous at the prospect of addressing this 500-strong black-tie crowd as I went out live on ABC TV that night, I was keenly aware of the privilege I'd been handed. After seven months of putting all these thoughts together, and becoming ever-more passionate about the theme, I surprised myself with how keen I was to get up on that stage and get my message out.

Within just a few minutes I was launched on several themes, including the pressure on how women look.

'Today's media landscape, particularly for women,' I said, 'is one now so focused on the glossy and the glamorous it often eclipses and undermines everything else.

'And it is everywhere. I kid you not — even in preparing for tonight's lecture, the most common question I was asked was not "What are you going to say?", but "What are you going to wear?"

'And when you're a woman doing breakfast TV, you quickly learn the sad truth that what you wear can sometimes generate a bigger reaction than even any political interview you ever do.'

Many of the female TV journalists in the room I could see were nodding knowingly.

'As a woman in the media, it has long saddened me that while we delight in covering issues of overt sexism – possibly the hottest topic in the media over the last twelve months – the media itself can be every bit as guilty of treating women entirely differently to men.

'And in terms of our audience, the cliché is so often true – it is women who can turn out to be a woman's harshest critic.

'Take this email that arrived in the *Today* show inbox, from a viewer called Angela, in March of this year ...

Who the heck is Lisa's stylist? Whoever it is has Lisa in some shocking clothes.

Today's outfit is particularly jarring and awful.

Just my 2 cents worth.

Get Some Style.

'Now, while I know I am far from being above criticism, good sense should tell me to leave that sort of semi-anonymous stuff alone. But some mornings, it was hard to resist ...

Dear Angela,

Thanks for all of your 'Get Some Style' feedback.

Please feel free to send me a list of all the outfits you don't like out of the 200 or so that I have to come up with each year, and I'll see what I can do.

Just so I can prepare, are we just talking about the outfits I wear for the *Today* show, or the ones I have to wear for red carpet and charity events as well?

You'll need to be very specific because, Angela, that is a lot of outfits to remember.

Please include suggested styles, colours, sleeve-lengths, skirt shapes, your preference for prints, fabric weights, jackets vs blouses, etc ...

Of course, Angela, given that I am a journalist – and not a supermodel – it is important that anything I wear allows me to feel comfortable for three and a half hours on set or perhaps outside when we're on location.

Oh, and I'm a married mother of three, so please, nothing too revealing.

And by the way, nothing I wear can ever clash with what Georgie is wearing. And I have a larger bust, so nothing too tight either, thanks. Oh, and I'm not very tall – did I mention I'm not a model? – so please take that into consideration as well.

And finally, I must never clash with Karl's ties. Or suits. Or the couch.

Look forward to hearing from you.

Best regards,

Lisa.

'I think I must have done Angela's head in with that response, because I never heard from her again.

'Even our most esteemed female media guests aren't immune from criticism. Not even when that guest is the Australian of the Year.

'Take this recent email from viewer Steve …

I don't think you guys should allow Miss Ita Buttrose on the show. She has so much to answer for. Before she started writing all that stuff in her magazine all those years ago, women were happy! They didn't need to vote, or have a license, they didn't even know what an organism was! Now they expect it … EVERY TIME !!!!! Steve.

'Why are women so often the targets of vitriol? Why too, in so many areas of Australian life, is it that the rules of engagement are still so different for women?

'I despair that every time a female journalist is profiled in the press, her age is usually mentioned by the second paragraph, as if it is a measure of her sexual currency and just how long it will be before it expires. And yet, does anyone here know or care how old Kerry O'Brien, Kochie, Tony Jones, Hugh Riminton, Ray Martin, Peter Overton or Laurie Oakes are? They are all brilliant at what they do, and the rule of thumb is that the more experienced they are, the better they are at their jobs. So why, so often, doesn't that same measure apply to women?

'I despair when so many gossip magazines use ridicule of women as their stock in trade. How many times do we see female celebrities used as bullying targets, almost always based on their appearance?

'I despair whenever I hear the words "Post Baby Body" accompanied by images celebrating women who in four amazing weeks have managed to immediately wipe away any physical trace of evidence that they had ever been pregnant in the first place. And we're meant to aspire to that?

'I despair when I see another "Celebrities With Anorexia" gossip cover, complete with before-and-after paparazzi shots, calculated to show each one of them at their sad, tortured worst. It's pure voyeurism and ridicule masquerading as concern.

'I despair when our Federal Cabinet has just one woman – and women are told in response that we must shoulder the burden of blame for this lack of female parliamentary presence due to our lack of "merit". If only we were more talented, we're told, we might get half a chance of a look in.

'I despair that so many young girls are growing up, held hostage via social media to the views others have of them, long before they even know who they are themselves.

'To the rising generation of female journalists in the room, and those watching at home, allow me to say that I appreciate you have come into the media at a difficult time.

'The wonderful thing is – and I want to end on a positive note – there are actually a lot of bright shining stars for us all to steer by.

'I encourage you to look, as I regularly do, to the women I most admire in this wonderful profession in which we find ourselves: from Leigh Sales, who had the unenviable task of stepping into Kerry O'Brien's shoes and now totally owns *7.30*; to the easy charm of Liz Hayes and her ability to draw out unexpected admissions from her interview subjects; Sarah Ferguson, whose every TV exposé is cause to lean in so as to not miss a word; Georgie Gardner's obvious compassion in every news bulletin she delivers; Emma Alberici's and Jenny Brockie's sheer professionalism and depth of experience; Mel

Doyle's extreme grace under professional pressure; Annabel Crabb's quirky individuality matched only by her sharp–as–a–tack political acumen; Tracy Grimshaw, my predecessor at *Today*, who picks up *another* Walkley nomination every time she sits down for one of her signature interviews; the wonderfully incisive writings of Julia Baird; Kate McClymont's forensic research and take–no–prisoners bravery; Deborah Thomas's seamless capacity to work across so many media platforms; Fran Kelly's warmth and piercing intellect as a broadcaster; Mia Freedman's trail-blazing bravery and inspirational innovation in the online world; Morag Ramsay's capacity as a producer to make the complex comprehensible; Jennifer Byrne's infectious enthusiasm for every subject she turns her hand to; and the gentle grace and warm wisdom the wonderful Caroline Jones brings on a Monday night, as this tribal elder and enduring pioneer of female journalists in this country introduces another episode of *Australian Story*.

'All of these women are at the top of their game. Their paths have been sure and steady: learning, growing, honing their craft, withstanding the temptation to compromise, and surviving, despite all the extraordinary pressures placed upon them.

'These are women for whom public approval comes from their desire to be authentic and get on with the job. Their very lack of desire to be "liked" – and hasn't *that* word altered in meaning over time? – is the very thing that drives their enduring and much-deserved respect.

'I am honoured to work in the same profession as them.'

And I still am.

CHAPTER TWENTY-EIGHT

Fifty Shades of ... WTAF?

'When people show you who they are, believe them.'
– Maya Angelou

CHATTING TO ROYALTY IS a very curious thing. You just know that whatever you discuss, this will more than likely be the eleventieth such chat the said royal will have had that day, so it's hard to know if it's your job or theirs to try to make your brief encounter interesting.

Weirdly, I'd been having quite a few such chats in recent times. First with Australia's own Crown Princess Mary of Denmark and husband Crown Prince Frederik at an Olympics function for our Aussie athletes in London. Without betraying what Princess Mary said about who she was cheering for during the Games, it was clear that you might be able to take the woman out of Hobart, but you just can't take Hobart out of the woman.

It's an even more curious and conflicting thing chatting with royals when they're British, and you happen to be married to the man just appointed as chair of the Australian Republic Movement. But it was ANZAC Day 2014, and I was in Canberra hosting a special episode of the *Today* show, beginning with the dawn service, which both the Duke and Duchess of Cambridge were attending. I'd also been invited by the director of the Australian War Memorial, Dr Brendan Nelson, to attend a small wreath-laying ceremony the royal couple were conducting at the AWM Pool of Remembrance later that morning. It was to be their very last appearance at the end of a successful 19-day tour of both Australia and New Zealand.

Pete, meanwhile, in his capacity as a Member of the Council for the AWM, was also attending. With a father, mother and four uncles who had all proudly served for Australia in various theatres of war, and Pete now writing books on so many of those landmark moments in our history, he was of course keen to take part in this solemn service. As for getting a close-up look-see at the most famous couple in the world? Not so much. To him it didn't seem quite right to make small talk with the very people whose line of succession he was so devoted to uncoupling from Australia.

As for me possibly meeting the royal couple? As I pointed out to Pete, I had been to their wedding, so really, it would be rude not to accept.

I'd met some of the British royals before – Charles and Camilla, in fact, at a Government House morning tea in Victoria two years earlier. A few select media had been invited, and once we'd each been offered tea and scones, the instruction was to stay in small manageable groups, and wait for the royals to approach you – definitely no approaching them first. And photos were an absolute no-no.

First up, was the oft-maligned Camilla, still seen by many as the woman who broke Diana's young heart in that 'crowded' marriage. I'd always been told she was totally charming in person, and she certainly was. Somehow our conversation turned to various horses she owned, some of which were racehorses.

I asked if she was any good at picking winners. She said she wasn't, but the Queen certainly was. She said that breeding racehorses was the Queen's greatest passion, and her knowledge of every one of them bordered on the encyclopaedic. She shared, too, that – much to her great annoyance – whenever the Queen advised her on how to get the best out of her own racehorses, she was always right, dammit! It was funny to think that even that far up the food chain, you can still have niggling in-law problems.

And with that, Camilla moved on …

Then, with a fresh cup of tea in my hand and halfway through munching on a jam and cream scone, Charles approached our small group. With my horse knowledge now all dried up, I decided to ask Charles how Harry was going with his recent redeployment to Afghanistan. He said that he presumed well, but he had hardly heard from him. According to his dad, Harry was a hopeless letter writer. Charles himself was writing to his second-born son every week, but to the future king's immense frustration, Harry, in return, would only communicate via quick, occasional emails. Charles said he had tried to make Harry aware that handwritten letters would not only one day serve as a personal record he would treasure and be able to then show his own children, but they were also important historically for the British public and the royal family itself. Nonetheless, Charles said, Harry simply wouldn't listen. 'And he's been that way for a while now,' he added with a smile, before he too wandered off to the next group.

Now, though, here at the War Memorial, I was about to meet Harry's older brother, William. The wreath-laying ceremony over, and Pete now retired to a chair at the back of this small courtyard, Kate wandered over first, as Dr Nelson introduced us.

Standing nearby was long-time UK *Sun* newspaper photographer, and favourite of the royal family, Arthur Edwards, and as a very polite Kate and I chatted (mostly about the weather – New Zealand had been great, Australia not so much), I could hear Arthur snapping away. Arthur had been a guest on our show many times, and he knew I would get a kick out of a keepsake of that moment. All I hoped was that there was no sign of a yawning Pete in the background.

Next came William. And if I could sense Kate's tiredness during our chat, William confirmed it. Just like his own first trip to Australia as a baby in 1983, William and Kate had brought Prince George with them. From William's account, George was proving a pretty boisterous lad and wasn't exactly a great sleeper. Now, he was just counting down the hours until that 24-hour plane trip home he confessed he was dreading.

My overall impression? It was nice to know that the royals, all of them, were human after all.

With the young couple gone, I went looking for Pete, but far from finding him asleep in the corner, he was instead attempting to corner his old football coach, Tony Abbott, on the virtues of Australia becoming a republic.

'Listen, Pete,' the PM told him firmly, but with a grin, as he tried to continue following just behind the royal couple, 'I really don't think this is the time or place we should be discussing this, do you?'

Typical of Pete – who, to be fair, was also smiling – he did.

*

There was no doubt Georgie Gardner was one of the best newsreaders in the country and we were lucky to have her superb skills at the desk every day, but in mid-2014, she announced she was leaving to spend more time with her family. With two children now in primary school, the hours were getting to her and it was 'time for Tim and the kids to have "present mummy" as opposed to "grumpy mummy"', as she described it on her final day.

The great pity for the show was that, in the strange science that applies to the successful-or-otherwise chemistry of breakfast TV, the very entertaining jousting that had been happening for years between Karl and Georgie would be gone. While the two had never exactly been what you'd call friends, their daily interaction was a constant, witty game of one-upmanship – which the viewers loved, and never more so than when Georgie won. They both gave as good as they got, and after seven years of watching that relationship at close quarters, I would say that by the time Georgie left, the score was dead even.

But now some of that quite uncomfortable tension was carrying through to off-air time, and Georgie had had enough. Politely, all she said was 'it's time for someone else to have this opportunity'. Equally politely, Karl said, 'We'll miss you.'

That someone was Sylvia Jeffreys, one of *Today*'s sharpest on-the-road reporters and sometime fill-in summer host for the show. She was particularly popular with Karl's younger brother Peter,

Nine's European correspondent who had just returned from a long overseas stint and was now settling back into Australian life and also doing a bit of summer holiday hosting himself. From their first moments on air together, it was obvious these two were meant for each other.

*

It had been just over a year since I'd delivered my Andrew Olle lecture, and without me initially realising it, Karl had really listened to my words on sexism in the media and quietly decided to conduct an experiment.

'Darl, I don't know if you've noticed, but I've been wearing the same suit for the last four weeks,' he told me in late 2013. I hadn't. His ties were changing as usual, but with the same nondescript white shirts on rotation, the unchanging navy-blue suit itself had passed me by. Karl told me he was going to keep going and see if anyone noticed. We waited for the fashion police sirens to wail, but now, a year on, not a single person had mentioned it, let alone complained. I wasn't at all surprised.

In that same time period, I'd seen possibly a thousand or so unsolicited bits of feedback on what I looked like, what I was wearing, my hair, my size – heck, even the way I was sitting. Some of it nice, but most of it calculated to hurt. But always, the way I looked was a topic up for discussion. And almost always it was from women.

Why was it, I wondered, that we women are too often still our own harshest critics? Why, after all our achievements, was a woman's appearance still deemed one of the most noteworthy things about her? What hope was there for real change when even one of the most strident feminists of our time, Germaine Greer, had gone on national TV and reduced Julia Gillard, the first woman to achieve the highest office in the land, to the size of her backside? It seems that unlearning sexist behaviour was still a job for us all – men *and* women.

I hoped that Karl's suit-for-a-year story would help move that conversation along. It did. The world went nuts for it. There was hardly a news or talk show that didn't discuss it. It even made headlines in the Middle East. Because, in the end, it all boiled down to one indisputable truth. Just as Karl had so successfully got away with being drunk on air, and I was convinced that were it me I would not have, similarly, if I had turned up on the show in the same dress for just two days in a row – let alone for a whole year! – the head-scratching and outrage would have been immediate. The world would have thought I'd gone barking mad.

Karl had proved his point superbly. And women everywhere thanked him for it.

*

It was 22 December 2014 and, just over a year into his prime ministership, Tony Abbott was having a small reshuffle of his Cabinet. That 'women problem' hadn't gone away, and he urgently needed to adjust the optics of his first term in office, as prime ministerial aspirant Malcolm Turnbull began to breathe down his political neck and agitate for a change of leadership.

As is customary in these moments, Tony Abbott was appearing on the show the morning after his reshuffle announcement to explain the reason for the changes. He particularly wanted to proudly spruik the 100 per cent lift in females on his front bench from one to ... two. No more 'good morning, lady and gentlemen' as he commenced his Cabinet meetings. Tony Abbott now seemed to think he had lady *abundance*.

Bafflingly, he had also reappointed himself as Minister for Women. So, my question to him that morning was an obvious one: 'Prime Minister, what would you say has been your biggest achievement as the Minister for Women over the last year?'

He hesitated for a moment. I got the distinct impression he'd never really thought about it. And then he launched.

'Well ... you know ... it is very important ... to do the right thing by families and households. As many of us know, women are particularly focused on the household budget and the repeal of the carbon tax means a $550-a-year benefit for the average family.'

That said it all. For Tony Abbott, women could only ever be seen through the lens of their domestic 'duties': of being a wife and mother, running families and looking after the house, doing the washing and the ironing, and paying the electricity bills. No mention from the Minister for Women of the recent exponential rise in female homelessness, or the growing scourge of domestic violence, or even the gender pay gap for which Australia still ranked as one of the worst amongst OECD countries.

As to his still disproportionately low number of female Cabinet ministers, he continued to defend it, because with roughly just 20 per cent of the Coalition's parliamentary numbers made up of females, Tony Abbott said 'there were still plenty of women in the corridors of power'.

Once again, his answer said it all. In Tony Abbott's world, he was happy with women just wandering the corridors. Perhaps cleaning them. Who knew? Either way, Tony Abbott certainly wasn't letting them in.

*

Jen Byrne and I had been mates for years going back to my old days at *Cleo* and hers at *60 Minutes*, when we would regularly run into each other at the gym in Park Street. She and her partner, Andrew Denton, had a son, Connor, not long after our Jake had been born, and as always in our belief that 'it takes a village to raise a child', Jen and Andrew had become very important members of our village.

Over the years we'd shared family holidays, many late-night dinners, compared notes on parenting, celebrated triumphs and given each other support in the tough times. We'd even worked out, if a pandemic ever came, where we would go and how we would get through it. Andrew and Jen had become two of our most treasured friends.

So, when an invitation arrived to attend the premiere of *Fifty Shades of Grey*, the film version of a book series that had sold a motza around the world, I asked Jen if she wanted to come with me to see what all the hot and steamy fuss was about. Jen was one of the most voracious readers I knew, but even as the host of the ABC's *The Book Club* program, Jen had never delved into E.L. James' tomes either, so we both came to the big screening with no particular expectations.

From virtually the opening credits, we could hardly believe our ears and eyes. All around us, women were groaning, then laughing, then groaning again, as the lead character, Anastacia Steele, completely submitted to the aggressive, controlling, jealous Christian Grey. Grey is a stalker of the highest order, who turns up at her work uninvited, breaks into her apartment, forces his way into her friendship group, and, when he crashes an afternoon spent with her mother, insists she describe him as her boyfriend. This was a relationship all about power – him having it, her having none. Jen and I couldn't believe it. This was the stuff that had been taking the world by storm?

So, the next morning I asked our new executive producer Mark Calvert if I could do a review of the appalling, downright dangerous drivel I had seen the night before. Sadly, Tommy had now left us to become executive producer at *60 Minutes*. When I gave Mark an idea of what I wanted to say, he said the show was already packed and it was a 'maybe'. By 7.40 it was time for Richard Wilkins' regular Thursday movie review, and when he gave *Fifty Shades* two stars out of five, I became even more fired up than ever. I now had something to say about that as well.

By 8am, when I asked again, Mark said he still wasn't sure if he could find the time, but to go ahead and prepare something. Then, just before the close of the show, I was told I had one minute to say whatever I wanted to say …

So, as we came back from the break, with Sylvia and Richard joining us on the couch, Karl briefly set things up, and introduced me …

'Welcome back … and it's now over to Lisa for her review of *Fifty Shades of Grey*.'

'Thanks Karl, because, yeah, I've got something that I want to get off my chest. Now, my husband had a big smile on his face last night when he discovered that I was heading off to see *Fifty Shades of Grey* …'

Karl: 'Why did he have a smile on his face?'

'Shoosh! This was the book series, after all, that left women all over the world wanting more … if you know what I mean. Sure, I was one of the few women I know who hadn't read the books, but hey, with 100 million copies sold, it must make a good movie, right?'

Karl: 'Right!'

'Wrong! *Fifty Shades of Grey* is, quite simply, the worst movie I've ever seen. With a script that makes Mills & Boon read like bleedin' Dickens, and lines like "I don't do romance!" Jamie Dornan as Christian Grey is the thirty-something jerk of a billionaire who never seems to work! An emotionally crippled narcissist no-one could love. Meanwhile, Dakota Johnson is the one-dimensional, lip-biting (could someone get that girl a *Chapstick*!), pathetic Anastasia Steele, who for no discernible reason falls in love with the aforementioned jerk and single-handedly sells women across the world short. Yes, *Fifty Shades of Grey* is more appalling than appealing. It's domestic violence dressed up as erotica. And if there is one thing this movie is not, it's erotic.'

Karl: 'Say it, sister!!'

Richard Wilkins: 'So, did you like it?'

'One star out of five, Dickie, and that's only because of the excellent choc-top I consoled myself with later. And I know you're wondering as to Pete, and no, he didn't get lucky last night … because after two hours of complete drivel, I need more than a choc-top to pop my corn.'

Sylvia: 'Amen, sister!!!'

I then asked Richard where the heck his two stars came from, to which he replied, 'Well, I thought the soundtrack was pretty good …'

*

'Mum, you've made it!' Jake was living on campus at Sydney Uni these days and on this Friday night, home for the weekend. But as he was sitting on the lounge, his computer open on his lap, he couldn't quite believe what he was seeing.

'Mum, your *Fifty Shades of Grey* video is at number one globally on Reddit and Lad Bible!' Apparently that was a good thing. And Louis agreed: 'Honestly, Mum, you don't understand ... that is seriously cool.'

According to Louis, both sites were huge with young guys, and for me that bit was seriously cool. If that meant some of those messages from the video – which in 36 hours had had a combined eight million views – reached a young male audience about how it's not OK for a man to stalk a woman, harass her, and isolate her from her friends and family, then that was a great thing. Good relationships are built on trust, respect and consent, and *Fifty Shades of Grey* had none of that.

Next morning, I woke up bleary-eyed, as I always did on a Saturday, grateful for the weekend and the luxury of waking up when the sun and my body thought I naturally should. I then checked my emails for the ratings, as usual, just after 9am. Another good number, and yes! we had won again. *Today*'s winning streak felt unstoppable.

There amongst the rest of my emails, though, was one from an address I didn't recognise. It was from Arianna Huffington, the powerhouse behind the hugely popular *Huffington Post* news site. I had no idea how she'd got my address, but she was writing to say that she had seen the *Fifty Shades* video. She loved it. In fact, she'd recently been in Australia, scoping for people and offices in order to open a bureau of her now eponymous site. She wanted me to be its Australian editor-at-large.

I was thrilled at the prospect of working with such a dynamic woman, but wholly unsure how Nine would feel about it. The network had next to no digital presence editorially, and in a meeting my manager Nick Fordham had with Nine News boss Darren Wick, he recognised that. Far from unhappy, Wick said that both he and CEO David Gyngell were thrilled that I'd got the offer and immediately encouraged me to take it with their full blessing.

He believed it was a brilliant way for me to spread *Today*'s reach across different audiences. Wick was a former executive producer of *Today* and knew only too well the hard work that went into the show, and he was desperate for us to finally get the show to number one. As Darren told Nick, everything helps. The deal was for me to write a column every month over the next three years.

*

It was a lazy Saturday afternoon in August 2015. I'd been up early as Billi's school water polo team had an important match, and we had to travel over to Drummoyne for a fairly chilly 8am start by the harbour.

Now, Karl was on the phone. I almost didn't pick up when it rang, because for years now, even though I had his number, Karl had been coming up as 'No Caller ID'. The last thing I felt like dealing with was a pesky marketing call, or some kind of random spam alert. But for no particular reason I had a feeling it was Karl.

'Hey, darl, great numbers, again!' he said. He was right. We'd won another week.

'We are smashing this!' he continued. 'Look, just wondering where you're up to with your negotiations on your contract? Mine's up at the end of the year, and yours is too, right?'

It was, and I told him I was pretty much nowhere at that point. Nick and I had talked, but we agreed that with the numbers on the show still rising, and with word that Gyng was in the middle of some pretty heavy network negotiations, Nick would hold off for another few weeks until the time to talk to Gyng was right.

'That's good, because you and I know we are stronger together, right?' he said. I was surprised, because Karl had never talked to me about his negotiations before; but now, suddenly, he seemed to want it all out in the open.

Karl said that with Georgie gone, and Ben having left to concentrate more on his radio career outside of Nine, we were the heart and soul of the show. Without us, he said, the network would be screwed. They needed us like never before. He wanted us to present to Nine as one entity, an unbreakable duo, with a dual contract on equal pay.

'I think we should do a *Friends*-style pact and go into this as a combined force. We come as a package. What do you reckon?'

He was referring to the deal the cast of the top-rating US sitcom *Friends* had so famously sealed when they decided, after their second top-rating season, to no longer negotiate their TV contracts separately, because even though some in the cast appeared to have bigger profiles, it was the combined chemistry of all six that made it so magical.

I was surprised and flattered he thought that about us. Karl had always been one to run his own race and play his cards very close to his chest. The ratings didn't lie, though. We were regularly winning, so I told Karl to call Nick, so the two of them could chat through his idea.

Karl immediately organised lunch, and when I spoke to Nick afterwards, he confirmed that Karl was indeed red-hot to do this. It was on. Karl promised to get back to Nick with a plan. So, we waited. Nick called Karl a couple of times to follow up, but the silence was suddenly as deafening as it was telling.

The first we knew that the plan was no longer in play was when we read it in the press. Along with the rest of the country.

Karl was now in negotiations with Channel 7. Solo. Again.

CHAPTER TWENTY-NINE

A changing of the guard

'I want to tell my daughters, that the value in their bodies has
nothing to do with being seen. The value in their bodies is in
how they will use their legs and lungs to carry them out into
the world, and their hearts and brains to think and feel.'
— Samantha Hunt, 'What Is a Teenage Girl?',
The New York Times, 22 January 2021

ALLISON BADEN-CLAY. MASA VUKOTIC. Jill Meagher. Stephanie
Scott. Lisa Harnum. Warriena Wright. They were all women
we didn't know, but women whose names had entered the headlines
and broken our nation's heart, because of the horrific way in which
their lives had so tragically ended — at the hands of violent men.

Violence against women in Australia had reached epidemic
proportions. Sixty-two women had died so far that year, and it was
only September. That was close to two Australian women dying
every week.

On 11 September 2015 — three days after Gold Coast mother
Tara Brown was bashed to death by her ex-partner in her upturned
car, after he had forced her off the road — I called on the *Today*
show for Tony Abbott to stand down as Minister for Women. I
needn't have bothered. Because the following Tuesday, Karl and I
hosted the show from the frosty lawns in front of Parliament House
to cover yet another imminent leadership spill.

And just like that, Tony Abbott was gone – making history in the process as Australia's shortest-serving elected prime minister since Harold Holt.

Malcolm Turnbull had now been handed the keys to The Lodge – becoming our fifth new prime minister in as many years.

*

Prime ministers weren't the only change that was in the air. Our CEO David Gyngell was leaving the network. I was genuinely sorry to see him go. I'd first met Gyng, as he was known, back in his younger days as a successful Bondi surf shop owner and James Packer's best mate. He'd been an inspiring leader at Nine – a passionate programmer and a healing force after Nine's rocky years under the heavy-handed influence of John Alexander. He knew how to look after people, and always got in touch when he thought you'd done a good job.

His replacement was announced as Hugh Marks, a former Nine legal counsel who was returning to the network after running TV production company Southern Star.

Marks was arriving at a time when the headlines were ramping up once again about Karl feeling restless. One story in *The Australian* newspaper declared that Karl was going 'part-time' on *Today*. It was the first I'd heard anything about it. An interview he'd done with Brisbane's *Sunday Mail* quoted Karl as saying he wanted to do 'more news-based stuff. A late show would be tremendous fun too, something more entertainment focused, not like *The Verdict*.'

The Verdict was a weekly panel show Karl had just started to host, along with his regular *60 Minutes* assignments – the former a rough attempt to replicate the success of *Q&A* on the ABC. It was also, I suspected, an attempt by Nine to arrest Karl's wandering eye during contract negotiations. Regular guests on *The Verdict* included politicians Mark Latham, Pauline Hanson, Bob Katter and Jacqui Lambie. But despite a big audience lead-in from *The Block*, the ratings were not what anyone had hoped for.

Meanwhile, most mornings, the papers were providing helpful

updates on what were becoming known as 'the annual end-of-year Karl rumours'.

The *Sydney Morning Herald* said that Karl was negotiating with Nine, the *Daily Telegraph* said that he was in talks with Seven, while *The Australian* said he was talking to both, and that 'there is a strong possibility Karl won't be returning to head the program with Lisa Wilkinson in 2016'. Karl seemed to be talking to everyone but me. When I finally addressed the issue one morning and asked him if any of it was true, Karl's reply was simple: 'All bullshit, darl.'

Whatever the truth, I had my own contract to sort out, and it was now clear I wouldn't be doing any of it with Karl. In any case, Marks had told Nick he didn't think there was any urgency to closing a deal with me. Being so new to the job, he was still looking at budgets, and didn't want to rush into anything, particularly while there was 'a bit to sort with Karl'.

Of course. By early December, Karl had already headed off overseas on his annual six-week holiday and, in his wake, left behind a rumour mill in overdrive. The smart money was on Karl going to Seven.

No matter, we had a show to get on with, and all this speculation about Karl not wanting to be on the show anymore was not helping anyone – least of all, our viewers. Both Ben Fordham and David Campbell were Karl's regular fill-ins, and I loved working with both of them. Maybe that arrangement with one of them was about to become more permanent? I simply didn't know.

*

In the still wee hours of this Tuesday morning, 8 December 2015, I had assumed my usual position in the Channel 9 makeup chair, one eye closed as my regular rust-coloured eyeshadow was being applied, while the other perused the morning news sites. And then I saw it. I couldn't believe my eye …

> KARL Stefanovic is set to take home more than twice what his *Today* show co-host Lisa Wilkinson will earn in 2016.

Stefanovic is set to reject an offer from Seven and renew his longstanding contract with Nine, according to the *Herald Sun*, having landed a $6-million multi-year deal.

It is understood he will earn $2 million a year for three years – effectively almost doubling his salary.

Media analyst Steve Allen said Stefanovic's reported new wage was 'kind of outrageous'.

'If this is true, I'm just gobsmacked,' Mr Allen of Fusion Strategy told *news.com.au*. 'Not just the salary difference, but the quantum of what he has managed to get.'

The 41-year-old will reportedly continue his transition into prime time on Nine with his new panel show *The Verdict* being commissioned for another series in 2016.

Industry sources have said that Stefanovic's multi-year deal would place him at the top of the Aussie TV heap.

In 2012, Stefanovic negotiated a $1.3 million deal with Nine, which more than doubled his $500,000 salary in his 2009 contract. Meanwhile, Wilkinson was reported to be earning $750,000 in 2012.

The three-year contracts for both anchors, who have shared the *Today* show panel for eight years, expired this year and were up for renegotiation. It's not known what Wilkinson's new contract looks like.

Mr Allen described negotiations between networks and managers as 'a game of poker'.

If those numbers were true, Karl had played it hard and won – big time. That new contract would surely put an end to the rumblings about him 'being over' the *Today* show. As far as I could tell, he now had everything he'd ever wanted. His own prime-time show in *The Verdict*, plenty of time away from the *Today* show desk and those early alarms to film stories for *60 Minutes*, and enough money 'to finally buy the family home by the water he'd long dreamt of.

*

Well, that was it then. No more school lunches to make, no more Easter hat parades, no more late nights scrambling to help with school projects, no more parent–teacher nights, no more end-of-year concerts, no more HSC angst.

Billi, our baby, was a baby no more. She had left school, her exams done, and just as Jake was leaving Sydney University – the same uni Louis, too, had been attending for the past year – Billi was about to begin her own student life there. With our children all now adults, Pete and I felt like we were entering the next phase of our lives together.

And in this last gasp of 2015, we were, as ever, all looking forward to our annual family Christmas at Newport. All the cousins were of course now grown, too, and conversing as adults who genuinely delighted in being together, along with all their aunts and uncles.

And sure enough, no sooner had all the Fitzes arrived on site than the board games, beach trips, singing, guitar-playing and talking till late into the night began.

For the past eight years, though, there'd always been a small interruption for me at Newport, as no sooner had I arrived and settled in than I had to duck away on Christmas Eve to co-host Channel 9's *Carols by Candlelight* in Melbourne, first with Karl, and now for the past four years, alongside my good buddy David Campbell.

For decades I'd watched Ray Martin take to the stage for this magical annual TV institution. Now, I was lucky enough to have that same role. It never failed to take my breath away as I walked out onto that stage and saw the candlelit faces of so many kids, wide-eyed and waiting, and in some cases desperately fighting sleep, until the big moment when Santa himself arrived. I knew the house back at Newport would be alive with a similar kind of buzz as the whole army of Fitzes prepared for the excitement that Christmas morning would bring. Even now with most of them in their early twenties, the Christmas traditions continued, including leaving pillowcases at the end of their beds ready for filling should Santa deem them as having been on the 'nice' list that year.

When the kids were really young, I always found that I was much better than Pete at communicating with Santa over what went into those pillowcases each year. Then, when I started heading off to do *Carols* on the very night that Santa made his drop, it became a job I had no choice but to entrust to Pete.

Many were the texts I sent as I headed to Melbourne on the 24th, with strict instructions from Santa for Pete, on who was to get what.

'Trust me, it'll be alright on the night ...' was always Pete's response. I was never so optimistic.

More than once on Christmas morning, when they were younger, the kids had come to me, confused, about why half the presents they'd asked Santa for had appeared in their brother's or sister's sack.

'Don't worry, darling,' I remember saying on one particular occasion, before shooting a look at Pete who was clearly trying to pretend he hadn't heard a word, 'it's probably just those people up the road leaving too much whiskey out for Santa again. He must have got a little confused. But good on you for *sharing*, sweetheart ...'

I was always sorry to be missing the Christmas Eve fun at Newport, but at least Nine were kind enough to charter a small plane each year for all the artists from Sydney to get back to their families in time for Christmas morning.

Once we'd landed, it was then a 45-minute drive up to Newport to grab an hour or two's sleep before dawn would break and the fun would begin: presents exchanged, photos taken, before a quick swim at the beach and a Christmas lunch that would stretch late into the afternoon.

With so little sleep, it was exhausting, but the loveliest kind of exhausting. As ever, I would look around at these happy family scenes and marvel at the extraordinary good fortune of my life: to be experiencing such precious times with all these wonderfully good and decent people, surrounded by so much genuine love.

Mum, now nudging near 90, was always warmly welcomed to Christmas lunch by the extended Fitz clan. Often, she'd sit there, not saying much, just with her hand on the head of the other old lady there with us – our blessed boxer dog, Scout, now nudging 12 herself, whose devotion to Mum was only equalled by Mum's love in turn for her.

As the rest of us cleared up after lunch before the traditional post-Christmas-lunch nap to sleep off the turkey, ham and Christmas pudding, Mum and Scout would find a spot in the cool shade of the big old coral tree in the backyard. In her later years, there really was no greater joy in Mum's life than being with her grandchildren and seeing them grow up happy and healthy, living in the bosom of a mob who so adored them.

*

In the early days of January 2016, with Newport over for another year, Pete and I went to visit what he liked to call his 'other family' in France, the people he'd grown so close to while living and playing rugby there for four years in the mid-80s: *la famille Fourche*.

Every few years, Pete would travel back to visit, and it was always a delight to stay with them in their house overlooking the ancient village of Donzenac and across to the farmhouse Pete had lived in during his time there. I loved how much they adored '*Peterrrrr*', as they called him, and he loved them in turn: *la pere*, Jackie; *la mere*, Monique; and his two 'sisters', Manu and Carole, and their families.

Over long lunches and dreamy late-evening family dinners by the fire, Channel 9 and the *Today* show seemed such a long, long way away, which was good. As far as I knew, my new contract was still not sorted, and year's end had come and gone with no word.

Before we left, stories had even started dropping in the press suggesting that maybe my contract wouldn't be renewed. Which could mean only one thing: after the big cash splash on Karl, the network needed to save some money, and this was their way of telling me. Or something. I just didn't know ...

And right then, I wasn't sure I cared. The Fourches were such lovely people, and their lives so full of simple pleasures honed in these parts for a thousand years. They were so far from the intense and sometimes savage world of TV contract negotiations that they were a salient reminder to me of what truly mattered.

Then on our third night in 'Donza', my manager Nick called in the middle of dinner, just as we were well into Monique's famous *rosbif* and our third bottle of red, while Pete was on his fifth cup of tea.

'I'm sorry, Leese,' Nick started, 'but Nine are only offering another two years. And even though they recognise that this could be the year that *Today* wins the ratings, there's no pay rise. They asked me to tell you not to feel bad, though, because times are tough, and no-one at the network is being offered anything beyond two-year contracts.'

Well, according to *news.com.au* and that pretty well-informed 'source' about Karl's three-year deal, that bit, at least, I knew wasn't true. But anyway. I was tired of all this ... *'ow-you-say? ... bull-sheet.* Right now, I just wanted it sorted, at least for two years, and, really, I had no choice. I knew I was paid well, clearly nowhere near as well as Karl ... but whatever.

'Thanks, Nick. OK, I'll take it,' I told him, and then went back to the loving bonhomie of the Fourches, knowing that one of Carole's pretty darn fabulous *mousse au chocolat*s was on the way. And I was *more* than fine with that.

*

I suppose it was inevitable. From the moment I showed my 13-year-old Billi a copy of *Dolly* magazine, and she in return showed zero interest (and, in fact, seemed largely unaware of its very existence), I knew that *Dolly*'s future was bleak; *Cleo*'s, too. And now it had been confirmed: both monthly magazines were closing.

For two titles that had played such significant roles not only in my early life, but the lives and careers of so many other Australian women, I couldn't help but feel incredibly sad. But with the arrival of the internet, and a more immediate world of information, fashion, lifestyle and entertainment content opening up, the demise of these once much-loved titles was all but guaranteed.

Ironically, women were now consuming more content than ever before, but it was via their phones, social media and podcasts. Forget the excitement and anticipation of waiting a whole month for that brand-new issue to arrive. Now, *anything* you wanted arrived in an instant.

No longer would these once thriving publications be that trusted, informed, spirited and supportive friend to coming generations. Nor would they be that fertile breeding ground for some of the best young, ambition-fuelled journalists in the country. In my 17 wonderful years at both *Dolly* and *Cleo*, I'd worked with some of the finest. In fact, at last count, more than 20 of them had gone on to become magazine editors themselves.

Some had carved out whole new media entities, like Mia Freedman with her hugely popular Mamamia site. Deborah Thomas had become one of *The Australian Women's Weekly*'s longest-serving and most successful editors. Carlotta Moye went from fashion assistant to editor to one of the most in-demand photographers in the country. Marina Go had not only become an editor but a serious corporate player across a number of heavyweight boards. Wendy Squires, Paula Joye, Nicole Bonython-Hines, and so many more either cut their teeth or honed their considerable skills at *Cleo*, and then spread their impact across other magazines and media outlets and their audiences.

Many of those colleagues had remained dear friends of mine ... and of each other. For me, those friendships at *Dolly* and *Cleo* were just like the pages of the magazines themselves: supportive, inclusive and empowering. And I'm sure that was a big part of why our readers connected so passionately with what we produced.

We were proud to be wholly Australian. And try as others might to take over our number-one positions, no other titles ever came close.

For many of us, *Dolly* and *Cleo* had been trusted guiding hands in enormously changing times in our lives. Now they, and those times, were gone. And I was so grateful for having known them both so well.

*

Oh, for god's sake, were they serious? Right there, leading the *Daily Mail* website: I'd been busted! Not for drugs. Not for having an affair. Not for stealing. Not for parking in a disabled spot.

Nope, in the world of the *Mail*, I'd committed a crime far, far worse. And I'm sure if they'd had the power to lock me up and throw away the key (as long as their paps could get a shot of it first), then they would have.

'That's Thrifty! *Today* show's Lisa Wilkinson sports same floral blouse, just four months apart, while hosting breakfast program.'

Yes, the pretty maroon blouse with its 'strategic cut-out above the bust' (as the *Mail* had so curiously put it) that I'd worn that morning was one I'd also worn four months before – or to be more accurate, about 125 outfits ago.

I know. What *was* I thinking?

And I know what *you're* thinking – I should be outraged, right? You're thinking, what sort of 'news' website devotes time and energy to keeping a daily pictorial log of what outfits a news presenter wears when, and how often, and then comes up with 400 words calling them out?

Well, I wasn't outraged at all. In fact, I was grateful. Because they had just proven once and for all what we all knew to be true: that men and women on television are treated entirely differently. You see, I'm the gal that sat next to the guy who wore exactly the same suit on air every day for a whole year. And no-one noticed. Even more ridiculously, the *Daily Mail* had wholeheartedly applauded Karl at the time for doing it. But let a woman try that? On just *two* days, four months apart?

So, what's a girl to do? The only thing I could do under the circumstances. Mad Dog Wilkinson was going to wear that baby once again. And I did, the very next morning.

That's right: same outfit, *consecutive* days. On national TV.

And sure enough, the *Mail*'s fashion police were on to me again. 'So nice she wore it thrice!' the headline screamed, next to a picture gallery undeniably proving their forensic investigation into the matter.

So that was it. Like Karl, I had just made news broadcasting fashion history. The first and only time that any female news presenter anywhere in the Western world had ever worn the same outfit at the same news desk, *two days in a row*.

Take that, Barbara Walters and Diane Sawyer. You call yourselves trailblazers? Meh …

*

It was a day we all knew was coming, but one we had long been dreading. Our beautiful, loyal, gentle boxer dog, Scout, was gone. At 12, she was a grand and dignified old lady of 84 four-legged years.

I wasn't even remotely ready, which is crazy, because the last few months had been so tough for her, and she was clearly heading down a hill for which there was only one possible end. I guess I was hoping she could fight her way through this, just as she always had before.

When she was just an 11-week-old puppy, she'd had a terrible fall from the top of a four-metre wall at home – puppy curiosity getting the better of her – and her life should've ended then. But she defied the odds and, at great expense, the local vet managed to screw her shattered little bones back together.

But the truth is, we would have paid anything to fix her, so quickly had she become the centre of our family's universe. The vet warned us that arthritis would be a problem in old age, and he was right. In recent months her back legs had started collapsing beneath her. And most of her days were being spent in her bed, where she was happy just to watch the world gently pass by.

But any early predictions of Scout's fragility when we first got her were wrong. She was strong, surviving – beyond her leg-shattering fall – numerous bouts of cancer, a heart attack, and her regular 'escapes' into our busy neighbourhood whenever one of us accidentally left the gate open. The neighbours knew our little escapee well. And loved her.

'Found Scout up the street again, Lisa,' they would tell me more times than I can remember. 'Just popped her inside the gate for you.'

Then today, a friend dropped by around lunchtime to find none of us home, but there was Scout, standing sentinel, as she always did by the driveway, in anticipation that one of us was just about to arrive back. It didn't matter to her which one of us it was. We all received the same greeting that was her specialty: an excited boxer happy dance, a tail that almost wagged itself off, a sniff of our hand, and a sneeze of excitement.

But when Pete arrived home soon after with no Scout waiting in the driveway, he knew something was wrong. Ten minutes later he found her. There she was, lying peacefully in the dappled afternoon light thrown by the weeping mulberry tree above. It was a favourite spot whenever her old bones needed warming. Maybe she was just asleep? But then when he called her name, there was no response and ...

And I hoped with everything in my soul that her end was peaceful. That, realising she was right at the bottom of that hill, she just closed her eyes and slipped away. Anything else was too much to bear.

So that afternoon we gathered to bury her, wrapped in that same precious red-and-white quilt from the lounge in the kitchen she and the kids loved so much. We chose a patch of ground beneath the swing in our garden where, when the kids were little, they would play while Scout sat by patiently watching, protecting, and waiting her turn until they threw her a ball, had a wrestle, and had *her* time to play.

Then, as the sun started to drop in the sky and deliver us one of the most perfectly autumnal afternoons any of us can remember, Jake lowered our girl into her final resting place. She had gone peacefully. And we wept.

Mum was heartbroken. Never again would she arrive at our house to see that other grand old lady rouse herself in warm greeting. And I think she sensed that, with Scout gone, her own time, too, must be drawing near.

CHAPTER THIRTY

Winning

'It is not enough to dream. You must act. Without action,
a door is just a wall.' – J. M. Storm

IT WAS ONE OF those bitterly cold evenings in mid-August that
make you yearn for the warmer days ahead. Pete and I had just
finished cleaning up after an early dinner and I was about to get
to work on preparing questions for an interview I had with the
PM, Malcolm Turnbull, the next morning. After deposing Tony
Abbott as leader in 2015, Turnbull had successfully managed to
return the Coalition to government in the recent election, but it
was a government divided, with the Party's hard right providing a
constant background rumble of disquiet.

Turnbull was not an easy interview. As sharp as he no doubt
was, his answers always tended to take a bit of a circuitous route,
so that meant the six minutes I had with the PM – generous by
breakfast-TV standards – needed to be focused. Seven or eight tight
questions would usually do it.

With the kids all out and Pete doing some writing of his own,
I figured I should be able to get an hour or two's uninterrupted
work done, until ... I heard my phone ping with the arrival of a
text. Strangely, it was from Karl's wife, Cass – something that didn't
happen often.

Although we rarely saw each other, Cass and I always got on well, often joking that I was the on-air wife and she was the off-air one. I was aware that the success of breakfast TV demands a closeness between its hosts that other workplace colleagues rarely share – and one that real-life partners might not appreciate. Fortunately, neither Cass nor Pete ever had an issue with it.

For Cass to be sending a text on a Sunday night, though, was unusual.

I read the text and gasped. Cass wanted to let me know that Karl had moved out a few weeks before. She was worried he hadn't yet told me and didn't want me mentioning anything on air about them that might make things uncomfortable. She said it would be out there soon enough and she didn't want me being surprised.

I looked at the text again as I wandered into the lounge room, and read it out to Pete.

'They split a couple of weeks ago,' I said, still not quite believing it, 'and I hadn't even realised?'

Somehow, Karl had gone through major trauma in his personal life and hadn't even blinked on air. I wasn't sure if it was testament to his professionalism, or me possibly just being so clueless about his life off-air. After all these years together.

'Are you sure that's right?' Pete asked, looking just as shocked. 'Surely you had some idea something was up?' I simply didn't.

Karl and Cass had been together for something like two decades – he the young handsome reporter, she the accomplished ABC newsreader he was so in awe of, who, as he'd always warmly acknowledged, had then given it all up to raise their kids and support him on his rocketing rise to the top.

Like most of us, Karl and Cass didn't have a Hallmark-greeting-card marriage, but they had just bought a waterfront property a month or two before and he had just signed a massive deal with the network. I presumed everything was great. The maths, the timing, the incredible suddenness of it all just didn't add up.

Karl obviously had his reasons, but I was sad for him, for Cass and for the kids, so I called Cass just to make sure she was OK and assured her I would of course respect her wishes.

But what was I to do with all this when I turned up at work the next morning? I didn't want to make it awkward for Karl. Whatever his reasons, I knew he wouldn't have made this decision lightly.

So, I said nothing the next morning about what I knew. And for three and a half hours, neither did he. I looked for signs. Of something. Anything. A moment of sad pause. A missed one-liner. A drop in his energy. A stumble. A whispered, 'Can I talk to you after the show?' But there was nothing. In fact, we had a great show. Karl was in fabulous form.

What I knew for sure, however, was that while right now Karl was managing to keep a lid on things, when word got out, this was going to be a huge story. This was simply the calm before what was going to be a massive media storm. The ripple effects would be enormous.

How long could a story like Karl's separation possibly hold?

I texted him randomly a couple of times after work and over the next few weekends to see if he wanted to go and have a coffee or a drink, but Karl was never great at getting back to me, so I just left it. Then, almost four weeks after that text from Cass, and just a few days before the news broke, Karl texted me. He and Cass were having a break, he said.

I didn't tell him that I'd known for weeks, but just said I was very sorry to hear it and hoped he was OK.

Then on Sunday 18 September, the floodgates opened and the story was splashed over newspapers across the country. Karl's face was everywhere. It's fair to say *Today*'s viewers were more than merely shocked. The tabloids went berserk. And social media melted down.

Heightening the mainstream media interest was the fact that, just as it all broke loose, we were closing in on beating *Sunrise* for the first time in 13 years, and we were right on the cusp of that golden TV number of winning 21 weeks out of a possible 40 over the official ratings year. All going well, we could finally get there by early October, just three weeks away.

How Karl got through the intensity of the following weeks, I'll never know, but every day he kept turning up at work, always focused, always professional, never giving anything away. And every day the paparazzi were following him. Everywhere. In the morning as we arrived in the dark, there they would be, in the shadows. When Karl left, suddenly a line-up of cars with their darkened windows would pull out from the kerb right behind him.

The weekly women's magazines found they'd hit a goldmine with the story and were splashing it on the cover almost every week. Blessedly, there were quite a few 'We Love Australia' trips planned for the show over the next few weeks, which we all hoped would give Karl a bit of a break from everything, but somehow, despite our itinerary being confidential, the paps always knew exactly which flights we were booked on. And sure enough, there they were at every airport, ready to pounce. To walk beside Karl and make your way through any of the big airports was to find yourself in the firing line, too. It was an instant education in the way this whole organised tabloid machine actually worked.

But after weeks of photos of the newly separated Karl all looking the same – head down, jeans and a T-shirt, sunglasses on, just going about his business – the insatiable appetite for new material and different photos only grew. And the paps changed their game.

At one airport, as we came through the security doors, I heard a pap continually goading him, 'Hey Karl, why did you leave your wife?' It was disgusting to witness, but Karl didn't flinch; he just kept walking. He refused to give them what they wanted – a blow-up. His restraint was extraordinary.

I, on the other hand, wanted to yell at them to back off, and it took every bit of strength I had in me not to. Sensing my fury, Karl just mumbled under his breath next to me, 'Don't react.' I didn't, knowing that the photos would then be all about some ridiculous 'Tensions flare between Karl & Lisa' story. Anything to sell more photos, get more clicks, sell more magazines. And make them all a fortune.

*

'We've done it! Dickie's at 1pm.'

It was a text from our executive producer Mark, and it came at 9.01am on Saturday, 22 October 2016. Twenty-one unassailable ratings weeks were now ours. That meant that whatever happened for the rest of the year, *Sunrise* couldn't beat us.

The *Today* show was back at number one in the ratings – for the first time since 2003. I was over the moon – and thrilled for everyone in our hard-working, talented team around the country.

'Dickie's' was Richard Wilkins' house in Cremorne on Sydney's lower North Shore … a house that had recently achieved celebrity folklore status for its not one, but *two* inground swimming pools – one in the front garden, and one in the back. A house, too, that had become party central for any kind of *Today* show celebration. Engagements, birthdays, anniversaries, Christmases, even Fridays, were all celebrated here in Richard's big open-plan living room with its very own well-stocked, nightclub-style 'bar room' next door, both of which spilled out onto his sprawling pool deck overlooking the waters of Middle Harbour.

Never, however, had I seen a happier or more packed *Today* show celebration than this. Almost everyone from our Sydney-based production team had raced to be there.

As soon as I saw Karl, we hugged. It was a hug for the ages. It was a hug for all those early mornings; all those late nights; the good times; the tense times; the moments of frustration; the triumphs; the exhaustion; the many, many, many laughs; and it was confirmation that almost ten years earlier Karl had been absolutely right …

As he'd said to me in those first days as we sat together at that desk, 'For this to work, then *we* have to work … We have to do good work and support each other … and the rest will come.'

And it finally had.

*

Meanwhile, there was another guy in the news who was soaking up a good portion of the headlines: Donald Trump. Somehow, despite a growing list of scandals, questionable tax records, a loose association with the truth, a close association with Russia, a well-documented adulterous history and his greatest fame coming from a reality show, there was a good chance he would become the next president of the United States.

So, with the US election about to get underway, Nine sent Karl to the US to cover what was turning out to be a reality show to beat them all.

In the election lead-up, many thought the chances of Trump making it all the way to the Oval Office would take a severe hit when a tape emerged capturing him bragging that when you were famous enough, you didn't need a woman's consent before making sexual advances.

'You can grab them by the pussy, they love it. When you're a star, they let you do it,' Trump said in the recording. 'You can do anything.'

Despite that, and against every prediction to the contrary, on 8 November, Trump romped in to become the 45th President of the United States.

It was quite the election for Karl to be covering, but watching from home, I could see that Karl looked tired. The intensity of the past few months were starting to show, and not long afterwards, Nine's Darren Wick put out a statement to say that Karl was taking an extended break.

'Obviously what he's working through with his family situation … he needs to have a break and just rest and spend time with his family. He's going to do that and come back fresh next year.'

It followed news that *The Verdict* would cease production and, in its place, Karl would host a new series called *This Time Next Year*. Based on a UK format, the series would examine everyday Australians achieving monumental personal goals – losing weight, overcoming a setback, or falling in love – over the course of a year. It would mean that, along with his *60 Minutes* commitments, Karl would have to regularly take time away from *Today*; and, as always, Ben and David would be waiting in the wings.

We were all starting to get used to that.

CHAPTER THIRTY-ONE

Coming up trumps

'Some guy said to me: "Don't you think you're too old
to sing rock n' roll?" I said: "You'd better check with
Mick Jagger."' – Cher

I T WAS UNMISTAKABLE. THERE was a seismic shift happening for women across the world. For many, Trump's ascendancy to the position of US president was deeply offensive and the final straw.

On 21 January 2017, the day after Trump's inauguration, the Women's March rallies said it all. Four hundred and eight marches in the US, and 168 in 81 other countries; more than seven million took part around the world. In the US, it was the largest single-day protest in history. According to the organisers, the goal was 'to send a bold message to our new administration on their first day in office, and to the world, that women's rights are human rights'.

Women wanted the world to know that they were through with playing nice, keeping quiet, being good girls, not rocking the boat. They were through with feeling unseen and unheard. If a self-confessed 'pussy' grabber could be voted in as the next leader of the free world, then they no longer had anything to lose. At those marches, women were mad as hell and they just weren't going to take it anymore.

It was time to lift the veil of secrecy and admit there was a common thread to so many of the issues that women faced on a daily basis. Trump's rise became the lightning rod for it all. In Australia, domestic violence, workplace inequality, women's safety, sexual harassment, maternity-leave funding, childcare, female homelessness, and the woeful lack of women in our parliament were top of the agenda.

The gender pay gap, too, had become a major issue, and nowhere more than in Australia. On average, in 2017, there was a $26,000 pay gap between men and women working full-time. And it was happening in every industry and occupation at every level. Even for those with a degree, that wage discrimination began the minute women graduated from university.

Young male dentists in their first job earnt, on average, $14,000 more than their female counterparts; male lawyers pocketed $4300 more; while young male architects got an extra $9000. Women also earnt less in non-managerial roles — $31 an hour compared with $35 for men. Even in that bastion of fair-mindedness, the ABC, the salaries of its highest-profile broadcasters were mistakenly published, showing that, without exception, females were openly paid less to do the same work as their male colleagues. The comparisons were damning.

So, if men were paid more than women for comparable jobs at the national broadcaster — a publicly funded organisation that trumpets its support of social equality — what chance did women in the wider world have?

Yep, the gender pay gap was everywhere.

*

By the fourth week of January, Karl and I were both back from holidays, and together again at the *Today* show desk. In our absence, Pete and Sylvia had been filling in; and with the two now on the countdown to their 1 April wedding, the viewers were loving it, and both of them.

Karl's break had been a particularly long one this time around — almost two months in fact, culminating in a quick trip to cover Trump's inauguration on his way home, a gig he had clearly relished.

The break appeared to have done him a whole lot of good, as he'd returned with a genuine spring in his step. The hope was that we could make last year's ratings win two in a row, although things had faltered a little in those final months of 2016 with all the off-camera distractions we were facing. Karl was full of stories of his holiday and Trump's inauguration. He also mentioned during one of the commercial breaks that he'd love to talk to me after the show. 'Can we meet upstairs in the office?'

As ever, Karl played his cards close to his chest when it came to his private life. His belief was that when you know someone too well and share too much, 'in jokes' are a hazard. It was true that we could certainly still surprise each other on air, so maybe he was right.

When I got to Karl's office, I found him as happy and relaxed as I'd ever seen him. He said that he felt like a brand-new person.

'I've just never felt so sure of where I'm going,' he said. Being overseas and getting away from all that intense scrutiny really did seem to have lifted a huge weight off his shoulders.

'And I've met someone,' he whispered.

Well, that certainly just took a turn. And explained a lot. That smile he had on his face got even bigger.

'Her name is Jasmine,' he said, and as he handed his phone to me, it was clear he couldn't wait to show me a picture. He was literally beaming, and I suspected that even he couldn't believe this 'former model, who's now a shoe designer based in LA' was in his life. He was, he said, madly in love.

'And,' he added, 'she's from Brisbane!' For Karl, being the passionate Queenslander he is, that detail was the cherry on top. The plan, he told me, was for 'Jas' to eventually return from LA, but for now it was a long-distance romance until he could get back over there.

'At least, if you do that,' I said, 'you can escape the prying eyes of the paps back here.'

Three weeks later, Karl was photographed on a luxury boat on Sydney Harbour. The pictures were blurry, taken from what must have been a drone. There was Karl. There was champagne. And there was a beautiful blonde who, it quickly became clear, was Jas.

The media exploded as never before. For all Karl's happiness, the next few months became a nightmare of headlines, pap photos, and speculation around the divorce. Some days I could see that he was really struggling – while remaining admirably stoic – with the constant spotlight upon him.

At one point, Karl was photographed in LA with Jas joyously embracing him at the airport, at the same time as Cass was photographed moving house.

On *The Kyle and Jackie O Show* one morning, the radio hosts spoke to entertainment reporter Peter Ford about Karl's split and the impact it was having on his career.

'His personal ratings – and Nine has done research to confirm this – are right down the toilet,' Ford said. 'Women are angry at him.'

When Kyle professed amazement, Jackie said she knew exactly why women were so angry.

'This is what a lot of women would think, Kyle. This is a lovely lady who's stood by him for years. They have a family and they saw him leave her.

'They think he's just left her for some young 20-year-old and he's cavorting around, kissing her, cuddling her, for everyone to see.'

She said that Karl leaving his wife and starting a relationship with a younger woman struck a jarring chord with many Australian women.

'They believe that could happen to me,' she said. 'They look at Karl and they're blaming him. And it probably will take quite some time to repair that.'

As to that research Peter Ford had spoken about, the entire *Today* team, including Karl, had been asked to attend a presentation of it in a very awkward meeting on the third floor. Each of us was given a full dossier detailing it all, and Jackie was right. It made for very uncomfortable reading.

*

It was so lovely to see the old gang again. It was our third school reunion in the many decades that had passed since we'd all left Campbelltown High, and a few years too since I had last managed to catch up with my high school friends Michelle, Therese, Chris, Julie and Sue. We were scattered all around the country these days, so for old times' sake we decided to make a sleepover of it, and grabbed a few rooms at the Campbelltown Catholic Club where the big night was being held.

It was going to be a great turnout, with many enthusiastic RSVPs, including one from one name in particular that leapt out at me. Raelene Schroeder, my long-ago tormentor, was coming along for the first time. I wondered what it would be like to be face to face with her again. Her name alone still gave me a tightness in my gut and an all-too-familiar feeling of vulnerability – even all these years on.

What kind of woman had Raelene become? I wondered. Would she be at all self-aware about the teenage terror she had wrought on so many? Would she regret it? I was interested, too, to see where life had taken her.

From the moment all my old friends and I checked into our rooms on the afternoon of the reunion, it was like time had stood still. We were all suddenly 16 again – all the old jokes were still funny, and we were still swapping shoes and clothes, but now, instead of talking about boys, we were talking about our kids, and in Sue's case, cooing over photos of her beautiful grandkids.

By the time we arrived at the celebration itself, dozens of our former schoolmates had already grabbed a drink. Thankfully, with almost 40 years' worth of living under our old school belts, the organisers, Geoff and Peter – two of the loveliest guys at school – suggested we all wear name tags to help jog our memories, as we all tried to identify faces, some of which were harder to place than others.

Inevitably, we gathered around the memory wall of old photos we'd all been invited to contribute to. The laughter, as we looked at those faded images of the baby faces we all once had, was infectious.

Then, as we stood in small groups and the party pies and crackers were handed around, Geoff and Peter welcomed us all with a short speech, including messages from some of our old schoolfriends that weren't able to make it. Then they read out a list of those we had sadly lost over the years.

It was all over quickly, and with no other formal proceedings or sit-down dinner planned, it looked as though people were thinking of drifting off, with many never having moved out of the small groups they'd been standing in.

Sensing the night was about to come to an abrupt end, Geoff asked me if, with all my years of practice, I wouldn't mind grabbing the microphone and interviewing a few people so we could hear about their lives and what they were up to.

Of course, Geoff! I decided to make my way around the room, so no-one would miss out and we could hear from everyone who was there.

And then I saw her, as one of the late arrivals. It was Raelene, by the bar, with one of her old support crew and chief henchwomen from back in the day, Jenny. Ah well, I suppose it had to happen …

It was wonderful to hear the many stories of the lives of our old schoolmates. Some – often those who were the quiet ones at school – had gone on to have brilliant careers as doctors, scientists, nurses and teachers. Others were simply enjoying watching their children and grandchildren grow up in this very different world we were all now living in.

Then I noticed something: every time I got close to Raelene and Jenny, they would quickly move away. Every so often, they would start talking loudly amongst themselves while others were in the middle of telling their stories. It was incredibly rude … and a couple of times I stopped and patiently waited for Raelene and Jenny to stop talking before we could continue.

Funnily enough, by the time I finally got to them, neither was all that interested in talking *into* the microphone.

It was quite something, after so long, to be this close to a woman I had once crumbled at the mere sight of. I could feel my heart almost beating out of my chest and I hoped that no-one noticed as I drew a deep, deep breath.

'So, Raelene, what's going on in your world these days?' I asked her, trying to sound casual, while taking in every aspect of that still very pretty face that had for so long been etched in my memory.

'Not much ... Living in Queensland, that's about it,' she said, looking anywhere but at me. And that *was* about it. She really didn't want to talk, and there was no use me pushing it.

Jenny was similarly uninterested in having much of a conversation with me – though she did tell me she had quite a few kids, and showed her *extreme* displeasure when I mentioned she must now be a grandma. I quickly moved on to the next person, proud of myself that I'd got through the encounter.

By now, there was only a handful left to chat to ... but none of us was prepared for what came next.

Gary had always been a gentle, quiet guy in class, and when I asked him about his life, he mentioned that his wife, Pam, who was sitting by his side, had been recently diagnosed with cancer, and the prognosis was not good.

Pam had attended nearby Camden High – a school that, it had been recently discovered, was built on the toxic site of an abandoned gasworks – and she was now one of many former students taking legal action after being variously diagnosed with cancers and unexplained tumours, or having children born with disabilities. It was a heartbreaking story, and everyone looked to Pam with enormous sympathy, until ...

'Ha-ha-ha-ha-ha-ha-ha,' came from the back of the room.

Everyone turned. Who on earth could possibly be so insensitive as to laugh out loud as such a tale of tragedy was being told?

Of course. It was Raelene and Jenny, who perhaps hadn't been listening and were lost in their own, no doubt riotous, conversation. Once again, I waited. After a moment or so, they stopped. I turned back to Pam and apologised on behalf of everyone, and she continued to tell the harrowing story of the many Camden High students who were suffering on so many levels.

But again: 'Ha-ha-ha-ha-ha-ha-ha ...'

This time I'd had enough. I quietly excused myself from Pam and Gary, slowly stood up from the chair I had been sitting in as we talked, and without even thinking, shouted, 'Raelene Schroeder and Jenny Levenson, would you two just *shut the FUCK up!*'

There was silence.

Stunned silence.

Everyone – most all of me – was a bit shocked that I had said such a thing. Especially so directly into a microphone.

I was a little unsure what to do next, but suddenly applause broke out – the strongest of it from those who knew best just how much I had suffered at the hands of those two, all those years ago.

Whatever else, it really did shut them up, for both turned on their heels and headed for the ladies room. Perhaps for a smoko, just like old times.

I didn't care. I wanted to move on … and was a little embarrassed that I'd lost my cool so publicly.

But after almost 40 years, I figured they had it coming.

*

Friday, 26 May 2017 was a red-letter day for me and one I couldn't quite believe had arrived.

It officially marked a whole decade of that 3am alarm.

Lunch that day was a small celebration at Catalina restaurant overlooking the waters of Rose Bay in Sydney's East. It probably wasn't the best choice of venue for Karl, as this was a restaurant well known to the paparazzi. So, with Karl ducking in early to try to avoid them, all the pap photos out the front ended up being of me with Ben Fordham. No matter. I was pleased at least that Karl had shown up.

As did so many of my long-time colleagues and friends at the network: Liz Hayes, Tracy Grimshaw, David Campbell, Georgie Gardner, Deb Knight and Sylvia, not long back from her recent stunning wedding and honeymoon with new hubby, Pete, in the Southern Highlands.

Nine's CEO, Hugh Marks, was also there and gave a short, cheery speech, albeit one devoid of any personal detail, because to that point I think I'd only met him twice – once in passing in the foyer at Nine just after he'd joined, and then again at a Christmas gathering at Georgie Gardner's house, where I discovered the two were good friends and neighbours.

The next day I got a lovely message from comedian Charlie Pickering, who had obviously seen the reports of the anniversary lunch, and texted to congratulate me on making ten years.

Charlie was a former co-host of Channel 10's *The Project* who had sat alongside Carrie Bickmore and Dave Hughes for five years, but was now hosting his own show on the ABC, *The Weekly*.

The Weekly is a brilliantly mish-mashed satirical take on the week's news, mixed with feature interviews, the comic genius of Kitty Flanagan, and Tom Gleeson's unmissable, excruciatingly excoriating segment, 'Hard Chat'. The five-minute segment had a committed cult following, mostly tuning in to see which celebrity would be silly enough to think they could ever take Tom on in a battle of wits and think they could win. Many had tried. Often it was a mistake. *Big* mistake. *Huge.* Because, in the end, Tom always won, through his exquisite talent for speaking truth to celebrity. It was viewing that was as uncomfortable as it was compelling.

Charlie had been after me for more than a year to come on the show as his interview guest. I was a huge fan and thrilled to be asked, but Darren Wick just wouldn't have it. We were banned from appearing on other networks. Or at least I was. Karl had made it onto 'Hard Chat', but as I later learnt, he did it without checking with the Nine bosses first. Karl, as always, running his own race, a race he always invariably won.

When I asked him once whether there were ramifications, he laughed and replied: 'What are they gonna do, dock my pay?'

Karl had balls when it came to that stuff.

The funny thing is, viewers always seemed to love it when anyone from one network suddenly popped up on another, not appearing to buy into the petty cross-network rivalries that so often made headlines. Nine's reasoning was: why gift other networks our Channel 9 star power, and therefore, ratings? And so for a year, the answer to Charlie had always been no. It all seemed so petty. I figured the *Today* show's recent ratings dip was one pretty good reason to say yes, so Charlie's audience could gift *us* some much-needed extra ratings.

But then, for some reason, when I told Darren Wick again that Charlie wanted me on the show to mark my ten years, he changed his mind and said yes. Whether I got Wick in a weak moment or if he really was worried about the *Today* show numbers, I'm not sure, but the following Wednesday, right after I came off air, I flew to Melbourne and headed to the ABC's studios in Elsternwick to record the interview for Charlie's show that night, before racing back to catch the last flight home.

It was the first time I had been to those iconic studios where once, every Sunday night at 6pm, Molly Meldrum would be in residence, usually next to one or other of the biggest pop stars on the planet, recording the latest episode of *Countdown*. I would be one of the last guests to ever appear there, as the studios were just about to be torn down.

The interview with Charlie started off pleasantly enough with chat about my early career in magazines, Kerry Packer, the country's current political leadership, and the like. Charlie was very complimentary, but just like his mate Tom, there was probably no chance this was ever going to be just some simple PR exercise.

And sure enough, halfway through, Charlie hit me with a question I wasn't expecting – a question on the gender pay gap. Most specifically, the one at the *Today* show.

Christ. Despite a lot of recent speculation as to why Karl and I were on such vastly different salaries when together we had taken the *Today* show to number one, I simply, stupidly, didn't arrive in that chair expecting the question. When I grew up, it wasn't polite to ask people what they earnt. But the gender-pay-gap issue had left polite behind long ago.

Once again I hadn't prepared an answer. Just like that time on Kerry Packer's verandah at Palm Beach all those years ago. Bloody hell, here I was doing this to myself again.

What was I supposed to say to Charlie in that moment, with three cameras trained on me, a live studio audience, and a massive national audience who would no doubt be leaning in for my response?

What could I say that didn't betray the frustrations of women around the nation who had been fighting tooth and nail for pay equality for generations? Solicitors, executives, salespeople, drivers, retail workers, accountants, administrators and, yes, journalists. The list went on ... women in every sector, all of whom knew full well that they were being short-changed when it came to negotiating an equal salary to their male counterparts but felt powerless to fight it as long as no-one spoke up.

Did I admit to him that, yes, the inequality across a number of aspects of my job was starting to get to me; and, yes, Nick had recently been talking to Nine about my contract but those talks were going nowhere, and this probably wasn't the best forum or time to air all of that, Charlie?

It was suddenly starting to get very awkward, but I had to come up with something ... and then I opened my mouth, really not sure what was about to come out. 'I have no idea what Karl is on,' I heard myself saying. 'Just as Karl has no idea what I am on.'

Charlie looked me right in the eye and said, 'I suspect ... that's bullshit.'

And Charlie was right. That was bullshit. I did have a pretty good idea of what Karl's deal consisted of. Someone who had been a part of those negotiations 18 months before had told me. I didn't believe the size of the contract at the time and wondered if that person had perhaps embellished the numbers. They hadn't. The truth was, the gender pay gap between Karl and me was so off the charts that no-one would have believed it – and much bigger than that figure that had been conveniently leaked to *news.com.au*. Nor was it a three-year contract as reported; it was for five.

With all of that in mind, what could I do in that moment but politely 'polish' around the edges of the truth. So, I just smiled politely and, I think, convinced no-one. Charlie had made his point. And perhaps so had I. For now.

The next morning, Karl was not happy. From the moment we both arrived in the studio, I could tell there was tension in the air, and during one particularly uncomfortable ad break just before the 7 o'clock news, he couldn't hold it in any longer.

'Have you been discussing my salary with all your leftie mates on the ABC?'

Sorry? Karl obviously hadn't watched the show the night before – or if he had he certainly hadn't mentioned it to this point – but I could see, opened before him on his in-desk computer, the *Daily Mail* website which had, predictably, put the usual clickbait spin on the conversation with Charlie.

Exactly what Karl expected me to say in answer to that question, I'm not quite sure, as three-minute ad breaks, microphones, cameras and nearby colleagues don't exactly make the ideal environment for discussing an issue like this – but one thing was for sure, there was a pretty frosty silence for the rest of the morning.

He obviously felt that I had somehow broken whatever code it was that he, and boys clubs everywhere, were signed up to when it comes to the gender pay gap. A gap that flourishes in the silence of women. And I had just gone and done the unthinkable: I'd opened my mouth.

It turns out there were a lot of people watching Charlie's show that night. Including a very nice Channel 7 executive I had worked with back in my days at *Sunrise*. He told me he'd seen the interview with Charlie and, after having been front and centre in those negotiations with Karl 18 months before, he thought it was about time I knew the truth of just how big that pay gap was.

While he didn't know what I was on, he certainly knew what Karl was on ... or at least the amount he had rejected at Seven, and that Nine had either matched or bettered. It only served to confirm what I'd already been told.

Karl, he said, had sold his loyalty to *both* networks at once, and the Seven executive was clearly still stinging from the experience. The deal, he said, was so huge, with every demand met, that it had to be taken all the way to Kerry Stokes; and after months of negotiations, it was on. Karl was going to Channel 7.

For weeks, he told me, Seven sat by and watched the headlines, just as I had: 'Karl was tired.' 'Karl was going part time.' 'Karl wanted prime time.' 'Karl was over breakfast TV.' He had played both networks off against each other brilliantly and in full public view.

Seven management, and Stokes himself, were furious. This particular executive's job had been put on the line as a result. This time, he said, they wouldn't forget.

There was no doubt about it: Karl certainly knew the art of the deal.

*

My own two-year contract was up at the end of December. And despite Hugh Marks's promise to Nick 18 months before that two years was all anyone was getting, I now knew that Karl had been signed for five. In the end, I figured good luck to him, but I was not happy that, once again, generous allowance on every level was always being given to the male half of this partnership.

But by the last week of June, Nick had just been knocked back for the second time on our request for an improved, more equitable contract for me. As the team and I headed off on yet another 'We Love Australia' tour, this time to celebrate the show's 35th anniversary, I knew I had a lot of thinking to do.

In all my time on the show, I had never given anyone there a moment's grief. Just nice magazine covers, family-friendly publicity, good market research findings, hopefully good journalism, and always, always the smiling, supportive team player sitting right by Karl's side. I was the quintessential 'good girl'. And I did it all happily. I had very little to complain about. I knew that I was already being paid incredibly well. But it was the massive gap between Karl and me that was at issue.

Because after ten years by each other's sides, bringing our different and complementary strengths to the show, covering for each other's weaknesses and taking the show to number one together, it was now clear that the huge financial spoils of our joint victory were very unevenly shared. I couldn't help wondering exactly what it was that Marks actually valued in his employees.

So when Nick rang, just as we had all arrived in the beautiful outback Queensland town of Winton, with the news that management had said that I could basically 'like my existing deal or lump it', Nick asked me what I wanted to do. How did I want to play it from here? He said the question I had to ask myself was, if they won't make some kind of gesture, if they don't go some way towards closing the gap, was I prepared to walk?

Those words came like a lightning bolt. Were we really at that point? This job I knew so well, the work I felt so proud of, the young producers I'd helped mentor, the beautiful audience I'd so firmly connected with ... would I, Nick wanted to know, be prepared to walk away from them all on a principle?

I waited, knowing that what I said next could alter the course of my career forever. But before I could even think about it properly, I said the words, 'Yes ... I would. I would walk.'

In some ways, it wasn't just me talking. Looking back, I'm sure I was channelling the collective frustrations of so many Australian women, some of whom were my friends, many more of whom I had done stories on, and an untold number more I'd read about. Knowing what I knew, and having lived my own experience, how could I, in good conscience, say or do anything else?

'If it comes to it, and I accept that it well might,' I said to Nick, with more force in my voice, now that I realised how comfortable I was with what I'd just said, 'I think I'll have to walk.'

I knew that if I stayed, accepted the existing deal and said nothing, no-one would be any the wiser. But by staying quiet, I would be complicit in perpetuating the gender pay gap for every woman who came after me. The conspiracy of silence that existed in the media was well known. More than one young reporter, and some high-profile hosts across various networks had contacted me over the years for advice, confessing their fears that if they spoke up, the consequences would be dire. Almost without exception, they'd been told there were plenty more standing in the queue behind them who would be glad to get their spot.

The next morning, as we broadcast from the main street of Winton for *Today*'s official 35th birthday celebrations, I had a bit of a moment that only served to confirm my resolve.

Just before we cut the birthday cake at the end of the show, our executive producer Mark had decided that Karl and I would have a race, each of us placed in quasi–horse floats and both pulled along by young local women dressed up as 'busty wenches' from another time. Our seating, as we hung on throughout that race down the main street? A toilet. One each, fortunately. But as I sat on that toilet, being pulled down the main street of Winton, and tried to smile for the cameras, I wondered if this was the moment when walking away was already feeling like a much better option.

That thought was only confirmed for me the next morning as we arrived in Glenrowan, 'Ned Kelly country', for that morning's broadcast. Where always I would pack a bunch of brightly coloured coats to visually punch through the bitter cold and initial darkness of these outside broadcasts, on this morning, the yellow coat I had prepared simply wasn't warm enough, so I threw on my only warm spare, which was navy in colour.

When I arrived on set, Mark was furious. 'Why aren't you wearing something brightly coloured?' I had a big bright pink scarf on, but for Mark that wasn't enough. 'Karl has got a black jacket on with a black scarf. You can't wear navy!'

Now I was furious. But we were surrounded by a lovely crowd of locals who had come out into the cold to be part of our audience for the morning, so as usual, I kept it nice, and through clenched teeth said gently to Mark, who was in my ear from the nearby broadcast truck, 'Can you please explain to me why I'm always the one that has to provide the bright colours? Is there any particular reason you're not asking Karl to change?' He had no answer. And, really, that was the problem. For so many of these issues, there was no answer. There was no rhyme or reason. That was just the way it was, and it was up to me if I wanted to keep going like this.

So, I rang Nick as we packed up that morning and headed to the airport for the next leg of our tour, and asked if we could have one last go at talking to Hugh Marks. But this time I wanted to be in the meeting. And it had to be face to face.

CHAPTER THIRTY-TWO

The kiss of death

'Speak your mind – even if your voice shakes. When you
least expect it, someone may actually listen to what you have
to say. Well-aimed slingshots can topple giants.'
– Maggie Kuhn

IT WAS A WEIRD thing to be standing in the shower thinking about
our *Today* show money guy, Ross Greenwood. It was the day
before my meeting with Hugh Marks. And as the shower ran, it just
so happened Ross was saying some pretty important things on his
Sunday morning radio show on 2GB.

He was talking about the fast-rising national shame of
homelessness that was happening for women over the age of 55. It
was a cause that was close to my heart as *The Big Issue* was one of
the charities that I'd been working with for almost 15 years. Even
though I knew the numbers around this growing scourge and had
met with hundreds of women over the years who'd told me about
their own experiences, I don't think I'd ever fully appreciated until
now exactly why that descent into homelessness for so many women
was becoming such a widespread and growing reality.

As Ross pointed out, the most recent figures showed that, on
average, men in Australia were retiring with $292,500 in their
super fund, while women were leaving their working life with just
$138,150. And that might be all well and good if that one man and

that one woman were in a relationship together, but the truth is, households change, as do circumstances, relationships break down, and it's always the woman – who on average lives longer and earns less – that is left high and dry.

As more women were choosing to go it alone or simply leave bad relationships, child rearing meant more years out of the workforce. Combine that with the lifelong effect of the gender pay gap, and it showed that the old-fashioned idea of having a well-paid man in your life to make up the difference was no plan at all.

Looking more broadly, Ross said, when it came to tertiary education, 52 per cent of graduates were currently women, which raised the questions: Why weren't there that many in boardrooms? Why were workplaces seemingly so female un-friendly? Why didn't employers close the pay gap, or seem to respect the contribution women make – not just in the workplace, but in the overall health of society?

In numbers too big to ignore, as Helen Reddy had once reminded us, women were paying the price, and it had just become an accepted fact that women retired poor. These were all seen as 'women's problems'. And yet, why did men who had the power to change such deeply unfair outcomes – men with wives, girlfriends, daughters, mothers, aunts and sisters – continue to allow this to happen in the workplace? Why weren't more men angry that, if this didn't change soon, some of the women in their own lives could become statistics too?

I wasn't even asking for Karl's pay, I was just asking for a slightly fairer share of the spoils that had come from the *Today* show's increasingly profitable position in the hugely lucrative breakfast TV market – even more so now that we were at number one. We were a show turning over $60 million a year, with well over half of that in profit.

So when Nick and I headed to Nine's famed third floor that day, right after I came off air, and we headed down the plush, hushed corridors of management towards Hugh Marks's office, I was incredibly nervous, but just a little fired up at the same time. And then, as I approached the reception area, with the smiling face of Hugh Marks's assistant Jane there to welcome Nick and me and usher us in, I suddenly felt like a little girl again, about to enter the headmaster's office.

The fact that the TV business is a cut-throat one should be no news flash to anyone, least of all me, so I was a little taken aback when, as I entered Marks's office, I found that he was already out from behind his desk and by the door to greet me, with … a kiss on the cheek. This was only the fourth time I'd ever met Hugh Marks. He was the CEO. Somehow, he had a presumption of intimacy that our limited interactions didn't really marry up with – particularly after his strained words with Nick, on my account.

But maybe that kiss on the cheek was meant to be a good sign? Maybe this meeting wasn't going to be difficult at all. Maybe me requesting a face-to-face meeting was going to thaw the ice in these, until now, intractable negotiations, and make it hard for him to justify the extraordinarily significant gender pay gap over which he was presiding.

Also in the room that day was the head of news and current affairs, Darren Wick, who himself had had a short and, by his own admission, brutal stint years before as executive producer at *Today*. He knew better than most the effort and energy both Karl and I had put into the show over the past decade, so I wasn't sure, but I hoped he would be onside. He'd been particularly warm in his praise of both Karl and me when we got the show to number one. So, I thought his appreciation for what I brought to the show was genuine. And there was a kiss from him, too.

Did the bosses greet their employees in this manner in other corporate environments? I wondered. To me it still felt odd. Especially under the circumstances.

So, as we all wandered over to the office's lounge area, I looked around the room for something, anything I could use as an opening chat point … and then I saw on the back of Hugh's chair a pretty cool-looking baseball-style jacket from Nine's wildly successful new show, *Ninja Warrior*.

'Congratulations on *Ninja*, Hugh,' I started. 'Ben and Rebecca did a great job hosting that. And Julie Ward is a brilliant EP. She was my first boss in TV back on *Beauty & the Beast*. In fact, our son Louis has applied to be a contestant,' I added.

It was the best I had. And for now it was enough, as Hugh thanked me. After exchanging a few more pleasantries, he said that I had the floor. So I took it.

And for the next 20 minutes, I put my case, while both men listened. I was pretty sure I didn't leave a single stone unturned. Every so often, Nick would add something, and then I would continue.

Karl and I were now ten years in, I started, and we worked! Not Karl on his own, not me on my own. Us. Together. Not since the hugely successful Liz, Steve and Tracy years had the show been number one. No other pairing in that crucial timeslot for Nine had succeeded. They'd tried Karl in four other combinations before me, and for whatever reason, it hadn't worked. It was no-one's fault, just a reminder of the incredibly inexact science of what sparks and what doesn't on breakfast TV, as Wick himself had always noted.

And yet, at every turn, Karl was given all the breaks, opportunities that I was not. The *60 Minutes* assignments. The prime-time shows. The Olympics. I had put my hand up for the possibility of all of those and been told 'no'. The reason? Karl was away so much doing those very assignments that it was crucial I stayed on the desk and kept the *Today* show home-fires burning – which, by the way, I not only accepted but understood. But if I was *that* crucial to the *Today* show's ongoing success, didn't that come with its own significant value with regards to my ongoing role?

I had no choice but to tell them that I knew exactly what Karl was on, and that I'd got it straight from two significant players in those negotiations. It was only then that both executives shifted uncomfortably … and exchanged a small glance. They said they were convinced they knew who had told me. But they were wrong. It didn't matter. The point was, I knew.

Hugh said he had heard me. 'Let me look at it. I know now exactly how you feel, and I'll get back to you.'

Right. Well, then, um … thank you. It was that awkward moment when you realise a tense meeting is over. I looked one last time around the office.

And right then, Hugh wandered over to his desk and handed me that *Ninja Warrior* jacket. 'Here you go, it's yours. You might like to give it to your son.'

I was going to make a joke about 'getting the coat off his back' but decided against it. It just didn't seem like the moment. But, always the mother, I left with that jacket for Louis.

The meeting generally seemed to go well. Hugh had listened and promised to look at it and said he would get back to us in a few weeks. Oh, and he'd given me another awkward kiss on the cheek before I left. Surely, that all pointed towards better times ahead?

*

It was such a joy to be in Italy with Pete for the first time since Chris and I had holidayed there almost 30 years before. We had a full two weeks planned of connecting with some of Pete's dear friends from his old Italian rugby-playing days, and heading to a part of the country we'd heard so much about but never seen: the amazing Amalfi Coast, south of Naples. The food, the history, the coastline, the colours, the stunning vistas, the long, languid twilights spent at summer dinners overlooking the Mediterranean – we were looking forward to it all. And within just a few days, I could feel myself breathing out for the first time in months.

Pete, too, had been feeling the pressure, but for him it was the demands of his next book deadline. As I took the chance to head out and pursue my other love, photography, Pete would find himself a comfy spot at a cafe somewhere and sit and write. All day. Looking up every so often to see the pattern of the daily Italian life he used to live and love, largely unchanged. On any given day, Pete would amaze waiters with the sheer amount of tea he could consume in one cafe sitting.

It had been five years since Pete had given up alcohol, cold turkey, and as he would tell anyone who would bother to listen, and even plenty of those who wouldn't, once he'd decided to give up the drink, it was one of the best decisions he'd ever made. The thing he'd worked out was that, for him, total abstinence was much easier than mastering moderation. As a man of great passions and enormous appetites, moderation in anything was always difficult.

For all the health benefits that being alcohol-free clearly afforded Pete, it made for a very healthy change in our marriage, too. As Pete would attest, we've never had a Mills & Boon union; we've always had a real marriage, with all the attendant stresses and strains that come with busy careers, kids, pets, bills, in-laws, renovations, a mortgage, loss and all the rest.

When Pete was drinking, he calculated that we had around 50 blissful days a year, 300 pretty good days, and 15 absolute shockers. But once he gave up alcohol, the 15 shockers were down to just three. That said, he was never prepared to say that the other 12 had been his fault. As he put it, 'Only some of them were, but I can navigate through your witches' hats better when I am sober!' (Charming, and very possibly true!)

But here in Italy, blissful days were assured. Everything was perfect. Maybe just a little too perfect ...

On day three of our holiday, Pete and I were just about to head out from our hotel in the coastal town of Amalfi and up into the hills of the ancient village of Ravello high above us, when I thought I'd take a quick shower to freshen up. I knew the floor was wet – the Italians do love a shiny marble tile – but the actual moment of falling seemed to take forever. My mind immediately went into slow motion, even though my body was in fast-forward, as I tried to calculate just how bad the fall was going to be. It was bad. Very bad.

The pain was like a red-hot dagger stabbing through my right wrist, and when I glanced down, it resembled an S-bend. As we raced to the nearest hospital, I was in more agony than I've ever felt, outside of childbirth. And even then ... those experiences gave me beautiful babies to look forward to at the end. There was nothing to look forward to here.

The hospital in Salerno looked like a tattered 1950s warehouse in Beirut, and I was quickly ushered into a waiting room that, I swear, not along ago must have stored fertiliser bags.

The X-rays were shocking. Or as the doctor put it, *'molto brutto'*. Very ugly.

Blessedly at last, there was pain relief – although it did take four separate shots of painkillers – and that was not before the doctor in question gripped my right hand and pulled and manoeuvred it to try and realign the broken bones. The sound of my own shattered bones twisting and crunching was indescribable. I swear they must have heard my screams back home. At that point I think I'd mentally checked out, because the next thing I remember was being aware of a wet plaster cast that went from just below my fingernails all the way up to just shy of my armpit.

When I asked Pete to ask the doctor in his still-pretty-good Italian why the need for the huge – and come to think of it, incredibly tight – cast, he said it was because it was needed to keep everything in place before I got home to be operated on. He then handed me a letter, something about permission to fly that didn't make any sense to me, mostly because that cocktail of drugs I was on had really started to work by now.

So, our perfect holiday was indeed too perfect – and it was now cancelled. But there was worse to come. As we boarded our flight out of Heathrow 24 hours later, my arm now throbbing and my fingers puffed up and purple with pain, the lovely Qantas flight attendant stopped me at the doorway, alerting me to the fact that I really shouldn't be flying long haul with such a fresh plaster. The risk of swelling mid-flight, she said, was significant, and I really needed to wait at least another 24 hours. And then I remembered the letter of permission from the doctor, which I still had in my bag. Suffice to say I really shouldn't have flown, and at a couple of points in the flight I almost passed out from the pain.

By the time we landed back in Sydney and went straight to Royal North Shore Hospital to have the cast sawn off, the prognosis for my entire right arm was grim. The blood supply had been all but cut off, and I was straight into surgery.

By the time I woke up in hospital the next morning, still groggy from the general anaesthetic, and up to my eyeballs on some pretty spacey drugs, I had no idea where I was, or how I had got there. Pete was there, though, right at my bedside, and he had some extraordinary news: 'Kerry Packer is alive!'

'Wow. That's amazing …' I said, looking around trying to get some sense of what the time was, and how I could find the nearest loo. 'Gee, my arm hurts.'

'Are you thrilled?' he asked.

It seemed a slightly strange question, but 'Yeah, of course,' I said. 'The main thing is, is Gretel thrilled? It's her I'm happy for.'

'What?' Pete asked. 'Why would Gretel be the happy one?'

'Well, if Kerry Packer is alive, I think Gretel is going to be pretty happy, isn't she? … Can I have some water?'

'No,' Pete said, 'I didn't say anything about Kerry Packer, I said, your portrait's won the Packing Room Prize at the Archibald! Remember that portrait you sat for six months ago? Peter Smeeth's entry? It's won the Packing Room Prize. And they're unveiling it at lunchtime today. Peter can't make it because he's giving the eulogy at his best friend's funeral at the exact same time. He wants to know if you wouldn't mind appearing on his behalf at the press conference to just say a few words?'

'Sure … Can I have some water? And can we take the painkillers with us?'

I only just remember appearing at the Art Gallery. I remember a lot of cameras, I remember reading out Peter Smeeth's very humble words, I remember that my Pete and the kids were there, and I remember me smiling … but then I remember going home to sleep. For days.

*

When I eventually got back to work ten days later, still in a pretty poor state and attending daily hospital physio for hours to try to get some movement back in my hand and fingers, something had very definitely changed at the *Today* show.

Our executive producer, Mark Calvert, seemed extremely distant. He was no longer coming down to the studio floor each morning for his customary five-minute, how-is-everyone pep-up chat … and on the few occasions he did, for some reason he couldn't look me in the eye. On my second day back, I'd told him that I was really struggling on air and might need to head to hospital because my fingers were blowing up again. His response was swift and unsympathetic. 'Can it wait, Lisa? I really need you on the desk.'

After a week, I just couldn't stand it anymore. Whatever Mark's problem was, I had to hear it straight, so I requested a meeting after the show. And for someone who had been so reticent to confront me, he suddenly wasn't holding back.

He told me I was basically a traitor to the network, and what on earth was this personal PR crusade I appeared to currently be on? For starters, the Archibald Prize appearance? Why didn't I check with him first?

I was stunned. 'You mean the one when I was just out of surgery, on major drugs and spoke on behalf of the guy whose best friend had just died?' I replied.

Why, he then wanted to know, hadn't I told him about the story I'd written for *Huffington Post* about my broken wrist?

'The one that I dictated to Pete so I could fulfil my monthly commitment to the same *Huffington Post* that the network was so keen on me writing for? You mean that one?'

I had no idea where this was all coming from. Mark was under intense pressure – I got that. The ratings were faltering, but I was sure we could get them back. So why was he losing it at me?

And then I had to go, as always, to Royal North Shore for my daily two-hour hand physio sessions. My hand just wasn't making the progress it should, and most mornings I was in tears. Then, six weeks in, the doctor told me if I didn't start doing more of the home physio on top of my two-hour sessions each morning, I was in danger of permanently losing all use of my hand. 'Move it or lose it,' were my doctor's chilling words.

Yeah, as years went, 2017 wasn't proving to be one of my favourites.

*

Wednesday, 13 September 2017 was a landmark day in the media. The tabloids were suddenly on notice. Aussie actor turned major

Hollywood star Rebel Wilson had just won a major court case against *Woman's Day*, for articles they'd written that she claimed were defamatory.

For many who had been the targets of these types of magazines and their oft made-up stories, a collective cheer went up: a record $4.5 million payout was awarded. It was a figure that must have been beyond Rebel's wildest dreams, and *Woman's Day*'s worst nightmares.

I couldn't help wondering what that might mean for Karl, who was still being hounded by the paps for those same magazines on a daily basis. Peter Meakin, now the boss of Channel 10 News and Current Affairs, must have been thinking the same thing as he called me to see if I would be happy to appear on *The Project* that night to discuss it.

'With your background in magazines, and the fact that you've seen Mr Stefanovic's life at close range over the last year,' he said, 'you're uniquely placed to bring something interesting to that conversation.'

I always loved the way Peter put things.

'Would you come on *The Project* for us tonight?' Meakin asked.

It was lovely to hear from my old Seven boss, but I told him that I doubted I would be allowed to. If he wanted to call Darren Wick himself, though, I'd be happy to. I warned Peter that I'd got away with an appearance on Charlie Pickering's show a few months before, but only just.

Within minutes, Peter called back. 'You've been approved. We'll have a crew out to your place at 5pm. Is that good with you?'

'Of course,' I told him. I was baffled as to how he'd got that over the line, but didn't balk.

Waleed Aly, Natarsha Belling and Pete Helliar were hosting *The Project* that night, and when they asked for my thoughts about the payout, I told them that, ultimately, it had to be a victory for truth in journalism, because even though we're only talking about tabloid magazines, now those anonymous sources they've always quoted to back up their stories would have to stand up in court and prove that what they were saying was true.

When Natarsha then asked me if others might now take a stand, Pete Helliar jumped in …

PH: 'Like Karl! Is Karl going to take a stand?'

Me: 'I couldn't tell you because I haven't spoken to Karl since the judgment, but he may have a wry smile on his face. And look, having watched all of that closely, I have to tell you it was ridiculous some of the stories that were written about Karl. It was almost comical, but I wasn't personally involved, and when you are involved, it's no laughing matter at all.'

Waleed: 'Alright, you haven't spoken to him, hmmm … (busily pretending to take notes) Tension on the *Today* show set …'

Me: 'No, no, no … that's only because he's hosting *A Current Affair* tonight, so we're having network wars right now!' I laughed.

PH: 'And we know which side you chose, Lisa! Well chosen!'

Me: 'I've gone for Channel Ten!' I said, sharing in the joke, and making a fairly pathetic attempt at a fist pump in the air with my right arm, now mercifully free of the cast, but still largely frozen and looking a lot like that of a store mannequin's.

Now, exactly why I said that bit about choosing Channel 10, I have no idea, but hey, it was all a bit of fun. And I really liked the team on *The Project*. Carrie and I had run into each other a few times over the years and met up for lunch since; Waleed and I had had cause to be in touch on a number of occasions, and met up at his Andrew Olle lecture in 2016. And even though I'd never met him, I could see that Pete Helliar was one of the really good guys of TV. They were all a class act on a show with a mission statement I really admired. 'News, delivered differently.' They took chances. Did editorials with genuine purpose and bite. And covered really important stories that other commercial networks simply wouldn't. All that mattered to the show was *if* it mattered.

The next morning, as I was sitting in my office after we'd come off air, chatting to one of our young producers, my phone rang. I looked down mid-sentence. Strangely, it was Peter Meakin. Why would he be calling again?

He wanted to thank me for last night's show. Everyone loved it, he said. He also wanted to know when my contract was up at Nine.

CHAPTER THIRTY-THREE

I don't like Mondays

'Women have to work much harder to make it in this world. It really pisses me off that women don't get the same opportunities as men do, or money for that matter. Because let's face it, money gives men the power to run the show. It gives men the power to define our values and to define what's sexy and what's feminine and that's bullshit. At the end of the day, it's not about equal rights, it's about how we think. We have to reshape our own perception of how we view ourselves.' – Beyoncé, *Beyoncé: Life is But A Dream*, 2013

AH, SATURDAY, AND THE whole team had just arrived back from yet another 'We Love Australia' tour, which this time had included Cairns in Far North Queensland, and the beautiful Yarra Valley in country Victoria. It had been a great trip, and wonderful as always to meet so many of our enthusiastic viewers, but once again I had missed our wedding anniversary, this one our 25th.

But Pete and I knew exactly how to make up for it. We'd decided, on the quiet, to get married again by renewing our vows down at the Bathers' Pavilion restaurant on Balmoral Beach, a spot that now held many happy memories for us, including being the venue for our wedding reception back in 1992.

With a tight capacity of just 100, spaces were limited, and our guiding light was: who are the 100 people we are most looking forward to growing older with? We decided to tell everyone on the invitation list that it was simply a dinner to celebrate our 25th anniversary, and to say thank you to them as our dear family and friends. The only ones who knew our secret were the kids, and everyone, almost without exception, had quickly RSVP'd yes, including Karl and Jas.

First, though, the two were heading off on a quick overseas jaunt, and as soon as we'd come off air on that Friday morning, Karl had called out cheerily from his car on the way to the airport, 'See you at Bathers' in a week. Can't wait!'

We couldn't either.

It was really Pete's idea. As soon as he'd seen me at the Logies a couple of years before in a beautiful white off-the-shoulder gown, he suggested that it was too special to wear just once, so why didn't we make the most of that dress and get married again.

The kids were thrilled, and now we were just days away from the big 'wedding' day, Saturday, 7 October. We had the dress, we had the celebrant, flowers were ordered, the menu, wine and champagne all chosen, and the cake was organised.

A nice boost on the morning of the celebration itself was that, with Ben Fordham having filled in for Karl that previous week, we'd won the ratings again; so it was nice to know at least that if Karl ever did leave the show, the audience certainly had a soft spot for Ben.

Then at 5pm that afternoon, with Billi as my bridesmaid, Jake as Pete's best man, and Louis walking me down the 'aisle' of the restaurant to the strains of Bruno Mars' '(I Think I Wanna) Marry You', Pete and I tied the knot again, in front of a very surprised gathering of those we loved most.

During the ceremony we were both caught a little by surprise by just how much it meant to us, too – mindful as we were, after 25 years of real married life, of all that went with those newly spoken vows. It was, without doubt, one of the happiest nights of our lives.

Then with dinner over, and three brilliant (and hilariously close-to-home) speeches from the kids, we cut the cake, and cheers went up from everyone.

Everyone, except Karl and Jas, with Karl having texted Pete two mornings before to say they'd extended their stay overseas and wouldn't be coming.

*

Byron Bay is just beautiful in October. And the perfect spot for a quick one-week second honeymoon. Walks to the lighthouse, endless beaches, blessed sleep-ins and, something I needed more than anything, a bit of much-needed thinking time. While an offer had finally come through from Hugh Marks a few weeks before, it was now not the only offer on the table.

For as it turned out, just as Peter Meakin had indicated in that phone call a month before, Channel 10 was very interested in me joining the network – most particularly, *The Project* – and for weeks Nick had been talking to them. I'd tried to put it all out of my mind. I really didn't like being in this position.

Nick asked me if I wanted him to let Marks know that there was now a serious offer on the table from Ten, but I insisted he didn't. Karl had the stomach for that sort of stuff, but I had no interest in playing one network off against another, and even less in doing it publicly. I simply wanted to work somewhere that valued what I could bring. In every job I'd ever had, and loved, it had always been about doing good work I could be proud of and – hopefully – be fairly rewarded for.

Nick had made it clear that Ten seriously did value me, and really hoped that I would decide to make the shift across. He knew I loved *The Project* and how genuinely thrilled I was at the possibility of working with such a talented team. I'd even had a great night at the Walkley Awards a couple of years before with their executive producer, Craig Campbell, too, so I had a pretty good idea of the genius that was going on behind the cameras as well. Nick told me on the Wednesday I was in Byron that he now had a formal letter of offer from Ten ready to go. All it needed was for me to say yes.

I felt sick about the whole thing. I told Nick I just needed to get to work on Monday, and see how I was feeling about it all. But something else was bothering me …

A month or so before, I had no idea whether I would even be allowed to take this time off after the wedding, as it coincided with Nine's 'Up Fronts': the network's annual opportunity to flag the next year's line-up of shows and 'stars' to advertisers. They were always huge affairs, and every year we were all very strictly instructed to attend. It was mandatory. No exceptions. Ever.

But for some reason this year, the word had come from Marks that I didn't have to be there, and that I should go and enjoy my week off. That was when I discovered Georgie Gardner would be taking on my usual role alongside Karl presenting the News and Current Affairs section on the night.

Oh. OK …

Neither Georgie nor Karl nor anyone in management had mentioned a thing to me about the strange pairing, which had apparently been in place for months. When I enquired with Mark Calvert as to why, I was told, 'No reason. They're just mixing it up a bit.' Still, I'd spent an entire morning filming a segment they would play for the event, so I decided to take my leave pass from the night as a win.

But on the Thursday morning in Byron, just as Pete and I were heading off on a walk along the beach, my phone started melting down with messages from Nine colleagues who wanted to know why I wasn't included in the Up Fronts the night before. I was sure that couldn't be right. But then one of those colleagues sent me a link to the lengthy video package I was meant to be in, and they were right.

Was that a cold wind blowing from down Sydney way? It certainly felt like it.

So, at 10am I emailed Mark, and by midday there had been no response. I called and left a message. Nothing. I rang Karl, too, to see if he was also baffled as to my exclusion. But my call went straight to voicemail.

*

As the day dragged on, there was still no response from Mark. Finally, at 7 o'clock that evening, in deep frustration, after a number of attempts I finally got through to our *Today* show publicist, Adrian, a lovely young guy who'd just joined the network. He was apologetic for the silence after all my messages, but there was 'a lot going on …', he said. Nevertheless, he'd 'got to the bottom' of what had happened.

'Look, it was simple human error. They shot so much footage and, in the end, it was just too long, and unfortunately you got left on the cutting-room floor,' he said.

'With respect, Adrian,' I started, 'you seriously expect me to believe that? How could anyone forget to include one half of the network's breakfast show team in a major news and current affairs presentation for 2018?'

'I know, crazy, huh? But look, here's the good news: the network has decided that you are their big pick to push for next year's Gold Logie, and they've put a story in tomorrow's *Tele*, so how good is that?

'Lisa? … Lisa, are you still there? … Leese?'

And sure enough, the next morning, there it was on page 13 of the *Daily Telegraph*, the lead item in 'Sydney Confidential': 'Nine Plans Gold Logie Bid For Lisa'.

When it came to Nine's tactics, I now, officially, had no idea which way was up.

*

It was my first day back at the *Today* show desk, and the first time I would see Karl after his no-show at the wedding.

In the ten days since, he hadn't contacted me at all. No phone message, no text, no apology, no congrats, just the memory of that text to Pete. I was curious to know when *I* would hear from him. In all the years we'd sat next to each other, even though there were the occasional frustrations on both sides, upsets were rare. But on this morning, I was upset. There were two precious spots at the wedding we could so easily have filled with dear friends, but Karl's late text meant those seats had gone empty.

By 5.10 on that Monday morning, Karl and I still hadn't crossed paths. Then, as I was seated on set having some quick hair and makeup checks before our regular 5.15am live cross to the early news, Karl arrived at the desk only just in time.

And he was instantly away … 'Morning, Airlie, we've got a great show for you this morning …'

Promo done. Then, quick as a flash, Karl threw a joke at the floor crew and he was gone. Really? So, I sat there for a moment. Wow. Nothing. Not a mention. Not a congrats. And certainly no 'Sorry for letting you down by my no-show at the wedding'. Not … anything.

What I felt in that instant was hard to put into words. More than anything, I felt just a little bit pathetic. What was this thing Karl and I had between us? I had presumed that along with our working relationship, there was a friendship as well. I must have been wrong. For all the early starts, the ratings we'd worked so hard to claw back, the significant wins, the disappointments, the hilarious on-air moments, the understanding we had of each other's strengths and weaknesses, the occasional private confidences we'd shared, the chemistry magic even we didn't quite understand … he could then still treat me with such uncaring disregard.

I watched as Karl headed back to his dressing room and the crew busied themselves with last-minute sound and lighting checks before our 5.30 start.

Did I finally know exactly where I stood with Karl?

So, I stayed at the desk. I didn't wander back to my dressing room as I normally would have. I had seen enough, so I just sat there and looked out into the cavernous space inside Studio 22, home to so many iconic Channel 9 shows and names, over the years. The stories these walls could tell. They could even tell one of a brand-new, and very nervous, *Cleo* editor walking out onto the set of *The Midday Show* to a welcoming Ray Martin, to announce that she'd just dropped the magazine's iconic centrefold. It had all happened right here.

With just minutes now to on-air, Sylvia took her place at the end of the desk and cheerily asked me how Byron was. 'You must show me the pictures. I love that place. And how's your arm? It was so great that you got by without your cast at the wedding.'

Whether Karl heard Sylvia's comments as he wandered back across the studio floor, on the way slapping one of our cameramen on the back, telling a joke to another, and then slipped into the chair beside me, I'll never know.

And then, that familiar theme music began. Our floor manager, Abby, always such a calm presence on the floor, counted us down: five, four, three, two ... and the red light was on.

Then, before I could draw breath, Karl leaned in. 'Well, good morning, great to have your company on this Monday, October 16. And good news, Lisa has returned from holidays ... in fact, didn't you get married again while you were away? Congratulations!'

I don't think the pause I took in that exact moment was picked up by the cameras, but in my mind it lasted an eternity. *Now* I get congratulations? Because the cameras are on?

What did Karl expect me to say at that point? 'Yeah, I did Karl and I invited you, you said yes, and at the last minute you didn't show up and haven't said a word to me since'?

It was the 5.30 half hour, the part of the show where we had long joked we could be our most raw and relaxed, because, let's face it, at that hour, no-one is watching. In that moment I was certainly feeling raw, but relaxed was not one of the many emotions I had in play.

What had happened a week before – a joyous celebration amongst our closest friends and family – really didn't seem to matter to Karl. And the fact that I might be disappointed seemed to count for little.

I glanced over at Sylvia. I could see that she had clocked Karl's words but quickly looked away, her smile never budging.

I took a deep breath, my eyes momentarily widening at what I had just heard, turned to the camera, and ...

'I did, Karl, but why would anybody care about that when it's news time. Sylvia, good morning ...'

And with that, no further words needed to be spoken. Karl knew I had cut him dead, something I had never done on or off air before. I was furious, possibly more at myself for having cared so much in the first place. With all those hours still ahead of us sitting half a metre apart, I knew it was going to be a long show.

For the next two hours, I exchanged not a single word with Karl outside of what was scripted when the red light was on – because for the first time, I just didn't trust myself.

But there was another reason I was quietly fuming. I couldn't help noticing the bizarre run-down for the show. Almost every interview was now Karl's alone. During the break I messaged Mark Calvert and asked: was that a mistake?

'No, it isn't,' was the sharp reply. I was suddenly reminded that Mark still hadn't responded to any of my emails or phone calls asking what he knew about me being cut from the Up Fronts the previous week.

What the heck was going on? I messaged him again as he sat in the control room, just a short distance away, and asked if I could see him after the show. I waited. This time, no response. To say I was having a rotten morning would be an understatement.

For two hours, I sat there feeling hollow and useless. *Today* was now the Karl show. What was the point of me even being there? The cameras were on me so there was nowhere to hide. And yet, I felt completely invisible.

Then at 7.30, something in me suddenly switched. Did I really want to sit there for another 90 minutes feeling miserable? I'd always promised myself to do every show as if it was my last.

So, I did. It was an instant mood switch which more than likely confused the bejesus out of Karl. But for the remainder of the show, I was determined to enjoy what little I'd been given to do beyond throwing to the news and weather every half hour.

This job was a privilege I had always treasured and should really only ever belong to those who felt that way. I wasn't going to throw another minute of it away. When I walked off set that day at 9 o'clock, I was proud of myself. I'd kept my promise.

But as I got back to my dressing room, that run order was still bugging me. I had to go and see Mark and find out what was going on. Why was Karl so completely dominating the show now? In fact, why hadn't Karl *himself* questioned the absurd imbalance of the run-down? And why hadn't Mark responded to any of my attempts to contact him for the last four days?

So, I quickly changed and headed up to the office to catch him before the usual 9.30am planning meeting for the next day's show.

Strangely, by 9.20 Mark had already left. No-one was quite sure why, when he would be back, or where he was, so I asked Lydia, the *Today* show's lovely longtime PA, to let him know I was hoping to catch up with him. There was always plenty to keep me busy in the office, so I started answering letters, emails and phone calls, and talking to a couple of producers about stories they were working on, and hoped Mark would eventually resurface. But by 11.15, there was still no sign of him. So, with an 11.30 appointment at the hospital – as always for intense physio on my hand – I called him on the way, but still he wasn't picking up. I left a message asking him to call, but … nothing. Something very strange was going on.

I don't know what compelled me, but as I sat in the doctor's waiting room, readying myself for yet another session of painful hand exercises and finger manipulation, I sent an email to Nick, and to Pete.

Subject: This morning's show

Guys,

I'm going to take a note of how the allocation of hosting roles go down between Karl and me in the coming weeks. (See attached.) Never know when I may need it as a record …

This morning I didn't have a single solo interview, and even the ones Karl and I would normally do together had been given to Karl alone. All I had was the 'girls chat' segment at 8.40.

What is this, the 1960s?

Cheers,

Lisa.

The good thing was Nick had a meeting with Hugh Marks scheduled for that afternoon. And after my email, Nick called agreeing that something was up and promising he would raise it at the meeting with Marks.

'How do you feel?' he asked.

I thought about it for a moment. Then said, 'Kind of sad for some reason.'

'Don't be,' Nick said. 'I'm sure it will all work out.'

*

Mum hadn't been well, so I dropped in later that day and sat with her in the afternoon sun of her apartment. She hadn't been eating properly, so I wanted to see what she might need picking up from the supermarket just before I connected up with the afternoon conference call at 5.15.

Those calls were always a good way to get a handle on the rough plan for the next day's show, and what I should be keeping an eye out for in the news that night. Karl was never a big fan of those calls and had long ago abandoned them, but I always liked getting a sense of what the team was working on, and for me, it was simple to fit a call in around the kids, while I was out running errands, driving between appointments, or today, while I was picking up a few groceries at Woolies.

I still hadn't heard from Mark after my earlier message requesting a meeting, so I hopped on the call early hoping to catch him. And even though there were others already on the line, I asked him if he got my message. 'Must have missed it,' he said. 'I'll get back to you later.'

As the chief of staff talked us through the next day's show, I made my way around the shopping aisles and ticked off both Mum's list and mine – bread, salad, washing powder, toilet paper, dog food … – while I listened: 'Psychologist Justin Coulson is joining us with advice on how to keep kids calm during end-of-school exams; Ray Hadley's in for What's Making News; Dr Joanna MacMillan with healthy food choices heading into summer; two judges from *The Block* Darren Palmer and Neale Whitaker are on to promote the show; Chris Urquhart is joining the circus just before the 8 o'clock news; and the cash mascots will be at the desk for the 7.45 Cash Call.'

Those bloody mascots. I hated those stupid mascots.

The conference call over, I hung up and grabbed a tin of tuna. Pete was on his way back from speaking at an event on the Central Coast for his latest book, so I figured he may have already eaten. Louis and Billi were at their usual Monday night formal dinner at college, and Jake, well, he said he might drop in for a quick dinner, so maybe I'll just make a simple tuna salad and …

And right then, my phone rang. It was Nick. I knew he'd had that meeting with Hugh Marks so I was interested to find out how it went.

'Hey, Nick …'

'Hey there. Where are you?' His voice was low and measured and I couldn't quite hear him above the noise of the passing shopping trolleys, and John Denver's 'Country Roads' playing over the supermarket intercom.

'You're very soft, Nick,' I said, uncoupling my phone from between my left cheek and shoulder as I juggled the groceries, and now holding it properly. 'I'm at Woolies in the canned fish aisle, why?'

'I'm just getting into the lift at Channel Nine. I'm trying to keep my voice down,' he whispered. 'I've just left Hugh's office.'

'Oh, of course, sorry, I've just got off the conference call for tomorrow's show,' I said. 'So how did you go?'

Nick: 'You're off the show.'

Me: 'Off what show?'

Nick: 'You're off the *Today* show.'

Me: 'Sorry, Nick? What do you mean by "*off*"?'

Nick: 'Permanently off. Never to appear again. Today was your last day.'

I …

'Nick, hang on … that can't be right. I just got off the call to the team for tomorrow's show. Mark was on that call. He said nothing. And what about Nine's offer that's already on the table?'

What the hell had just happened?

Nick could tell I was in shock.

'I'll meet you at your place in ten … are you OK?'

I looked around. I wasn't sure that I was. I was in a fog of complete disbelief.

I had just been dismissed from Channel 9. Effective immediately. In aisle six at my local Woolies. And I was holding a can of tuna.

I hung up from Nick, and gently placed that tin of tuna back on the shelf. I then put the bag of lettuce back in the fruit and vegetable department. The toilet paper, the dog food, the washing powder, all returned one by one to where I had just found them, hoping that as I wandered the aisles, what I had just heard would start to make sense. But it didn't. Those words kept going through my head: 'Never to appear again.'

Had everyone in Woolies heard what I did? Was it my imagination or had they dialled down John Denver and dialled up that whole conversation at full volume over the loudspeaker? I was pretty sure it hadn't just been broadcast, but I knew that the news of my dismissal surely soon would be.

Finally, with all the groceries back on the shelves, I placed my now-empty green basket neatly back in the pile by the checkout, my head down, desperate not to meet anyone's gaze, and walked in silence to the car. I wasn't in tears. I wasn't anything. Apart from numb. Did I really just get sacked? The woman Nine was apparently so proud of, they were lining me up for a Gold Logie?

While this news of my dismissal was still probably hours from going public, the humiliation I felt at that moment was overwhelming. Because a few suburbs away, a man who had stood up at my ten-year celebration and declared how incredibly important I was to the show and to the network had now turned around and shown me the door before slamming it behind me. Turns out that kiss I'd felt so uncomfortable about at that meeting with Hugh Marks was not one of admiration. It was the kiss of death.

What on earth had I done so wrong to get such a brutal 'don't-come-Monday', on a *Monday*? All those years, all those early mornings, all my loyalty to a show and a job I'd loved so much, now over.

As I headed across the car park to find my car, I tried to get Pete on the phone. I knew he was heading back from that commitment on the Central Coast, but we hadn't spoken for more than an hour, and now, for some reason, he wasn't picking up.

Who could I call? Not Mum, I knew she would be devastated for me and I didn't want to upset her, particularly not with her failing health. I needed someone who could tell me – even if it was a lie – that it was going to be OK.

Should I call Karl?

But hang on … was *this* why I hadn't heard from him after the wedding? Was *this* why he never said a word about that total freezing-out of me in the show's run-down this morning?

Oh. The penny was starting to drop.

What about Mark Calvert? Did he know he suddenly didn't have a co-host of the show he executive produced? Why hadn't *he* been returning my calls?

Oh. The penny just dropped a whole lot further.

As I pulled into the driveway, I could see that no-one was home. No sign of any of the kids wandering about in the kitchen, and even our new boxer puppy, Maggie, was nowhere to be seen. Everything was quiet. I walked through the kitchen door and wandered into the lounge room. I just needed to sit, by myself, and take in the events of the last ten surreal minutes.

People change and lose their jobs all the time. In the scheme of things, this was no biggie. Wasn't this what I wanted … to have the situation I'd been wrestling with for weeks taken out of my hands and decided for me?

For a moment, I thought back to the wise words of Brian Walsh on that very first day on set at *Beauty & the Beast*: 'Oh, for fuck's sake, get over yourself. It's only television.' I knew he was right, but right now, I just couldn't escape from the stinging humiliation that I knew was coming.

To try and get a grip and put it all into some sort of perspective, I focused on something Pete always said when various seeming calamities had popped up in our lives. 'There are three questions you and I must ask,' he'd say. 'Is Jake OK? Is Louis OK? Is Billi OK?'

The answer was a resounding yes to all three. And *my* mum was OK. And our house hadn't burnt down. And both Pete and I had our health. I was simply parting ways with Nine on a principle. We had fallen out on the issue of the massive gender pay gap I'd been experiencing for years. Of all the hills to die on, I was OK with the fact that this was the one I'd chosen.

But as the sun's late afternoon rays streamed into the lounge room and hit my face, I caught my reflection in the windows. The TV makeup of that morning's show was still in place, but as heavy as it was, it was unable to mask the very raw me that stared back.

'Never to appear again,' I whispered to myself. There, I'd said it out loud.

Never again would I sit in that studio, the one where I'd experienced so many extraordinary moments, interviewed so many inspiring people, had the great honour of co-hosting almost 9000 hours of live TV and four nail-biting federal elections.

It felt to me like the world had stopped. I was suddenly feeling very, very alone – and not at all unlike the bullied teenage girl I once was.

The kitchen door slammed. 'Leese, it's Nick. Where are you?'

As Nick walked into the lounge room, his deep concern was obvious. 'Are you OK?'

I told him I wasn't sure.

'I called Pete. I don't think he's too far away,' Nick said.

The kitchen door slammed again. 'Darling, it's me. Where are you?'

CHAPTER THIRTY-FOUR

Night of the Long Knives ... and Champagne

'Not all storms come to disrupt your life. Some come to
clear your path.' – Paulo Coelho

As writer Hunter S. Thompson once said, 'The TV business
is uglier than most things. It is normally perceived as some
kind of cruel and shallow money trench through the heart of the
journalism industry, a long plastic hallway where thieves and pimps
run free and good men die like dogs.'

A place perhaps, also, where often good women's careers are so
inconsequential and short-lived, they weren't even thought worthy
of mention by Mr Thompson.

When I first moved from what felt like the relative safety of
magazines into the much more fickle world of television, I always
presumed it would be little more than a passing chapter in my
career. That first series of *Beauty & the Beast* was only meant to
run for thirteen weeks, so there was no-one more surprised than
me that those thirteen weeks had stretched out to more than 21
continuous years.

Along the way I had somehow largely avoided the more
unpleasant side of the business. I'd worked with some brilliant
people, and always made the work, the journalism, the audience,

my priority. In any business, though, particularly one involving billions of dollars, where supersized egos are often rewarded, if you take the big risks, you have to be prepared for the big falls. I always approached every day as if it were my last, knowing that, more than likely, one day someone was going to tap me on the shoulder. And now they had.

I needed Nick to help me understand why, in that meeting, it had come to this. As Pete and I sat with him in the lounge room and pressed him for detail, Nick said that it wasn't clear. Hugh Marks had simply said he wanted me off the show and gone from the network immediately. Not just when my contract ended on 31 December, but now. Right now. This was my last day at the network.

No farewell show to say goodbye to our wonderful viewers, no goodbye to the team at the desk I'd shared so much with, not even a chance to say goodbye to the real stars of the show, the team behind the scenes: our brilliant producers, who every morning put words in our mouths and facts at our fingertips, and usually worked even crazier hours than all of us out the front, with absolutely none of the glory; the hard-working floor crew I'd shared so many bleary-eyed mornings with; and the super-talented hair and makeup team whose job it was every day to, as if by magic, turn the puffy eyes and wet hair of 4am me into something much more acceptable for the cameras.

Exactly what had angered Marks so much for him to take such drastic action, however, remained a mystery. Did he want to make an example of me? He had a business to run, and with the rising tide of discontent over so many aspects of the treatment of women in the workplace, including the gender pay gap, was he wanting to set an example of me to all those other women at Nine? *Look at what I did to one of our longest-serving female hosts when she started asking for better treatment. This could be you too.*

Was that his thinking? I'll never know, because Marks never called to tell me himself. It all came via Nick – and a press release that was apparently now being prepared. As Nick explained it, it was a very short meeting. He tried to get more detail but Marks was finished.

'Surely,' Nick said, 'this should be talked through with Lisa first? Surely, after more than a decade of loyal service to the network, she deserves that?'

Apparently not. According to Nick's account, as Marks called the meeting closed and Nick was seen to the door, my manager turned one last time and said, 'Hugh, are you sure you really want to do this? Basically, you're taking one of your most loyal key talents out in the street and putting a bullet in the back of her head just because she is asking for fairer pay. I don't think you understand what a PR disaster this is going to be for you, Nine and the *Today* show.'

Marks looked at him and said, 'Nick, it's done.'

So, as Nick, Pete and I sat there in the lounge room continuing to talk over all the details, I realised I had to start making some plans. If they were writing a press release, and this news was not far from being made public, I had to make sure that a comment from me was included in whatever statement was put out. But first I had to let the family know. I didn't want them hearing this from anyone but me. So, one by one, Pete and I called the kids.

'No more early mornings, Mum!' Louis said triumphantly on loudspeaker, 'No more stupid mascots, no more sitting on dunnies being dragged down the street by women dressed up as wenches!' (Oh Jesus, Louis saw that ...)

Billi was next, and she was upset for me, but Pete quickly reminded her of the three questions – as all three of you kids were OK, sure this was a pain and, yes, a bit of a shock, but in the scheme of things, not serious.

As ever, that put it all in perspective, but when Pete tried the same thing with Jake, our beautiful eldest son interrupted with just the one question he had: 'Dad,' he said softly, 'is *Mum* OK?'

The answer was, I wasn't, but I would be. Because what had been momentarily lost in these last, crazy 90 minutes, was the fact that I was incredibly lucky. I had an alternative: I was now free to take the offer from Channel 10.

For all the brutality of what had just happened, the universe had gone ahead and made the decision I'd been wrestling with for me.

That *Today* show chapter had just – somewhat more abruptly than I would have ever liked – been closed.

The head of Ten, the person Nick had been dealing with throughout these negotiations, was Beverley McGarvey – yes, a woman, and one Nick had been raving to me about for weeks – and she was on the other side of the world, at a TV trade fair in Cannes.

Nick texted her with four simple words: 'We accept your offer.'

His phone rang almost immediately. Bev wanted to know, were we serious?

We most definitely were. Let's do this.

Let's do this!

Everything was moving so fast, it was hard to keep track.

I then had to make one final call of my own. To Mum. I spared her the brutality of my sacking, and instead told her about how excited I was to be moving to *The Project*. She was confused and asked if I'd been 'getting good advice on whether this was the right thing to do', which was so Mum, God love her. I told her I had. Then, she told me she always quite liked that show 'and that lovely blond man on it, the comedian, Peter Hillyard. He's funny.' I told her I agreed. So Mum was good.

By 7.52pm, my statement had been added to the Channel 9 press release, and all the main players had signed off on it. At the same time, Ten were preparing their own press release, for which they, too, needed a quote.

So, Nick called Hugh's team and said they could put the statement out. We were ready. But what came back was quite bizarre. Nick was told that they weren't going to distribute it. They had a press release they weren't going to release to the press? They said they were going to wait for journalists to ring them.

'But if they don't release it,' I said to Nick once he was off the call, 'how will anyone know that I'm leaving? That makes no sense.'

Nick was just as confused.

There was only one thing that did make sense.

'That's OK,' I said. 'I don't work for them anymore. I've got a copy of it. *I'll* release it.'

And so I did. On Twitter. Turns out having a decent social media following can come in very handy sometimes.

So, I kept my tweet above the press release simple ...

'I have some news. I'm sad to say that today was my last day on @thetodayshow. The following statement is from Channel Nine ...'

Nine today confirmed we have been unable to meet the expectations of Lisa Wilkinson and her manager on a contract renewal for a further period. We express our gratitude to Lisa for her 10 years with the *Today* show and are disappointed we find ourselves in this position. Nine will be going in another direction and will be considering our options in the coming weeks ...

The partnership between Lisa and Karl has taken the show to the success it is today and we thank Lisa for everything she has done for the show and for Nine over the past 10 years. We all wish her well for the future,' said Nine CEO Hugh Marks.

Wilkinson said, 'I want to thank Channel Nine for the privilege of co-hosting the *Today* show for the last ten years. I would particularly like to acknowledge my colleagues Karl, Sylvia, Georgie, Tim, Richard, Stevie and Natalia, as well as all the hard-working producers and the entire team behind the cameras ...'

And then I hit 'send'. I was genuinely unsure how people would react, but react they did. Within an instant my phone was buzzing with notifications, texts and calls. But I couldn't look, as I still had to finalise my words for the Ten release. And by 8.56pm, Nick told me the release was done and ready to go.

By this stage I discovered that Pete had been keeping the wider family and a whole bunch of our friends across what had been going on these last couple of hours ... including Deborah, Andrew and Jen, and Mia Freedman, along with several others. The first I knew was when, just five minutes after Billi arrived home to give me a big hug, Mia was at the door with two enormous bottles of champagne.

Mia and I had been close friends, going right back to our days at *Cleo*, and now, as a tireless champion of women's issues and the boss of the largest independent women's media site in the country, this was a day and an outcome she was here to celebrate.

But now that Ten press release had to go. Time for another tweet …

'Thanks so much to everyone for all your lovely messages. I have some more news. This statement is from @channelten. I'm absolutely thrilled …'

LISA WILKINSON JOINS NETWORK TEN

Network Ten is delighted to announce that Lisa Wilkinson is joining the network in a senior hosting and editorial role, effective January 2018.

Lisa will join the team of TEN's award-winning news and current affairs program, *The Project* … [and] will work alongside *The Project* hosts, Carrie Bickmore, Waleed Aly and Peter Helliar, as well as hosting *The Sunday Project*.

Network Ten Chief Operating Officer, Beverley McGarvey, said: 'Lisa Wilkinson is one of the most respected journalists and television presenters in Australia and we are thrilled that she has agreed to join Network Ten's fantastic stable of on-air talent …'

And I hit send again, just as Ben Fordham, who had heard the news via his brother, Nick, turned up with some more champagne in hand.

It was a surreal moment. As Pete, Ben, Nick, Mia, Billi and I all sat around our kitchen table sharing headlines, comments and texts we were all receiving, the news was spreading all over social media – with Australian women, particularly, charging forth in overwhelming support, comparing their own stories and immense frustrations over the gender pay gap. What had started out for me as one of the most confusing and upsetting of afternoons was turning into one of the most empowering nights. Somehow, what had happened to me at Nine, only to then have Channel 10 say 'we'd love to have her and treat her right,' really resonated with Australian women.

Of the many calls that I saw come through that night, there were just four that I managed to get to. Carrie and Waleed were the first, and both couldn't have been more welcoming, just as I was so thrilled that we would all actually get to work together.

The next call was from Michael Pell, my former boss at *Weekend Sunrise* under Adam. My friendship with Michael had never faltered after I left Seven, even though he'd gone on to replace Adam as executive producer of *Sunrise*. I had enormous respect for the way he ran the show, and as competitors go, the only pity was that I liked him so much. His phone had been running hot with the news of my departure, even though he was all the way over in Seattle, on a Qantas junket with a whole bunch of other journalists. He said he was ringing to thank me for leaving *Today*. It was a joke, I knew that. But after a day like I'd had, a joke was exactly what I needed.

And the last call was from Sylvia Jeffreys, and what she said to me in that call will stay with me forever. Out of everyone I had been working with at *Today*, Sylvia was the one I knew I would miss the most.

Each time I took a phone call in the lounge room – the scene of so much upset just hours before – and then returned again to the kitchen, I found one or other of our group calling out updates. Every major news website was covering it. Everyone seemed to have an opinion too, as Nick, Pete, Billi, Ben and Mia read out, one after another, the comments that were pouring in.

One particularly stunning moment came when, with *Sky News After Dark* on in the background, one of their female panellists Rita Panahi, a long-time critic of mine, came down firmly on my side of the equation, saying she knew what it was to be underpaid as a woman herself, and said, according to a disbelieving Pete, 'Good on Lisa!' Yep, this was an issue that reached right across the divide.

One of the most telling moments, though, came when Pete read out a new statement Nine had just given to *The Australian* newspaper: 'Nine will take the *Today* show in a different direction, although we are not yet sure what that direction will be.'

*

It had been an exhausting day and night, and, one by one, Ben, Mia and finally Nick had headed home. Billi decided to stay the night (it *was* pretty good champagne), and by the time I traipsed upstairs to bed, I think I'd experienced in the previous 24 hours every possible human emotion there was: disappointment, elation, anger, frustration, confusion, surprise, pride, loss … and gratitude, for the overwhelming support of so many Australian women who'd had their own struggles and were thrilled by what was being seen as a victory over the boys' club.

But really, now it was time for bed. Pete was already fast asleep, and as I was standing in the bathroom cleaning my teeth, downstairs I could still hear the distant muted ping-ping-ping of messages coming through on my phone.

Stories had already started appearing in the *New York Times* and on the BBC in the UK, and now friends overseas were reading about it there. I knew I should have turned that phone to silent, but somehow, as I crawled between the sheets, I just couldn't muster the energy.

And then I heard it. My 3am alarm, beckoning me to work. I raced down the stairs, not wanting to wake Pete or Billi and grabbed it before it did too much damage throughout the house.

And then I smiled as I did something I hadn't been able to do on a weeknight for well over a decade. I turned my phone – and my alarm – off.

*

I was shocked when I opened my eyes the next morning. The bedroom door was closed and sunlight was streaming in. Stunning, full-blown, well-past-dawn sunlight. My god, what time was it? My panic was instant. Sunshine. I'm not meant to see sunshine when I wake up! Was it the weekend? Shit, I've slept in!

I was living that bad dream I'd occasionally had over the years: that one where I've slept through the alarm, and no-one from the

Today show has called, because, basically, they realised they could do the show without me. Turns out, they very definitely could.

And then it all came flooding back ... yesterday, last night ... it had all *really* happened. I really was gone from the *Today* show.

I rolled over and turned my phone on. 8.16am – a full five beautiful hours past my normal alarm. I took a moment to reflect on everything that had just happened, how my whole world had been turned upside down since that call I'd taken in aisle six at Woolies. And then I pulled the sheets over my head. Damn, that sun really was bright at this time of the morning.

As I lay there staring up close at the textured thread of the white sheets, and the light box effect all that sun was having inside that safe bubble I'd just created, I heard Pete's footsteps coming up the stairs, and then the door gently being opened.

'It's OK. I'm awake,' I croaked. 'I'm just hiding.'

Pete laughed, and pulled the sheets from over my head, before leaning down and kissing me on the forehead, in the same gentle way my dad used to, to make things better.

I looked at Pete, not at all sure of how I was feeling. Perhaps looking for clues from him. How *should* I be feeling?

'Gee, that was a good sleep,' he said. 'I've checked on you a couple of times and you were out cold. I'm glad you slept through.'

'Did that really all just happen?' I asked, as he took one of my hands and sat on the bed.

'It not only happened ... it's still happening.'

Huh?

'Well, this might be our new life for a little while,' he said as he handed me a copy of the *Daily Telegraph*. 'I Break Up With *Today*!' the very clever headline read, with a huge photo of me looking elated, and covering almost the entire front page – and plenty of pages after that, with lots of industry and social media reaction to the news. Well, that didn't take long.

Pete went on: 'And when I went to the newsagent to get it, there were about a dozen paparazzi and camera crews lining the street. I told them you probably wouldn't be coming out, but they're obviously not going anywhere.'

LISA WILKINSON

I looked down at my phone, still vibrating with notifications. Ninety-six new text messages. Sixty-five voicemails. My email inbox, too, was overflowing.

'Anyway,' Pete continued, 'I told them it had been a big night and you're sleeping in for the first time in ages, and that they were wasting their time but thanks for the interest. I don't think it put them off though. They're still out there. And I just saw a few more arriving.'

I got up and looked out the bedroom window, and through the bushes I could see them all.

'Look, why don't I make you a coffee and you can come and watch what they did on the show about you leaving,' he offered. 'I've paused it for you on the TV downstairs. They addressed your departure. You might want to take a look.'

Suddenly, my safe bubble under the sheets was once again looking very appealing.

'Was what they did ... nice?' I asked. 'I mean, they got rid of me, so it's OK, you can tell me if it wasn't.'

'Just take a look,' Pete said.

So together, we went downstairs. As the kettle boiled, Pete walked over to play me my *Today* show farewell – the one I wasn't allowed to be at – the very public full stop at the end of my breakfast TV career.

There, frozen on the screen, was the always professional, always dependable Deb Knight sitting in the chair that was no longer mine, alongside Karl, Sylvia and Richard.

And then Pete hit 'play'.

'Farewell to our beloved Lisa after ten years on *Today*,' Karl started.

'For ten years Lisa has dragged herself out of bed at three-thirty in the morning, fed the dogs and cats, put a load of washing on and come into work to inform you of what was happening in the world.

'For ten years she handled those hours with grace, beauty, intelligence and a wicked, wicked sense of humour. It's safe to say it's come as a bit of a shock and will take a while for it to sink in. So for now, just this, Lisa. Thank you.

456

'Thank you for the laughs, the sage advice, the calmness – oh, the calmness – the support. Thanks for being a great colleague, a great interviewer; thanks for being a great dancer and a truly, truly terrible singer.

'Thanks for being a great mum; I know you value that more than anything else. And thanks for being a great friend. Whatever you do or wherever you go, you do so having made your mark on this show and this man.

'Mostly, you go with all my love. We will see you soon ... maybe after midday. Enjoy the sleep.'

Wow. Just wow. I turned to Pete. So that's how Karl feels? Really?

Then, there was a farewell package summing up my ten years. To be fair, whoever had been asked to put it together wouldn't have had a lot of time, and I was amazed there was anything at all, but it could be best summed up as: Lisa playing tennis, Lisa dancing, Lisa singing, Lisa dressed in various costumes ... and Lisa with a giraffe taking a carrot from her mouth. But at least I looked like I was having fun. Which I almost always was. Because, despite the ending, I really did love that job.

Meantime, I checked a few more of the messages on my phone. So many women in the industry were sending their support – dozens from colleagues at Nine and some really touching ones from women at other networks, from Leigh Sales, Juanita Phillips and Sarah Ferguson to Mel Doyle, Natalie Barr and Kylie Gillies. The always supportive Steve Liebmann, too. Even Hugh Jackman and Deborra-Lee Furness had heard about it and sent their love and congratulations.

The most amusing of all was from my former boss and the man whose support had always mattered to me while I was at Nine, David Gyngell, texting from his new life up Byron Bay way: 'Well played.'

But the one that really stood out and gave me the biggest smile as I scrolled back to the top of all the messages was from Ross Greenwood: 'Welcome to a new world Lisa, where 3am is a dream, not a wake-up call. Thanks for a terrific 10 years. Cheers Ross.'

If only he knew the part he had played. So I messaged him back.

Hey Ross,

Thank you. I've loved working with you too. And you should probably know it was a really passionate piece you did on radio back in the middle of the year on the shame of the gender pay gap and why you believed it was time to stop this nonsense that really spurred me on.

Anyway, onward and upward from here. Warmest wishes always, Lisa.

*

Mum had seemed a little confused the night before. She was an avid *Today* show viewer, and I was sure that, if she'd tuned in that morning, seeing her daughter missing from that seat might have been a little more upsetting than she was expecting. So I called her, and it had been, no matter how much I tried to explain how happy I was with the ultimate outcome.

And then it dawned on me. In Mum's eyes I had been publicly humiliated and rejected. Cast aside by an organisation she had seen me work so hard for, and I wondered if maybe she was reliving her own feelings of abandonment – feelings that I knew still lived deep in her soul. So I went to see her ... saying a quick few polite, positive words to the paps sitting at the top of the driveway as I left, hoping that would be enough to keep them happy.

I promised Mum that I would be OK, and assured her once again about how thrilled I was to be going to Channel 10. I even read to her some of the lovely messages I'd been receiving, and I think that helped.

But the backlash from Hugh Marks – who was clearly not happy under the circumstances of my speedy re-employment – was soon apparent. According to Marks, in one of the many interviews he gave in the following days, 'There are six, seven, eight women I could name right now who could fill Wilkinson's position. She is no loss.'

Hunter S. Thompson was right. But Marks was not done. For shortly afterwards in another interview, 'If she got what she wanted, we would have had to cut ten producers' jobs.'

Yes, there were *lots* of big salaries at Channel 9; but who is the one, whose proposed increase in salary – still much, much less than Karl's – risked the livelihood of ten producers?

That would be me: the *woman*.

I was greedy. Didn't know my place. And had, apparently, been on some sort of personal publicity crusade by renewing my vows. Ah, yes, how clever of me. Pete and I had actually been plotting this coup for 25 years! So sneaky. If nothing else, surely they had to admire my patience and long-term planning!

Meantime, another 'insider' at *Today* told the *Herald*, 'To be honest, there is a sense of renewed energy here. We have something to prove now, because most of us work as a team.'

So, are we all clear now? Women asking for a fairer go on pay parity? Yer lettin' the team down, darl.

By this point all I could do was laugh. I didn't know how long this was going to go on for. The media interest, even globally, was extraordinary. The whole issue had hit a major nerve. Alerts on my phone continued to go crazy. There were requests for interviews from around the world, including now *The Times* of London and the *Washington Post*. I declined, not wanting to further feed a beast over which I had no control. I hoped that these few days would see us hit peak crazy and then tail off. I just had to wait, stay quiet and ride this out.

But nobody told the paparazzi that, who had now set up permanent camp outside our house. The prying lenses of complete strangers had captured and published images taken through our kitchen window. They'd followed the kids. I was chased down streets. Into cul-de-sacs. I saw a poor unsuspecting road worker come within centimetres of being run over by a speeding pap, determined to get yet another shot of me for the fourth day in a row. He finally cornered me in a Woolies car park. It was not nice.

I hated it all. I didn't want to be photographed. I didn't want another *Daily Mail* headline. I didn't want to hear my name on the radio. And I did everything I could to stay out of it.

Every day I wore black, in the same sunglasses, looking down. And still they got published. And on one ridiculous day, when I'd come back from visiting Mum and parked in our driveway, I decided to climb over and get out on the passenger's side so they couldn't see me through the bushes. Sure enough, the next day, front page of the *Daily Telegraph*, there was me crouching behind the car, looking a whole lot like a criminal hiding from the cops. For the first time, under that intense level of scrutiny, I started to understand what Karl had been going through for more than a year.

What made it all easier to bear, though, was how lovely people generally were being: the emails and letters I received, the strangers who stopped me in the street to thank me for taking a stand. Mostly they were women, but there were also many men, too – often fathers of daughters – and they were so kind I simply couldn't have been more humbled.

But after a week of too many headlines, too many untruths, too many moments finding myself looking in the rear-vision mirror at every car that was following just a little too closely behind me, I had to take a break. It was getting too much. Social media, the weekly 'women's' mags, and gossip writers had hit a wellspring of clickbait, and my name was in the middle of it all.

I had to get out of my own way, and simply shut everything down and take a big break from it.

But just before I did that, I saw one last beautiful note from a long-time viewer of the show that made everything worthwhile.

It was a DM on my Instagram from a single mum, Lesley, who told me she had recently graduated from ten years of part-time uni and entered a law firm only to experience her own pay battles at work. Along with her two kids, Lesley had watched the *Today* show for as long as she could remember and wanted me to know about the reaction she'd witnessed in her household one week on from my departure. As she told it, after a few days, her son had heard his sister say that I wasn't going to be on the *Today* show anymore. She wrote …

'Why did Lisa leave the show?' he asked me as he was tying his shoelaces for school – clearly not happy about the decision, and maybe a little confused as to why he hadn't been consulted.

(Sorry, but that's how much ownership we take in the show – and you – at our place!!) At that moment Lisa, I realised that you had handed all of us who believe in true equality and want to pass those important lessons on to our children – boys and girls – a gift.

I also knew that what was happening in our house was probably echoing a conversation that was going on in households around the country. It was a perfect teaching moment, because I'm also ashamed to admit I hadn't spoken up to anyone about what was going on in my own workplace. To that point I hadn't shared my own work pay battles with my kids.

So I wanted to explain the issue but keep it really simple for him: 'Well, the girl wasn't being paid as much as the boy.'

My son then stopped tying his shoelaces, and looked up at me while he took it in.

'Well that's just silly,' he responded, just as simply. And there it was: the perfect response. From an 8-year-old boy!

Lisa, both my son and daughter – and me! – are going to miss you in the mornings. I don't know if we'll keep watching because I can see that there is stuff going on behind the scenes to indicate that there was much you had to put up with that never made it to air. And it doesn't make it as much fun to watch anymore.

But thank you for giving me that important teaching moment. Because I know that both my children have now learnt that what just happened will forevermore be seen as 'silly'. Good luck to you always, Lesley.

That message brought tears to my eyes. Whatever happened from here, whatever slings and arrows were coming my way, whatever was written about me, it was all worth it for that one moment, and that little boy tying his shoelaces before he, and his big sister, headed off into the world.

CHAPTER THIRTY-FIVE

And then there was Brittany ...

'Each time a woman stands up for herself, without
knowing it, possibly without even claiming it, she stands up
for every woman.' – Maya Angelou

Mᴜᴍ'ꜱ ʜᴇᴀʟᴛʜ ʜᴀᴅ ʀᴀᴘɪᴅʟʏ gone downhill, and on this warm
Saturday morning in early March, as Kyle and I sat at her
hospital bedside, she was weak but happy to see us and chat. For
hours.

It was a recurring theme with Mum over the years that whenever
any of us visited or chatted with her on the phone, it wouldn't be
long before she would say, 'Well, darling, I know you're busy, I don't
want to hold you up ...' But not today.

Just four weeks earlier, I'd been in Melbourne for the Friday
night hosting of *The Project*, and Louis had gone to urgently collect
Mum from her apartment and take her to Royal North Shore
Emergency to determine exactly what was going on with her health.
Week by week she'd bounced around various hospitals almost as
much as had her changing prognoses. From Emergency to ICU, to a
ward, to respite, to a ward, ICU again, then back to Emergency, and
so on. And with every transfer, every new set of doctors and nurses,
every new attempt at a precise diagnosis, it was obvious that Mum
was losing strength. There had been a few dire days, and then, like
the fighter she'd always been, Mum would rally.

On one memorable afternoon, Billi and I dropped in to see her in yet another new ward where, as always, she was every nurse's favourite patient.

'Your mum is such a sweetheart; we've just been having a lovely chat,' they would say, as we were shown to yet another new bed with Mum's ever-diminishing frame beneath the bedsheets.

Mum was always quick with a smile as soon as she saw us, and on this day, Billi had brought along a few things she knew Mum would like: a new nightie and dressing gown, a bunch of flowers and, as a treat, a Magnum ice-cream. Mum loved them all, except the Magnum. Despite her failing body, somehow, even at the age of almost 90, those early messages of the need for physical acceptance were still drilled in deep, and she said to Billi that as lovely as the thought was and as much as she would love to eat it, she would resist.

'I am finally down to the weight I was when I was 18,' she rasped triumphantly, 'and I think I might finally fit back into a bikini again. So, you have it, darling.'

Even though we all laughed, knowing Mum, she was probably only half joking.

But now on this Saturday with Kyle, propped up on several pillows, nurses coming and going checking various monitors and writing notes on her patient record at the end of the bed, Mum was at peace.

She told us she'd had the loveliest time the day before chatting with Jake for hours. Just the two of them together, a grandmother and her grandson, sharing memories, while Jake talked about his plans and provided the afternoon's soundtrack. 'Whatever song you want, Grandma! I've got them all here,' he'd said, holding up his phone and showing her, as he'd explained it to Mum, 'this thing called Spotify'.

Mum was not what you'd call an early adopter of technology. She had lived a life never having sent an email, never Googling anything, and certainly never owning a computer. And when on a couple of occasions I'd tried to show her something on my own computer I thought she'd be interested in, she always maintained a safe distance.

Kyle had bought her a mobile phone, which more often than not she forgot to charge, while I'd sorted an iPod for her so she could have all her favourite songs at her fingertips, which she never used. Even the basic technology of her apartment could be a challenge for her, and on Brett's wonderfully regular visits, he would always have to sort out the answering machine, the fridge, the pilot light on the gas, or the headphones for her much-loved transistor radio.

So on this occasion, to have her first-born grandchild – that little baby she once rocked for hours on our front verandah as they both waited for 'Mummy' to come home from work – play every one of her favourite songs as requested was, she said, one of the happiest days she had ever spent.

The playlist that day said it all. Louis Armstrong's 'What A Wonderful World', Ronnie Milsap's 'Lost in the Fifties Tonight', Sister Janet Mead's 'The Lord's Prayer', Eva Cassidy's version of 'Imagine', and a lot of Frank Sinatra … 'Fly Me to the Moon', 'You Make Me Feel So Young' and 'September of My Years'. Mum loved Frank Sinatra. It just so happened that my beautiful, handsome dad, the man she had spent almost 40 years with, was the spitting image of ol' blue eyes; and, Frank's superb voice aside, I was sure that that was a big part of why his songs had been featuring so heavily that day.

There was one other song, too: Peggy Lee's 'Is That All There Is?'. It had been a huge hit when I was a kid, and Mum and I used to sing it together whenever it came on the radio, but even then, it always made me sad. It was about a woman looking back at the end of her life, with all its many joys and disappointments, continually asking the question: is that all there is? And deciding they may as well dance and have a ball … if that's all there is.

Once or twice as a kid, I remembered seeing Mum and Dad dancing in the kitchen to that song. And I saw Mum happy.

I hoped that when she'd listened to it on that Friday with Jake, that again she'd been happy. I hoped she knew that if her life was now close to done, for all its early difficulties, all the fears that never quite left her, that she realised she had triumphed over her beginnings. She had overcome most of her demons to be an incredible grandma, a kind and supportive mother to all three of her children, and a faithful and loving partner to Dad.

And now, just three days after Jake had played all those songs, he was playing them again. This time, though, we didn't know if she could hear them. Mum was in a coma in ICU at Royal North Shore Hospital. Around her were her three children, three grandchildren and Kyle's partner, Trish, all of us taking turns at holding her weary, aged hands lined with tubes – their contents hopefully easing this final journey she was on.

We'd had the call at 7 o'clock that Monday morning: 'Come now!' Even as we raced from home, by the time I was parking the car the call came again: 'It's happening.'

And yet, in one final shout out to the universe that this good woman just wasn't going down without a fight, Mum hung on against all the odds – all day – as we sat there in our masks and PPE, watching the beeping monitors grow weak and then pick up again.

Pete was overseas that weekend and unable to get back in time to say his goodbyes, but he managed to do one thing that day for which I will forever be grateful. He called his good friend Monsignor Tony Doherty, the long-time Dean of St Mary's Cathedral, to deliver Mum the Last Rites. Even though she had long since abandoned so much of what the church had to offer, there was something about her Catholic beginnings that just never left her.

And so, at 5.23pm on 5 March, a full ten hours after we'd received that first call, Mum took her last light breath, and the machines finally fell silent.

After 89 years of fighting to keep going, Beryl Wilkinson, the little Catholic girl who'd had such a tough start to life, was gently seen out by her loving family and one of the most senior Catholic clerics in the country. It would have humbled her, and was exactly what that timorous little girl deserved.

*

It's a funny thing, parenting. Much as you try to get it right, it's hard to see the long game. There is no book that tells you if any of this stuff that you're doing is working. Or gets in. Most of us are just putting one foot in front of the other and trying not to trip.

My simple belief is that as long as kids feel safe and seen and heard, then you're most of the way there. Kids are smart, too, and for all your loving guidance, they do work a lot of things out for themselves, and it's those moments when they surprise you that can really take your breath away.

As we all made our way into the North Chapel at Northern Suburbs Memorial Gardens and Crematorium to say our goodbyes to Mum, with a huge contingent of familiar faces from the old days at Campbelltown who'd made such a wonderful effort to be there, I was about to be reminded just how surprising your children can be.

Jake said that he wanted to say a few words at the service. Included in those words was a poem by Lee Pitts, called 'These Things I Wish For You' from a grandmother to her grandson, which was all about the virtues of hand-me-down clothes, homemade ice cream, leftovers and even the occasional black eye for standing up for something you believe in. Mum had read it to Jake once, or maybe more often than that; I didn't know. But it had clearly struck a beautiful chord between them, and now, before the hushed rows of gathered friends and family, he spoke first of what a wonderful grandmother she'd been and then recited the poem.

I couldn't have been prouder or more moved. That poem was a testament to Mum's values, and I was so happy to know that Jake had embraced them too.

At the wake straight afterwards, so many were sharing their own stories of Mum, but the most wonderful moment came when 30 or so long-time members of the Harlequins Rugby Club, who had made the trip from Campbelltown, gave a rousing rendition of the club song. All these years on, they remembered and honoured Mum's tireless contribution, alongside Dad's, to their community; and in many ways, it was a Campbelltown farewell to both of them.

Then, there remained just one last thing left to do. Before we headed home for a family wake of our own, we placed a bunch of the white hydrangeas from atop Mum's coffin right by Dad's plaque in the crematorium gardens, hoping that maybe now the reunited couple were dancing together once again …

*

One of the many things I'd always loved about *The Project,* whenever I'd watched it over the years, was the feeling that I was seeing the best of society reflected back at us. It was a place where conversations started and the complex was explained. Every night there was something confronting, provocative, thoughtful, considered … and fun. It was, as promised, news delivered differently. With an ever-growing list of reality shows now dominating the airwaves and designed to bring out the worst in its participants and everyone watching, *The Project* was a show that consistently displayed the best of what people can be. And I was so thrilled to now be a part of that.

Within days of joining the team, I knew that everything I'd gone through in 2017 had been worth it. Just so I could be here. With these people. Doing this work. Learning, growing, expanding on and challenging all that I previously knew.

Just as those calls from Carrie and Waleed had been so very welcoming on that night – which our family had now affectionately dubbed 'The Night of the Long Knives' – so were the entire team wonderfully welcoming now. Pete Helliar – or Hillyard, as Mum had called him – really is the nicest guy in TV … and I immediately understood why the show was as good as it was.

Some of my favourite people from my years at *Today* – both in front of and behind the camera – were now at *The Project* too, including Gorgi Coghlan, who had gone from strength to strength in the intervening years; as well as the man responsible for making my move to Ten happen, Peter Meakin, and our former chief of staff, Chris Bendall. A particular joy, too, was co-hosting *The Sunday Project* with Hamish Macdonald, a journalist whose investigative and foreign correspondent work I'd long admired.

It was amazing how quickly I relaxed into it. It was something Jake pointed out to me one night over a family dinner that had lingered late – something we'd rarely got to do when that early alarm used to beckon. 'Mum,' he'd said, smiling, 'we finally got you back.'

My *Project* brief was broad; and along with all the human interest stories, political interviews, editorials and daily news I could throw myself at, Craig Campbell, the executive producer, was keen that I head overseas for big celebrity interviews as often as time allowed.

I certainly hit the ground running. Within weeks, I was at Caesar's Palace in Las Vegas to interview Celine Dion who, as divas go – in her dramatic high-collared cream coat-dress and black patent thigh-high boots – certainly didn't disappoint. As we were chatting before filming, while the team organised the last of the lighting and camera angles, she had asked me if I was married. I told her I was, and mentioned that Pete was an author; and then, right on cue, as I was placing my phone on the ground, he happened to call. A call Celine insisted on answering ... and they ended up having a great chat.

In fact, Pete seemed to develop a bit of a habit for inopportune calls when, on another occasion, just as I had finished an interview with New Zealand Prime Minister Jacinda Ardern, it happened again. This time, the two had met before, and with the PM a huge rugby fan, they had plenty to discuss. This time, it took a full ten minutes to wrestle my phone back from the coolest woman on the planet.

Serena Williams, meanwhile, proved to be the toughest customer I'd ever interviewed. Just 48 hours before we sat down together, the 23-time grand-slam tournament winner had made global headlines for her explosive on-court performance after losing the US Open 6-2, 6-4 to first-time grand-slam tournament winner Naomi Osaka.

On the day we met in New York, Serena was the most-talked-about woman in the world. It was her first interview since that volatile display at Flushing Meadows. The only problem was, Serena herself didn't want to talk, and in the moments before the cameras started rolling, it felt like her incandescent fury on court had now morphed into frozen dismissiveness and eagerness to be quit of me.

The interview had been arranged months before as part of a breast-cancer awareness campaign for her sponsor Berlei; and while Serena was obliged to fulfil her contractual duty, anything beyond that had been the subject of deep negotiations with her team in the next room.

We had already been warned that if we asked about the controversial Mark Knight cartoon published in Melbourne's *Herald Sun* the previous day that had mocked Serena and made global headlines, she would walk out.

We agreed that we wouldn't, but equally made it clear that we had not come all this way ... just to come all this way. As a news program, we had to ask questions specifically on the US Open, and her people eventually agreed to three.

So, after 15 minutes discussing the very important issue of breast-cancer screening, her injury struggles, the battle to stay at number one, the magic of motherhood, and her good buddy Meghan Markle, I dove right in with the US Open questions: about her coach's admission that he was giving her tips from the sidelines, the verbal attack on the umpire, and whether she was comfortable robbing Naomi Osaka of her big moment of triumph. Then I asked whether she regretted smashing her racquet in anger.

Serena hesitated and glanced off camera. It must have been a cue, because at that point, a very loud, very insistent blonde woman from her team jumped up at the back of the room. She was seriously not happy.

'Sorry, that's four questions about the US Open.' Serena kept looking at her as if to indicate that this new player in the room was now in charge of proceedings and, hey, what could she do?

But I knew exactly who was running this show. It was Serena. So, I carried on speaking to the tennis star directly.

'Are you comfortable or not?' I asked the tennis star gently, focusing only on her.

'Change topic,' said the blonde, who hadn't introduced herself and whose name I didn't know.

Serena didn't want to look at me. But I continued, looking right at her – the most powerful woman in the room. And, on her good days, on the planet.

'I'm in your hands, Serena,' I said, making it clear that I wasn't taking instruction from anyone but her. 'I'm in your hands ...'

It worked. I got her back … and even though I felt like I'd just done three tough sets of mental mind games with the tennis legend, I survived – and, as I left that day, couldn't help feeling just a little more sympathy for Osaka.

Not all assignments have been as tense as that one. In fact, if there is an exact opposite to 'tense' it would be the super speedy round-the-world trip Craig sent me on that took in three separate cities and three separate interviews all in the space of six days. First up, London, to interview David Beckham; then straight on to New York for a sit-down with Bradley Cooper; and on the way home, a quick stop in LA for a chat with Jon Bon Jovi.

He had to be joking. He wasn't.

'What a waste on a happily married woman!' was all any of my single girlfriends had to say when I told them. In fact, plenty of my married girlfriends laughed and said the same. I laughed, too: 'It doesn't seem like a waste to me at all!'

Every one of my girlfriends promised to forgive me if I came back and declared a favourite by the end of this ridiculous trip of dreams.

In David Beckham's case, I couldn't get over his impeccable manners, the softness of his voice or, endearingly, how much he talked about family life at home with Victoria and their kids. His entire office was decorated with the framed black-and-white photography of son Brooklyn, and he said that one of his greatest joys these days was picking up his seven-year-old daughter, Harper, from school each day. (Something I suspected might be a bit of a joy for all the mums at the school gate each afternoon, as well.)

When I got to New York the next day, *A Star Is Born* had just been released and Bradley Cooper, the actor-turned-director, charmed our entire crew when, 90 seconds into our interview, he suspected there was an issue with our sound and suggested we take a moment, try and get it right, and start again. He said he really wanted our interview to go well and was happy to wait while it was fixed – something celebrities and their minders rarely do. Normally, the clock is always ticking. Not with Bradley.

And then there was Jon Bon Jovi who, to be honest, I knew the least about, even if like everyone I had screamed 'Livin' On A Prayer' at the top of my lungs at more weddings, parties, anything, than I could count. He had me from the moment he started talking about his wife of 30 years, Dorothea, and their four kids with such love and pride. Despite his enormous success in rock and roll, he turned out to be one of the most unaffected celebrities I've ever chatted to. That head full of proudly salt-and-pepper hair only added to his appeal ... and so, in a very close race, I told my girlfriends that Mr Bon Jovi was my favourite in that crazy week.

And then there was the royal wedding. My second. And once again the world's media descended on the UK, this time to chronicle the wedding of Prince Harry to Meghan Markle. It was lovely to see Diana's second son seemingly so settled. There was something too about this union that made it all just that little bit more intriguing. Was change finally coming to the British royal family?

Maybe it was the preacher who quoted Martin Luther King and touched on the legacy of slavery. Or perhaps it was the gospel choir singing 'Stand By Me', while the cameras cut to Camilla looking confused. Was this finally a modernisation of the royals, whether they wanted it or not? In hindsight, it was crazy to think, even for a moment, that this accomplished, independent American actress would ever allow herself to meekly collapse to fit the Windsor mould, and abandon her strong beliefs in the service of the antiquated pomp and privilege of the monarchy.

Meghan was never going to be a Stepford duchess; she had opinions, she was politically aware – heck, she had an actual life before the royals. And it was all so mesmerising to watch from the sidelines.

Unlike last time with the wedding of Harry's older brother, I wasn't in a specially constructed studio, or hanging with my loo mates Barbara Walters or Diane Sawyer; I was mixing it on the ground, with the hundreds of thousands lining the streets on the four-kilometre 'Long Walk' up to Windsor Castle. Our small team had an absolute ball as we raced around putting together packages for *The Sunday Project*, which I then hosted out of London the following evening.

As our small team made the long walk back to our car from Windsor Castle, I passed many of the international broadcast set-ups, including … yes it was … the *Today* show set. With the wedding over, the raised stage emblazoned with that very familiar *Today* show logo was all but empty now, but I could see that some of the hard-working crew I knew so well were packing up. It was wonderful to chat with all of them, and they told me I had apparently just missed Karl and his new co-host, Georgie Gardner, who had both just headed for Heathrow.

No matter; it was lovely to see so many old faces in the crew, but it surprised me how long ago my time at *Today* now felt. Pete had told me once of a saying in the Wallabies that when you leave a team, it's like pulling your finger out of a glass of water: the space it once took up is instantly filled – and there are new and instant loyalties and dynamics that exist that you are simply not a part of. That was precisely the case here. They had moved on, and so had I.

Meanwhile, the big interviews continued: chatting to George Clooney about lockdown haircuts and the joy of his kids; Dame Helen Mirren on the importance of living authentically; Angelina Jolie on hanging out with Aussie mates; and Michelle Pfeiffer, who had no idea that her name had become slang in the Australian cricket team for taking five wickets in an innings (a 'five-for' morphing into a 'five-fer' into a 'Pfeiffer', a 'Michelle Pfeiffer', and finally a 'Michelle'). Geddit? She got it, was overjoyed, and told me she couldn't wait to tell her cricket-fan husband. True fame for Ms Pfeiffer at last!

And of course, there was the one and only Barbra Streisand, who told me mid-interview that she hated being interviewed – before proceeding with one of the most surprisingly honest chats imaginable, with some pretty full and frank assessments on the performances of both Beyoncé and Lady Gaga, which made world headlines.

Interviewing Lady Gaga herself at her LA home in mid-March of 2020 was a particular treat, despite meeting at a time when coronavirus was just teetering on the edge of exploding across the US and the world.

When the crew and I arrived 30 minutes ahead of schedule at what we thought was Gaga's address, we were momentarily confused by the unmarked driveways in this pocket of the Hollywood Hills where the singer lived, and unsure if we were at the right house. It was at this point that a van pulled up right next to us, and a driver jumped out and opened the door, only to reveal an utter explosion of colour and sequins and tulle and fabulousness to be carried up the driveway. Yep, we were definitely at the right address.

Inside, minders were stationed at various points as we moved further into the home's inner sanctum, all there to ensure Gaga's safety. When I was then ushered into her home recording studio, it was not before I'd been through three separate sanitising stations, ID checks and reminders to keep my Gaga distance. 'Absolutely no touching!' I was warned.

I'm really not sure what I was thinking when I chose my outfit that morning – a rather demure grey frock – to interview a woman who had once worn a dress made entirely of meat, but let's just say, if there were still any bosses out there looking for a little lady ready to take dictation, I was dressed for it.

Gaga herself arrived in a banging rock-chic ensemble, all black leather, jewelled chains, winged eyeliner and a dramatic high ponytail to top it off. When I whispered my embarrassment about the demure way I was dressed just before we started, Gaga clocked it, assured me it was fine, and then as soon as the cameras started rolling shared, 'No-one heard you say this, but you do not look like a secretary.'

I confessed, 'I feel very conservative in this outfit.'

'That's just because I have no pants on and a leather jacket!'

We had a great chat and, by the end, we'd bonded over one issue in particular – our shared experience as teenagers: 'Being bullied has taught me the importance of spreading kindness in the world, because it's something we can fix.' And she was right. Then, much to my surprise, she leaned in for a huge, non-socially-distanced hug.

And then I rushed once more to LAX. The last plane out to Sydney was almost gone, just as COVID was shutting everything down.

And I only just made it.

*

But for all the fun of the celebrity interviews I've done for *The Project*, it's been the stories of real people living through extraordinary and sometimes heartbreaking experiences that stay with me.

I particularly think of Sam Ballard, a beautiful young man in his twenties who was left paralysed after swallowing a parasite-infected slug, and whose extraordinary mum, Katie, was fighting to get a fairer deal amid the bureaucratic red tape of the NDIS. And Gareth, the now single dad from Townsville, whose beautiful wife, Beck, had died from cystic fibrosis three months before her best friend delivered their baby son, Rixon, by surrogate.

There were the Qantas pilots who cried in the retelling of the moments they flew to the Mojave Desert in Southern California to deliver the unused jets for which a pandemic-ravaged Australia no longer had use. Now, with no job, they had pivoted as a group to become bus drivers and, despite the trauma of their clipped wings, continued to give each other strength.

There were the children of rugby-league legend Steve Folkes, Hayley and Dan, who discovered their dad had CTE (chronic traumatic encephalopathy), and were part of a successful push to change the rules around concussion in the game.

I will equally never forget: the beautiful siblings of Will Mainprize, desperate for help to find their brother after a typhoon capsized the ship he was on off the coast of Japan; or meeting NSW south-coast locals who had lost everything after the devastating 2020 summer bushfires.

Particularly haunting was hearing the horrific details of the sexual abuse allegations laid by Brett Sengstock against the former head of the Hillsong Church, Frank Houston. At the time of writing, those allegations have resulted in Houston's son, Brian, the current worldwide leader of Hillsong and a close personal friend of Prime Minister Scott Morrison, being charged for allegedly concealing that sexual abuse.

*

And then there was Brittany ...

It was mid-January 2021 when a young woman from Canberra called Brittany Higgins contacted me, saying that she had a story to tell – one that would be as difficult for her to recount as it would be for the nation to hear, and one that would make a lot of the most powerful people in this country very uncomfortable.

After many phone calls, she had arranged to take a day off from her job in the office of Employment Minister Michaelia Cash to travel up from Canberra. We finally met in a Sydney hotel just 24 hours after sexual assault survivor Grace Tame had been named Australian of the Year. Brittany was accompanied by her partner, David Sharaz, while I was with my *Project* producer, Angus Llewellyn.

Over the next six gruelling hours, Brittany told us her account of allegedly being raped by a fellow parliamentary staffer on a couch in the office of her then boss and government minister, Linda Reynolds, late one night in March 2019. Deeply traumatised, she told us she had then turned to three of the most powerful women in Australian politics for help. According to Brittany, instead of being treated for what she was – a young woman in desperately deep distress needing help – she was now a pressing political problem the government wanted to make disappear.

As excruciatingly private as her situation was, though, word of Brittany's alleged rape was becoming common knowledge within the walls of Parliament House. Turning from those three women to the system within her workplace whereby she could make legal complaint, she had found there was no independent body or human resources department within Parliament House designed to deal with allegations of sexual assault. That meant that, if everything Brittany was telling me was true, Parliament House was the easiest place in Australia to rape a woman and get away with it.

And Brittany was not alone. Other women in Parliament House had their own stories to tell, but the pressure not to speak – and certainly not to the media – was enormous. When some of those women had appeared on *Four Corners* a few months before with allegations of their own, Brittany was confronted the next morning by female colleagues making devastatingly disparaging remarks:

criticising them for speaking up, breaking party ranks, and then urging Brittany not to tell her own story. 'You'd never do that, would you …' they'd half pleaded, half warned.

So now, after almost two soul-destroying years of being dismissed, disrespected and denied her chance to seek justice, Brittany had had enough.

Angus and I listened to it all, stunned. Right now, she knew that if she ever had any hope of justice, then sitting down in front of our cameras and telling us her story was the only option she had left. As a media adviser herself, she knew that once she spoke publicly, what came next was going to be ugly, and there would be major ramifications.

'They will come after me,' she said.

Who will?

'The government.'

With horrifying precision, Brittany predicted exactly the response that would come from Scott Morrison, those who ran things in the Prime Minister's Office, Minister Reynolds and Minister Cash: the talking points, the language, the denials, the teary performances for the cameras, the obfuscation, the leaks to sympathetic pro-government journalists. Enormous forces would come into play to silence her, she told us. But still she wanted to do it.

Brittany told us her hope was to release the interview on 14 February, the first day of the first parliamentary sitting week of the year, in order for it to have the greatest impact. Brittany told me she was also going to share her story with News Corp's Samantha Maiden. One TV interview, one print interview … and that would be it.

One week later, I sat down with Brittany for more than three harrowing hours, as this brave young woman told her story for our cameras in the starkest and simplest of terms.

From the moment Brittany's story went to air, Australia reeled.

My greatest fear was that after a few days of the churn and burn of the fickle political news cycle, the spin doctors in Parliament House would make sure – just as Brittany had predicted – that there was nothing to see here, and her important story would be forgotten.

But Australian women were never going to let that happen. Because for an untold number of them, Brittany's allegations of being sexually assaulted, of being shamed, of being silenced, was their story, too. There was just something about Brittany's story, and Brittany herself, that touched people, that made it feel safe for them to also speak up. Often, for the very first time. In the same month Brittany spoke out, there was an historic 61 per cent surge in women reporting sexual assaults to the NSW Police.

Stories so many had long kept hidden were being shared. And believed. We have Brittany's extraordinary courage to thank for that.

The most underwhelming reaction, however, came from the prime minister, Scott Morrison, who had at first downplayed the horror of a staffer having been allegedly raped just 50 metres from his own office door.

Then the morning after watching our interview, as the story made front-page news around the country, the prime minister called a snap press conference.

'Jenny and I spoke last night,' he told the gathered press pack, 'and she said to me, "You have to think about this as a father first. What would you want to happen if it were our girls?"'

The female fury in response to those comments, and the idea that we had a prime minister incapable of understanding the seriousness of such heinous allegations of criminality unless through the imaginary context of it happening to his own daughters, swept the country and inspired the March 4 Justice rallies exactly one month later.

There was one word that kept reverberating: Enough! Women of all ages and generations had had enough of the injustice. Enough of the cover-ups. Enough of the indifference. Silence was getting women nowhere.

I was inundated with the stories of other women who had never before spoken of what had happened to them. Friends, colleagues, strangers, private messages on social media, people who stopped me in the street. Always the reasons for never speaking out before were the same: feelings of shame, the fear of not being believed, or possibly being scoffed back into silence. For many it was just easier to try to forget, but it was clear they never did.

Of the thousands of heartbreaking accounts I heard, one was from the daughter of a survivor. She wanted me to know just how powerfully Brittany's story had affected her family. And it has stayed with me ever since ...

> When my mother saw the march, she was badly affected as it brought up the time when she was molested by her singing coach, a Professor at the Sydney Conservatorium. She saved so hard for these private lessons and was accepted because of her skill. She was 18 at the time, and innocent. She is now 91. The sheer powerlessness has never left her. She has carried this for 73 years, never telling a single soul. Now she has. She never went back to singing. A career lost.

*

It is extraordinary how much support you get when you live your truth. When you realise that a life driven by love and gratitude trumps all else. That it's wise to distance yourself from those who diminish you. That kindness is life-affirming. That disruption can be good. And that at the end of our lives, the question should be not what we have done, but how well we have loved.

Too often, we forget that being a woman is an incredible gift. It can be amazing and joyous and powerful, and we need to show girls that however often they might cry, they will almost certainly end up laughing three times as hard. That it is possible to come to peace with our bodies. That it's OK to be scared, and even better to do something that's unfamiliar and raw. We need to teach that vulnerability is a strength, because that's when courage takes over, and that can only happen when fear is present first. And that it's important sometimes to just sit a while and think.

Oh, and stop waiting for that person to text – that one who keeps you waiting is unlikely to be there for the long haul in any case.

We need to teach that age is not something to fear. Getting older really is the greatest gift, and that's the secret no-one tells you. It's a time to embrace all that hard-fought wisdom, to live a life that's full and honest, and burn more brightly with the dreams of what you still strive to achieve.

What gives me hope are the rising generations. Their strengths, their passions, their focus. I see it in the eyes of young women like Ash Barty, Brittany Higgins, Grace Tame, Greta Thunberg, Poet Laureate Amanda Gorman and Nobel Peace Prize laureate Malala Yousafzai. I see it in the eyes of my own children, the children of friends and so many of the brilliant young people I work with.

Once, it was one or two people who would stand up or speak out, and now we're seeing entire generations who are standing together – and not just for things that benefit them directly. We're seeing good men stand up and speak for women; we're seeing white people stand up for those of colour; we're seeing straight people stand up for the LGBT+ community. We are seeing the current generation caring more and more about the environment that future generations must inherit – and understanding the need for action now. We're seeing more people standing up for what they know is right, rather than just accepting what has always been.

As I look to my own children, I hope I have given them the benefits of all my knee scrapes, without saving them too much from the pain of knowing their own. I've tried to teach them all I know, but what I was never prepared for is how much they have taught me. And that's the point really, isn't it? That with each new generation, we can try to fix the mistakes of the past.

So much has shifted since I was a kid, and I'm so glad it has. And yet, I feel so fortunate to have been born when I was, to have had the parents I did and for it all to have unfolded in a way I never could have imagined.

And that's the funny thing, really. Because I always thought it wasn't meant to be like this. But maybe it was ... all along.

Acknowledgments

To all those who helped me with this book – from old friends who helped refresh my memories, to family members who could still recall things from many, many decades ago, to former colleagues whose own reminiscences helped with precious detail – my warmest thanks.

It was lovely to relive some of the moments we shared together, and to fill in a couple of gaps with details that I only learnt in the course of putting this manuscript together. (I might note in passing, however, that while all the events described in this book occurred, on occasion I have changed some names – Therese, Raelene, Jenny, Mandy, Tia, Gary and Pam – for simple reasons of privacy. I equally record that very occasionally I have tweaked the chronological order of scenes, for the purposes of simplifying the storytelling structure.)

I also want to extend my enormous gratitude to my publisher, Catherine Milne, whose constant words of encouragement and gentle guidance kept me focused and sane throughout, and who gave me the precious latitude I so often needed on deadlines. My eternal thanks also to my two brilliant editors, Rachel Dennis and Lu Sierra, both of whom went way above and beyond the call of duty.

In terms of the writing, I am blessed to have a husband who believed long before I did that I could do this, and always gave me great advice, particularly on a few of my darker days. Thank you, Pete, for your always unwavering love, and your constant faith in me.

As to my eldest son, Jake, a better writer than Pete and me combined, I warmly acknowledge two things: his first-class instincts on storytelling, and his loving patience with his techno-phobe mum that somehow kept this whole show on the road – on one evening in particular, when I was ready to give up. Thank you, darling.

Louis, as ever, your hugs are without peer and you gave them unconditionally when I needed them most. And to Billi, my daughter, now a young journalist in her own right, your serious sass and sensibilities throughout this journey – much of which was spent in a house in lockdown – always, always helped steer me true.

And to every one of my friends for whom I largely disappeared throughout this writing process, thank you for your patience, rainchecks, quiet encouragement, occasional tissues, and regular check-ins. They meant the world to me. Thank you too to BJ and Ant, for the constant coffee, the excellent muffins, and the endless hours you let me stay writing at the corner table, sometimes with tears in my eyes, sometimes smiling. Thank you for always letting me stay well beyond closing. And finally to Adrian, I will never be able to thank you properly for the role you played in the Night of the Long Knives, or for your care and friendship since.

I am in all of your debt.